E-Learning: Methods, Tools and Advances

E-Learning: Methods, Tools and Advances

Edited by **Albert Traver**

New Jersey

Published by Clanrye International,
55 Van Reypen Street,
Jersey City, NJ 07306, USA
www.clanryeinternational.com

E-Learning: Methods, Tools and Advances
Edited by Albert Traver

© 2015 Clanrye International

International Standard Book Number: 978-1-63240-167-0 (Hardback)

This book contains information obtained from authentic and highly regarded sources. Copyright for all individual chapters remain with the respective authors as indicated. A wide variety of references are listed. Permission and sources are indicated; for detailed attributions, please refer to the permissions page. Reasonable efforts have been made to publish reliable data and information, but the authors, editors and publisher cannot assume any responsibility for the validity of all materials or the consequences of their use.

The publisher's policy is to use permanent paper from mills that operate a sustainable forestry policy. Furthermore, the publisher ensures that the text paper and cover boards used have met acceptable environmental accreditation standards.

Trademark Notice: Registered trademark of products or corporate names are used only for explanation and identification without intent to infringe.

Printed in the United States of America.

Contents

Preface

In my initial years as a student, I used to run to the library at every possible instance to grab a book and learn something new. Books were my primary source of knowledge and I would not have come such a long way without all that I learnt from them. Thus, when I was approached to edit this book; I became understandably nostalgic. It was an absolute honor to be considered worthy of guiding the current generation as well as those to come. I put all my knowledge and hard work into making this book most beneficial for its readers.

This book provides an insight into the latest technological advancements in the fast emerging domain of E-learning. With the resources provided by communication technologies, E-learning has been adopted by many universities and also by various training centers and schools. This book provides a systematic compilation of various topics related to the subject and emphasizes on the importance of E-learning. It reflects the progress of E-learning, with discussion about tools, techniques, improvements and potentials for long-distance learning. The book is dedicated to methodologies and tools employed for E-learning, keeping in mind collaborative methodologies and specific environments. It also provides an analysis on E-learning, highlighting researches about E-learning features and assessment of different methodologies. Lastly, it discusses recent advancements in E-learning, stressing on topics like knowledge enhancement in virtual environments, novel schemes for architectures in tutorial systems and presenting various case studies.

I wish to thank my publisher for supporting me at every step. I would also like to thank all the authors who have contributed their researches in this book. I hope this book will be a valuable contribution to the progress of the field.

Editor

Part 1

Methodologies and Tools

1

Wikis and Blogs in E-Learning Context

Teodora Bakardjieva and Boyka Gradinarova
Varna Free University, Technical University of Varna
Bulgaria

1. Introduction

Much has been written about the effect that web technologies are having on commerce, media, and business in general. But outside of the 'edublogosphere', there's been little coverage of the impact it is having on education. Teachers are starting to explore the potential of blogs, media-sharing services and other social software - which, although not designed specifically for e-learning, can be used to empower students and create exciting new learning opportunities.

In the present chapter characteristics of some sample Web 2.0 tools for PKM (Personal Knowledge management) are discussed. Educational uses of wikis and blogs are outlined. Blogs and wikis represent new repositories of information and knowledge for personal and institutional purposes. System architecture of semantic blogging framework is shown. Challenges and future perspectives of Web 2.0 in e-learning are presented.

Social software driven approach represents a shift towards a new open and knowledge-pull model for learning. The platform, developed and prototypical in use at Varna Free University, is based on concepts like social tagging and networking and therefore offers its users a new perspective of Web 2.0 driven learning.

Open source Learning Management Systems (LMS) have an advantage in universities and developers can build and integrate easily open source web 2.0 tools into the LMS.

This chapter suggests that Web 2.0 tools provide an opportunity for new developments of the e-learning concept and discusses these new approaches developed with the objective of operationalising this social perspective in the context of managing personal knowledge. At the centre of this approach are the challenges of personalization and collaboration. Rather than integrating different tools into a centralized system, the idea is to provide the learner with tools and hand over control to him/her to select and use the tools the way the learner deems fit. Chatti et al. (2006) discuss the potential use of social software in learning environments. Open blogs and cloud platforms such as Facebook have great educational potential (Meyer, 2010). Setting up an e-learning system is very easy now. Almost anyone can now establish an online learning community using open source learning tools that comprise Web 2.0 features. That's why it is now possible for any organization to afford personalized online courses with a learning management system having advanced features to support mutual communication and collaboration. Production and delivery of e-learning programs is far easier with the arrival of Web 2.0. Discussion forums, wikis, blogs and podcasts are just a beginning in the field of online learning.

E-learning has evolved through a series of overlapping stages. Stage 1 consisted of communication and course management tools, from web page to, course management systems, PowerPoint, email, bulletin boards, and chat rooms. Web 1.0 definitely improved the learning experience. It facilitated student-faculty and student-to-student communication. It gave students access to a broad range of databases and research resources. It made it much easier for students to conduct searches. It broadened the range of resources we brought into our classes, including audio and visual resources. And it allowed us to reinforce student learning by presenting material visually. But too often, Web 1.0 involved an impoverished definition of interactivity.

E-learning's second stage emphasizes active learning, collaboration, and enhanced interaction. Wikis, blogs, mashups, podcasts, tags, and social networking are the buzz words. These technological innovations offer opportunities to students to engage in inquiry and to share resources and create collaborative projects.

2. Web 2.0 in e-learning

Web 2.0 is a term which is hard to define because of the amorphousness of the concept. Web 2.0 (O'Reilly, 2005) or the Social Web has introduced new concepts and tools that are able to operationalise a more social-centric vision. Online social networking systems, such as LinkedIn, MySpace and Facebook, allow people to manage their interaction with others on a massive scale. Blogs, microblogs (e.g. Twitter) and instant messaging tools (e.g. Skype) have provided communication tools to interact more effectively with others in opened communities. Wikis and social bookmarking aimed at directly supporting PKM and fostering collective intelligence. This trend has appeared so relevant and so promising that many specialists consider this approach to be the future of knowledge management, hoping that these tools will contribute to realizing the challenge of managing knowledge (Kakizawa, 2007; McAfee, 2006; Shimazu and Koike, 2007). This perspective raises a number of questions related to the application of a vision that was born from the need to incorporate more of the social dimension (Nabeth et al., 2002; Thomas et al., 2001) and to better fit the individual needs of knowledge workers (Razmerita, 2005). PKM on Web 2.0 is achieved by a set of tools that allow people to create, codify, organize and share knowledge, but also to socialize, extend personal networks, collaborate on organizing knowledge and create new knowledge.

After O'Reilly, Paul McFedries (2006) presents a tentative definition according to which web 2.0 is "a second phase of the evolution of the World Wide Web in which developers create Web sites that act like desktop programs and encourage collaboration and communication between users". McFedries identifies the main characteristics of the Web 2.0 "movement", highlighting the social perspective of relation, collaboration and user-participated architecture:

- content is user-created and maintained (peer production, user-content ecosystem);
- user-created and maintained content require radical trust;
- application usability allows rich user experience;
- combining data from different sources leads to creation of new services (mashup);
- services get better as the number of users increases in architecture of participation.

In the last few years, there has been an increasing focus on social software applications and services as a result of the rapid development of Web 2.0 concepts. Nowadays, the web is a platform, in which content is created and shared facilitating social connection and information interchange. Social software technologies include wikis, blogs, podcasts, RSS and social tagging. Web 2.0 tools are designed for ease of use and rapidity of deployment, making possible powerful information sharing (Boulos et al., 2006). Web 2.0 is informed by a "constructivist" understanding of learning in which students devise their own conceptual models for understanding.

Collaboration is the best feature of Web 2.0 that can help e-learning. It was not technically difficult to introduce a collaborative tool on top of a learning system accessible over web. However, fostering collaboration among a group of users is a challenge and Web 2.0 makes it very easy. Using Web 2.0 tools, people do not only passively consume information; rather, they are active contributors, even customizing tools and technology for their use. Web 2.0 facilitates social networking and collaboration and therefore is also referred to as the Social Web. The underlying principle of the Social Web is to make use of the "wisdom of the crowd" and "user generated content". The wisdom of the crowd is a term coined by Surowiecki (2005) who argues that large groups of people are smarter than an elite few. No matter how intelligent they are, large groups of people are better at solving problems, fostering innovation, coming to wise decisions and even predicting the future. In this highly interconnected, dynamic world, new ways of cultivating and exploiting knowledge sharing with customers, suppliers and partners are forcing companies to expand their knowledge management concepts and agendas (Mentzas et al., 2007). There is also the second phase of knowledge management where companies try to exploit a much richer form of knowledge assets, including blogs, wikis and social networks, focusing on the social, collaborative dimension of Web 2.0.

In Table 1 characteristics of some sample web 2.0 tools are highlighted.

Web Application	Description	Characteristics
Social networking, online social networks	Category of Internet applications to help connect friends, business partners, or other individuals together using a variety of tools.	Architecture of Participation
Social network Search engines	Social network search engines are a class of search engines that use social networks to organize, prioritize, or filter search results	Architecture of Participation
Blogs	A weblog, (or blog), is a website where entries are made displayed in chronological order. They often provide commentary or news on a particular subject, typically combining text, images, and links to other blogs, web pages, and other media related to the specific topic.	User-created and maintained content
Blog guides	Specialized search engines for searching blog and news Contents	Architecture of Participation
Social tagging, (folksonomy)	Ad hoc classification scheme (tags) that web users invent as they surf to categorize the data they find online	Architecture of participation, trust
Social bookmarking	Saving and applying keywords to one's personal collection of Web site bookmarks on a site that enables other people to share those bookmarks	Architecture of participation, trust

Web Application	Description	Characteristics
Web Syndication, Web feed management	Web syndication is a form of syndication in which a section of a website is made available for other sites to use through to making Web feeds available from a site in order to provide other people an updated list of content from it (for example one's latest forum postings, etc.).	User created and maintained content, content aggregation
Tag clouds	A list of tags user in the site with some kind of visual indication of each tag's relative popularity (ex. large font). Web sites that implement tag clouds functions allow both finding a tag by alphabet and by popularity.. Selecting a single tag within a tag cloud will generally lead to a collection of items that are associated with that tag	Architecture of participation
Peer production news	Websites combining social bookmarking, blogging, and syndication with a form of non-hierarchical, democratic editorial control. News stories and websites are submitted by users, and then promoted to the front page through a user-based ranking system	User created and maintained content, trust
Wikis	Collaborative web sites that allows users to add, edit and delete content	User created and maintained content, trust
Collaborative real time editing	Simultaneous editing of a text or media file by different participants on a network.	User created and maintained content
Content aggregation and management, mashup (web application hybrid)	A website or web application that combines content from more than one source	User created and maintained content, trust,architecture of participation

Table 1. Sample web 2.0 applications: description and "social networking" characteristics (Pettenati & Ranieri, 2006).

The traditional approach to e-learning has been to employ the use of a Virtual Learning Environment (VLE), software that is often cumbersome and expensive - and which tends to be structured around courses, timetables, and testing. That is an approach that is too often driven by the needs of the institution rather than the individual learner. In contrast, e-learning 2.0 (as coined by Stephen Downes) takes a 'small pieces, loosely joined' approach that combines the use of discrete but complementary tools and web services - such as blogs, wikis, and other social software - to support the creation of ad-hoc learning communities.

The learning process is social, personal, dynamic and distributed in nature, a fundamental shift is needed towards a more personalized, open and knowledge-pull model for learning, as opposed to the centralized, static and knowledge-push models of traditional learning

solutions (Chatti et al., 2007). Web 2.0 leads to this new generation of technology enhanced learning. The communication with the students can be realized through blogs and wikis and the concept of tagging and folksonomies offers a great potential for learners to express their own vocabulary (Vanderwal, 2005).
Web 2.0 supports knowledge networking and community building. For example, wikis create an opportunity for collaborative content creation and social interaction. Further, these tools do not require advanced technical skills to use their features, allowing users to focus on the information exchange and collaborative tasks themselves without first mastering a difficult technological environment (Kirkpatrick, 2006). Such "transparent technologies" (Wheeler, Kelly, & Gale, 2005) allow the user to concentrate more on the task because they can "see through" the technology with which they are interacting.

3. Web 2.0 tools for PKM

PKM tools can be classified into six categories:

1. Personalized WebPages that enhance organizing and presenting information and sharing it with others. An example of a personalized webpage service is iGoogle, MyYahoo, Live.Com, etc. These sites allow people to create personalized WebPages by subscribing to specific content through RSS feeds and aggregating different types of information (e.g. blogs, favorite websites, weather forecasts), widgets or applications (e.g. calendars, dictionaries) in one place. This integration of different information sources facilitates access to information and the possibility of creating knowledge.
2. Personalized search tools that provide for retrieving and sharing of information. Swicki (http://www.eurekster.com) is a personalized search portal on topics of one's choice powered by a community. A Swicki learns from the community's search behavior; thus, it is easier to find something interesting.
3. Social bookmarking that provides a simple way for a community of people to share bookmarks of internet resources. Heystaks (http://www.heystaks.com) is tool that offers the collection, classification and sharing of web search results. Search results can be added to one's own lists called stacks, but it is also possible to join existing lists and benefit from others. Lists can be declared private or public, and can be shared with colleagues and friends. Links can be evaluated to indicate their quality to others. Using Heystaks, the management of bookmarks becomes a social activity.
4. Personalized live discussion forums that assist in analyzing, evaluating, presenting and sharing information. With Tangler (http://www.tangler.com), it is possible to create a live discussion forum and to share discussions with others.
5. Virtual worlds that encourage sharing of information. SecondLife (http://www.secondlife.com) or Vastpark (http://www.vastpark.com) are 3D platforms that allow users to create their own virtual world that they can own and share with others. It can be used for 3D gaming, building 3D presentations or creating social networks in shared worlds where users communicate, cooperate, learn and collaborate.
6. Blogs and wikis that support editing, presenting and organizing information or knowledge by individuals or in collaboration with others. A special category of wikis is personal wikis. They allow people to organize information on their desktop or mobile computing device in a manner similar to normal wikis. They are installed as a standalone version and can be seen as personal information managers. An example of a

personal wiki is Pimki (http://pimki.rubyforge.org), which includes mind maps, search functions or to-do lists. Pimki is a PIM (Personal Information Manager) loosely based on Instiki's Wiki technology (http://instiki.org/show/HomePage).

4. Introduction to wikis

Wiki applications facilitate collaborative editing supported by revision mechanisms that allow the monitoring of changes. Wiki technology can be used as a community platform but also as a personal authoring environment. Wiki was developed in 1994 by Ward Cunningham. Wiki comes from the Hawaiian word "wiki-wiki" meaning fast. "WikiWikiWeb" was created in 1995 by Ward Cunningham as an online manual for software programmers to share knowledge (Taylor, 2005). Jimmy Wales built on this idea and created Wikipedia, and now everybody is familiar with Wikipedia, which is itself a Wiki in the form of an online encyclopedia that can be edited by any user. Educators are now experimenting with using Wikis in pedagogically sound ways. Each user has the ability to modify any part of the Wiki space, analogous to a mini-website. Users create new nodes in the hierarchy each time that they want to elaborate, change or add content. Using Wikis can allow for a numerous opportunities for collaboration between students, but students do not have to be in the same physical location to meet with each other. These kinds of programs "allow for cooperation between the instructor and students or among students by using different formats of social interaction" (Godwin-Jones, 2003).

Evaluating the quality of contributions in such collaborative authoring environments is a challenging task (Korfiatis et al., 2006). However, based on the "wisdom of the crowd" principle, one collects and aggregates enough data until there is a consistently reliable answer. Oren et al. (2006) acknowledge that wikis are successful for information collection, but point out that they do not fully satisfy the requirements of PKM. A semantic wiki allows users to make formal descriptions of resources by annotating the pages that represent those resources. Whereas a regular wiki enables users to describe resources in natural language, a semantic wiki allows users to additionally describe resources in formal language. Semantic wikis augment ordinary wikis by using the metadata annotations, and thus may offer better information retrieval and knowledge reuse.

Wikis enable users to collaboratively create and edit web content directly, using a web browser. In other words, a wiki is a collaborative web site whose content can be edited by anyone visiting the site, allowing them to easily create and edit web pages (Chao, 2007). Wikis can serve as a source of information and knowledge, as well as a tool for collaborative authoring. Wikis allow visitors to engage in dialog and share information among participants in group projects, or to engage in learning with each other by using wikis as a collaborative environment in which to construct their knowledge (Boulos et al., 2006).

As defined in Leuf and Cunningham (2001), the proper term "Wiki" is used to refer to the essential concept rather than to any particular implementation, the latter being called simply a "wiki". From a technical standpoint, the Wiki concept rests on the World Wide Web, and the underlying HTTP protocol defines how the client-server communications occur. At the functional level, the essence of Wiki can be summarized as follows:

- a wiki invites any and all users to edit any page or to create new pages within the wiki site, using only a simple web browser without any additional add-ons;
- wiki encourages meaningful topic associations between pages by making the creation of page links almost intuitively easy;

- rather than serving as a carefully crafted site for casual visitors, a wiki seeks to involve the visitor in an ongoing process of creation and collaboration that constantly changes the web site content;
- semantic wikis extend wikis with formal annotations describing the content and create views;
- semantic wikis introduce background knowledge;
- semantic wikis for PKM - formal structure gives automated support and flexibility of wiki gives people freedom.

4.1 Background

Wiki modifications are easy because the processes of reading and editing are both quite simple. In essence, a wiki is a simplification of the process of creating HTML web pages. Simply clicking an "edit this page" link allows instant revisions (Lamb, 2004). Wikis are editable through a browser, and the editing interface is generally simple and easy to use.

Wikis provide a mechanism to record every change that occurs over time as a document is revised. Each time a person makes changes to a wiki page, that revision of the content becomes the current version, and an older version is stored. Versions of the document can be compared side-by-side, and edits can be "rolled back" if necessary. This means that it is possible to revert a page (if necessary) to any of its previous states.

Further, the administrator of the site has control over access, determining which portions are user-editable. Some wikis restrict editing access, allowing only registered members to edit page content, although anyone may view it. Others allow completely unrestricted access, allowing anyone to both edit and view content (Olson, 2006).

Many wiki systems are adding functionalities such as web-based spreadsheets, calendars, documents, photo galleries, private workspaces, hierarchical organization, WYSIWYG (what you see is what you get) web editing, importing Word or Excel files, and even integration with centralized content management systems (Lamb, 2004). WikiMatrix (2007) provides a tool to compare the features of various popular wiki engines.

Educational benefits of wikis revolve around the fact that they offer an online space for easy interaction and collaboration. Both teachers and students can easily create web pages using wikis without prior knowledge or skill in web development or programming, eliminating the extra time necessary to develop these skills. A wiki offers the ability to interact with evolving text over time as well, allowing teachers and learners to see assignments as they are drafted, rather than commenting only on the final draft. Considering the complications of scheduling after-hours meetings for students, a wiki can also be extremely useful for communication within groups. Further, as more organizations adopt wikis for internal and external collaboration and information dissemination, interacting with them at the educational level builds important work skills.

4.2 Observations and discussions

Varna Free University incorporated a wiki module in its e-Learning system (Fig 1), which encouraged both tutors and students to harness their collective intelligence in order to achieve their common educational goals and the exploration of new and effective uses of the Wiki tool is also presented.

Moodle has the most transparent and easiest navigation especially for a generation of students well trained in text editing in programs such as Microsoft Word (Fig. 2, Fig.3, Fig.4, Fig.5).

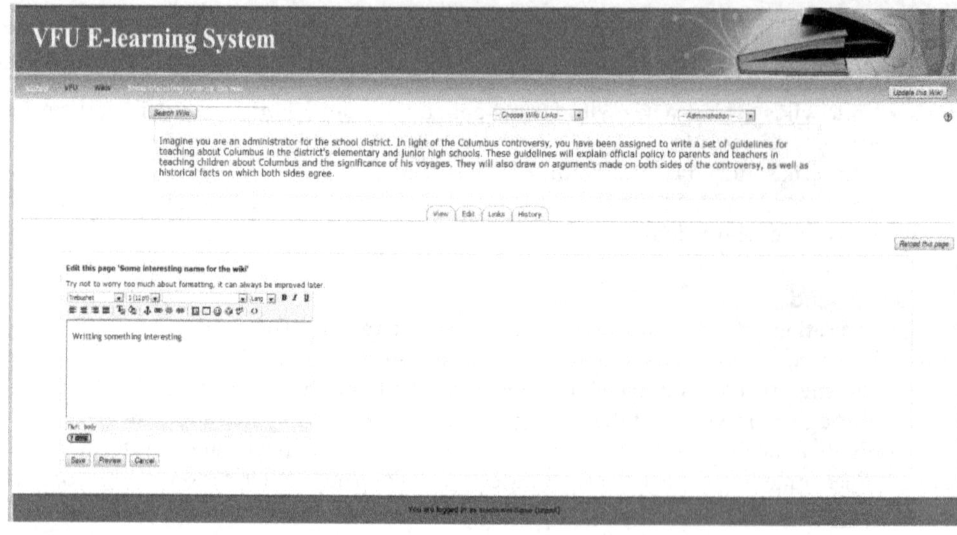

Fig. 1. VFU E-learning System.

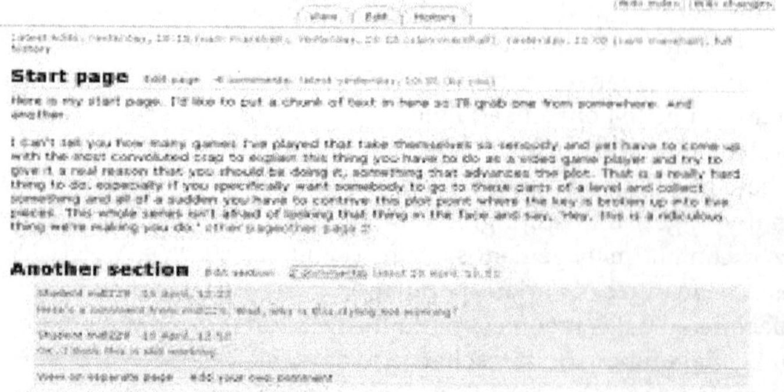

Fig. 2. Wiki HTML Editor.

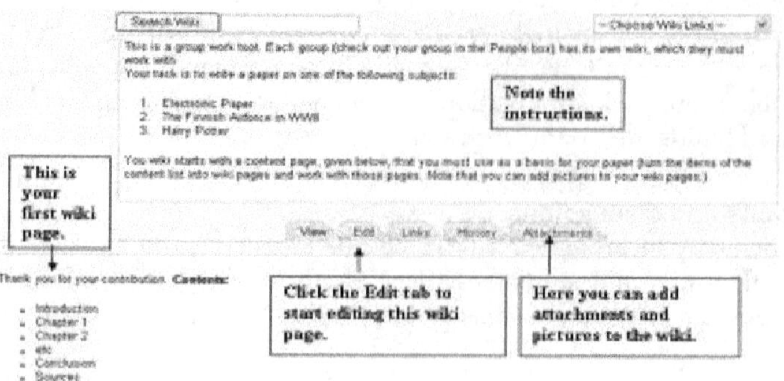

Fig. 3. Wiki in Moodle

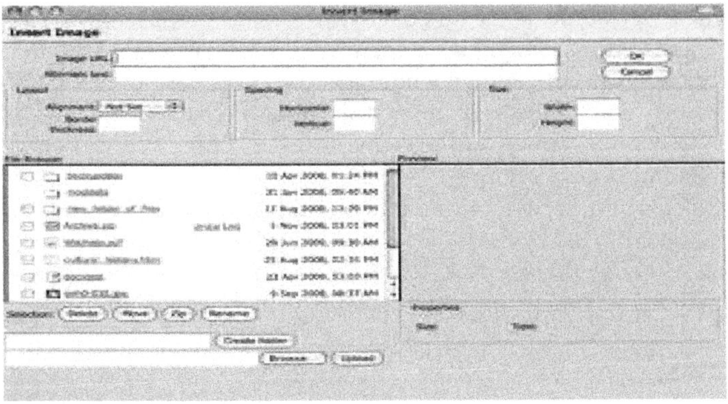

Fig. 4. Adding images to a wiki in Moodle.

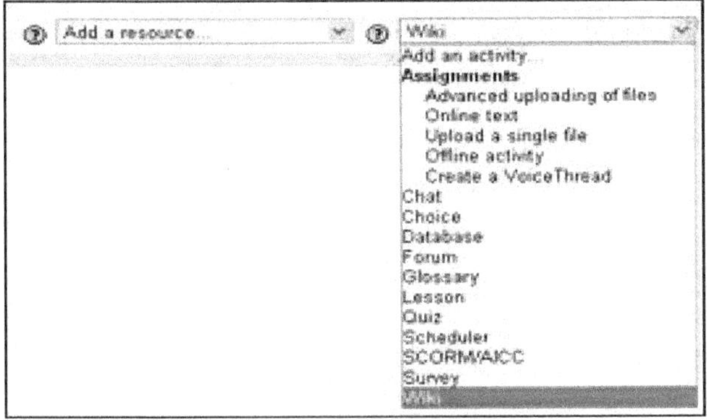

Fig. 5. Moodle Wiki Editing.

Wikis find application in the educational process and in the university management system as well. Placement centers use wiki pages to store and organize content for job postings and career development. Wikis act as a sounding board so that students can voice opinions about university policies.

The free-form, collaborative nature of wikis makes them easy to apply in creative ways. Any sort of group process can be facilitated using a wiki. Creating a wiki for group lecture notes after a lecture gives students a chance to combine their notes. Those that missed information get it from their peers. The group decides what information is critical and gives it proper emphasis. Group lecture notes are done.

The most straightforward use of a wiki is as a tool for group collaboration for creating group projects. A teacher assigning a group project gives students a place to work by creating a wiki with the group mode enabled. This gives each group their own space to record research, to develop outlines and to create the final product. The teacher creates a submission date on which to turn off editing capabilities for students so that he/she can grade the final projects. Afterwards, the teacher enables visible groups so that everyone can see each other's work. Also, a teacher develops a wiki for a student group and urges people to submit ideas around a brainstorming topic. People can add ideas as they occur and link to other pages for elaboration.

A teacher might assign students the task of contributing to another wiki on the Web, on any study topic, perhaps by assigning students to groups and challenging them to collaboratively create an article they would feel confident posting to a public-information space. Students use the course wiki to create drafts of the article they will eventually publish to the community at the end of the semester.

This type of assignment has a number of benefits:

- It gives students additional motivation to do their best, since they know their work will be viewed and critiqued by the public instead of just by their instructor.
- It can act as a summarizing activity for an entire semester's worth of material.
- Students will know their work will be used by other people, not just graded and filed away.

Response	Ease of use	Enhanced learning	Useful for exam prep	Fair assessment of students' efforts
1 - strongly agree	15	13	25	22
2 - agree	65	24	27	40
3 - neutral	13	59	30	17
4 - disagree	7	4	18	21
5 - strongly disagree	0	0	0	0

Table 2. Student Survey of Wiki Projects (MBA 257 - 60% response rate).

An inquiry was made among 257 MBA students and as a result they had mainly positive reactions to the Wiki projects. Some students commented that Wiki was a useful tool and a good way to put a summary of the lecture content together in a way that all students could benefit. Others mentioned that it allowed them to carry on dialogue with varying view-points that offered a more holistic learning experience. There was dissatisfaction about the fact that it is hard to grade participation because often people post the same things. Pointing out the pedagogical benefits from the project we have to stress on the assessment. As seen in the survey results above, this is one area in which students were the least satisfied. Students were assessed on their participation in the Wiki. Any user can see who has made a contribution, the date and time of each contribution.

Another difficulty in integrating Wikis successfully comes from the switch to a student-centered approach. Using student-created Wikis as a major content source shifts the creation and ownership of knowledge base from the teacher to the student. The role of student in this Wiki project is that of primary content producer. The teacher's role changes to one of facilitating and correcting errors. As mentioned above, Wikis are quite straightforward, and Moodle has Wiki interface that resembles common word processing programs, so students may find it easy to use.

4.3 Conclusion to wikis

Using Wikis in an LMS such as Moodle can be a useful teaching tool and can support a student-centered learning experience. Maybe the two most important factors to consider when implementing a Wiki are how to integrate the Wiki project and how to assess student learning and participation in the Wiki project. Students are quick to realize when a project is an add-on requirement and perceive this as extra busy work. The teacher must provide a clear assessment procedure that will be as objective as possible. For this purpose student self-assessments can be used and this procedure could also include more specific requirements concerning the number and length of each post, or could include a note grade instead of pass-fail based on content and form.

By carefully designing the implementation, integration, and evaluation of a Wiki, a new, enjoyable collaborative space can be created which allows for much more efficient, asynchronous, and evaluated interaction between groups of students and teachers. Also, the flexibility of this medium allows for extremely varied adaptations in an extraordinarily large range of educational contexts.

Some educational uses of wikis can be outlined:

- Students use a wiki to develop research projects, with the wiki serving as ongoing documentation of their work.
- Students add summaries of their thoughts from the prescribed readings, building a collaborative annotated bibliography on a wiki. Wiki is used for publishing course resources like syllabi and handouts, and students comment on these directly for all to see.
- Teachers use wikis as a knowledge base, enabling them to share reflections and thoughts regarding teaching practices, and allowing for versioning and documentation.
- Wikis map concepts. They are useful for brainstorming, and editing a given wiki topic can produce a linked network of resources.
- Wiki is used as a presentation tool in place of conventional software, and students are able to directly comment on and revise the presentation content.
- Wikis are tools for group authoring. Often group members collaborate on a document by emailing to each member of the group a file that each person edits on their computer, and some attempt is then made to coordinate the edits so that everyone's work is equally represented in a single, central wiki page.

Wikis usage in an e-Leaning system can be a powerful teaching tool that enhances and increases collaboration outside of class.

5. Introduction to blogs

Blog posts or blogs are primarily textual and can vary widely in their content. They can be devoted to politics, news and sharing opinions or dedicated to technical developments. Blog entries are usually maintained in chronological order, but are usually displayed in reverse chronological order. Nardi et al. (2004) identified five reasons why blogs are used:

1. to update others on activities and whereabouts;
2. to express opinions to influence others;
3. to seek others' opinions and feedback;
4. to "think by writing";
5. to release emotional tension.

Blogging is increasingly finding a home in education (both in school and university), as not only does the software remove the technical barriers to writing and publishing online - but the 'journal' format encourages students to keep a record of their thinking over time. Blogs also of course facilitate critical feedback, by letting readers add comments - which could be from teachers, peers or a wider audience.

Students use of blogs are far ranging. A single authored blog can be used to provide a personal space online, to pose questions, publish work in progress, and link to and comment on other web sources. However a blog needn't be limited to a single author - it can mix different kinds of voices, including fellow students, teachers and mentors, or subject specialists. Edu-blogging pioneer Will Richardson (author of the main books devoted to Blogs, Wikis and Podcasts) in 2001 used the blog software Manila (http://manila.userland.com) to enable his english literature students to publish a readers guide (http://weblogs.hcrhs.k12.nj.us/bees) to the book The Secret Life of Bees. Richardson asked the book's author, Sue Monk Kidd, if she would participate by answering questions and commenting on what the students had written - to which she agreed. The result was a truly democratic learning space.

Richardson marked 10 years since his first blog post, a full decade of writing and sharing online. He defines the education reform: "We don't need better, we need different" (Richardson, 2011)

Today's students are immersed in the digital age, but can our educational system keep up? Best-selling author Will Richardson's comprehensive collection of posts from his acclaimed blog (http://weblogg-ed.com) outlines the educational reform we must achieve to stay ahead of the curve:

- Project-based learning
- Student-created media that develops critical thinking
- Extending learning beyond the classroom and school hours
- Cooperative and collaborative learning
- Student empowerment and career readiness

The necessary shift will not magically happen, but experts agree that it must happen now. This compilation will inspire educators and parents to engage in the technology their children already embrace, and to take an active role in transforming education to meet the challenges of the digital revolution.

5.1 Observations and discussions

Herring et al. (2004) defined three types of blogs: personal journals, "filters" (because they select and provide commentary on information from other websites) and "knowledge logs". The majority of blogs are the online diary type. Bloggers are interested in reading new information, sharing knowledge and being connected with other users. While blog writers are more extroverted, blog readers are more consumerist.

The use of blogs and semantic blogs has recently been associated with a decentralised form of knowledge management (Cayzer, 2004, Breslin & Decker 2007). Semantic blogging is a technology that builds upon blogging and enriches blog items with metadata. For publishing information such as research publications, there is need of some structure and semantic blogging provides this. Items may be classified using ontologies. Semantic links may exist between items (Cayzer, 2004b). Semantic blogging uses desirable features of both blogging and the semantic web to deal with the challenges of traditional blogging. The semantic web is well suited for incrementally publishing structured and semantically rich information. On the other hand, the easy publishing nature of blogging can boost the semantic web by publishing enough data and resources (Cayzer 2004a; Cayzer, 2004b).

Semantic blogging can help users discover items of interest in blogs. Navigation through the blogosphere can be more flexible and meaningful due to interconnections among various items and topics. Aggregation of useful materials across multiple blogs and the semantic web is possible. Semantic blogging can extend blogging from simple diary browsing to informal knowledge management (Cayzer, 2004b). Publication is easy in semantic blogs too because only some additional metadata data have to be added compared to traditional blogs. The users do not need to put any effort to enjoy the additional features provided. Hence, there is not much effort added in using a semantic blog instead of a conventional one. The rich metadata and semantic structure work behind to give the user the added value experience of semantic blogging. However, the semantic capabilities currently implemented for semantic blogging are still limited. It is difficult to obtain blog entries relevant to a topic in an aggregated and organized form.

There is newly developed framework for semantic blogging capable of organizing results relevant to user requirement (Shakya, 2006). Attempts for implementation of that framework are made at Varna Free University (VFU) to provide more effective navigation and search by exploring semantic relations in blogs.

The system is built upon a blogging infrastructure backed up by an RDF metadata store. The metadata schema enriches the blog entries input. The metadata schema also helps the query processor to search by metadata. Users input queries to the system according to their information requirement. The query processor searches for matching blog entries and instances in the ontology of the domain of application. Integrated with the ontology is the inference engine, which can deduce implicit relations from the ontology. All the blog entries related to the relevant ontology instances are obtained from the blogontology mapping. The total relevant blog entries obtained are finally organized into an aggregated and navigable collection by the organizer. The system also produces output in RSS format which computers can understand and aggregate.

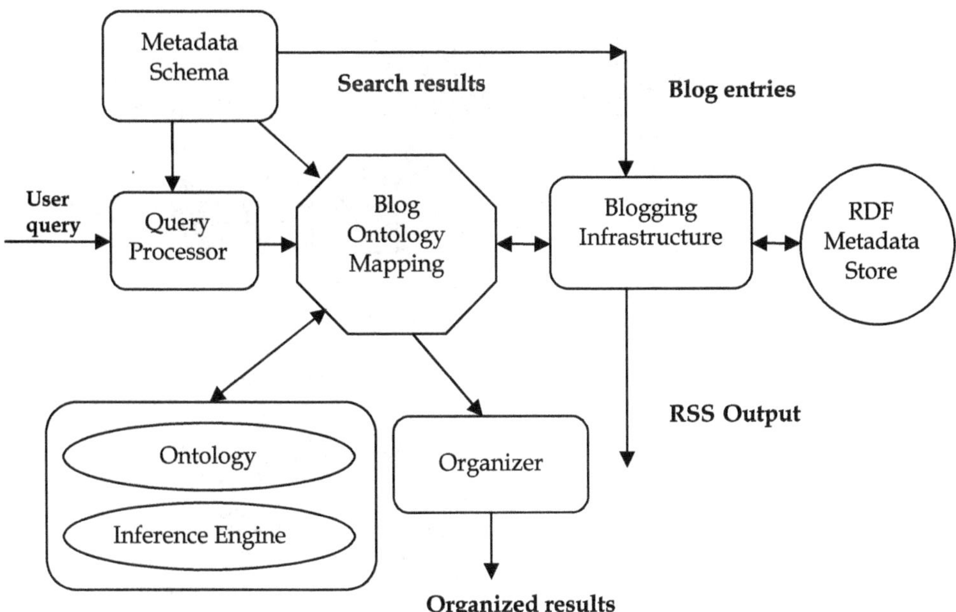

Fig. 6. System architecture of the semantic blogging framework.

Some edu-blogs that are used at Varna Free University (Fig. 7, Fig. 8, Fig. 9):

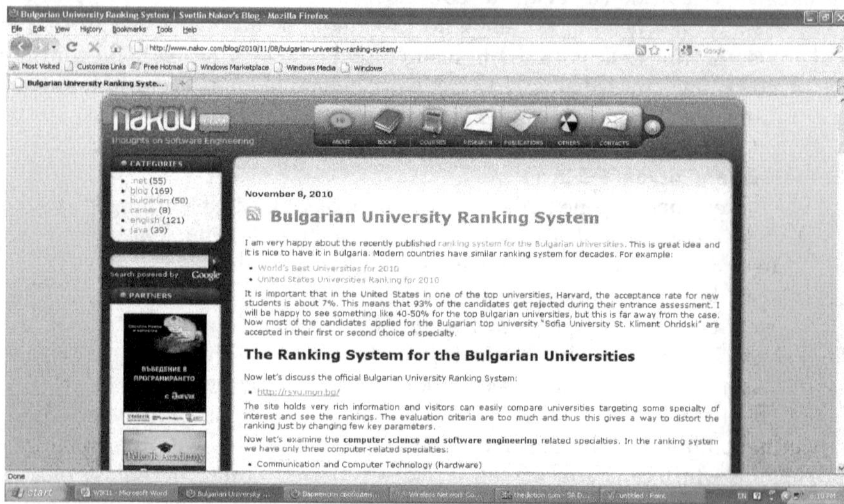

Fig. 7. Edu-blog for the Ranking System for the Bulgarian Universities.

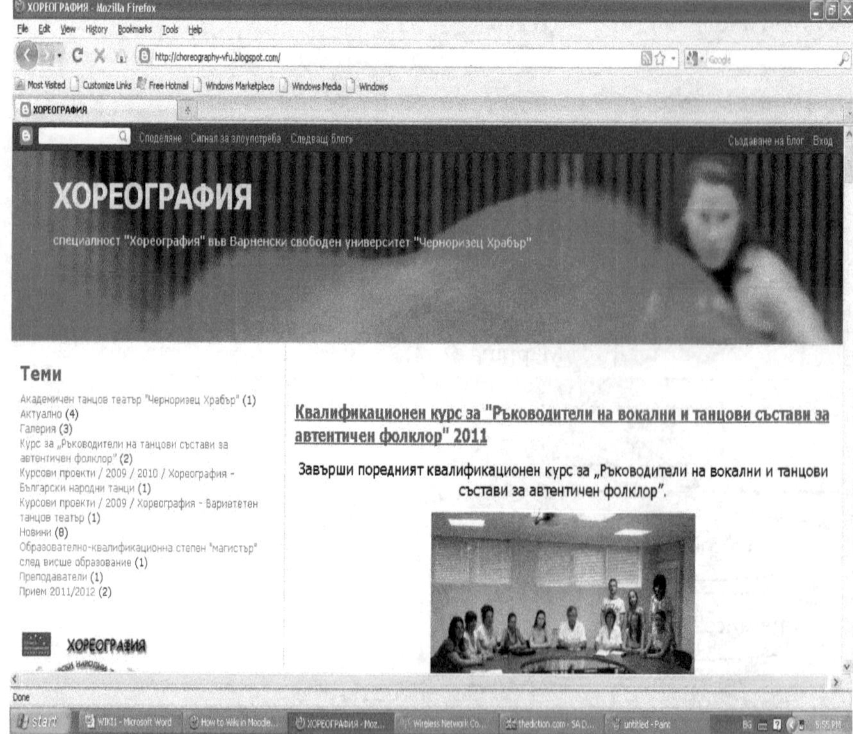

Fig. 8. Edu-blog for Choreography

Fig. 9. Edu-blog for Spatial Design.

5.2 Conclusion to blogs

Teachers are using blogs to provide up-to-date information and commentary on their subject areas, as well as posting questions and assignments and linking to relevant news stories and websites.

Ontology has been introduced to utilize semantic relations, enhanced by inference. Blog entries are mapped to the ontology using language processing. Search results are organized by introducing semantic aggregation. Blog entries are enriched by metadata and an annotation mechanism has also been developed. The framework has been tested and evaluated by implementing a system for the Institute of Technology domain ontology at VFU. Experiments have shown quite good results. Single sample ontology is created for demonstration.

6. Challenges

The wave of new web 2.0 technologies, such as blogs, wikis, and especially e-portfolios, and open source content management software such as WordPress enable students as well as instructors to create, load and edit content. This increases active learning, and provides means to collect, organize and assess student work in more authentic ways than tests or essays.

However, learning management systems still have major advantages, in that they provide an institutionally secure environment, enable the management of learning, and integrate with administrative systems. Thus designers are looking for ways to integrate web 2.0 tools with learning management systems (Mott, 2010).

Also as students get more tools and more encouragement to use these tools for learning, there is the possibility of creating 'personal learning environments', software interfaces that the learner can add to or edit, to facilitate their learning. These might include a portal to their courses that would include access to an LMS, but would also include links to their blog, e-portfolio, and social networks such as Facebook (Bates, 2011)

Students now have access to mobile phones with cámera and audio recording capabilities and access to video editing through software on their laptops and video publishing through YouTube. Students now can collect data, organize and edit it, and publish it. In addition, through the Internet, they can access a multitude of resources far beyond the limits of a traditional class curriculum. They can do all this outside the confines of the classroom. This is resulting in new course designs focused on learner-generated content, but working to overall academic guidelines and principles established by the instructor.

The traditional best practice instructional system design model of analyze, design, develop, implement, and evaluate (ADDIE) is giving way to the new, dynamic web 2.0 tools, and learner-generated content.

As a result, we are beginning to see some high quality design models that are developed, in response to changing input from students, the arrival of a new technology course, or breaking news in the subject area. This allows courses to appear more spontaneous and more authentic, grounded in the real world. These new developments are happening more in the area of training and vocational education than academia, although they have potential especially for professional programs.

7. The future is mobile & learning analytics

The major technology development during 2010 was the launch of Apple's iPad. The iPad has yet to prove its worth as an educational tool. It is valuable for 'consumption', for example access to media and e-books, but has more limitations on 'production', as it stands at the moment. Version 2 includes more 'production' functionality, such as a camera, and software to facilitate multimedia creation. With the movement towards learner-generated content this is a major limitation of tablets so far for educational purposes. Furthermore, phones, tablets and laptops are converging, so that, combined with cloud computing, the full functionality of a computer will eventually be available on the smallest devices.

Also there were further improvements in 2010 on the functionality of mobile phones, although educational applications remain tiny compared with other areas, such as entertainment and publishing. One barrier to educational applications is the multiplicity of mobile operating systems; another is the lack of a clear model of design for mobile learning. The release of the HTML5 standard for web applications, which will provide a 'standard' platform for mobile applications, is unlikely before 2012.

Open content is most likely to be used in a context where courses are explicitly designed around the concept of open content. Instead, students would be encouraged, within certain guidelines and academic criteria, to search the Internet and to collect local data to create their own blogs and wikis that would demonstrate their knowledge within a particular subject domain. Another strong development in these resources is the increased use of multimedia such as video, animations, simulations and, to a much lesser extent, games.

The application of business intelligence software to learning and learners is likely to be the next perspective in e-learning. Institutions accumulate a great deal of data about students. This is rarely used for the purposes of academic decision-making, mainly because it has up to now required a huge effort to analyze such data in terms of specific decisions. Learning analytics do this through software that 'sits on top' of the several different databases used in universities, such as student information systems, learning management systems, and financial systems.

8. Main conclusions

The social software driven approach reflects the nature of learning and knowledge as being social, personal, distributed, flexible and dynamic. It represents a shift towards a more personalized, open and knowledge-pull model for learning. The platform, developed and prototypical in use at Varna Free University, is based on concepts like social tagging and networking and therefore offers its users a new perspective of Web 2.0 driven learning.

Web 2.0 brings new possibilities and tools to e-learning. Social software supports active social networking processes and a community model to foster knowledge sharing and collaboration. Blogs and wikis represent new repositories of information and knowledge for personal and organisational purposes. High quality contributions are assured not only by guidelines, but also by reputation and rating the contributions. Through social software, students especially in LLL process are more motivated to share knowledge with others. Organizations have to decide whether they want to build their own internal proprietary solutions with blogs, wikis and/or social networks or with the use of existing tools. Although anyone can use social software and edit a blog or a wiki, not everybody does. Effective social structures may create incentives and guide fruitful collaborations.

The Web 2.0 era has emerged as a shift of perspective from a world of plentiful information that has to be searched using powerful search engines to a world in which the social process has become central for identification and access to information and knowledge. In this new world, a variety of tools have been developed to better manage the social capital (with social networking systems such as Plaxo, LinkedIn), to communicate more effectively with blogs, and/or to harness collective intelligence with systems such as wikis.

Open source LMS, such as Moodle, have an advantage here in that designers in universities with access to open source developers can build and integrate open source web 2.0 tools into the LMS quite easily.

This chapter suggests that Web 2.0 tools provide an opportunity for new developments of the e-learning concept and discusses these new approaches developed with the objective of operationalising this social perspective in the context of managing personal knowledge. Web 2.0 enables a new model of e-learning that contributes to collective intelligence through formal and informal communication, collaboration and social networking tools. This new model facilitates virtual interaction, social processes, collaboration and knowledge exchanges on the web. A characteristic of such systems is the fact that they are open and designed to invite collaboration and to facilitate social interaction.

There are numerous ways that faculties can use the Web 2.0 tools to enhance student's interaction in online learning. Incorporation of Web 2.0 tools such as blogs and wikis into online and hybrid courses has the potential for improving student engagement in learning. As shown through examples from our teaching and from the literature, these tools can facilitate rich interaction among students, the faculties, and the online interaction, the cornerstone of effective online learning.

In blogs and wikis externalisation of personal knowledge is self-initiated. Furthermore, despite using Web 2.0 tools it is still difficult to find the right piece of information. Better search functionalities and sorted entries are an issue that needs to be addressed in further development. Semantic Web technologies enhance Web 2.0 tools and their associated data with semantic annotations and semantic-enhanced knowledge representations, thus enabling a better automatic processing of data which in turn will lead to enhanced search mechanisms.

9. References

Bates, T. (2011), E-Learning Outlook for 2011 http://www.tonybates.ca/2011/01/16/e-learning-outlook-for-2011/

Bates, Tony (2010), Blackboard acquires Elluminate and Wimba: the end of LMSs? http://www.tonybates.ca/2010/07/11/blackboard-acquires-elluminate-and-wimba-the-end-of-lmss/

Boulos, M. N. K., Maramba, I. & Wheeler, S. (2006) Wikis, blogs and podcasts: A new generation of web-based tools for virtual collaborative clinical practice and education, BMC Medical Education, 6(41). http://www.biomedcentral.com/content/pdf/1472-6920-6-41.pdf (Last visited January 2011)

Breslin, J.G, S. Decker (2007), "The Future of Social Networks on the Internet: The Need for Semantics", IEEE Internet Computing, vol. 11, no. 6, pp. 86-90pp.

Cayzer, S. (2004a). Semantic blogging and decentralized knowledge management. Communications of the ACM, 47(12): 47-52. http://portal.acm.org/citation.cfm?id=1035164&coll=GUIDE&dl=ACM&CFID=49 229987&CFTOKEN=13649580&ret=1#Fulltext

Cayzer, S. (2004b). Semantic Blogging: Spreading the Semantic Web Meme. http://citeseer.ist.psu.edu/698724.html Last visited July 2011

Chao, J. (2007) Student project collaboration using Wikis. Proceedings of the 20th Conference on Software Engineering Education and Training (CSEE&T2007), Dublin, Ireland: July 3-5.

Chatti, M.A., Jarke, M. and Frosch-Wilke, D., (2007). The Future of e-Learning: a Shift to Knowledge Networking and Social Software, International Journal of Knowledge and Learning, IJKL, 3 (4), p. 404-420

Chatti, M.A., Srirama, S., Kensche, D. & Cao, Y. (2006). Mobile web services for collaborative learning, Proceedings of the 4th International Workshop on Wireless, Mobile and Ubiquitous Technologies in Education (WMUTE 2006), 16–17 November, Athens, Greece.

Godwin-Jones, R. (2003). Blogs and Wikis: Environments for Online Collaboration. Language Learning and Technology 7(2): 12-16. http://llt.msu.edu/vol7num2/pdf/emerging.pdf Last visited July 2011 Stephen Downes, E-Learning 2.0:Notes from Stephen Downes http://www.downes.ca/ http://www.speedofcreativity.org/2006/10/08/elearning-20-notes-from-stephen-downes/

Gradinarova. B. (2009). Importance of web 2.0- mediated competence for the educational demands on learners. In Proceedings of the 10th International Conference on Computer Systems and Technologies and Workshop for PhD Students in Computing on International Conference on Computer Systems and Technologies (CompSysTech '09),

Kakizawa, Y. (2007), "In-house use of Web 2.0: Enterprise 2.0", NEC Technical Journal, Vol. 2 No. 2, pp. 46-9.\

Kirkpatrick, M. (2006) The flu wiki: A serious application of new web tools. http://marshallk.blogspot.com/2005/07/flu-wiki-serious-application-of-new.html (Last visited March 2011)

Lamb, B. (2004) Wide open spaces: Wikis, ready or not. EDUCAUSE Review, 39(5) (September/October), 36-48. http://www.educause.edu/pub/erferm04/ermO452.asp?bhcp=l

Leuf, B. & Cunningham, W. (2001) The Wiki Way: Quick Collaboration onthe Web. Boston, MA: Addison Wesley

McAfee, A.P. (2006), "Enterprise 2.0: the dawn of emergent collaboration", MIT Sloan Management Review, Vol. 47 No. 3, pp. 1-28.

McAfee, A.P. (2006), "Enterprise 2.0: the dawn of emergent collaboration", MIT Sloan Management Review, Vol. 47 No. 3, pp. 1-28.

McFedries, P.: The Web, Take Two Technically Speaking. IEEE Spectrum, June (2006)

Mentzas, G., Kafentzis, K. and Georgolios, P. (2007), "Knowledge services on the Semantic Web", Communications of the ACM, Vol. 50 No. 10, pp. 53-8.

Meyer, M. (2010) Creating an Open Web 2.0 Cloud E-Learning Experience, 2010 Educause Annual Conference http://www.educause.edu/E2010/Program/SESS124 (Last visited March 2011)

Mott, J. (2010) Envisioning the post-LMS era: the Open Learning Network Educause Quarterly, Vol. 33, No. 1

Nabeth, T., Angehrn, A. and Roda, C. (2002), "Towards personalized, socially aware and active knowledge management systems", in Stanford-Smith, B., Chiozza, E. and Edin, M. (Eds), Proceedings of E-business and E-work - Challenges and Achievements in E-business and E-work, Vol. 2, IOS Press, Amsterdam, pp. 884-91.

Olson, C. (2006) New tools for learning. http://faculty.eicc.edu/golson/tools.htm (Last visited March 2011)

O'Reilly, T.: What Is Web 2.0. In Internet: http://www.oreillynet.com/pub/a/oreilly/tim/news/2005/09/30/what-is-web-20.html

Oren Eyal , Max Vëolkel, John G. Breslin& Stefan Decker (2006), Semantic Wikis for Personal Knowledge Management, S. Bressan, J. KËung, and R. Wagner (Eds.): DEXA 2006, LNCS 4080, pp. 509–518, 2006, Springer-Verlag Berlin Heidelberg http://www.johnbreslin.org/files/publications/20060919_dexa2006.pdf

Paul, C. and Schofield, A. (2010) *e-Portfolios for teacher candidates* Vancouver BC: UBC Faculty of Education (retrieved from http://ctlt.ubc.ca/2009/09/22/e-portfolios-for-teacher-candidates/, December 6, 2010)

Pettenati M.C., M. Ranieri, Informal learning theories and tools to support knowledge management in distributed CoPs, E. Tomadaki and P. Scott (Eds.): Innovative Approaches for Learning and Knowledge Sharing, EC-TEL 2006 Workshops Proceedings, ISSN 1613-0073, p. 345-355, 2006.

Razmerita, L. (2005), "Exploiting semantics and user modeling for enhanced user support", electronic version, Proceedings of HCI International 2005

Rogers, E. (2011) How Web 2.0 Is Influencing E-Learning http://ezinearticles.com?HowWeb-2.0-Is-Influencing-E-Learning&id=5968742 (Last visited March 2011)

Shakya A.(2006), A Semantic Blogging Framework for better Utilization of Information, Thesis submitted in partial fulfillment of the requirements for thedegree of Master of Engineering http://citeseerx.ist.psu.edu/viewdoc/download?doi=10.1.1.115.7250 &rep=rep1&type=pdf (Last visited July 2011)

Surowiecki, J. (Ed.) (2005), The Wisdom of the Crowds, Anchor Books, New York, NY

Taylor, C. (2005). It's a Wiki, Wiki World. Time 165(23): 40-42.

Vanderwal, T., (2005). Explaining and Showing Broad and Narrow Folksonomies, http://www.vanderwal.net/random/entrysel.php?blog=1635 (Last visited March 2011)

Wheeler, S, Kelly P., & Gale, K. (2005) The influence of online problem- based learning on teachers' professional practice and identity. ALT-J 2005, 3(2):125-137.

Wiki, Matrix - Compare Them All. (2007) Retrieved April 19, 2007 from http://www.wikimatrix.org/

Will, Richardson, Blogs, Wikis, Podcasts and Other Powerful Web Tools for Classrooms http://weblogg-ed.com/

Will, Richardson, Learning on the Blog http://www.corwin.com/books/Book235915?siteId=corwin-press&subject=C00&q=richardson

2

E-Learning Tools as Means for Improving the Teaching-Learning Relation

Augustin Prodan[1], Paulina Mitrea[2],
Mădălina Rusu[1], Cornelia Revnic[1] and Remus Câmpean[1]
[1]*Iuliu Hațieganu University Cluj-Napoca*
[2]*Technical University Cluj-Napoca*
Romania

1. Introduction

Generally, educational activities consist of teaching and learning processes. Teachers disseminate knowledge towards learners through teaching processes, while learners acquire knowledge through learning processes. The purpose of teaching methods is to facilitate the settlement of teaching-learning relations between the dual teaching and learning processes. A teaching process is really working if and only if the associated learning process is working. Therefore, we are successful in teaching if and only if our partners (students, colleagues, etc.) obtain successes in learning (Prodan, 1996). These assertions are true in all educational contexts, from traditional face-to-face courses to new electronic educational environments offered by e-teaching and e-learning technologies. In a face-to-face course, pedagogical virtue is mainly radiated by physical presence of a good teacher. This is the reason why our approach to e-learning is so called blended learning, which combines traditional face-to-face and computer-based learning, with focus on principles of active learning.

The main goal of our work is to improve the teaching-learning relation by means of e-learning tools. For this purpose, we used Java and XML technologies to implement practical and intelligent e-learning tools (Prodan et al., 2002, 2004, 2006, 2008, 2010), which we began to incorporate in a Moodle based e-learning system (Martinez & Jagannathan, 2008).

We started our researches concerning e-learning technologies in the last years of the previous century, when we created a pool system consisting of e-courses to be used in a context of open learning. We observed that open learning is the most important component of the real learning, because the real learning is achieved for the most part through open learning. In an open learning context, learners have more control, they have the freedom to choose where, when and how to learn, each learner having his own pace. The benefits are for both slower and faster learners. The foreign students learning in a second language have extra time they need to understand the meaning of words by using dictionaries. However, we considered this new type of open learning not as a substitute, but as a supplement for traditional learning (Prodan, 1998).

We rely on new paradigms of artificial intelligence (Bayesian Inference, Case Based Reasoning and Intelligent Agents) for creating e-learning scenarios to be used in a context of active learning. An e-learning scenario combines simulation and interactive visualization and allows the learners to explore the knowledge bases with some well-defined learning purposes. For each application object, our system contains a simulation class and a visualization class. These classes are then configured to obtain a particular simulation with a specific visualization. In an e-learning scenario, visualization is an active part of the system, serving as an additional interface for modifying dynamically some parameters. The simulation and visualization classes are coded in Java, using XML format to describe the configurations for both the components and their relationships.

We use Internet as communication support in our e-learning technologies. Internet provides a general communication space, which we use as the base line infrastructure for creating e-learning spaces. We created e-learning spaces around various subjects, such as biostatistics (Prodan et al., 2004), pharmaceutical botany, analyzing medical images (Prodan et al., 2006, 2008, 2010), etc. Previously, each teacher used a private e-course organizational structure for learning management.

The main final result will be a student-centred, cost effective, Moodle based e-learning system (Martinez & Jagannathan, 2008), supporting the benefits of blended learning pedagogical models (Francis & Raftery, 2005) and allowing to improve the teaching-learnig relation.

In section 2 we present a short literature review for some e-learning tools we intend to consider in our effort to enhance the teaching-learning relation. In section 3 we propose an e-learning environment based on a Java framework for designing and implementing e-learning tools. Section 4 shows some results and experiments with e-learning scenarios and finally section 5 states some conclusions and future work.

2. E-learning tools

E-learning comprises all forms of electronically supported learning and teaching, the support being provided usually by e-learning tools. In the teaching-learning equation, the learning side is more important. This is the reason why the word "e-learning" is more frequent used than "e-teaching". Generally, the efficiency of the learning depends on teaching-learning relation and we think that it is possible to improve this relation by e-learning tools. We use Java and XML technologies to create original e-learning tools and we think the best way to follow for improving the teaching-learning relation is by using electronic portfolios and by incorporating all these e-learning tools in a Moodle based e-learning system. The subsection 2.1 illustrates some general ideas about electronic portfolios, while subsection 2.2 presents the reasons why we decided to approach a Moodle based e-learning system.

2.1 Electronic portfolios

Our students have different backgrounds, interests, levels of motivation and approaching to studying, therefore we considered that open learning is adequate to them. To improve the teaching-learning relations, we included electronic portfolios in our e-learning technologies. The Java framework provides the infrastructure for preparing e-learning scenarios based on practice and real world experiences, as practice is essential in learning activities. Our e-learning scenarios promote active learning, forcing the students to take part in real world activities, simulated on computer.

To better the human contact between students and instructor, we approached new strategies labelled as blended learning, combining e-learning and traditional face-to-face classroom instruction, with a focus on active learning. We implement e-learning scenarios relying on learner centred paradigm, where learners are encouraged to develop skills and strategies in

their own way. Learning is not considered simply as an outcome of teaching, because it is an activity having as input the results of teaching and training. Blended learning should be viewed as a fundamental redesign of the instructional model. A blended learning context can provide the independence and increased control essential to developing critical thinking. Along with the increased control that a blended learning context encourages is a scaffolded acceptance of responsibility for constructing meaning and understanding (Garrison & Kanuka, 2004). To be a critical thinker is to take control of one's thought processes and gain a metacognitive understanding of these processes, i.e., learn to learn.
In education, portfolios are described as a meaningful collection of students' work stored in a traditional folder (Farr, 1990). There are various types of portfolios, organized according to the purpose they are used for:

- Learning portfolios - used for supporting the learning processes and the on-going professional development;
- Teaching portfolios - used for supporting the teaching processes;
- Assessment portfolios - used in evaluation processes;
- Employment portfolios - used in seeking jobs.

The electronic portfolio was introduced later and represents the same collection of students' work, only this time the storage is not the traditional folder, but an electronic storage environment, such as web pages, files organized in folders and stored on a CD or on a dedicated server, etc (Barret, 2001). An electronic portfolio simply means that the portfolio is technology based. There are many benefits of electronic portfolios, versus traditional portfolios. Electronic portfolios take up little physical space, can hold a great deal of information and may be accessed with minimal effort. A learning portfolio is a collection of student work over a period of time, resulted from activities in the e-learning environment. Electronic portfolios may improve the teaching-learning relations (Rusu & Prodan, 2006). The students have a constant project to work on being actively involved in the learning process, and their motivation has increased visibly. Both the teachers and the students agreed that portfolios provide a better assessment than the traditional testing: learners can have their learning process assessed and are offered the chance to reflect on their own work. Portfolios allow constructive feedback from tutors, increasing cooperative learning and students' motivation. Portfolio assessment helps students enjoy the assignments, while enabling them to learn more easily and take an active part in their development.

2.2 Moodle based e-learning environment

This year we decided to approach Moodle in our e-learning environment. The main reason for such a decision is that Moodle was meant to embody better a student-centred paradigm, enabling to improve the teaching-learning relations. Moodle is an open source LMS (Learning Management System), so we benefit from the availability of the source code and the right to modify it. Also, Moodle gives us a lot of flexibility and is inexpensive, allowing us to face the present-day budget crisis. Other important qualities of the Moodle result just from his title. The word Moodle is an acronym, standing for Modular Object-Oriented Dynamic Learning Environment. Being modular, we can add and remove modules, considering our actual needs and requirements, and our previous experience. The programming paradigm used in Moodle is Object-Oriented as in Java. We created in Java an e-learning infrastructure and e-learning scenarios, focusing on real life objects. It is no difficult to move all our Java classes into Moodle, the programming paradigm being the

same. Moodle is a powerful tool able to provide dynamic web pages, employed to create dynamic teaching-learning relations. In our previous e-learning experiments, we used this valuable characteristic. To implement the e-learning scenarios, we used Java technologies for dynamic processes and XML technologies for dynamic content (data and documents).
A valuable pedagogical advantage of the Moodle, arising at both teaching and learning level, is constructivism. Teachers construct their own teaching strategies and cooperate for enhancing these strategies, using a feedback with reactive suggestions. Also, learners use e-learning modules that allow peer to peer interaction and cooperation, acting and thinking cooperatively.

3. E-learning environment

We defined and implemented a Java framework for designing and implementing intelligent and practical e-learning tools, to be used by both the students and the teaching staff in a context of open learning. This framework provides the infrastructure for preparing e-learning scenarios based on practice and real world experiences, as practice is essential in learning activities. Our e-learning scenarios promote active learning, forcing the students to take part in real world activities simulated on computer. Also, we designed e-learning tools based on bootstrapping methods (which are quite valuable for reasoning in uncertain conditions), with the purpose to simulate laboratory experiments in both didactic and research activities.
An e-learning scenario is in fact like a traditional lesson, and the ideal solution is to simulate a teaching-learning relation with a virtual teacher able to interact with the learners and to instruct them (Prodan et al., 2008). A good traditional teacher learns all the time from previous didactic experiences. Based on this historical feedback, the teacher exploits prior specific successful episodes, and avoids prior failures. We introduce a similar feedback mechanism in our technology of elaborating e-learning scenarios (Figure 1). The feedback information, collected from learners' remarks and from prior results and successes, is stored in case bases. The relevant cases are retrieved and adapted to fit new situations from new e-learning scenarios, or to improve the previous ones. In addition, our approach in creating an e-learning scenario relies upon a special sort of goal oriented intelligent agents

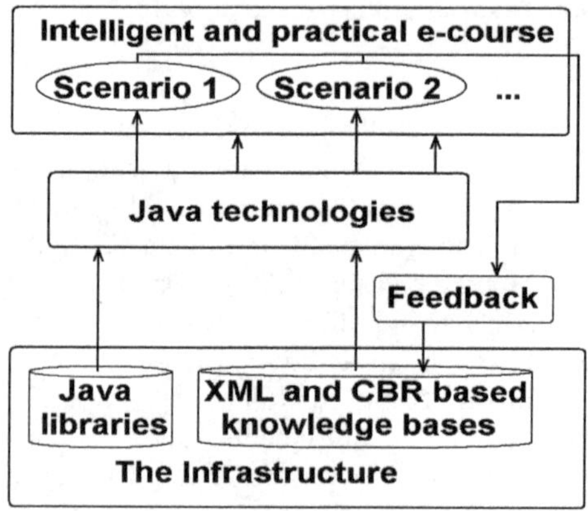

Fig. 1. The generation of the e-learning scenarios.

(Nwana, 1996), able to incorporate knowledge, teaching methods and pedagogical characteristics into e-courses (Kanuka 2008). We intend to implement a simulation of some intelligence based actions and initiatives, that are to be incorporated into e-learning scenarios, with the purpose to map, to plan and to monitor the pace and the progress of a learning process. Following the traditional model, the cases of positive experiences from previous e-learning scenarios are stored into case bases created with XML and CBR (Case-Based Reasoning) technologies (Leake, 1996).

An e-course consists of a set of e-learning scenarios, each e-learning scenario being generated by virtue of some well-defined learning objectives. To generate intelligent and practical e-learning scenarios for a particular e-course, we created first a particular infrastructure containing the knowledge from particular domains of the target e-course. For this purpose, we generated consistent Java and XML based knowledge bases, containing integrated knowledge of the best teachers. In addition, we implemented in Java a set of simulation algorithms describing real world phenomena, processes and activities we have to include in e-courses. When generating a new e-learning scenario, we use a feedback mechanism based on our historical experience from previous e-learning scenarios (Figure 1). Also, we use Java technologies to generate intelligent and practical e-learning scenarios, based on new AI (Artificial Intelligence) paradigms, such as Case-Based Reasoning, Bayesian Inference and Intelligent Agents (Prodan et al., 2006, 2008, 2010). A learner can access the e-course and launch an e-learning scenario either locally, or via WWW in a context of distance learning.

When generating an e-learning scenario, we focus on pedagogical context and have all the time in mind the following pedagogical characteristics:

- **Friendly interface** - When the learners have the initiative to enter the e-course, a teaching-learning relation is initiated through the user interface. Hence, it follows that if our purpose is to facilitate the learners' access to knowledge, our system provides a friendly, easy to learn, efficient and agreeable graphical user interface.
- **General information** - When a learner enters for the first time into an e-course, we have to visualize some general information about that e-course, the objectives of the e-course, specific information about e-learning scenarios and how to use them.
- **Objectives** - Each e-learning scenario is generated by virtue of some well defined learning objectives. When a learner launches a particular e-learning scenario, it is necessary to visualize the objectives corresponding to that scenario. By doing so, we help the learners to see what it is expected to be able to do after they will traverse the respective e-learning scenario.
- **Orientation facilities** - When the learners use e-learning scenarios to navigate in an ocean of information and knowledge, browsing through XML based knowledge bases and hyperdocuments, they want to know at any time their position. We implement in e-learning scenarios many techniques to facilitate the navigation, such as maps, marked routes, bookmarks, diagrams, queries, etc.
- **Layered structure** - An e-course has a layered structure from simple to complex, allowing each learner to access an optimum layer, depending on his purpose and previous knowledge.
- **Customization** - The functionality of an e-learning scenario is adapted to ability and purpose of each learner. Customization can be either static or dynamic. Static customization is an easy task, being carried out by a set of parameters before run time. Dynamic customization is more difficult, because it is necessary to collect information about learner during e-learning scenario execution.

- **Global and local coherency** - To improve global coherency of an e-learning scenario, we implement adequate visualization and orientation techniques. As concerning local coherency, each link must have a well-defined destination and it is necessary to minimize the fragmentation, to avoid the confusion and getting lost.
- **Learning by doing** - We think that practice is essential in learning activities, because learning by doing increases substantially the effectiveness of learning processes. We elaborate practical e-learning tools, allowing the learners to work on experiments with real world items.
- **Active learning** - The experienced learners can take part in activities of design and elaboration of some particular e-learning scenarios for beginners.
- **Homework assignments** - Previous studies show that most traditional learners appreciate the homework assignments. However, in traditional teaching-learning relations, the teachers do not have the means to react properly to the individual problems the learners have when working out the assignments. This problem is overcome in case of a simulated teaching-learning relation, because the virtual teacher is always present in a running e-learning scenario.
- **Virtual teacher evaluates the solution** - Before the final solution is sent to the virtual teacher, each learner can obtain some hints and suggestions to handle the problem. After the final solution is sent, the learner gets the outcome for self-evaluation.

3.1 Stochastic modelling and simulation

We approached e-courses in domains of biostatistics, stochastic modelling and simulation, using as infrastructure a set of Java class libraries for stochastic modelling and simulation, created and implemented by us (Prodan & Prodan Radu, 2002). The papers (Prodan et al., 1999, 2000) demonstrate the advantages of stochastic models for representation of real world activities and focuses on a Java package, which includes a collection of classes for stochastic modelling and simulation. In order to employ mathematics and statistics to analyze some phenomena processes and activities of the real world, we first construct a stochastic model. Once the theoretical model has been constructed, in theory we are able to determine analytically the answers to a lot of questions related to these phenomena and processes. However, in practice is very difficult to get analytically the answers for many of our questions. This is the reason why we must implement the probabilistic mechanism using a programming language, then to perform a simulation study on a computer. Due to actual spread of fast and inexpensive computational power everywhere in the world, the best approach is to model the real phenomenon as faithfully as possible, and then rely on a simulation study to analyze it. We created and implemented a collection of Java class libraries for stochastic modelling and simulation. The stochastic models constructed accurately represent real world phenomena processes and activities, particularly in medicine, pharmacy and health care. We use these Java libraries as an infrastructure to build intelligent and practical e-learning tools, integrated in an electronic educational environment.

We have considered three levels of simulation. The first level consists of simulating random numbers, as they are the basis of any stochastic simulation study (Figure 2). Based on the elements of the first level, we created a second level of simulation applied for distributional models, stochastic processes and Monte Carlo methods. We implemented a hierarchy of Java classes which model the classical distributions and we created a collection of Java class libraries for stochastic modelling and simulation (Prodan & Prodan Rodica, 2001).

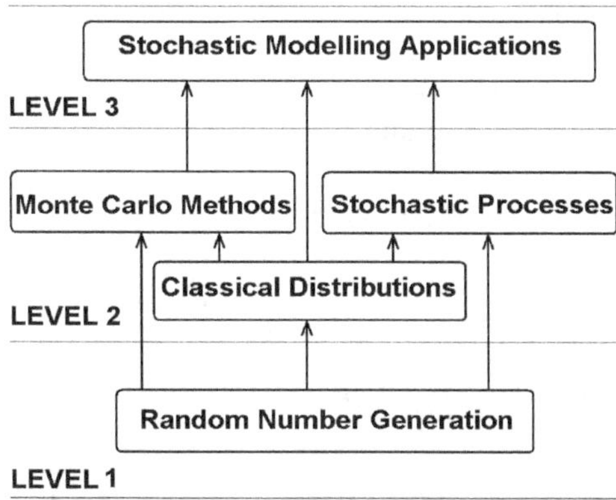

Fig. 2. The simulation levels.

The first two levels of simulation are the basis for the third level, which is devoted to applications. We used distributional models, stochastic processes and Monte Carlo methods to implement some stochastic modelling applications that accurately represent real world processes, phenomena and activities, particularly in medicine, pharmacy and health care (Prodan & Prodan Rodica, 2001; Gorunescu et al., 2002).

3.2 Java infrastructure for distributional models

The classical random variables are the simplest stochastic models, also called distributional models, which enter into the composition of other complex models. We propose a hierarchy of Java classes for modelling the classical distributions. Each distribution class encapsulates a particular simValue() method (Figure 3).

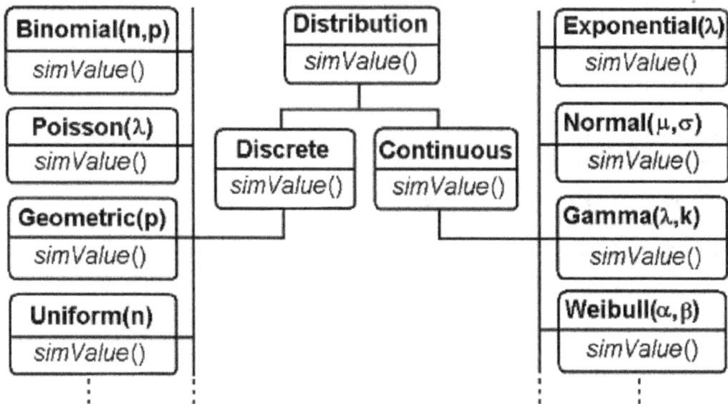

Fig. 3. The hierarchy of Java classes for distributional models.

Each distribution is determined by a set parameters and a distribution function. Based on these elements we defined a Java class for each distribution, obtaining a generic distributional model (Figure 4). This Java class is used to create one or more objects, which are instances with particular values for parameters. Also, a simulation algorithm is defined for each class, which is able to generate a specific value for the corresponding distribution. So, there is a set of simulation algorithms belonging to the whole hierarchy of Java classes, these algorithms being implemented via the polymorphic method called simValue(). The particular implementation of the simulation algorithm for each class is based on one or more of the following techniques: the Inverse Transform Technique, the Acceptance-Rejection Technique and the Composition Technique (Ross, 1990).

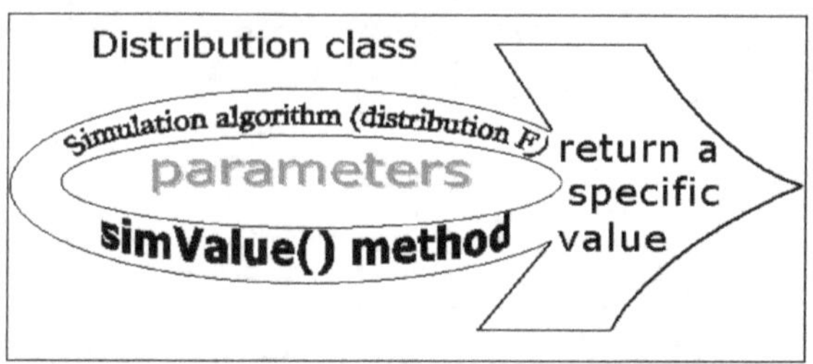

Fig. 4. The generic distributional model.

The hierarchy of Java classes for modelling the classical distributions is included in a JAR (Java ARchieve) library. To generate a single value from a particular distribution, it is necessary to import the corresponding distribution class from the library, then to instantiate an object of that class, and finally to call the polymorphic simValue() method based on this object (Figure 5). An instance of a particular class can be used to simulate a sequence of values for the corresponding random variable, by calling simValue() as many times as needed.

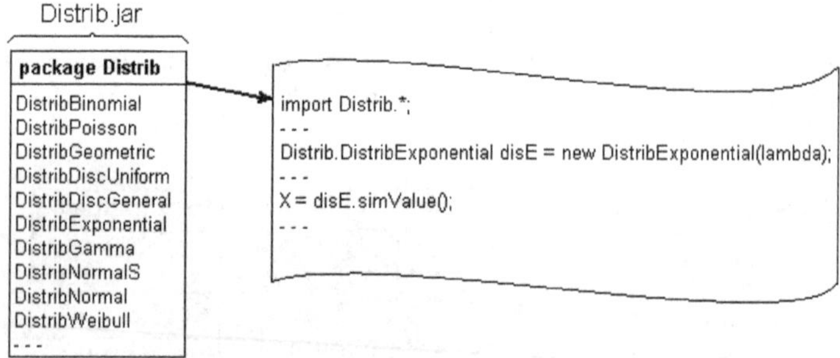

Fig. 5. The import of the distribution classes from the JAR library.

To make a simulation study for a distribution, it is necessary to generate more values, a sequence of values. One may choose to continually generate additional values, stopping when the efficiency of the simulation is good enough. Generally, one may use the variance of the estimators obtained during the simulation study to decide when to stop the generation of additional values. For example, if the objective is to estimate the mean value $\mu=E(X_i)$, i = 0, 1, 2, ..., one may continue to generate new data values until one has generated a number of data values for which the estimate of the standard error is less than an acceptable value.

3.3 Bootstrapping e-tools for simulating laboratory works

Laboratory works play a fundamental role in learning environments, allowing learners to operate on experiments with real world items. Practice is essential in learning activities, because learning by doing increases substantially the effectiveness of the learning processes. Practical exercises are designed to prompt conceptual reasoning and critical thinking which prompts the application of science to everyday situations. Heavy emphasis is put on detailed laboratory reports, written answers to exercises, completed homework assignments, tests and group work. Often we must repeat the same laboratory experiment many times, to make our utmost for all the students to participate and watch it. Students learn to ask questions, design experiments and analyze data, facts and theories. Also, statistical methods play a fundamental role in our university's didactic and research activities. Both the students and the teaching staff use traditional statistical methods to infer the truth from sample data gathered in laboratory experiments.

However, there are some reasons to minimize the number of laboratory experiments. In some cases, the repeated laboratory experiments mean the consumption of a great deal of substances and reactants. In other cases, there is a range of ethically motivated reasons to reduce the number of animals (frogs, guinea pigs, etc) used in experimentation. As the previous conditions are quite contradictory, we have to search for a solution that balances them. We perform an actual laboratory experiment only once for each group of students, then we repeat the same laboratory experiment by simulations as many times as necessary, each student being able to take part in analyzing data, making exercises and inferences.

We implemented bootstrapping methods into software tools, as applications in our simulation system (Figure 2), with the purpose to simulate laboratory experiments in both didactic and research activities (Prodan & Câmpean, 2005). Usually, the result of a laboratory experiment is a set of output values v_1, v_2, …, v_n, named original, or actual sample. The experimenter (student, teacher, or researcher) uses this sample to perform data analysis and statistical inferences, then to draw conclusions. Bootstrapping methods involves repeating the original data analysis procedure with many replicate sets of pseudo-data. We implemented a general discrete distribution (Figure 10) to generate sets of pseudo-data, based on original set of data v_1, v_2, …, v_n. By resampling the original data, we generate artificial samples on which we make inference of interest as for the original sample. Using a bootstrapping e-tool and the computer power, the experimenter can repeat the original experiment without any consumption of substances and reactants, and without use of animals, obtaining pseudo-data as plausible as those obtained from the original experiment. Our bootstrapping tools use the computer power to obtain reliable standard errors, confidence intervals and other measures of uncertainty for a wide range of problems. Moreover, the bootstrap can produce a more accurate confidence interval than would produce based on normal approximation.

4. Results and experiments

In the first phase of our research we designed and implemented a hierarchy of Java classes for distributional models which we included in a JAR library, to be used as an infrastructure for stochastic modelling and simulation. We present in subsection 4.1 the main distributions we implemented in this library. Based on this infrastructure we created e-learning scenarios to be used in a context of active learning, relying on practice and real world experiences. Subsection 4.2 shows some of these e-learning scenarios.

4.1 The implementation of distributional models

We implemented a hierarchy of Java classes for distributional models (Figure 3). Java is the standard programming language for Internet applications (Prodan & Prodan Mihai, 1997); this is the reason why we used this language to create the infrastructure for e-learning scenarios. We present below Java classes implemented for some distributions, as well as simulation examples.

Binomial distribution

```
package Distrib;
public class DistribBinomial extends DistributionDiscrete {
  public DistribBinomial(int n, double p) { // Constructor
        this.n = n;
        this.p = p;
  }
  public double simValue() { // Simulation of a value
        double U, rap, pp, F;
        U = Math.random();
        rap = p/(1-p);
        pp = Math.exp(n*Math.log(1-p)); // probability X=i
        F =  pp; // F(i)=P{X<=i} distribution function
        double k = 0;
        while (U > F) {
          pp = (rap*(n-k)/(k+1))*pp;
          F = F + pp;
          k++;
        }
        return k;
  } // simValue()
  public double initRecursion() {// Initial value for recursion
        return Math.pow(1-p, n); // P{X=0}
  }
  public double valRecursion(int k) {// Value for recursion
        return (double)(n-k)*p/(k+1)/(1-p);
  }
  int n;
  double p;
}///;
```

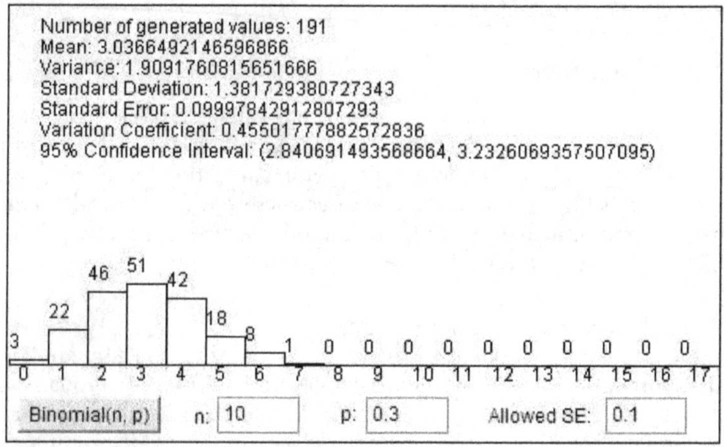

Fig. 6. Simulation from binomial distribution.

Poisson distribution

```
package Distrib;
public class DistribPoisson extends DistributionDiscrete {
  public DistribPoisson(double lambda) { // Constructor
        this.lambda = lambda;
  }
  public double simValue() { // Simulation of a value
        double U, pp, F;
        U = Math.random();
        pp = Math.exp(-lambda); // probability X=i
        F =  pp;  // F(i)=P{X<=i} distribution function
        double k=0;
        while (U > F) {
          pp = lambda*pp/(k+1);
          F = F + pp;
          k++;
        }
        return k;
  } // simValue()
  public double initRecursion() { // Initial value for recursion
        return Math.exp(-lambda); // P{X=0}
  }
  public double valRecursion(int k) { // Value for recursion
        return (double)lambda/(k+1);
  }
  double lambda;
}///;
```

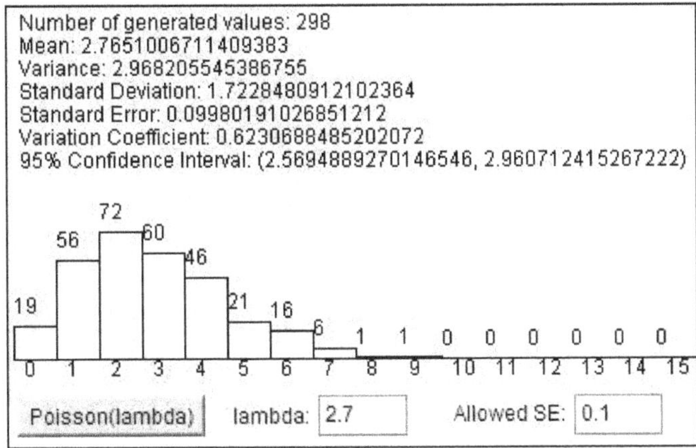

Fig. 7. Simulation from a Poisson distribution.

Geometric distribution

```
package Distrib;
public class DistribGeometric extends DistributionDiscrete {
  public DistribGeometric(double p) { // Constructor
        this.p = p;
  }
  public double simValue() { // Simulation of a value
        double U; // geometric random variable in (0,1)
        U = Math.random(); // Generate a random number
        return (int)(Math.log(U)/Math.log(1-p));
  } // simValue()
  public double initRecursion() { // Initial value for recursion
        return p; // P{X=0}
  }
  public double valRecursion(int k) { // Value for recursion
        return 1-p;
  }
  double p;
}///;
```

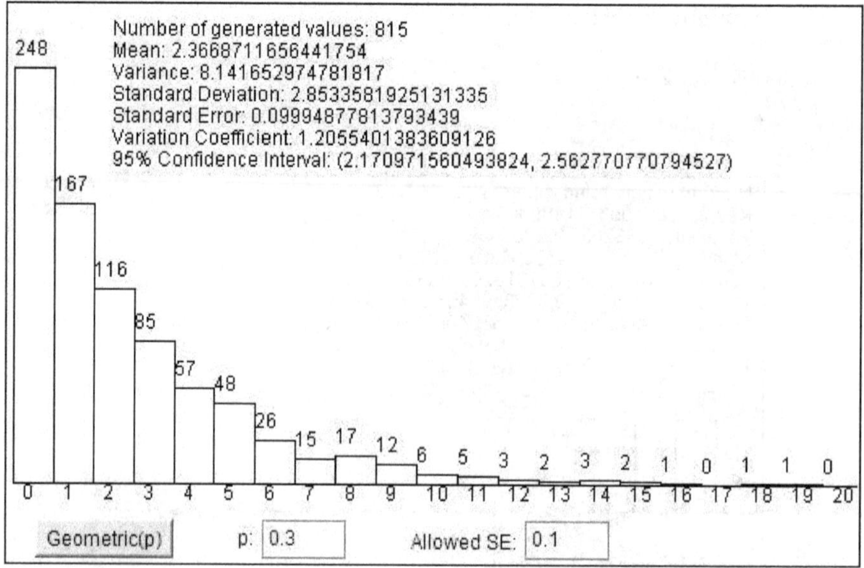

Fig. 8. Simulation from a geometric distribution.

Uniform discrete distribution

```
package Distrib;
public class DistribDiscUniform extends DistributionDiscrete {
  public DistribDiscUniform(int numb) { // Constructor
        n = numb;
        p = (double)1/n;
  }
  public double simValue() { // Simulation of a value
        int X; // Random variable
        double U; // Uniform random variable in (0,1)
        U = Math.random(); // Generate a random number
        return (int)(n*U);
  } // simValue()
  public double initRecursion() { // Initial value for recursion
        return p; // P{X=0}
  }
  public double valRecursion(int k) { // Value for recursion
        return (double) 1;
  }
  int n;
  double p;
}///;
```

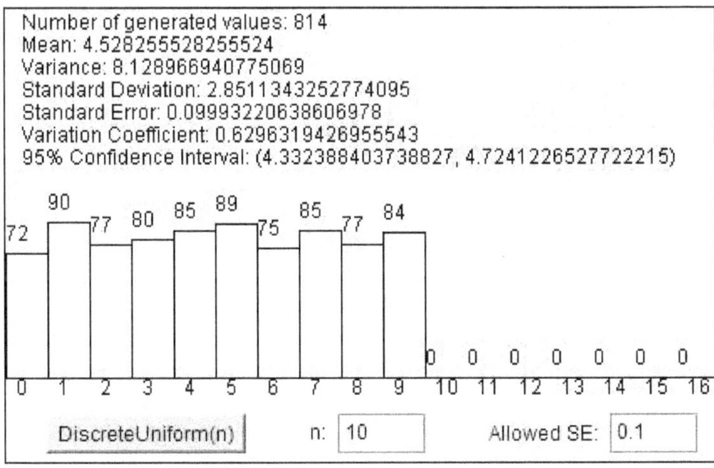

Fig. 9. Simulation from a uniform discrete distribution.

General discrete distribution

```
package Distrib;
public class DistribDiscGen extends DistributionDiscrete {
   public DistribDiscGen(int n, double[] p) { // Constructor
            this.n = n;
            this.p = p;
            for (int i=0; i<p.length; i++) {
               if (pMax<p[i]) pMax=p[i];
            }
            c = pMax*n;
   }
   public double simValue() { // Simulation of a value
            Distrib.DistribDiscUniform dDU = new DistribDiscUniform(n);
            do {
               Y = (int)dDU.simValue();
               U = Math.random();
            }
            while (U > (double)(p[Y]/(c/n)));
            return Y;
   } // simValue()
   int n, Y;
   double pMax=0, c, U;
   double[] p = new double[n];
}///;
```

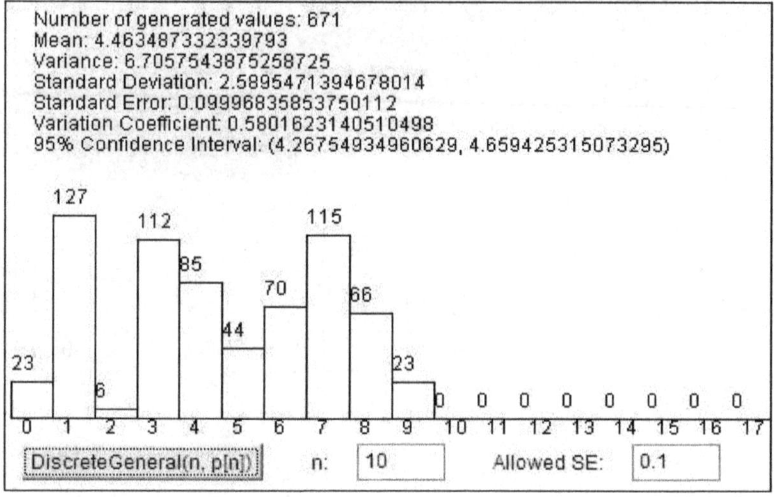

Fig. 10. Simulation from a general discrete distribution.

Normal standard distribution

```
package Distrib;
import Distrib.*;
import java.util.*;
public class DistribNormalS extends DistributionContinue {
   public double simValue() { // Simulation of a value
         double y1, y2, y, Z, U;
         Distrib.DistribExponential Y1 = new Distrib.DistribExponential(1);
         Distrib.DistribExponential Y2 = new Distrib.DistribExponential(1);
         Random R = new Random();
         do {
            y1 = Y1.simValue();
            y2 = Y2.simValue();
            y = y2-Math.pow(y1-1, 2)/2;
         } while (y<0);
         U = R.nextDouble();
         if (U<0.5) Z = y1;
         else Z = -y1;
         return Z;
   } // simValue()
} ///;
```

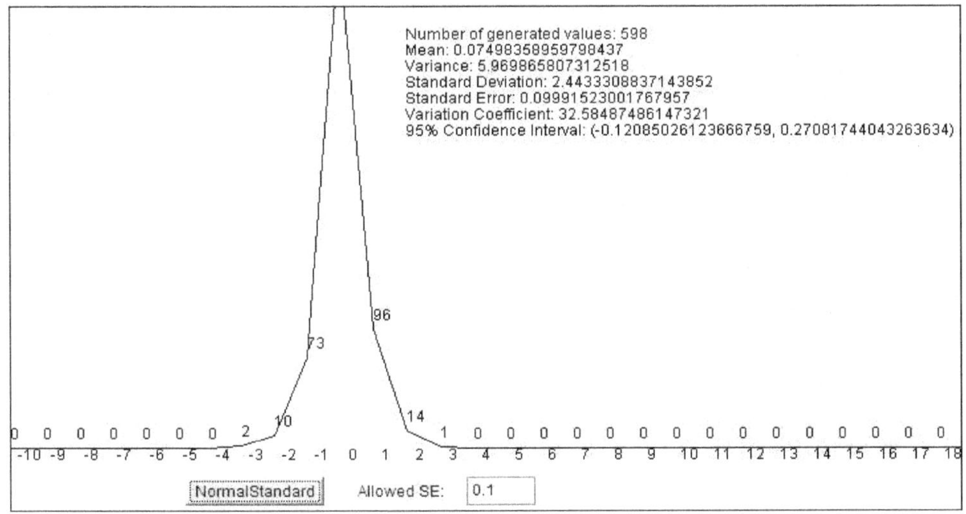

Fig. 11. Simulation from normal standard distribution

Normal distribution

```
package Distrib;
public class DistribNormal extends DistributionContinue {
  public DistribNormal(double miu, double sigma) { // Constructor
        this.miu = miu;
        this.sigma = sigma;
  }
  public double simValue() { // Simulation of a value
        double Z;
        Z = NS.simValue();
        X = miu+sigma*Z;
        return X;
  } // simValue()
  double miu, sigma, X;
  Distrib.DistribNormalS NS = new Distrib.DistribNormalS();
}///;
```

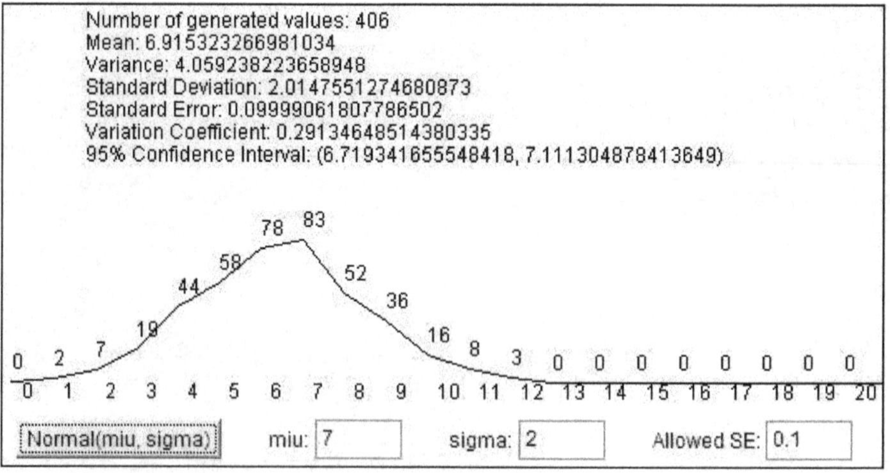

Fig. 12. Simulation from a normal distribution.

Exponential distribution

```
package Distrib;
public class DistribExponential extends DistributionContinue {
   public DistribExponential(double lambda) { // Constructor
          this.lambda = lambda;
   }
   public double simValue() { // Simulation of a value
          U = Math.random();
          X = -1/lambda*Math.log(U);
          return X;
   } // simValue()
   double lambda, X, U;
}///;
```

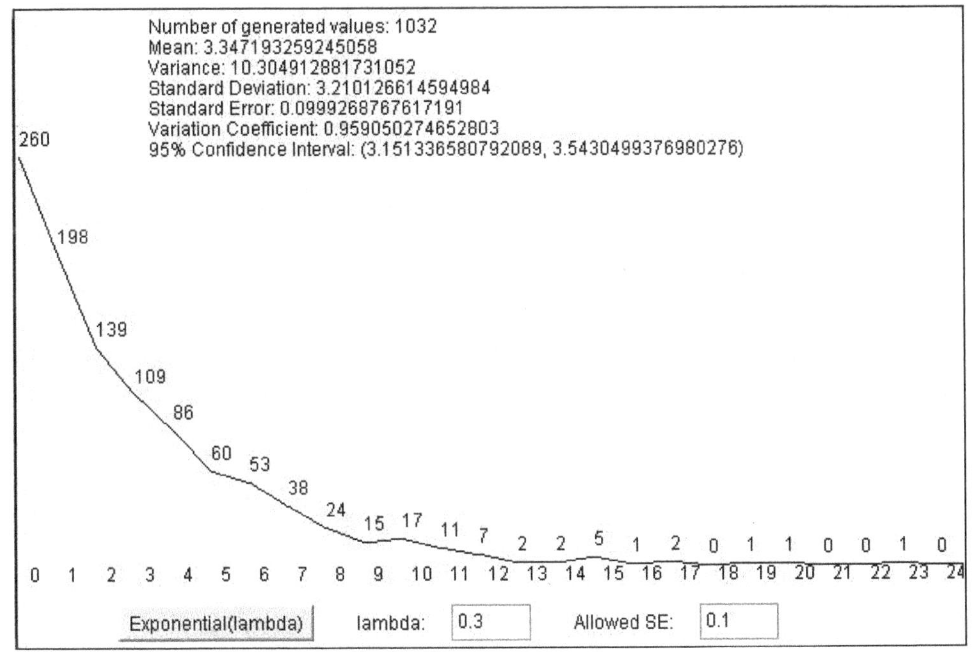

Fig. 13. Simulation from an exponential distribution.

Gamma distribution

```
package Distrib;
public class DistribGamma extends DistributionContinue {
   public DistribGamma(double lambda, int n) { // Constructor
            this.lambda = lambda;
            this.n = n;
   }
   public double simValue() { // Simulation of a value
            double U, X=0;
            for (int k=1; k<=n; k++) {
                     U = Math.random();
                     X = X-Math.log(U)/lambda;
            }
            return X;
   } // simValue()
   double lambda;
   int n;
}///;
```

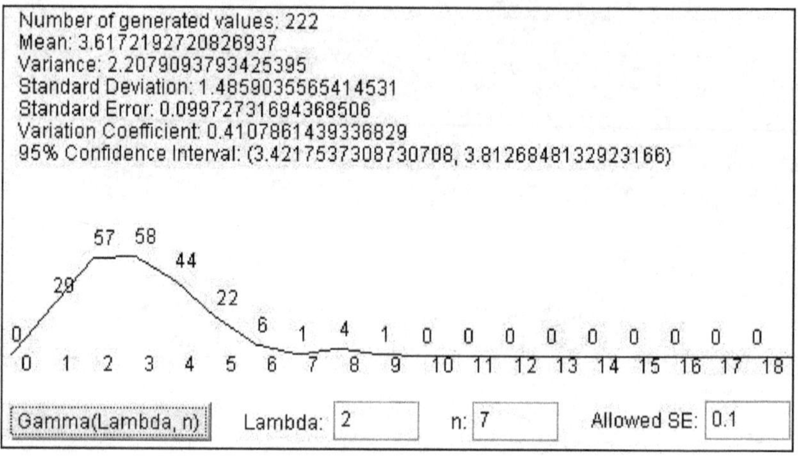

Fig. 14. Simulation from a gamma distribution.

Weibull distribution

```
package Distrib;
public class DistribWeibull extends DistributionContinue {
  public DistribWeibull(double alfa, double beta) { // Constructor
        this.alfa = alfa;
        this.beta = beta;
  }
  public double simValue() { // Simulation of a value
        double U;
        U = Math.random();
        X = 1/alfa*Math.pow(-Math.log(U), 1/beta);
        return X;
  } // simValue()
  double alfa, beta, X;
}///;
```

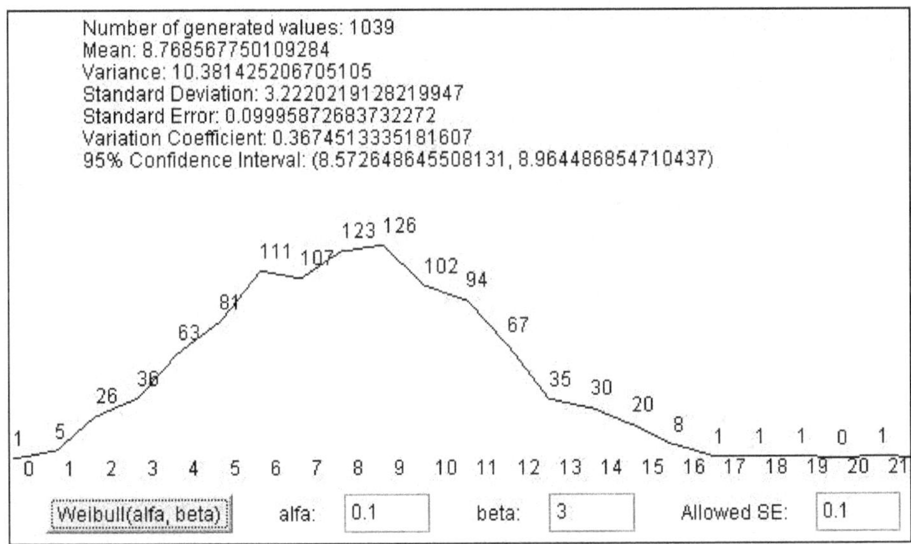

Fig. 15. Simulation from a Weibull distribution.

4.2 Experiments with e-learning scenarios

Based on the simulation system presented previously (Figure 2), we create and implement various models as applications, to be used as e-learning scenarios. We create e-learning scenarios by looking at problems that can be put in a probabilistic framework. Every new concept is developed systematically through completely worked out examples from current medical, pharmaceutical and health care problems. In addition, we introduce in each e-learning scenario specific probability models that fit out some real life problems, by assessing the probabilities of certain events from actual past databases.

4.2.1 E-learning scenarios for distributional models

As an example, we propose an e-learning scenario for students in medicine and health care. A learner that traverses such a scenario will be able to apply a binomial distributional model in studying the chance of patients suffering from a particular type of cancer, to survive for at least a six month period after diagnosis. We would have to appeal to previous studies and information from actual databases to assess the chances of a patient surviving. This might indicate, for instance, that the probability of survival is $p = 0.3$, and consequently the complementary probability of death is $q = 1 - p = 0.7$. In real life, we are frequently interested what might happen to a group of patients we are studying. For example, we may formulate the following problem, as a piece of the current e-learning scenario:

"*Of the* 11 *patients in a particular cancer program, what is the chance of 7 or more of them surviving at least six months past diagnosis?*"

If p_k is the probability that k patients survives (where $k \leq 11$), to solve the previous problem we have to compute the sum $P = p_7+p_8+p_9+p_{10}+p_{11}$. The binomial distribution B (11, 0.3) can be applied to calculate these probabilities. If the learner is a beginner in Probabilities and Statistics, maybe needs to get immediately an explanatory text about binomial distribution B (n, p). Then it is possible to directly apply the formula and compute the probabilities for binomial B (11, 0.3). Using the formula $p_k = 11!/(k!(11\text{-}k)!)(0.3)^k\ (0.7)^{11\text{-}k}$, for $k \leq 11$, one obtain the values $p_7 \approx 0.017$, $p_8 \approx 0.003$, and $p_9 \approx p_{10} \approx p_{11} \approx 0$. Finally, the learner can give the solution for the previous problem: $P = 0.017 + 0.003 = 0.02$. The e-learning scenario may be resourceful in showing additional information when necessary. The learner may ask whenever for any information, but intelligent software tool may have also the initiative to show some information when it considers that is an adequate moment. We think that Bayesian inference is suitable for deciding when the learner needs some supplementary information. We have to combine Bayesian inference with a sort of intelligent agents, to prepare and to configure a suggestive visualization, based on a friendly and efficient dialogue with the learner. As an example, for any learner may be useful to see a visualization of the previous probabilities p_k, where $k \in \{0, 1, 2, ..., 11\}$, in a very suggestive column format, and to recognize the solution to previous problem shown with dashed columns (Figure 16).

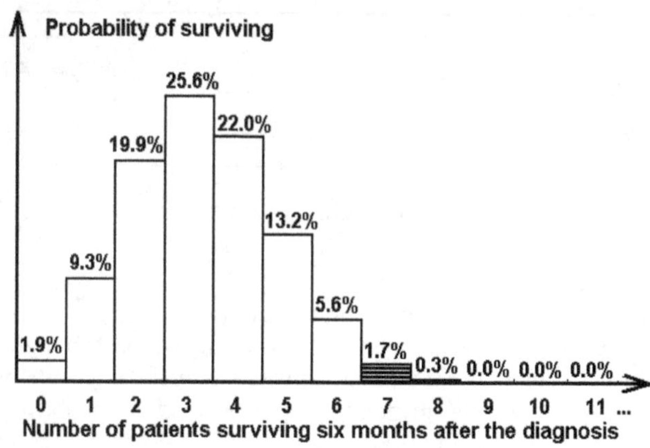

Fig. 16. A graphical solution for the patient surviving problem, based on the binomial distribution B (11, 0.3).

The previous distribution model, which is binomial distribution B (11, 0.3), may also be applied in an e-learning scenario for students in pharmacy. For example, suppose they have to test the effect of a dose of digitalis on frogs. In this case, the problem can be formulated as follows:

"Injection of a certain dose of digitalis per unit of body weight into a large number of frogs causes the death of 30% of them. What is the probability that the number of deaths will be 7 or more, when this dose is injected into each of a group of 11 frogs?"

It is obvious that we may use the same statistical template to create a similar e-learning scenario for students in pharmacy, but with specific texts.

4.2.2 E-learning scenarios for simulation studies

To make a simulation study for a distribution, it is necessary to generate more values, a sequence of values. The learner has the possibility to interactively select a distribution, to set some parameters, to visualize the results of a simulation and to form some conclusions. For example, the learner may choose to generate N = 995 values from previous binomial distribution B (11, 0.3) and to visualize them in a column format. In addition, the learner may visually verify the results of a simulation by comparing them with theoretical values, computed by theoretical formulae (Figure 17). There is an obvious relation between theoretical values and the values presented in Figure 16, as in the previous scenario we used the binomial model B (11, 0.3).

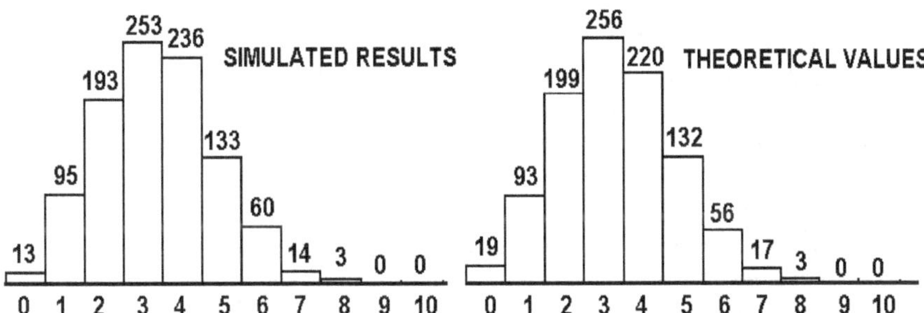

Fig. 17. Simulated versus theoretical values in case of the binomial distribution B (11, 0.3).

The learner may choose to continually generate additional values, stopping when the efficiency of the simulation is good enough. Generally, the learner may use the variance of the estimators obtained during the simulation study to decide when to stop the generation of additional values, i.e., when the efficiency of the simulation study is acceptable. The smaller this variance is, the smaller is the amount of simulation needed to obtain a fixed precision. For example, if the objective is to estimate the mean value $\mu = E(X_i)$, i=0, 1, 2, ..., the learner should continue to generate new data until are generated n data values for which the estimate of the standard error, SE $= s/\sqrt{n}$, is less than an acceptable value given previously and named *Allowed SE*, s being the sample standard deviation. Sample means and sample variances are recursively computed. The final values of these parameters, the confidence interval and other statistics are showed as the result of the simulation study. Figure 18 shows a comparison of the results for two simulations from binomial distribution B (11, 0.3), first simulation with allowed standard error of 0.1, and second simulation with allowed standard error of 0.05.

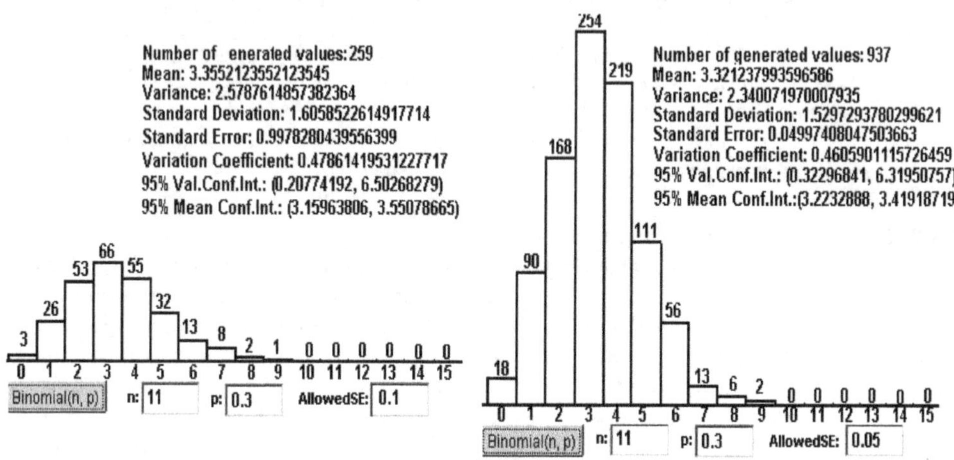

Fig. 18. A simulation with *Allowed SE* = 0.1, versus a simulation with *Allowed SE*=0.05, in case of binomial distribution $B(11, 0.3)$

The number of generated values is determined by the value *Allowed SE* introduced by the learner, as the simulation stops when the condition $s/\sqrt{n} \le$ *Allowed SE* is true. For the left side simulation, with allowed standard error of 0.1, are generated 259 values, while for the right side simulation, with allowed standard error of 0.05, are generated 937 values.

When simulate from a continuous random variable X, a generated value $x \in X$ is approximated with a given *precision* expressed by the number of decimal digits after the decimal point. The learner has the possibility to choose a precision of one, two, or even more decimal digits. If a coarse approximation is accepted, no decimals are considered and the real value x is approximated by $int(x)$, that is by integer part of the x. In this case the continuous random variable X is rudely approximated by a discrete one, and the results of a simulation can be graphically expressed in a segmented line format, each segment joining the top sides of two neighbouring columns. If a precision of one decimal digit is selected, a more refined segmented line can more precisely visualize the results of the same simulation. With a precision of two decimal digits, a more refined visualization is obtained. The higher this precision is, the higher is the *resolution* realized in visualization. Figure 19 compares two visualizations for the same set of generated values from the standard normal distribution N(0, 1), the first visualization being with a precision of one decimal digit (Figure 19, graph a), and the second with a precision of two decimal digits (Figure 19, graph b).

As can be seen in this figure, when the precision grows with one decimal digit, the resolution grows ten times. With a precision of one decimal digit, ten numbers are considered between two successive integers, while if the precision is of two decimal digits, one hundred numbers are considered between two successive integers. When necessary, intermediate resolutions can be considered. Figure 20 shows a similar comparison for the exponential distribution with parameter $\lambda = 0.3$.

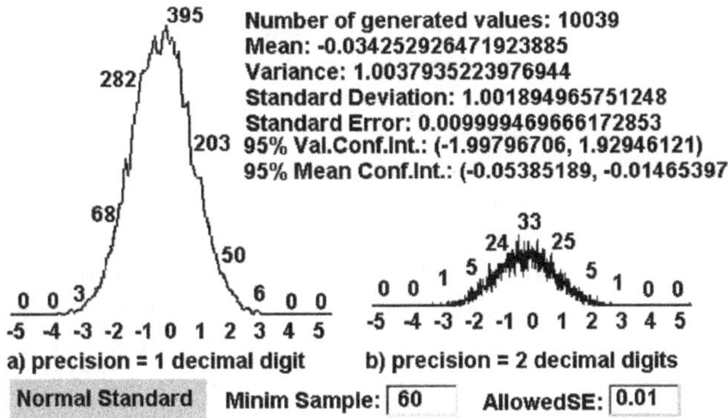

Fig. 19. The same set of generated values from the Standard Normal distribution N (0, 1), visualized with a precision of one decimal digit, versus a precision of two decimal digits.

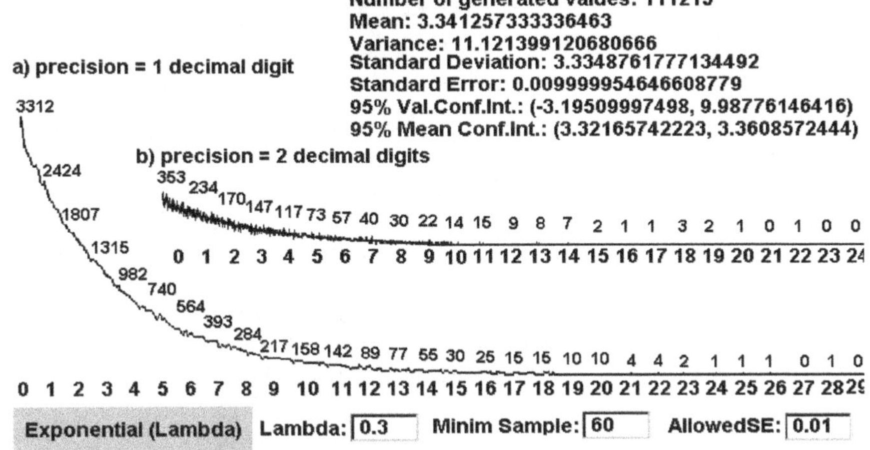

Fig. 20. The same set of generated values from the exponential distribution E (0.3), visualized with a precision of one decimal digit, versus a precision of two decimal digits.

4.2.3 A Markov model for geriatric patients' behaviour

We modelled the flow of patients through chronic diseases departments (Gorunescu et al., 2002) and based on these models we created e-learning scenarios. The planning of medical service within a chronic healthcare department is a complex problem the staffs has to face, because patients of long-term services occupy the beds for long periods of time and a high quality medical care costs a lot of money. Under these circumstances, a balanced policy between a high quality service measured by the number of beds and suitable costs becomes a necessity for the administration in order to get full value for the money they have spent. With this end in view, using the simulation of distributional models and stochastic processes, we modelled the patient flow through chronic diseases departments. The use of stochastic compartmental analysis, which assumes probabilistic behaviour of the patients around the system, is considered a more realistic representation of an actual situation rather than simpler deterministic model. In order to simulate the model, we have split it into two parts: the arrival of patients and the in-patient care. Patients are initially admitted into acute care consisting of diagnosis, assessment and rehabilitation. The most of patients either are released and therefore re-enter the community, or die after such a period of acute care. However, a certain number of patients may be considered to be unable to look after themselves, and therefore pass from acute into long-stay care where they may remain for a considerable amount of time, or they will eventually die.

The arrival of patients is modelled as a Poisson process with a parameter estimated by using the inter-arrival times (Prodan et al., 1999). These times are independent exponential random variables, each with parameter λ (the rate of arrivals) and with the corresponding density function $f(t) = \lambda e^{-\lambda t}$, $t \geq 0$. Figure 21 shows a simulation of the Poisson arrivals at rate $\lambda = 2.75$ per day.

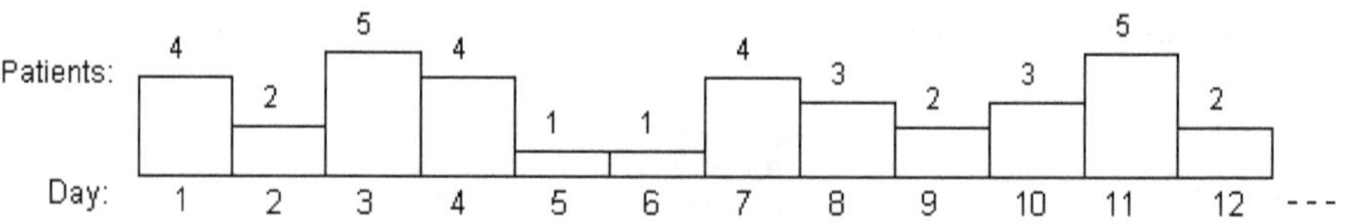

Fig. 21. The Poisson arrivals at rate $\lambda = 2.75$ per day.

The in-patient care time is modelled as a mixed-exponential phase-type distribution, where the number of terms in the mixture corresponds to the number of stages of patient care. A common scenario is that there are two stages for in-patient care: acute and long-stay, composing in this case two exponential distributions with parameters λ_1 and λ_2, representing the corresponding access rate for each stage. In this case, the mixed-exponential phase-type distribution has the density function $f(x) = \rho\lambda_1 e^{-\lambda_1 t} + (1-\rho)\lambda_2 e^{-\lambda_2 t}$, which implies a mean care time of $\rho/\lambda_1+(1-\rho)/\lambda_2$ days per patient (Prodan et al., 2000). Figure 22 shows a simulation for the in-patient care time with parameters $\rho = 0.93$, $\lambda_1 = 0.04$ and $\lambda_2 = 0.001$, resulting a mean care time of 93.25 days per patient.

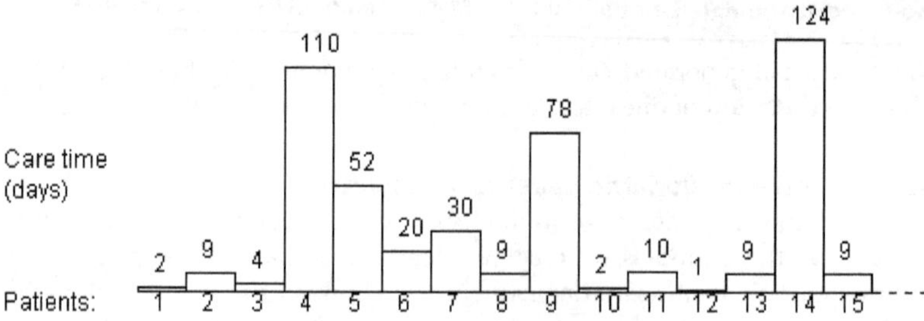

Fig. 22. The simulated results for in-patient care time.

This model enables us to study the whole system of geriatric care and can be used to look at the time patients spend in hospital and the subsequent time patients spend in the community. Interesting real phenomena can be studied during simulation experiences, such as rejection at entrance due to a brimful department, the resources being limited. Both medical staff and hospital administrators agreed that such a model could be used to maximize the efficiency of the chronic diseases departments and to optimize the use of hospital resources in order to improve hospital care. We used this model in training health care teams, based on e-learning technologies.

4.2.4 E-learning tools for wound image understanding

Medical images are valuable in both didactic and research activities, for students in medicine, pharmacy and health care. Computerized image processing contains methods for non-invasive wound evaluation, allowing an accurate diagnosis in a large category of patients with damaged and wounded skin. Generally, wounds have a non-uniform mixture of yellow slough, red granulation tissue and black necrotic tissue. Relying on a high quality of image acquisition, we can analyze a succession in time of more images for the same wound and assess changes in wound healing, i.e. the recovery or worse evolution. Our aim is to create and implement in Java an automatic method which can be used as a reference standard for colour and texture wound analysis. The purpose is to create e-learning scenarios for wound image understanding and wound healing simulation, by applying this method to large amounts of wound image data stored in XML based knowledge bases (Figure 23).

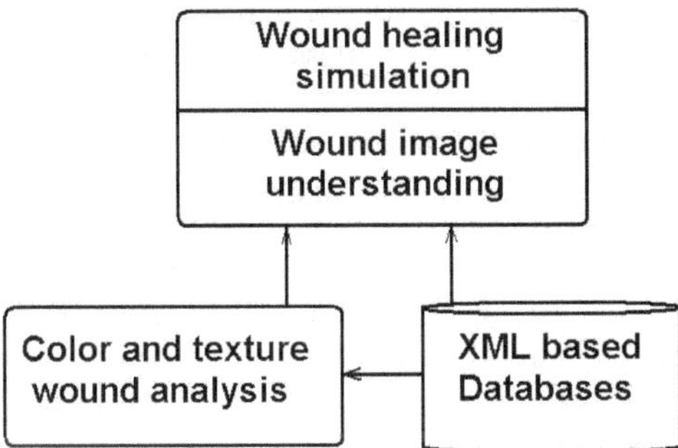

Fig. 23. The general method applied for wound image understanding and wound healing simulation.

Our main objective is to develop appropriate skills in wound management for a learner that traverses such an e-learning scenario. The e-learning scenarios are practice driven and relevant to professional practice, being used by students in medicine, pharmacy and health care, at graduate, postgraduate and residency levels.

For a given wound, we must find out some quantitative and qualitative attributes for assessing the healing state. As quantitative attributes we measure its surface area and its volume (evaluating depth). The original image is processed with the purpose to emphasize the distinction between wound and non-wound area. We use some general methods to enhance the image, because we must exaggerate the distinction between wound and non-wound. As an example, for individuals with fair skin, we lighten the images and then view them using shades of green with the red and blue minimized. This way more clearly exhibit the borders of the wound than in the original image. Removal of the red and blue leaves the wound black and the rest of the image green. For images of individuals with dark skin, both the red and green are accentuated while the blue is minimized. This procedure also leaves the non-wound area green, but colours the wound red. In either case, the wound can easily be distinguished from the non-wound without difficulty.

Our work is based on a continuous collaboration with physicians and wound care experts, because it is necessary to make a rigorous classification for various categories of wounds. We collected large amounts of wound image data and we calculate statistical parameters as mean, median, standard deviation, confidence interval, skewness and kurtosis for them. These historical data are included in XML based databases, to be used as inputs to classification algorithms. The general purpose is to make distinction between infected and non-infected, inflamed and non-inflamed wounds. Based on colour analysis, we build a statistically significant differentiation of mild, moderate and severe wounds. Our system analyses the differences in calibrated hue between injured and non-injured skin, obtaining a repeatable differentiation of wound severity for various time intervals. As an example, burn wounds are characterized according to their depth as:

- Superficial - with bright red colour and the presence of blisters (usually with brown colour);
- Deep - with red-whitish colour and with dark dots;
- Full thickness - with creamy or dark brown colour.

Assuming normality, the first two moments (mean and standard deviation) characterize very well the colour distribution. However, sometimes the first two moments alone are inadequate to discriminate between wound and non-wound skin. Therefore further details of the colour distribution are required. Skewness and kurtosis of the colour data proved to be more useful for this purpose.

We implement e-tools that will enable to assess the current state of the wound and to gain insight into the wound evolution, by comparing the series of wound data collected over time. Based on this knowledge we can design an e-tool for simulating the process of wound healing. The colour image processing is the most acceptable automatic method of objectively and reproducibly analyzing skin wounds and lesions. Also, this method has the main advantage of being completely non-invasive.

5. Conclusions and future work

The main aim of our research is to acquire better results in education based on improving the teaching-learning relation by means of e-learning technologies. We think that an important contribution to a high quality teaching-learning relation have the charm and eloquence of a good teacher. At the same time, it is our belief that e-learning technologies can improve the teaching-learning relations. We may try, but it is very difficult to extend the virtue and charm of a good teacher beyond the face-to-face relation and to include these qualities in e-learning scenarios. The use of Internet as the base line infrastructure for communication is essential, but is not enough for our purpose. It is necessary to transfer the spirit of a good teacher in e-learning scenarios. In our e-learning system, the learner has the possibility to interact with specific Java applets, to select specific values for some parameters, obtaining this way specific simulations and visualizations. As the real teacher is not physically present during an open learning process and the electronic technologies do not contain pedagogical characteristics, we have to simulate a valuable teaching-learning relation and to incorporate the teaching activities in our e-learning software, obtaining intelligent and practical e-learning tools (Prodan et al., 2006, 2008, 2010).

As future work, we have to create new e-learning scenarios and to find new methods for improving the teaching-learning relation by means of e-learning tools. The best way to follow for improving the teaching-learning relation is by using electronic portfolios and by incorporating the e-learning tools in a Moodle based e-learning system. Both the teachers and the learners agreed that electronic portfolios improve very much the teaching-learning relations and provide a better assessment among students than traditional methods (Rusu & Prodan, 2006). Also, our Moodle based learning management system provides dynamic and flexible student-centred authentic e-learning experiences, improving this way the teaching-learning relations.

6. Acknowledgment

This chapter was supported by UEFISCU PNII Partnership grant 11018/2007-2010 (MoDef).

7. References

Barrett, H. C. (2001). Electronic Portfolios. A chapter in *Educational Technology, ABC CLIO.* Available from: http://electronicportfolios.com/portfolios/encyclopediaentry.htm

Farr, R. (1990). Setting directions for language arts portfolios. *Educational Leadership*, Vol.48, No.3, pp. 103

Francis, R. & Raftery, J. (2005). Blended Learning Landscapes. *Brookes eJournal of Learning and Teaching*, Vol.3, No.1, ISSN 1744-7747, Available from http://bejlt.brookes.ac.uk/vol1/volume1issue3/perspective/francis_raftery.html

Garrison, D. R. & Kanuka, H. (2004). Blended learning: Uncovering its transformative potential in higher education. *The Internet and Higher Education*, Vol.7, pp. 95-105

Gorunescu, M., Gorunescu, F., and Prodan, A. (2002). Continuous-time Markov Model for Geriatric Patients Behavior. Optimization of the Bed Occupancy and Computer Simulation, *Korean Journal of Computational and Applied Mathematics,* Vol. 9, No. 1, pp. 185-195

Kanuka, H. (2008). The Theory and Practice of Online Learning (Second Edition), edited by Terry Anderson, AU Press, ISBN 978-1-897425-08-4. Available from http://www.scribd.com/doc/51302878/4/Heather-Kanuka

Leake, D. B. (1996). *Case-Based Reasoning: Experiences, Lessons, and Future Directions*, AAAI Press/Mit Press, ISBN 0-262-62110-X, Menlo Park, USA

Martinez, M. & Jagannathan, S. (2008). Moodle: A Low-Cost Solution for Successful e-Learning, *DevLearn, Learning Solutions Magazine*, November 10. Available from http://www.learningsolutionsmag.com/articles/71/moodle-a-low-cost-solution-for-successful-e-learning

Nwana, H. S. (1996). Software Agents: An Overview. *Knowledge Engineering Review*, Vol. 11, No. 3, 1996, pp. 205-244

Prodan, A. (1996). Quelques barrières à franchir dans la relation enseignement-apprentissage, In: *Flash Informatique,* EPFL, spécial été, 3 septembre 1996, pp. 23-26, Available from: http://ditwww.epfl.ch/SIC/SA/publications/FI96/fi-sp-96/sp-96-page23.html

Prodan, A. & Prodan, M. (1997). *Java Environment for Internet*. ProMedia Plus, Cluj-Napoca, ISBN 973-9275-07-9

Prodan, A. (1998). Towards a new type of open learning. *Clujul Medical,* Vol. LXXI, No. 3, pp. 424-431, ISSN 1224-550X

Prodan, A., Gorunescu, F., and Prodan, R. (1999). Simulating and Modelling in Java, *Workshop POOSC'99 (Parallel/High-Performance Object-Oriented Scientific Computing)*, Lisbon, TR FZJ-ZAM-IB-9906, Forschungszentrum Julich GmbH, pp. 55-64

Prodan, A., Gorunescu, F., Prodan, R. and Câmpean, R. (2000). A Java Framework for Stochastic Modelling, *Proceedings IMACS'2000, (16th IMACS World Congress on Scientific Computation, Applied Mathematics And Simulation)*, Lausanne, CD Ed. Rutgers University, New Brunswick - NJ, USA, ISBN 3-9522075-1-9

Prodan, A. & Prodan, Rodica (2001). Stochastic Simulation and Modelling, *Proceedings ETK-NTTS'2001 (Exchange of Technology and Know-how – New Techniques and Technologies for Statistics)*, Crete, pp. 461-466

Prodan, A. & Prodan, R. (2002). A collection of Java class libraries for stochastic modelling and simulation, *Proceedings ICCS'2002 (International Conference on Computational Science)*, Amsterdam, Springer, Sloot et al.(Eds.), Part. I, LNCS 2329, pp. 1040-1048

Prodan, A.; Câmpean, R. & Rusu, M. (2004). Stochastic Modelling and Simulation in Medicine and Pharmacy, *Proceedings ECMI 2004* (European Conference on Mathematics for Industry), pp. 242-247 Eindhoven, Netherlands, 21-25 June 2004

Prodan, A. & Câmpean, R. (2005). Bootstrapping methods applied for simulating laboratory works, *Campus-Wide Information Systems*, Vol. 22, No. 3, pp. 168-175, Emerald, ISSN 1065-0741, ISBN 1-84544-399-X

Prodan, A.; Rusu, M.; Câmpean, R. & Prodan, R. (2006). A Java framework for analyzing and processing wound images for medical education, *Proceedings of the ECMS 2006* (European Conference on Modelling and Simulation), pp. 421-426, ISBN 0-9553018-0-7, 28-31 May 2006, Bonn, Germany

Prodan, A.; Rusu M.; Câmpean,R. & Prodan, R. (2008). Artificial intelligence for wound image understanding, *Proceedings of the ICEIS 2008* (International Conference on Enterprise Information Systems), pp. 213-218, ISBN 978-989-8111-48-7, 12-16 June 2008, Barcelona, Spain

Prodan, A.; Rusu, M.; Revnic, C.; Câmpean, R.; Mitrea, P. & Prodan, R. (2010). Intelligent e-Tools for Wound Image Understanding and Evaluation, *Proceedings of the IEEE/ICDS 2010 International Conference on Digital Society* (ICDS 2010), pp. 8-13, IEEE Catalog Number: CFP10738-CDR, ISBN: 978-0-7695-3953-9, 10-16 February 2010, St. Maarten, Netherlands Antilles. IEEE Computer Society Digital Library,

Available from http://www.computer.org/portal/web/csdl/doi/10.1109/ICDS.2010.11

Rusu, M. & Prodan, A. (2006). Electronic portfolios as means of improving the teaching-learning relation, *Proceedings of the ICICTE 2006* (International Conference on Information Communications Technologies in Education), pp. 17-21, ISBN: 1-895802-26-8, ISSN: 1109-2084, 6-8 July 2006, Rhodes Island

Ross, S. M. (1990). *A Course in Simulation*. Macmillan Publishing Company, New York, USA, 2nd edition

3

Methods and Tools for Increasing the Effectiveness of E-Learning

Donika Valcheva and Margarita Todorova
"St. Cyril and St. Methodius" University of Veliko Tarnovo
Bulgaria

1. Introduction

In its different forms the e-Learning offers a set of considerable priorities over the traditional teaching: personalized tuition, reduced costs, opportunity for team work, flexibility of the learning material, etc. The evaluation of the effectiveness of e-learning is very important for both - the whole analysis and the improvement of a given system. The effectiveness can be defined by a definite target function, where regardless of its analytical aspect; a given number of indicators are included. Their importance can be defined by appropriate, objectively estimated coefficients' weights.

The right assessment for the rate of importance of the different indicators ensures an adequate rate of objectivity of the whole process of e-learning evaluation. In this chapter method for assessment the effectiveness of e-learning is discussed. It consists of some stages, which are deeply described in the chapter.

The chapter suggests a 3D model which could be used as a tool for increasing the e-learning effectiveness. It also offers an approach for applying this 3D model for increasing the e-learning effectiveness. This approach has methodical value in line with the idea for dynamic adjustment of the individual learning profile of each student in order to increase the personalization level in the e-learning process.

An approach for personalization of the e-learning with preliminary processing and simulation of the teaching and learning process for priori assessment of the effectiveness and transformation of the existed e-learning content towards the individual student expectations is described, tested and visualized in this report. The presented approach has methodical value, according to the idea for dynamically adjustment of the individual learning profile of each student with the aim to increase the personalization level in the e-learning process.

The success or failure of any e-learning initiative can be closely correlated to learner motivation. This chapter presents a method for defining the Students' Motivation in E-learning, which uses the main concepts of the Keller's ARCS Model and the Gagne's events.

2. Method for assessment the effectiveness of E-learning

The implementation and usage of e-learning require large investments of time and money. That is why the evaluation of its effectiveness is necessary to be done. In the last few years a lot of research work has been made in that direction (Todorova & Todorov, 2004; Todorov,

2005; Georgieva, Todorov, Smrikarov, 2003; Hughes, 2008; Sonwalkar, 2001; Todorova & Kalushkov & Valcheva., 2008; Вълчева & Тодорова, 2009).
The quality of e-learning is directly connected with the concept - measurement of the characteristics of the e-learning components.

2.1 Defining a system of indicators for evaluation the effectiveness of e-learning

For defining the efficiency of the different forms of e-learning some groups of indicators have to be defined. These indicators may be used not only for evaluation the effectiveness of existed e-learning platforms but also for designing and implementation of new ones.
In this method the following basic groups of indicators are used (Todorova & Todorov 2004; Valcheva & Todorova, 2005a):

1. Software group of indicators;
2. Hardware group of indicators;
3. Didactical group of indicators;
4. Communications group of indicators;
5. Information group of indicators.

The offered system of indicators is open and its content can be changed and modified depending on the concrete applications and goals of the education. In tab. (1-5) are presented the indicators within each group.

Indicator	Description
1. Personalized teaching	The tools for self-teaching helps the students to study according to their capabilities and free time, to choose the form and the way of providing the material on the basis of their own predilections;
2. Interoperability	To support content from different sources and multiple vendors' hardware/software solutions, the system should be based on open industry standards for Web deployments (XML, SOAP or AQQ) and support the major learning standards (AICC, SCORM, IMS and IEEE);
3. Reliability	To give acceptable results even if there is invalid inputs. The assessment gives an opportunity refusals and situations that involve refusals to be predicate;
4. Flexibility	To exist an opportunity for changes in the content;
5. Portability	To be independent from the users' operating system and to be used by widespread browser such as Internet Explorer, Netscape Communicator etc.
6. Functionality	To be useful;
7. Accountability	The classifying, testing and the assessment have to be automated in such a way that the participants to be distributed according to their responsibilities in the process of learning;
8. Security	The system should selectively limit and control access to online content and resources for its diverse user community;
9. Costs indicator	Measures the costs for purchasing the system, its exploitation and support, etc.;

Table 1. Software indicators for evaluating the effectiveness of e- learning

Indicator
1. Parameters of the micro-processor;
2. The memory capacity;
3. The speed of the Internet access;
4. Presence of additional multimedia hardware components that gives an opportunity for usage of multimedia application.

Table 2.Hardware indicators for evaluating the effectiveness of e- learning

Indicator
1. The material should be presented in a logical sequence. Broken into small, incremental learning steps;
2. The material should be linked to other sources, with reading assignments clearly specified;
3. The material should be Illustrated by examples and/or case studies when new information is presented;
4. Encouragement for critical thinking, creativity, and problem-solving;
5. Relation to other material the learners may have studied or experiences they may have had;
6. Usage of illustrations, photographs, animation, and other forms of multimedia in order to present facts and reinforce concepts;
7. Abbreviations and symbols are defined;
9. Appropriate language level for the intended audience.

Table 3. Didactical indicators for evaluating the effectiveness of e- learning

Indicator
1. Opportunity for team work;
2. Opportunity for communication by e-mail;
3. Opportunity for communication by on-line conferences, discussions, chat, etc.;
4. Multilanguage support.

Table 4. Communication indicators for evaluation the effectiveness of e- learning

Indicator	Description
1. Usefulness	Depends on the concrete goals, interests, motivation and knowledge of the student;
2. User satisfaction	The information is evaluated according to the user gratification;
3. Information value	It depends on the extent of its authenticity, actuality and clearness.

Table 5. Information indicators for evaluating the effectiveness of e- learning

2.2 Defining weights of the indicators' coefficients for evaluation the effectiveness of e-learning by the expert evaluation method

One of the appropriate methods for defining the weights of the indicators coefficients is the expert evaluation method.

2.2.1 Concepts of the expert evaluation methodology

The method can be divided into three stages (Valcheva & Todorova, 2005b):

1. Framing of the questionnaire, which must consists of the following very important parts:
   - List of the indicators for evaluating the effectiveness of e-learning, which rate of importance have to be assessed by the experts;
   - A cell, where every interviewee can put his mark (the evaluation scale is preliminarily determined by the questioner)
   - Information for the competence and the resource of the argumentation of the different experts, participating in the interview.
2. Defining the circle of the experts that will be interviewed, and implementing the interview.
3. Defining the rate of competence of the experts, eliminating the inadequate opinions and processing the results. The rate of the experts' competence is defined by:

$$C = \frac{b_1 + b_2 + b_3}{36}, \quad (1)$$

where b_1, b_2, b_3 are defined according to respectively - the official position and rank of every expert; the time, spend on working at the problem; and the resource of his argumentation. The coefficient varies in the interval from 0 to 1 and the experts' opinions, which rate of competence is less than the preliminarily determined value has to be eliminated from the later processing of the results.

The meaning of b_1, b_2, b_3 can be defined in the following way (tab. 6-8):

Official position and rank	Without degree	Doctor	Doctor of science
Assistant	2	4	-
Associate professor	4	6	8
Professor	8	10	12

Table 6. Meaning of b1

Time, spend on working at the problem (in years)	0	1	2	3	4	5	>5
	0	2	4	6	8	10	12

Table 7. Meaning of b2

Resource of the argumentation	
By intuition	2
Acquaintance with the problem state	8
Practical experience	10
Implementation of theoretical analysis on the problem	12

Table 8. Meaning of b_3

The next stage of the method includes the procession of the results, obtained by the provided interview. On the basis of the received experts' assessments the weight coefficients of the suggested groups of indicators and actually the indicators themselves are processed, and the agreement rate of the experts is determined.

1. The procession of the results consists of the following stages:

4.1. Defining the weight coefficients of the suggested groups of indicators:
4.1.1. Processing the average assessment of the experts F_t for the rate of importance (weight coefficients) of each group of indicators by the formula:

$$F_t = \frac{1}{m}\sum_{j=1}^{m} h_{tj} \tag{2}$$

where h_{tj} - the assessment of the j expert for the weight of the t group, m- the number of the experts and t obtains value from 1 to 5, according to the defined number of groups.
4.1.2 Procession of the normalized assessment k_t for each of the groups:

$$k_t = \frac{F_t}{\sum_{t=1}^{5} F_t} \tag{3}$$

4.1.3 Procession of the weight coefficients of the indicators within the groups:
4.1.2.1 Defining the average assessment S_i of the groups of experts for the rate of importance of each indicator within the group:

$$S_i = \frac{1}{m}\sum_{j=1}^{m} r_{ij} \tag{4}$$

where r_{ij} - the assessment of j expert for the weight of the i indicator, m- number of the experts.
4.1.2.2 Processing the normalized assessment for the weight of each indicator:

$$S_{inorm} = \frac{S_i}{\sum_{i=1}^{n} S_i} \tag{5}$$

where n- number of the indicators.
4.1.2.3 Formation of the weight coefficients, according to the group weight, to which they belongs:

$$x_i = k_t . S_{inorm} \tag{6}$$

In that way the sum of the weights coefficients of the indicators within a given group is equal to the weight coefficient of the whole group:

$$\sum_{i=1}^{n} x_{it} = k_t \tag{7}$$

2. For determination of the agreement rate of the experts, the average quadratic diversion δi is calculated:

$$\delta_i = \sqrt{\frac{1}{m}\sum_{j=1}^{m}(a_{ij} - \overline{a_i})^2} \tag{8}$$

where

$$a_{ij} = \frac{r_{ij}}{\sum_{j=1}^{m} r_{ij}} \tag{9}$$

$$\overline{a_i} = \frac{1}{m}\sum_{j=1}^{m} a_{ij} \tag{10}$$

Based on (8) and (10) the variation coefficient V_i, is calculated, which characterized the agreement rate of the experts, participating in the research:

$$V_i = \frac{\delta_i}{\overline{a_i}} \tag{11}$$

The smaller is the value of Vi, the higher is the rate of the experts' agreement.

2.3 Processing of the results from the customer assessment of e-learning effectiveness

Normalizing the customer assessments for each indicator. For the assessment of each *I* indicator from the *j* customer the y_{ijnorm} is calculated:

$$y_{ijnorm} = \frac{y_{ij} - y_{ij\max}}{y_{ij\max} - y_{ij\min}}, \tag{12}$$

where $y_{ij\max}$ maximal assessment from the scale and $y_{ij\min}$ is the minimal.
Defining the average value of the normalized assessments:

$$\overline{y}_{inorm} = \frac{1}{m}\sum_{j=1}^{m} y_{ijnorm} \tag{13}$$

Forming the assessment in accordance with the *i* indicator by the formula:

$$A = \frac{1}{n}\sum_{i=1}^{n} x_i \overline{y}_{inorm} \tag{14}$$

where A $\in [0,1]$.

3. 3D Model as a tool for increasing the effectiveness of E-Learning

The advent of e-learning is a consequence from the increasing necessity of a learning process which is effective, flexible, adaptive to the individual student's learning style and accessible everywhere and at any time. The interest in e-learning problems, common aspects and applications is continuously increasing (Sonwalkar, 2001; Schreurs, 2006; Schreurs & R.Moreau, 2006; Schreurs et al., 2006; Quinn Clark N, 2008).

3.1 3D model for e-learning: background and main concepts

This chapter presents a new 3D model for e-learning, in order to solve some of the problems, related to the lack of personalization, discussed in the introduction. This model is based on the following circumstances (Valcheva & Todorova & Asenov, 2010a, 2010c):

- Each student has individual learning style
- Formalism and low level of personalization in the traditional form of learning - each curriculum consists of N disciplines distributed in K educational years.
- In order to increase the effectiveness of e-learning, it should offer students the freedom to choose the most relevant learning content and also great variety of learning materials.

3.2 Description and visualization of the model

The model of the most effective way of studying, according to the different learning modalities is defined in the space of the learning process state. The space is three-dimensional and each of the axes presents the effectiveness vector, which is defined as ranged triad from:

{discipline, course version for a given discipline, the prognosticated assessment for effectiveness of the e-learning process}.

The goal of the modelling process is to define and to visualize the surface of the effective e-learning by prognosis assessment for the e-learning effectiveness.

The prognosis is realized by comparison between two vectors on the basis of scalar subtraction:

- Vector of the teaching impact and
- Vector of the student's learning style.

The Vector of the teaching impact in the model presents the quantitative assessment of the teaching characteristics of each version of the courses. The Vector of the teaching impact and the Vector of the student's learning style are chosen with one and a same dimension - (L), and each of the coordinates (p) from 1 to L presents a connected set of properties impact/modality, respectively for the Vector of the teaching impact and the Vector of the learning style. For example if property 1 of the Vector of the teaching impact presents "presenting the new knowledge by graphics", then the Vector of the learning style will be defined as an analogical modality "ability of the student to learn effectively by graphical presentation of the new knowledge".

In this way other modalities and approaches for data presentation could be defined and presented in the model such as: presentation and absorption of knowledge by text description, voice and sound, animation, problem solving, simulators, games, etc.

An unique Vector of teaching impact **VEij(1,L)** is defined for each version *j* of a given course *i* . A Vector of learning style **VSk(1,L)** is formed For each student *k*

The prognosis assessment of the e-learning effectiveness for each version *j* of each course *i* and student *k* - **LDijk** is defined by the following formula (15):

$$LD_{ijk} = \sum_{p=1}^{L} | \ VE_{ij}(p) - VS_k(p) \ | \ \ i \in \{1,N\}, j \in \{1,M\} \tag{15}$$

For each student ***k***, M-scalar assessment is processed and according to (16) the course version $LD_{ij_{best}k}$ is found where the scalar assessment is minimal:

$$LD_{ij_{best}k} = \min\left(LD_{ijk}\right) \ , \ \ j \in \{1,M\} \tag{16}$$

The minimal value of the scalar assessment corresponds to the minimal absolute discrepancy between the teaching impact of the concrete course version and the learning style of the k-student.

Applying criterion (16) for each course $i \in \{1,N\}$ most appropriate for the k-student's learning style course versions are formed.

In visualizing the 3D model the points, which are presented with ranged triad coordinates for the k-student are approximated with parts of planes– fig.1: {i-course, j-version, LD_{ijk} - scalar assessment according (15)}

The graphical result of the visualization presents applying the criterion (16) and the possibility to prognosticate the way of defining $LD_{ij_{best}k}$ versions for ***i*** courses. The presented result is a surface of the effective e-learning. Very clear marked local minimums present the versions of the courses, for which the k-student will have least difficulties in absorbing the learning content and the effectiveness of the learning process is expected to be maximal- fig. 1. Fig.2 shows the opposite - the course versions for the same student, which are most difficult for him, according to his learning style. The learning styles used for visualizing the model are exemplary. It is not subject of this chapter to present tools and methods for defining learning styles.

The presented results in fig. 1 and fig. 2 are for one student, 10 courses in the curriculum and from 1 to 5 versions for each course.

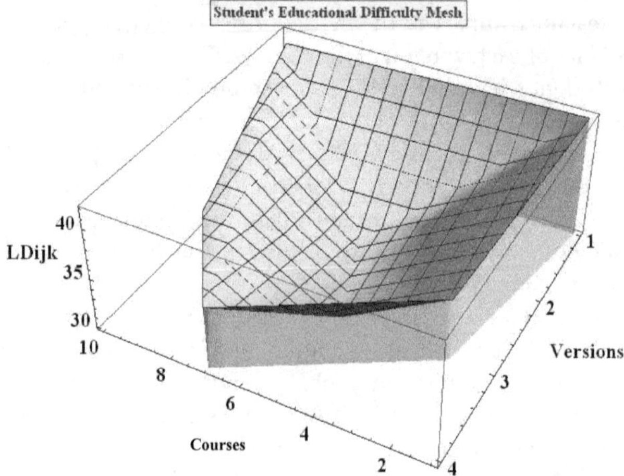

Fig. 1. Course versions, in which the student k will have less learning difficulties

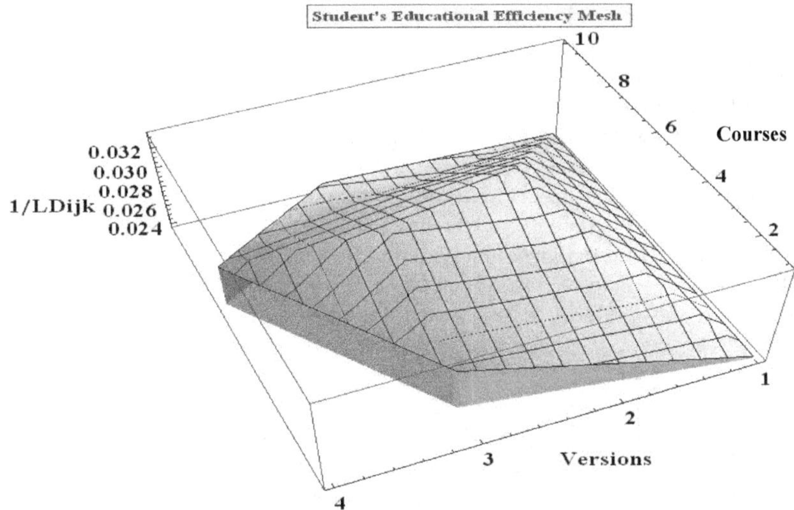

Fig. 2. Course versions, in which the student k will have most learning difficulties

3.3 One approach for applying the 3D model of e-learning

The approach (Valcheva & Todorova & Asenov, 2010b) presented on fig. 3 consists of 7 stages:

Stage 1 - the e-modules (E-module 1-n) are described by experts with metadata (E-module metadata) and are stored in database (E-learning DB). The experts are the teachers doing research in the field of e-learning.

Stage 2 - includes the student's registration and determination of his individual learning style. This is presented in the approach by the data structure SLP IDj.

Stage 3 -includes the student's request for learning (the request is presented in the approach by KSR IDi).

Stage 4 - in this stage the 3D simulator defines the best versions of the existing e-learning modules for the individual learning style of each student by applying the 3D module. The input data for the simulator are the students request KSR IDi and the student's learning profile - SLP IDj.

Stage 5 - the selected most effective e-learning module is offered to the student and the online activities are started.

Stage 6 - includes an opportunity for actualization of the student profile. It is possible to change the input data about the students learning style because of some outside factors.

Stage 7 - end of the session and saving the updated information

On fig.3 is presented a block scheme of an e-learning personalization approach with a preliminary processing and simulation of the teaching and learning processes for priori assessment of the effectiveness and for transformation of the exiting e-learning content towards the individual student's expectations. This approach is based on existing e-learning content (e-learning modules), which is assessed with a definite system of criteria for acquiring the important for the personalization content - E-modules metadata. From the point of view of the models for data presentation, it could be accepted that each course is presented by metadata structure.

The choice of the structure and the content of the metadata is based on the idea that each module can be described according the personalization needs and the presented metadata content must be understandable for the experts, which will process the courses in Stage 1 from the presented approach (fig.3).

One example for metadata structure for presenting e-learning module is shown in Table 9. The presented structure in Table 9 is an example and it aims at visualization of the formalization level by metadata. The experts' task is to assess the proportion of the learning modalities that each course offers and thus to define to which learning style it is most appropriate.

The last three elements from the metadata structure have direct connection with the learning styles and the 3D model (stage 4 from the presented approach). On stage 2 of the approach questionnaire with the students is conducted in order to be defined for student **j** his personal style of learning, presented in the approach by the data structure SLP IDj (fig.3).

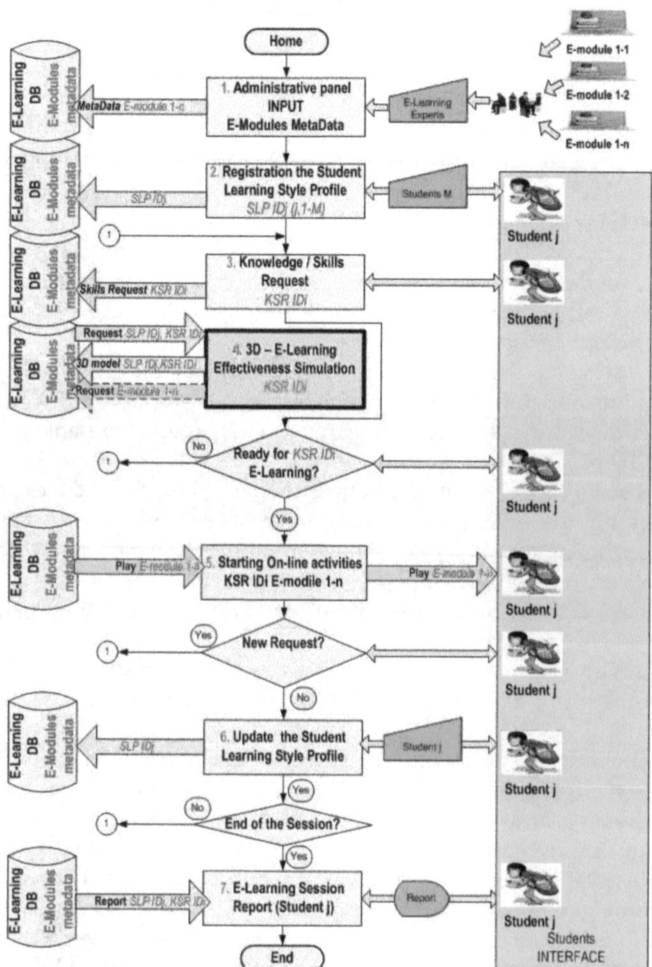

Fig. 3. Block scheme of an approach for e-learning personalization

Metadata structure	E-module 1-n1	E-module 2-n2	E-module 3-n3
Field of science	"…………"	"…………"	"…………"
Subject	1-"…."	2-"…."	3-"…."
Date of creation	12.05.2010	17.05.2010	21.02.2010
Language (s)	EN,BG	EN	BG
Author	"………….."	"………….."	"………….."
Average duration (hours)	0,8	1,2	0,9
Learning by seeing in % from the whole learning process	70%	20%	50%
Learning by hearing in % from the whole learning process	20%	50%	20%
Learning by doing in % from the whole learning process	10%	30%	30%

Table 9. Example of Metadata structure for describing e-learning module

Table 10 shows the content of the data structure SLP ID_j, which presents the profile of student j.

Data structure for presenting students' profile for students j, j+1, j+2	Student j	Student j+1	Student j+2
Name of the student	"………."	"…………"	"………."
ID	XXXX	YYYY	ZZZZ
1-st preferred language	BG	BG	EN
2-nd preferred language	EN	EN	RUS
3-rd preferred language	RUS	RUS	BG
Effectiveness of acquiring knowledge by „seeing" in %	70%	20%	50%
Effectiveness of acquiring knowledge by „hearing" in %	20%	50%	20%
Effectiveness of acquiring knowledge by „doing" in %	10%	30%	30%

Table 10. Example of metadata structure for presenting student's profile

The presented structure in Table 10 is a production of the structure for formalization of the learning content by metadata. In this way informational support of the 3D simulator for assessment of the effectiveness of e-learning (Stage 4 of the approach) is ensured, based and developed on the basis of the 3D model.

Data structure (Stage 3) KSR IDi is used for formalization of the students' request for e-learning content. For good quality of applying the experimental approach, it is necessary for the personalization of the e-learning to assess not only the personal learning style of the students, but also their individual needs for learning (Table 11).

Data structure for presenting the individual requests of student j, j+1, J+2	E-module 1-n_1	E-module 2-n_2	E-module 3-n_3
Name of the student	"..........."	"..........."	"..........."
ID	XXXX	YYYY	ZZZZ
Field of science	"...."	"...."	"...."
Subject	1-"...."	2-"...."	3-"...."
Expected average duration (hours)	1,5	2,0	2,0
Actuality of the content – published not later than – data	01.01.2010	01.01.2010	01.01.2010

Table 11. Example of formalization of the students' request for e-learning content

The output information for applying the 3D model as a tool for e-learning effectiveness assessment is formed On the basis of the data structure from Tables 9, 10, 11. The information from Stages 1, 2, 3, according to fig. 3 is stored in database - E-Learning DB.
The 3D simulator for e-learning effectiveness assessment (Stage 4) is based and developed according the 3D model of e-learning. The input data for the simulator is the student's request KSR IDi and the profile of the student **j** - SLP IDj. In the concrete example we assess all N courses with subject „1-..", which are described with metadata in E-Learning DB – E-Module 1-1, E-Module 1-2, E-Module 1-N.
On stage 5 the most effective e-learning module according to the individual student's learning style and needs is offered and the real learning process is conducted. In finishing the learning session in the experimental approach there is an opportunity for new testing of the student – Stage 6. The actualization of the student's profile gives possibility for feedback after finishing the course.
In the experimental approach this feedback is not directed towards assessment of the e-learning content or way of presenting the material, but towards improving the student's self-assessment about his preferred learning style. In this way one of the basic disadvantages in the presented approach – the formation of the learning styles by self-assessment is not always subjective. With each module the student corrects the proportion of the three perceptual modalities in his individual profile.
The presented experimental approach for applying the 3D model for assessment of the e-learning effectiveness is important not only for presenting and applying the 3D model, but also it has methodical value, according to the idea for dynamic adjustment of the individual learning profile of each student with the aim to increase the personalization level in the e-learning process.

4. Method for defining students' motivation in E-Learning

The success or failure of any e-learning initiative can be closely correlated to learner motivation. Even the most elegantly designed training courses will fail if the students are not motivated to learn. Many students are motivated only to "pass the test.". The developers of e-learning course must strive to provoke a deeper motivation in learners to learn new skills and transfer those skills back into the work environment.
Some reasons for decrease of the students' motivation:

- Learners can feel isolated.
- Difficult navigation within course.

- Confusing instructions for tasks.
- Irrelevant material for learners' needs and learning style
- Technical breakdowns.

As a first step, the e-learning course developers should ask the prospective learners questions such as:

- What would the value be to you from this type of course?
- What do you hope to get out of this course?
- What are your interests in this topic?
- What are your most pressing problems?
- What is your learning style?

The answers to these types of questions are likely to provide insight into learner motivation, as well as desirable behavioral outcomes.

4.1 Motivation models

According to (Keller, 1983, 1984, 1987) the most popular motivation models are:

4.1.1 The Time Continuum Model

The model is presented in the form of a handbook for developing instruction and draws on approaches from linguistics, cognitive psychology, and motivation research. The model is not based on any one scientific theory or philosophy. Wlodkowski's Time Continuum Model of Motivation identifies three critical periods in the learning process where motivation is most important. Those periods are the beginning of the learning process, during the learning process, and at the end of the learning process. Each of those three periods has two distinct factors associated with it, yielding six basic questions to aid motivational planning. The factors to be considered at the beginning of the learning process are attitudes and needs. When planning the beginning of a learning experience, the designer should consider how the instruction will best meet the needs of the learners, and how a positive learner attitude can be developed. It is suggested that when possible, the instruction should focus on the physiological needs of the learners and experiences familiar or relevant to the learners. The instruction should allow for choice and self-direction in assignments. A needs assessment should be performed prior to developing the instruction to aid in appropriate planning. Stimulation and affect are to be considered during the learning experience. To maintain a stimulating learning environment, learner participation via questions, humor, varying presentation style using body language and voice inflection, and the use of different modes of instruction from lecture to group work to class discussion are strategies suggested. Wlodkowski's primary strategy is to make the learning experience as personalized and relevant to the learner as possible. Finally, competence and reinforcement are to be considered at the end of the learning experience. Frequent feedback and communicating learner progress are the author's main methods for developing confidence in the learners.

4.1.2 Keller's ARCS model for motivation and Gagne's events of instruction

John Keller synthesized existing research on psychological motivation and created the ARCS model. ARCS stand for Attention, Relevance, Confidence, and Satisfaction.

Attention The first and single most important aspect of the ARCS model is gaining and keeping the learner's attention, which coincides with the first step in Gagne's model. Keller's strategies for attention include sensory stimuli, inquiry arousal (thought provoking questions), and variability (variance in exercises and use of media).

Relevance Attention and motivation will not be maintained, however, unless the learner believes the training is relevant. Put simply, the training program should answer the critical question, "What's in it for me?" Benefits should be clearly stated.

Confidence The confidence aspect of the ARCS model is required so that students feel that they should put a good faith effort into the program. If they think they are incapable of achieving the objectives or that it will take too much time or effort, their motivation will decrease.

Satisfaction Finally, learners must obtain some type of satisfaction or reward from the learning experience. This can be in the form of entertainment or a sense of achievement. A self-assessment game, for example, might end with an animation sequence acknowledging the player's high score. A passing grade on a post-test might be rewarded with a completion certificate.

This model is not intended to stand apart as a separate system for instructional design, but can be incorporated within Gagne's events of instruction.

Gagne's nine learning events are the most popular and effective model for creating e-learning contents. Gagne proposed that the content should have nine distinct instructional events to be effective. They are:

1. Gaining attention (reception)
2. Informing learners of the objective (expectancy)
3. Stimulating recall of prior learning (retrieval)
4. Presenting the stimulus (selective perception)
5. Providing learning guidance (semantic encoding)
6. Eliciting performance (responding)
7. Providing feedback (reinforcement)
8. Assessing performance (retrieval)
9. Enhancing retention and transfer (generalization).

4.2 Method for defining the students' motivation in E-learning, which uses the main concepts of the Keller's ARCS model and the Gagne's events

For defining the students' motivation in e-learning, we use as a base the ARCS model and the Gagne events. The reason for this choice is that these models can be easier implemented and applied according to the specific nature of the e-learning process.

After finishing given e-learning course the students could be kindly asked to fulfill a questionnaire, based on the concepts of the Keller's ARCS Model and the Gagne's events, in order their motivation to be defined. The results of this investigation will be very useful for the course developers (teachers, trainers or software developers), because they will obtain important feedback information about the students' motivation and satisfaction after finishing the course. Thus the quality of the e-learning courses can be measured and if necessary the learning content can be modified. The questionnaire will consist of the following questions, divided into 4 sections, according to the Keller's ARCS Model and the Gagne's events: The scale that could be used consist of the following possible answers:

- "Absolutely yes",
- "Yes, but not so much",
- "Absolutely no".

Attention section

The course offered me appropriate for my learning style e-materials

The interface design and navigation were easy to work with

The visual aspect of the content (i.e. rite size and color of fonts, proper line spacing,, relevant diagrams, positioned at right places) has a positive impact on the accessibility of the content

The objectives of the course are clearly stated.

Relevance section

The new content was based on my previous knowledge and skills in this field

The received new information will be very important for my future work and study

The course offer me links to additional information in the field

Confidence section

During the course I felt myself sure I can manage with the problems

During the learning process I received feedback and support from my teachers

My success in this course is a direct result of the amount of effort I have put forth.

Satisfaction section

I am satisfied with the results of my study, after finishing the course

I am feeling rewarded

I will use the newly received knowledge and skills in my work

5. Conclusion

The effectiveness of the e-learning depends on the quality and quantity of the applied e-learning materials, the needed time for taking the course and the results at the course end. As the time necessary for learning the new information that given course offers is shorter and the results at the end are better, the effectiveness of e-learning is higher.

Serious problem nowadays in e-learning is the lack of personalization of the teaching and learning process. In the Internet space can be found countless courses in one and the same theme, presented in different way, with different level of usage of multimedia elements, directed to different learning styles, with different duration and complexity. The user has the very difficult task - to find in the ocean of e-learning courses, the most appropriate for his learning style, basic knowledge and skills. This is not always possible, and even when the choice of an appropriate course is a fact, the chance the initial goal (gaining knowledge and skills in a given field) to be reached for a short time is not high. It is necessary to be created an approach, which will ensure knowledge (skills and competencies) acquiring and opportunity for preliminary selection from great number of e-learning modules with the aim for personalization of the e-learning environment according to the individuality of each student and his expectations about the final results.

The personalization in the e-learning may be described as a composition of procedures, approaches and techniques for giving the students the tools for self-learning, which will give them the opportunity to study according to their own capabilities, learning style, knowledge and skills, to choose the type of the e-learning material and the way of presentation of the new material, according to their own interests, needs and learning style.

One of the approaches for improving the personalization in the e-learning process is ensuring access to appropriate e-learning materials, according the individual learning style of the student. The learning style is the way of adoptions and procession of the information. Every person develops preferred and successive behavior and concrete approaches for studying. This is connected with three processes, which form the differences in the styles:

- **knowledge** – how the knowledge is acquired;
- **conceptualization** – how the information is processed;
- **motivation and emotions** – the way of taking decisions and emotional preferences.

One of the most important themes in psychology of learning is motivation. In order to include motivational factors in online learning, factors known as depending on the learner, assessment of the learner's motivation is required and this is the problem addressed by this research.

As a result from the presented in this chapter research some important concepts for keeping the learners motivated could be summarized in the following list:

- Defining the target audience and their learning preferences;
- Course designers must realize that learning styles are different: visual learners, kinesthetic learners, auditory learners. E-learning courses must cater for all otherwise learners will lose interest;
- Defining clear learning objectives of the course;
- Use of interactivity/Games/Simulations - using interactivity in e-learning contents has many benefits. It keeps the learners involved, breaks the monotony of a single way communication, enhances the learning experience by participation and facilitates active experimentation;
- Use of real life scenarios - Cognitive Theories say that any new information is compared to existing cognitive structures called 'schema'. Meaningful information is easier to learn and remember. It is very important for the students to know where they can apply the newly received knowledge.
- Assessment of the students' motivation.

The future work is directed to finding methods and tools for increasing the use of interactivity in the e-learning matherials. The modern computer (hardware and software) technologies offer wide range of opportunities for creation of interactive multimedia e-learning resources, appropriate for the different learning styles.

6. References

Вълчева Д., Тодорова М. (2009). Методи и средства за повишаване ефективността на електронното учене. Списание "Computer Engineering", Vol.3, №2/2009, ISSN 1313-2717, София, България.

Иванов И. (2003) Стилове на учене. Втора национална научнопрактическа конференция "Психолого-педагогическа характеристика на детството", Попово', Университетско издателство "Св. Кл. Охридски", 29-39.

Georgieva G., Todorov G., Smrikarov A., (2003) A model of a virtual university - some problems during its development, Proceedings of the International Conference on Computer Systems and Technologies CompSysTech'2003, Sofia pp IV.29-1 - IV.29-7

Hughes, J. (2008). A Framework for the Evaluation of E-Learning. Available from http://www.theknownet.com/ict_smes_seminars/papers/Hughes_Attwell.html

Keller, J. M. (1983). Motivational design of instruction. In C. M. Reigeluth (Ed.), Instructional-design theories and models: An overview of their current status. Hillsdale, NJ: Lawrence Erlbaum Associates

Keller, J. M. (1984). The use of the ARCS model of motivation in teacher training. In K. Shaw & A. J. Trott (Eds.), Aspects of Educational Technology Volume XVII: staff Development and Career Updating. London: Kogan Page

Keller, J. M. (1987). Development and Use of the ARCS Model of Motivational Design. Journal Of Instructional Development, 10(3), 2-10. John Keller's Official ARCS Model Website

Quinn N. (2008) Models for Intelligent Assistance Delivering the Dream. Available from http://www.astd.org/LC/2005/0805_quinn.htm

Schreurs J., Moreau R. (2006). EFQM and Kirkpatrick in a Framework for Evaluation of E-learning. Proceedings of the World Conference on E-Learning in Corporate, Government, Healthcare, and Higher Education, E-Learn 2006, Honolulu, Hawaii, USA, October 13-17, 2006. page 1780-1785. AACE, ISBN 1-880094-60-6.

Schreurs J. (2006) TQM in E-Learning: A Self-Assessment Model and Questionnaire. International Book Series "Information Science and Computing" - Methodologies and Tools of the Modern (e-) Learning, Available from http://www.foibg.com/ibs_isc/ibs-06/IBS-06-p01.pdf

Sonwalkar, N. (2001). A New Methodology for Evaluation: The Pedagogical Rating of Online Courses, Syllabus. Available from http://www.syllabus.com/article.asp?id=5914

Todorov G. (2005). Software technologies. Veliko Turnovo, Bojka.

Todorova M., Kalushkov T., Valcheva D. (2008), Influence of ICT on Learning Modalities, International Conference EDU-World. Pitesti 2008, Romania.

Todorova, M., Todorov G. (2004). Efficiency of Virtual Learning. International Conference SAER 2004.

Valcheva, D., Todorova M. (2005b) Defining Weights of the Indicators' Coefficients for Evaluation the Effectiveness of E-Learning by the Expert Evaluation Method. САИ-2005, София, България.

Valcheva, D., Todorova M. (2005a) Defining a system of indicators for evaluation the effectiveness of e-learning. International Conference on Computer Systems and Technologies - CompSysTech'05, Varna, Bulgaria.

Valcheva D, Todorova M. Asenov O. (2010a). A 3D Model as a Tool for Increasing the Effectiveness of E-learning. Serdica Journal of Computing, Volume 4, N. 4, 2010 (pp.475-486).

Valcheva D., Todorova M., Asenov O. (2010b). One Approach for personalization of e-learning. International Conference on e-Learning and the Knowledge Society –e-Learning'10, Riga, Latvia.

Valcheva D., Todorova M., Asenov O. (2010c). 3D Model of E-Learning. International Conference on Computer Systems and Technologies - CompSysTech'10, Sofia, Bulgaria.

4

XML Data Access via MOODLE Platform

Aleksandra Werner and Katarzyna Haręźlak
Silesian University of Technology,
Poland

1. Introduction

Nowadays, exchanging information plays a crucial role in both human communication and business tasks realization. More and more often, this process is performed with usage of computer systems. However, their variety, resulting from differences in time of their creation, exploited tools and platforms, enforces a necessity to their integration to achieve effective co-operation of business entities. Unfortunately, such computer systems contain data in incompatible formats and large amounts of information must be converted. Moreover, in the newly created software, an idea of outsourcing of functionality can be observed, what entails a need for an access to the same data by different applications. Cooperation of sales systems with one invoice system is a great example of such situation.

The aforementioned systems collaboration requires standardization of the exchanged data. The XML language is one of the most popular standards used for this purpose. XML data is stored in a plain text format independent from a software and hardware, making a process of creating data that is intended to be shared by different applications, easier.

XML is the meta-language for structured data description. There are no mandatory objects defined, only a set of rules of their creation. This is a reason why there are many fields of XML usage. For example it is used in financial and economic institutions of European Union. Furthermore, text editors, like MS Word (Rice, 2006), allow for saving documents in XML format, which is utilized in many companies to write their internal documentation and in social life for exchanging documents between citizens and offices.

For these reasons, knowledge concerning rules of constructing XML documents, ability to analyse their content and ways of their storage seems to be worth acquiring.

XML document consists of data described in accordance with the defined XML format and has to meet specified conditions to be regarded as correct. XML document can be analyzed on various levels of abstraction (Bray&Paoli&Sperberg-McQueen, 1998). On the highest level, a document is a tree with at least one, root element consisting of pair of tags - opening **<tag>** and closing **</tag>.** Other elements must be located inside the root. Between tags, contents can be placed. Element can be an empty one, which is marked by one tag in form of **<empty_element/>.**

Further analysis shows that XML document can be treated as a combination of tags and text data. The task of tags is to define a structure of a document. Correctness of such document can be considered in two terms:

- document is complete enough to be interpreted by a web browser,
- document has proper syntax structure.

Creating XML document can be realized with usage of any text editor but more conveniently is to utilize tools dedicated to manage XML files. Among them, for example, there can be enumerated (O'REILLY xml.com):

- Adobe FrameMaker, available from http://www.adobe.com.
- XML Pro, available from www.vervet.com/.
- XML Writer, available from http://xmlwriter.net/.
- XML Notepad, available from http://www.microsoft.com/download/en/default.aspx.
- eNotepad, available from http://www.edisys.com/Products/eNotepad/enotepad.asp.
- XML Spy, available from http://www.altova.com/.

They differ in various features - some of them have to be paid for and others are free, some of them are difficult in use, and other are easy to exploit. But none of them allows for organizing complete teaching process. Therefore, the possibility of constructing such comprehensive procedure in the MOODLE environment was considered. The goal of the research was to provide the complete tool supporting educational process of XML data management.

Solution of this problem was carried out in accordance with the principles of the major methodologies for software development, taking into consideration the scope of the problem being solved. The particular steps of project development covered:

- formulating the goal and assumptions of the research,
- analyzing the field of research and dividing the general knowledge about XML language into groups of issues,
- specifying the desired functionality in scope of XML data management,
- developing the algorithms covering given functionality,
- selecting the technologies needed to achieve the desired results and implementing the appropriate mechanisms.

Thanks to the ability to split the issues concerning the XML language into the smaller subgroups, the principles of Agile software development (Martin, 2002) were applied during the project realization. The effects of each iteration were demonstrated to potential users and their remarks were taken into consideration in subsequent steps. Preliminary results obtained during the research confirmed initial assumptions regarding usability of the elaborated mechanisms, so their evaluation for a wide group of beneficiaries is planned as a future work.

A documentation of work progress and obtained results presented in a chapter has the following structure. The first part includes general information about the MOODLE platform and XML language (sections 1, 2). The second part, including sections 4.1 and 4.2, presents the original solutions allowing for creation and analysis of XML documents. Point 4.3 describes synonyms defining tools, enhancing flexibility of these mechanisms usage. These issues are also discussed in section 6.1, where the activity of a specially designed block structure is explained. This section provides the mechanisms for creating the individual educational path (point 5) as well.

The third section describes more advanced mechanisms for the XML activity, including both DTDs and XML Schemas (point 6.2). Besides, the mechanisms for XML usage in relational databases are described in the 7th point of the chapter.

In the conclusion, the obtained results are summarized and directions for future work are formulated.

2. The MOODLE platform

IT development, the more and more popular access to the Internet and variety of tools enabling using it in the field of teaching (Nedeva, 2005), encourage many educational institutions and companies to expand their offers with e-learning courses (Daku, 2009, Dobrzański&Brom&Brytan, 2007). Owing to that, quicker access to knowledge and learning costs reduction can be achieved. Course materials can be studied by the employees or students at a convenient time and place, which gives them a chance to equalize possibilities of getting an education.

However, when using the available e-learning tools, two problems are observable.

- So far, usage of e-learning platforms is limited to theory presentation and exchange of teaching materials, whereas, in some knowledge branches - especially in the field of technical science - teaching practical usage of theory, experience achieved in real environments and learning from one's own mistakes play an important role. Current functionality of e-learning platforms does not provide such possibilities.
- Second problem results from asynchronous type of learner-teacher communication, which makes both sides dependent on their mutual activity. Solutions of complex problems are usually more extensive than just a yes/no answer. It should be taken into consideration that very often many aspects of the solution should be analyzed, which can have a massive effect on delays in remote communication. Thus, an automatic estimation of solutions inconvenience should be introduced.

Dealing with the aforementioned problems will enrich and make teaching process more effective on various levels of education. What is more, in many cases, capabilities of tools, supporting e-learning are higher than only knowledge presentation and make elimination of described inconveniences possible.

Because, one of the most popular and free environments for e-learning is Modular Object-Oriented Dynamic Learning Environment [MOODLE] (MOODLE Home Page -Statistics, Braccini&Silvestri&Za&D'Atri, 2009), it was used in the research in order to extend it with the new mechanisms.

MOODLE course management allows teachers to build their courses in an optimal way for their learners and subject matter. The platform capabilities include many different mechanisms - i.e. activities, giving trainees possibility to test and to resolve given problems in practice and passive resources, allowing the knowledge presentation. The Open Source distributed MOODLE environment, has the specific (i.e. modular) organization. Besides, it cooperates with a database server - one of the following can be used: MySQL, PostgreSQL or MS SQL Server (MOODLE Home Page - About MOODLE). This features caused, it was very suitable tool for introducing new mechanisms to a group of already existing activities.

Due to the fact, in previous papers (Haręźlak&Werner, 2009; Haręźlak&Werner, 2010), the MOODLE module structure was explained in details, now only the key issues will be described.

After installing the whole environment (i.e. Apache Server, PHP and chosen database server), all MOODLE courses modules, such as: chat, forum, glossary, lesson, quiz, etc, are placed in one folder */www/mod* of WAMP server installation path[1]. Every module has its

[1] All information about the MOODLE software structure relates to Windows operating system.

separate folder of a corresponding name and the similar structure. The most important - and obligatory in each folder - files, are: **mod_form.php** and **view.php**. First file is responsible for a contents of page seen by a teacher during editing an activity, while second one - for contents of page seen by course participants during executing an activity. Thus, the new module implementation is in practice reduced to creating a new folder with a known structure, and to providing the desired functionality of component files by the PHP or Java Script coding.

Taking the important role of XML language in the exchange of a wide variety of data into consideration, the new custom XML mechanisms were developed in order to make the completion of educational tasks possible.

Therefore tasks (activities) with a different exercise level of difficulty were prepared in a module. Among them, two groups can be enumerated. First of them consists of simple operations on an XML file:

- creating a simple XML document,
- analysing of an XML file content,
- inserting a single row of data and loading data from an XML file.

In the second one, more complex tasks, regarding database mechanisms for XML data management, are considered:

- designing and creating database structures, dedicated to XML data collecting,
- building XML schemas and assigning them to the database structures,
- retrieving relational data as XML and querying XML data with usage of advanced methods.

The chapter will present novel mechanisms guaranteeing comprehensive, interactive XML language learning.

3. Sample XML data structure

The analysis of the proposed solutions will be conducted on the basis of the example presented below. The XML document instance that describes titles, authors and supervisors of students thesis (Master and BA) in the Polish universities, will be taken into consideration. Let's assume, the task formulated in XML module by the tutor, is:

Write the well-formed instance of the XML document for the universities students' thesis data. First, data about the name of the university should be stored. Then – subsequently – for each student after defence, the student register number, the type (Master or BA) and title of thesis, the year of defence, finally, the name of student's promoter and his titles should be placed.

Additional requirements: use the tag <List> for the root element. Don't use tag attributes - only Element components. All data about the Master or BA thesis of the specified student should be described in 1 element. The description about each kind of a student's thesis should be contained in separate elements. The solution should contain an example data for 2 students from different universities. Suppose, first student is after Master and BA defence in Silesian Technical University, while second – only after BA in AGH University.

There are a lot of possibilities to formulate the given XML document instance for the given task. Two sample alternative XML documents of given requirements, where the names of the tags are not significantly different (*University* vs. *UnivName*, *TypeBA* vs. *BA*, etc.), are shown in fig. 1.

```
<?xml version="1.0" encoding="UTF-8"?>
<List>
  <UnivName>
    Silesian Technical University
    <student>
      1357321
      <BA>
        2008, PhD Adam Winkler
      </BA>
      <Master>
        2011, Prof. Jan Boltz
      </Master>
    </student>
  </UnivName>
  <UnivName>
    AGH University
    <student>
      1357321
      <BA>
        2008, PhD Adam Winkler
      </BA>
    </student>
  </UnivName>
</List>
```

```
<?xml version="1.0" encoding="UTF-8"?>
<List>
  <Univeristy>
    Silesian Technical University
    <student>
      1111122
      <TypeBA>
        2005, PhD Anna Michna
      </TypeBA>
      <TypeMaster>
        2008, PhD Anna Michna
      </TypeMaster>
    </student>
  </Univeristy>
  <University>
    AGH University
    <student>
      1111133
      <TypeBA>
        2011, PhD Joe Winter
      </TypeBA>
    </student>
  </University>
</List>
```

Fig. 1. Two sample alternatives of XML document instance.

The XML Schema shown in the fig. 2 defines the structure of described sample XML document, will be used to present mechanisms introduced in the MOODLE platform.

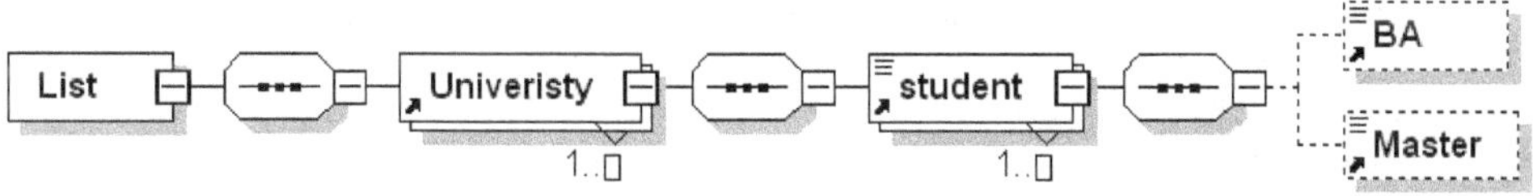

Fig. 2. The XML Schema of an example XML document.

4. Defining an XML document

As it was presented in the Introduction, XML documents can be utilized in many areas of life, but to be useful, they have to be prepared accordingly with a given structure, comprehensible for every interested part. Therefore, the most basic skills needed for the XML data management are an ability to formulate and analyze well-formed XML documents. Their teaching is supposed to be conducted in two directions. On one hand, the knowledge concerning rules of creating XML documents should be presented. On the other hand, there is a need to take care of gaining an experience in this field. Basis for obtaining such experience is an individual, practical usage of theory supported by feedback regarding types and places of made mistakes.

Due to that fact, functionality for XML document defining was designed for the MOODLE platform (Fig. 3), in which verifying of a document instance correctness was the most important problem to solve. It was accomplished with usage of both the MOODLE platform and database objects. Two groups of tables were introduced. The first one is dedicated to the teachers and serves as a container for descriptions of proper documents structures. The second one is indented to collect course participants' solutions. Validation of this solution is performed by the comparison of the contents of both groups. The appropriate functions are responsible for realization of this process.

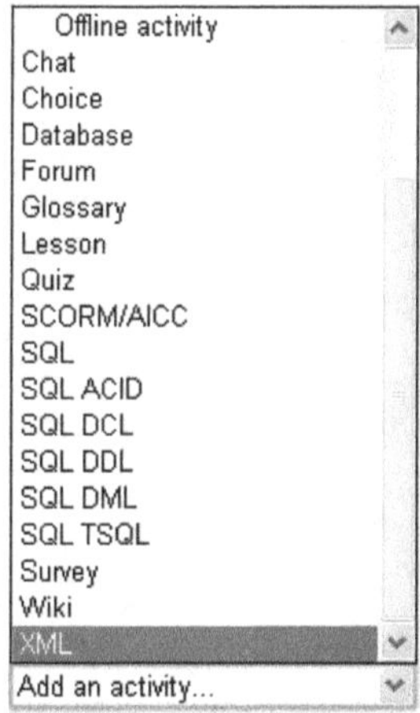

Fig. 3. The new XML activity.

4.1 Defining a structure of an XML document template

In the first research phase there was assumed that a teacher preparing tasks to be solved by course participants knows mechanism of the MOODLE platform well and does not have to know issues concerning computer science. So, mechanisms, introduced into this environment, had to be prepared in a way enabling teacher to use his/her skills.

The initial step in the research was to adjust a teacher's window to new functionality, which is XML document structure management. For this purpose, the **mod_form.php** file for a new activity, called XML, was modified (Fig. 3). Changes regarded both its construction and logic, it contained. Structure of the window was extended with a few elements. The most important one is the *htmleditor* named `xml_entry` (Fig. 4), which is designed to be filled

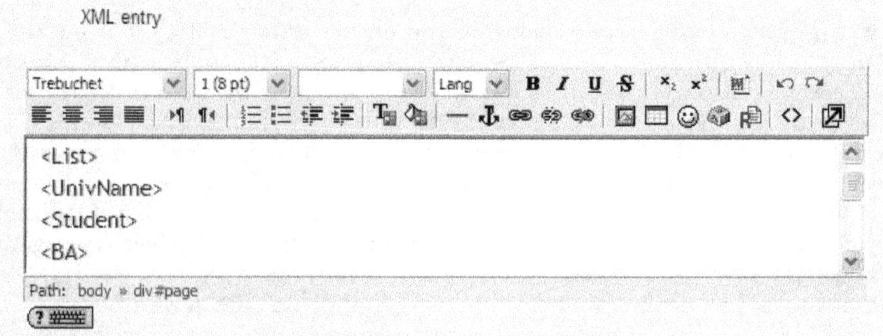

Fig. 4. The `xml_entry` htmleditor element visible in the teacher's window.

with an XML document template structure. Because content of this element will be different for various tasks, the identifier of a task should be entered as well (`task_number`, Fig. 5).

```
$mform->addElement('htmleditor','xml_entry',get_string('XML entry','xml'));
$mform->addElement('text','task_number',get_string('task number','xml'));
```

Task number 4

Fig. 5. The `task_number` text element visible in the teacher's window.

The provided XML template, for further use, has to be inserted into the database. Therefore, the *validation* function, which is run during the process of saving the newly defined activity, was equipped with required logic. Details of a database and credentials can to be provided by a teacher in next four fields (Fig. 6):

```
$mform->addElement('text','dbhost',get_string('dbhost', 'xml'));
$mform->addElement('text','dbname',get_string('dbname', 'xml'));
$mform->addElement('text','dblogin',get_string('dblogin', 'xml'));
$mform->addElement('text','dbpassword',get_string('dbpass', 'xml'));
```

or can be prepared by a module administrator with usage of a *setDefault* function, as is presented below:

```
$mform->setDefault('dbhost','moodle_server');
```

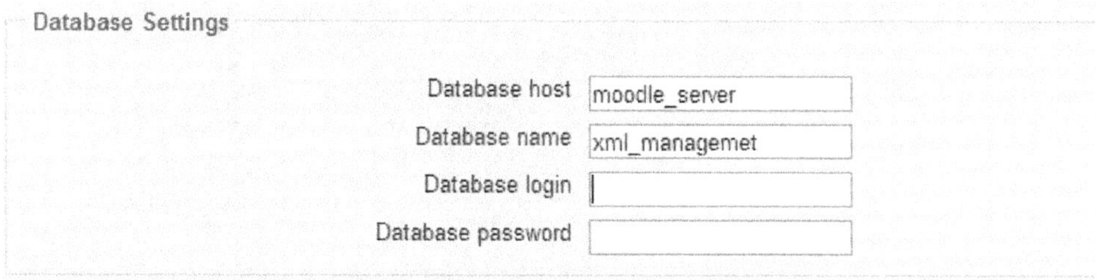

Database Settings

Database host moodle_server

Database name xml_managemet

Database login

Database password

Fig. 6. Elements defining parameters for a database connection.

This database, as mentioned above, must possess a special *Tag_templates* table, in which each tag from a template structure and its level in tags tree are stored in one row. Additionally, this information is complemented by the number of the task being created. However, before it is possible, XML template must be divided into substrings - one for each tag. This operation is also performed by the logic of the *validation* function. Unfortunately, usage of *hmleditor* element entailed problems regarding recognizing limiters of tags - e.g. < and > characters. They belong to a set of special symbols of HTML language and are represented by strings in form of *<* and *>* respectively. In consequence, obtaining string representing a tag must be preceded by extracting these chars. This problem can be avoided by using *textarea* elements:

```
$mform->addElement('textarea','xml_entry',get_string('XML entry','xml'));
$mform->addElement('textarea','synonyms',get_string('Synonyms','xml'));
```

During the process of XML template transformation a level of a tag is calculated as well. For example, if the aforementioned sample structure was taken into consideration, the result of acting of the *validation* function would consist of elements presented in the Table 1.

List	1
UnivName	2
Student	3
BA	4
Master	4

Table 1. Sample result of the *validation* function acting.

The *Validation* function is also responsible for checking contents of *Tag_template* table. If rows of another template for the considered task are found, they are replaced by a newly defined set.

4.2 Validating solution correctness

When the whole process of defining XML document template is finished, new activity can be utilized by course participants in the same way as all predefined in the MOODLE platform objects and is accessible in a list of participant's tasks. Window of the XML activity includes tree elements (Fig. 7): task contents, text area for its solution and *Check structure* button, which starts a procedure of verifying a correctness of a solution.

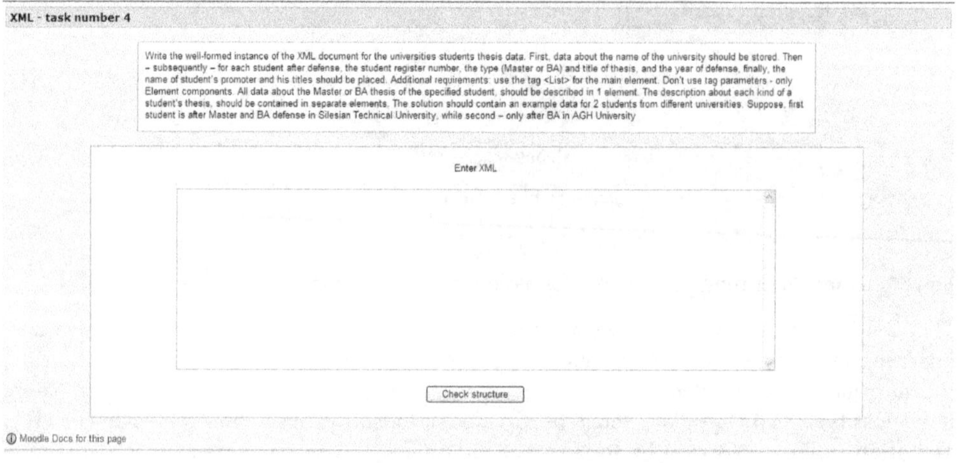

Fig. 7. View of a XML course participant's window.

This procedure, included in logic of the **view.php** file, is based on data inserted to the *Tag_templates* table and similarly, begins with splitting solution into substrings. Because a base for this partitioning is the symbol of a new line, the requirement ending each tag and value by this character has to be fulfilled. For each substring a level is calculated, which, subsequently, is compared with the level defined for a related tag in a template. In case of detecting a difference participant receives an appropriate message (Fig. 8). At the end of the process, an existence of a corresponding opening and closing tags is checked. A proper solution is acknowledged with a suitable notification (Fig. 9).

Fig. 8. View of a participant's window with a badly prepared solution.

Enter XML

```
<List>
<School>
Silesian Technical University
<Learner>
1357321
<BA>
2008, PhD Adam Winkler
</BA>
<Master>
2011, Prof. Jan Boltz
</Master>
</Learner>
</School>
<School>
AGH University
```

Check structure

Your solution is correct !

Fig. 9. View of a participant's window with a properly prepared solution.

Independently, every analyzed element is remembered in *Solutions* table. A row of this table includes task number, tag, its level in a structure defined by a participant and user identifier assigned to her/him. Owing to that, a teacher is able to analyze the result of a participant's work. Additionally, a new row, containing data on task and a participant solving it, is added to *Grades* table. If a solution is acceptable, the *passed* column is checked in this record. In other case column named *attempt* is incremented. The number of possible attempts is defined by a teacher in a task configuration window, through the additional element introduced into the **mod_form.php** file (Fig. 10):

```
$mform->addElement('text','attempts_number',get_string('attempts','xml'));
```

Number of attempts 3

Fig. 10. The `attempts_number` text element visible in the teacher's window.

4.3 The synonyms

Analysis of tasks' solutions can indicate that course participant prepared a good solution of a task, but used different tags from those defined in a template. XML elements must follow a few naming rules (e.g. names cannot contain spaces), but any name can be used, because no words are reserved. Therefore mechanisms for defining synonyms were developed. Again, the **mod_form.php** file was utilized. The set of elements defining teacher's window was extended with one more html editor for synonyms providing (Fig. 11).

```
$mform->addElement('htmleditor','synonyms',get_string('synonyms', 'xml'));
```

A synonym format is specified to facilitate an analysis of entered words. Each tag with additional words should be surrounded by square brackets: "*[*" ,"*]*". First word in that scope should be a tag ended by ":" character. After that, synonyms for a given tag, separated by a space, could be placed. Once more, example of the universities students' thesis data will be taken into consideration.

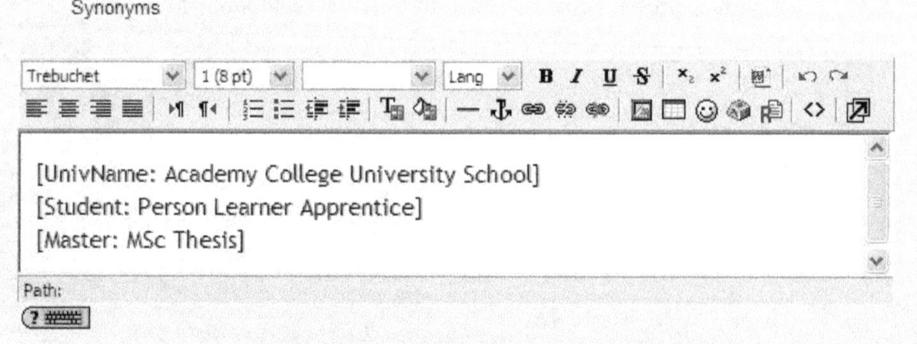

Fig. 11. The `synonyms` html editor element visible in the teacher's window.

To define alternative words for *UnivName*, *Student* and *Master* tags, teacher should prepare following script:

```
[UnivName: academy college university school]
[student: person learner apprentice]
[Master: MSc thesis]
```

Such script has to be placed within the *synonyms* element when task is being defined or edited. Subsequently, it is analyzed by the *validation* function, in which the operation of additional HTML symbols removal comes first. Next, each row of the script is being prepared to be loaded into the database. Two versions of database structures for storing synonyms were analyzed. On one hand, they can be inserted into one column and treated as one text. On the other, they can be spread into two tables - one being a kind of synonyms dictionary with one record per synonym and second one associating tags with their synonyms. This solution allows for writing a synonym once and then map it to many tags, but requires more tables' joins than in the first case. However, both of them were implemented and comparing their effectiveness is planned in the further research.

The simplified algorithm of the procedure for validating participant's solution correctness, which takes mechanism of synonyms management into account, is shown in the listing 1.

Enter XML

```
<List>
<School>
Silesian Technical University
<Learner>
1357321
<BA>
2008, PhD Adam Winkler
</BA>
<Master>
2011, Prof. Jan Boltz
</Master>
</Learner>
</School>
<School>
AGH University
```

Check structure

Your solution is correct !

Fig. 12. View of a participant's window with a solution using synonyms.

```
get participant's solution;
while (next_line_read){
    check participant_tag in the tags_template table;
    if (not found){
        check participant_tag in the Synonyms table(s);
       if (not found){
          show error message;
          set error_var;
       }else
          get tag for a participant_tag;
    }
    if (not error_var){
        check a level of participant_tag;
        if (level_error)
              show error message;
    }
}
```

Listing 1. The simplified algorithm of validating participant's solution correctness.

Thanks to the developed synonyms management functionality, mechanisms for validation of participants task solutions become more flexible. In case when function, which implements this functionality, discovers differences in template and student tags, it can still consider a given solution as a correct one (Fig. 12) if it finds a tag, provided by a student, in the synonyms table/tables.

Moreover, in case of a need, a once-defined set of synonyms can be extended by usage of the mechanism described in subsequent parts of the chapter.

5. Creation of an educational path

Process of acquiring necessary skills can develop at a different speed for different course participants. Sometimes presented knowledge requires only few tasks to be done, in other cases it should be practiced many times. For this reason, the simple mechanism, determining the number and difficulty of tasks to be solved by a given participant, depending on his/her current progress, was proposed in the developed activity. In the present stage of the research, it is based on a number of attempts allowed to obtain a proper solution of a task. This number should be specified by a teacher during defining the task (`attempts_number` in **mod_form.php** file - as it was presented in the fig. 10), but if it is omitted, the default value is taken into account.

This value is calculated for a participant accordingly with its activity (column *Attempt* in the *Grade* table) and is used by the logic of the **view.php** file to check how he/she dealt with a given task. Among cases being considered by this logic, the following can be enumerated.

1. Course participant has not attempted to solve a task yet - as a result, task window is opened for a task defined by a teacher.
2. Course participant has already solved a task - an appropriate message and three buttons are displayed; one for task redoing, second for solving a new task, with the same difficulty level and third for cancelling the action (Fig. 13).

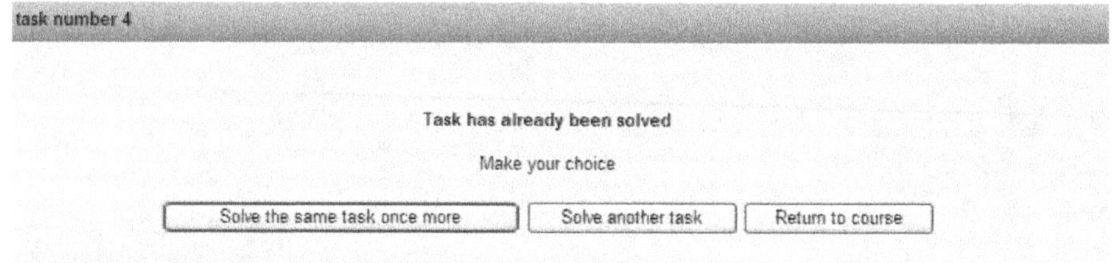

Fig. 13. View of a participant's window with a given task already solved.

3. Course participant undertakes the next attempt to solve a task, which previously was not solved correctly, but an attempt number is less than the highest acceptable (e.g. less than defined by a teacher) - in such situation, acting of the **view.php** file logic is the same as in the first case.
4. Course participant undertakes the next try to solve a task but an attempt number is greater than acceptable - discovering such situation results in displaying a message, which includes task number that should be completed before a next attempt to the current one occurs (Fig. 14).

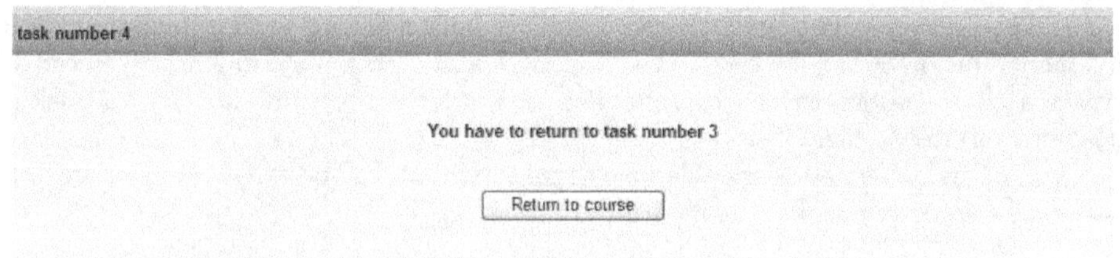

Fig. 14. View of a participant's window with a given task not solved properly.

5. Course participant gets back to solving a task, because he/she didn't manage to solve one of the subsequent tasks. In such case, the subject of the task should be changed, but its difficulty should stay on the same level. Activity of this kind entails creating a new template solution and preparing a new set of synonyms. That process can be automated

by usage of text files with standardized names. Their responsibility is to define new contents enabling the configuration of the task in accordance with the attempt number. The basic part of the file name (so called *prefix*), together with its path, should be provided by a teacher, in task definition window through `file_name` element (Fig. 15).

```
$mform->addElement('text','file_name',get_string('file name','xml'));
```

File name c:\xml\task4

Fig. 15. The `file_name` text element visible in the teacher's window.

Its content is then used for constructing full files names. Among them there are:

- *prefix_cont_attemp_number.txt* - containing task subject for a given attempt number,
- *prefix_temp_attemp_number.txt* - containing template of the solution for a given attempt number,
- *prefix_synonym_attemp_number.txt* - containing synonyms for a given attempt number, prepared in accordance with the aforementioned format.

Let's assume that a course participant did not manage to solve the task marked by number 5, because he/she exceeded number of allowed attempts. According to the proposed rules he/she was directed to get back to task number 4. In the first attempt, it is defined to solve the problem presented in Sample XML data structure part, but now the content of the task have to be changed. Let's assume once again that a file *prefix* provided by a teacher has the same value as it is shown in the fig. 15. This means that files used for the second attempt of the task will be searched for in *c:\xml* folder with following conditions:

- *c:\xml\task4_cont_2.txt* - for a new task content,
- *c:\xml\task4_temp_2.txt* - for a new task solution template,
- *c:\xml\task4_synonym_2.txt* - for the new task synonyms.

In case one of these files cannot be found, the first attempt configuration is used.
Simplified algorithm ensuring the described functionality is presented in the listing 2.

```
get passed value for a given task and a given user;
if (passed){
   show message "Task has already been solved" ;
   show appropriate buttons;
}else{
   get attept_number for a given task and a given user;
   If (attempt_number > 1){
        get file_name value for a given task;
        search for appropriate files;
        if (found) {
          define a new task content using prefix_temp_attemp_number.txt;
          prepare a new task solution template using_
           _prefix_temp_temp_number.txt
          insert a new template into a database;
          prepare new task synonyms using prefix_synonym_temp_number.txt
          insert new synonyms into a database;
       }
   }
  open a course participant's window;
}
```

Listing 2. Simplified algorithm of an educational path creation.

The basic structure of teacher's window including all described elements is presented in the fig. 16.

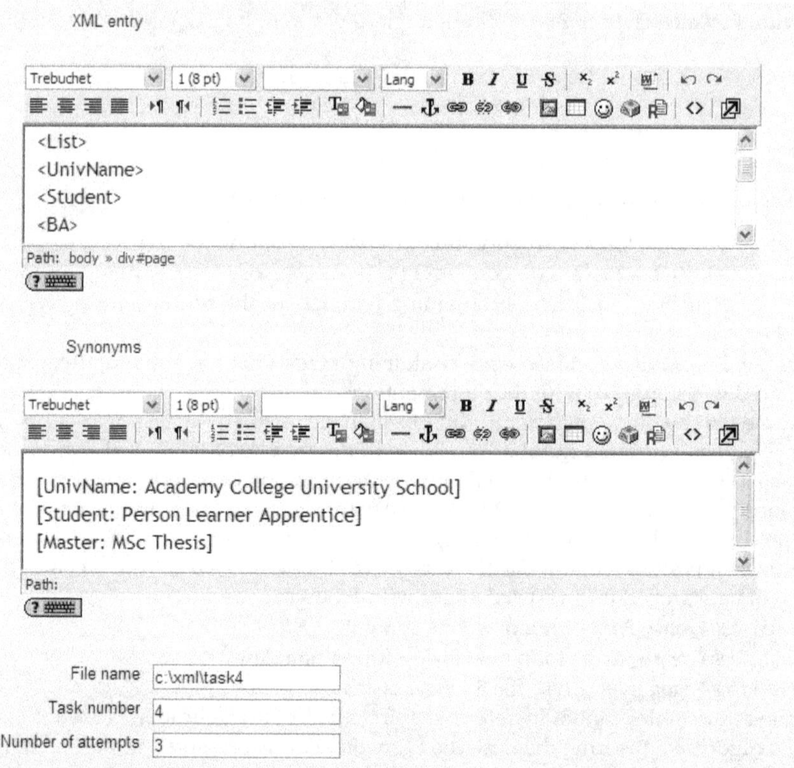

Fig. 16. The teacher's window with all described elements.

6. Advanced mechanisms for the XML activity

The basic functionality of XML activity was tested in terms of its usability. The results of tests indicated the possibilities of further e-learning platform extension. One of them regarded the possibility of the earlier defined set of synonyms extension. Besides, they concerned more advanced XML language issues, directed to the group of participants being at a higher education level.
Therefore, the suitable mechanisms for these inconveniences were proposed.

6.1 The synonym block

Another proposal to solve the difficulty of XML tags discrepancy is to use a specially implemented *Synonym* block. This mechanism provides the e-learning platform with the functionality for defining words and their synonyms, as it is shown in fig. 17.
There were several reasons for the choice of this type of the MOODLE environment component. The main one was the possibility of adding this kind of object to any module and any course, and, hence, achieving an opportunity to its later usage in other than the

XML modules. The SQL modules that were developed in the previous research (Haręźlak&Werner, 2010) can be a good example of such situation.

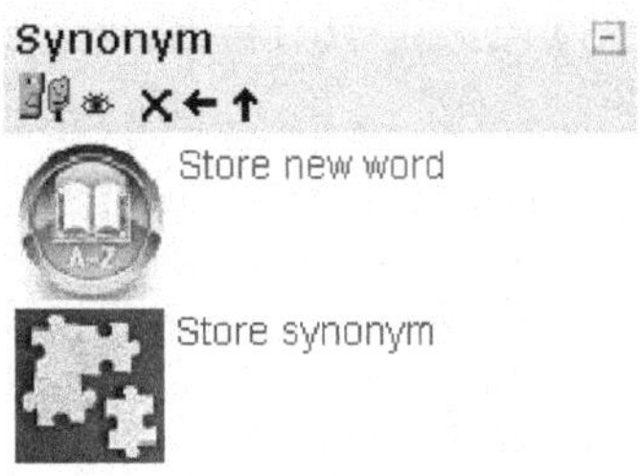

Fig. 17. The Synonym block.

In that case, the synonym block might be useful in situations, when the schema of a database queried by learners by the usage of SQL module, would change. Then, the typical action performed by a course trainer, would be to rewrite all query tasks (i.e. SQL activities) added to the topic previously and to change the names of the altered columns to a new ones. Whereas, giving the teachers the ability to use the synonym block element, would eliminate this disadvantage.

In order to define a new block, the */blocks* folder of the MOODLE home directory was changed. As it was mentioned before, the MOODLE software has the modular structure and all its units have similar construction. The same applies to the block element. In practice, in order to define a new synonym block, a new subfolder with the name corresponding to the name of being defined block, with a known set of PHP and HTML files is created. The chosen, mandatory, elements of */synonym* folder, are listed in table 2.

Chosen elements of /synonym folder	Content description
/db	Defines the structure of back-end MOODLE database table, that is created especially for defined block. It is used during block installation
/images	Includes two icons shown in fig. 17 that are next to the links forwarding the user to word or synonyms defining pages
/lang	Includes subfolders with translation files that consists of string mappings, realizing different language versions of block fields' headers
block_synonym.php	Provides block class definition with functions displaying - inter alia - the title and version of synonym block
synonym.php	This file name must be the same, as the name of defined block

Table 2. The elements of /synonym folder.

Besides, there are a few HTML files that provide block class, in */synonym* subfolder with specific - instance or global level - configuration.

The most important file is the **block_synonym.php**, where - inter alia - two Web links, referencing to separate PHP files, providing the desired functionality, are specified:

```
$this->content->items[] = '<a href="word.php">Store new word</a>';
$this->content->items[] = '<a href="synonym.php">Store synonym</a>';
```

Thus, the major modifications of the new block functionality were made in above mentioned files. It is worth emphasizing that these files are located both - in MOODLE home directory and its */course* subfolder. Such duplication was necessary to make files accessible for MOODLE users both - at the site, and the course, levels (Fig. 18).

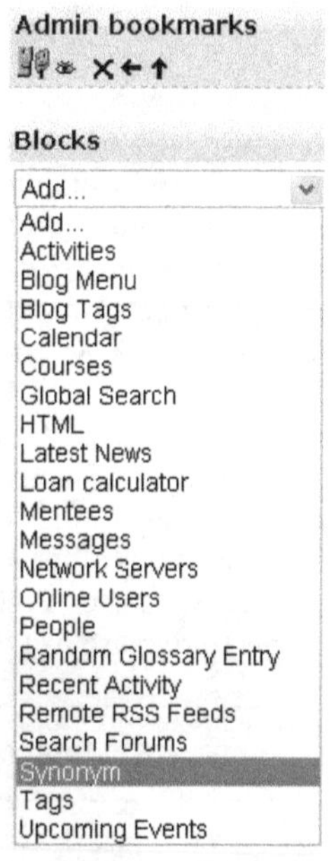

Fig. 18. Adding the Synonym block at the site level.

New added data - i.e. word itself, word id, annotation and the number of course, the word is defined for is inserted into described earlier synonyms table. The last attribute was intended to enable the word definition only to the selected course that – consequently – reduces the number of searched table rows. New rows are inserted to these table by the use of the especially prepared files - **word.php** and **synonym.php** ones.

The existence of two separate PHP files causes that in an independent manner - i.e. not necessarily at the same time - words and their synonyms can be defined.

The result of the **word.php** file acting is presented in fig. 19.

6.2 DTD documents and XML schema

As it was shown, the validity of XML document can be checked by a lexical analyzer. But in terms of the W3C organization (XML Essentials) valid XML document is a well formed XML document, which also conforms to the rules of a Document Type Definition (DTD) or by its successor – XML Schema.

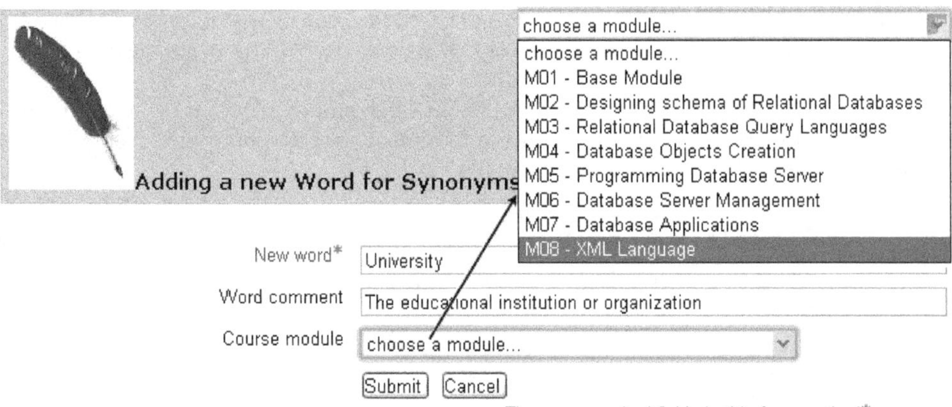

Fig. 19. Defining a new word for synonyms window.

The DTD may be declared inside the XML file (then it should be wrapped in a *DOCTYPE* definition) or in an external file (then, XML file should be assigned to the DTD definition by `<!DOCTYPE root-element SYSTEM "DTDfilename">` element). There is the possibility to extend MOODLE platform with required DTD or XML Schema validation functionality (Webmaster Tutorial - PHP Tutorials), however such validators are also available on-line. As an example, http://www.w3schools.com/xml/xml_validator.asp web page is presented in fig. 20.

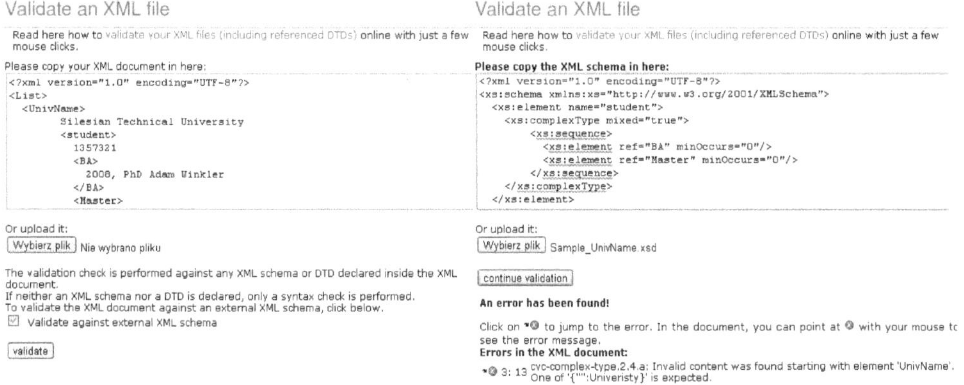

Fig. 20. The sample of two-step XML Schema validation window.

In addition to XML instance against DTD/XML Schema validation, another important problem was solved in the described XML module.

In order to provide mechanisms for comprehensive study of the rules regarding constructing of DTD and XML Schema documents, the suitable algorithms were implemented.

For example, one of the module tasks is to study the sample XML instance, written in a task body and correct given DTD document to fit the specified XML. The mechanism which had to be implemented in the MOODLE platform to check the coincidence of learners' responses with the "model" answer defined by a teacher, was coded in PHP by the usage of auxiliary files.

To grade the correctness of trainee solution (Fig. 21), the sample (i.e. accurate), well-formed, DTD document defined by a teacher is uploaded into a supplementary text file, while the sent answer - into the second temporary text file.

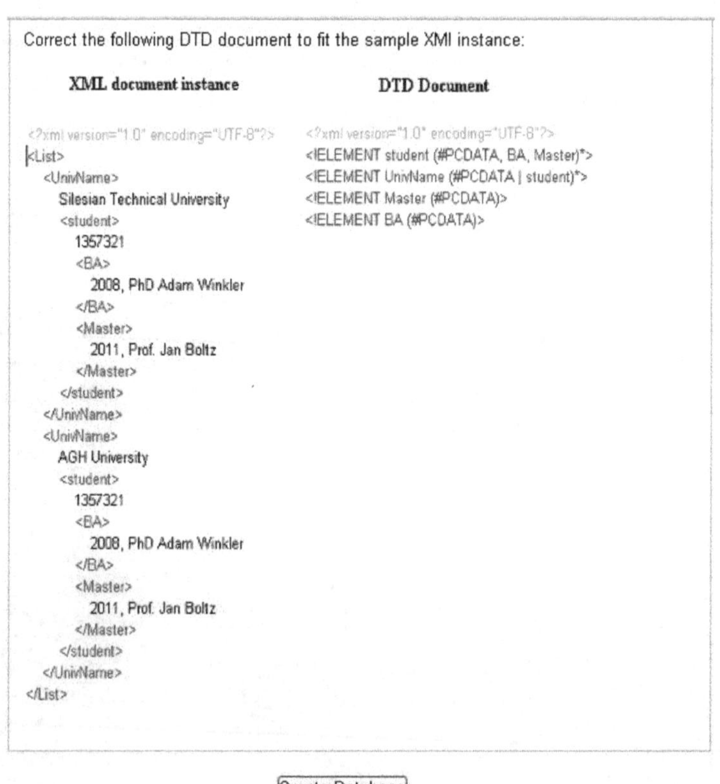

Enter DTD

```
<!DOCTYPE List [
<!ELEMENT student (#PCDATA | BA | Master)*>
<!ELEMENT UnivName (#PCDATA | student)*>
<!ELEMENT Master (#PCDATA)>
<!ELEMENT List ((UnivName+))>
<!ELEMENT BA (#PCDATA)>
]>
```

Execute Save Answer

You are succesfull! The DTD document is now OK!

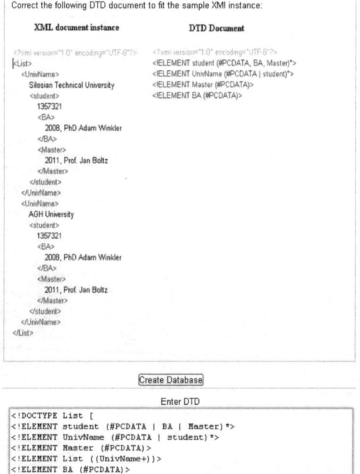

Fig. 21. The DTD correctness task window.

Both files are stored in the MOODLE backend server. Because of the fact, a lot of course participants can execute the task at the same time, the temporary file name generated for a particular MOODLE user solution is dynamically composed in a following manner:

XML_*UserId_ModuleId_TaskNo*.txt.

UserId, ModuleId and *TaskNo* represent course participant, module and task unique identifiers respectively and are accessible through PHP variables `$XML->dblogin`, `$course->id`, `$XML->id`, where `$XML = get_record('XML', 'id', $cm->instance)`. Additionally, to avoid the situation, the numerous spaces will influence the solutions discrepancy, the undue spaces and whitespaces are eliminated from sent answer by the use of regular expressions in form of `preg_replace("@\s+@"," ",$file)`. Generally, the whole algorithm is as follows:

```
Set variables, pointing to both files;
Open files for reading;
Get the contents of both files;
Remove undue spaces and whitespaces from the file contents;
For (each DTD entry) do {
  Compare an entry with its exemplar;
  If (the entries are the same) {
    Return the message of successful task solving;
  }
  Else {
    Return the message of incorrect task solving; }
}
Close the files;
```

Although the XML Schema defining rules differ from the DTD ones, the problems that had to be solved by providing the MOODLE environment with adequate mechanisms were similar. But it must be emphasized, that XML module tasks referring to XML Schemas play another, crucial, role in the topic of storing XML in relational database. Thus, numerous of the new XML functionalities were formulated with regard to a database used in this scope.

7. XML usage in relational databases

Nowadays, a lot of relational databases - e.g. Oracle and MS SQL Server - provide XML Schema support for the numerous purposes. Validation of the XML documents against registered XML Schema definitions is one of them. As a part of the XML Schema registration process, a database automatically creates the storage for a particular set of XML documents, based on the information provided by the schema. If the document fits to the schema, it is shredded into relational data conforming to the underlying relational table.

In described XML activity, the schema registration functionality was introduced. To enable participants the registration of their own XML schemas, suitable PHP script was added to a **view.php** file. In this type of tasks, the *Execute* button is used to perform the requested action, as it is shown in fig. 22.

In fact, the registration process involves an appropriate built-in procedure. For example in Oracle database repository it was *DBMS_XMLSCHEMA.RegisterSchema* procedure. Consequently, in the **view.php** file, the learner schema stored in a string variable, is only

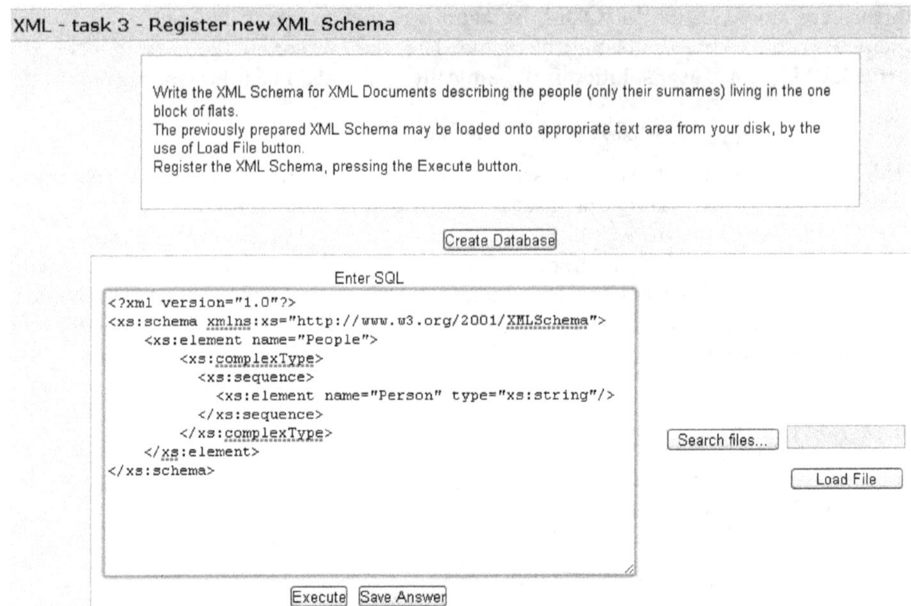

Fig. 22. The sample XML Schema registration.

one of the required procedure arguments. Therefore, after pressing the *Execute* button in the XML module window, the following code is performed (listing 3):

```
$conn = oci_connect($dbuser, $dbpassword, $dbname);
If ($conn) {
  $sql_statement = OCIParse(
    $conn,
    "begin DBMS_XMLSCHEMA.RegisterSchema (
      $SchemaName, $userschema, TRUE,TRUE,FALSE,TRUE, $SchemaOwner);
    end;");
  $command=oci_execute($sql_statement);
  If ($command) {
      echo "Schema is registered successfully";
  }
}
```

Listing 3. PHP code of XML Schema registration.

The schema registration is only the first step to enable storing the XML data in a relational database. Next, it can be, for example, schema-based table creation, as shown in the following example:

```
CREATE TABLE XmlTable OF XMLType
  XMLSCHEMA "http://www.XMLModule.com/sample.xsd"
  ELEMENT "List";
```

or posting a schema-based document to be inserted into a schema-based XMLType view. In this case, the database system checks whether the XML document being inserted into the table or view, conforms to the XML schema on which the view is defined. To illustrate this process, two tables in Oracle database - *Student* and *University*, with fields corresponding to tags of sample XML (Fig. 2), were created. Additionally, a new *univNo* column was added to each table, in order to enable table joining. The appropriate view definition is shown below (Listing 4).

```
CREATE OR REPLACE VIEW univ_v OF XMLType WITH OBJECT ID
    (EXTRACT(OBJECT_VALUE, '/UNIVERSITY/@univNo').getNumberVal())
AS SELECT XMLELEMENT
    ("UNIVERSITY",
          XMLFOREST(univNo, univName),
          (SELECT XMLELEMENT("STUDENT",
                XMLAGG(
                  XMLELEMENT("STUDENT",
                     XMLFOREST(studNO as "Student", BA , Master)
                  )
                )
           )
           FROM Student s, University u WHERE s.univNo = u.univNo
          )
    )
FROM University u;
```

Listing 4. XMLType view definition.

There are two ways to keep data in a XMLType storage structure, in Oracle database system:

- Store XML in CLOB XMLType.
- Store XML as structured data, by the use of object-relational storage. In this situation, the shredded XML document is inserted into the underlying relational table, as a new row.

In the **view.php** file only the second possibility was implemented (Building Database-Driven PHP Applications), as it is shown in listing 5.

```
$sql = $_POST["query"];
$tmp = str_replace(";", " ", $sql);
$sql = $tmp;
$sql_statement = OCIParse($connection,$sql);
oci_execute($sql_statement);
If ($r) {
  oci_fetch($sql_statement);
  $strXMLData = oci_result($sql_statement, 'RESULT');
  $doc = new DOMDocument("1.0", "UTF-8");
  $doc->loadXML($strXMLData); }
```

Listing 5. XML data result.

It is worth emphasizing that XML data retrieved from the database with applied DOM fidelity consists of the same information as it was inserted into the database, with the exception of insignificant whitespaces.

In order to print out the result in a proper way (i.e. XML-formatted), the *htmlspecialchars($strXMLData)* function was called. Otherwise, only "pure" data - i.e. entries without tags, will be printed. The XML-formatted result of a sample query is shown in fig. 23, while "ordinary" one - in fig. 24.

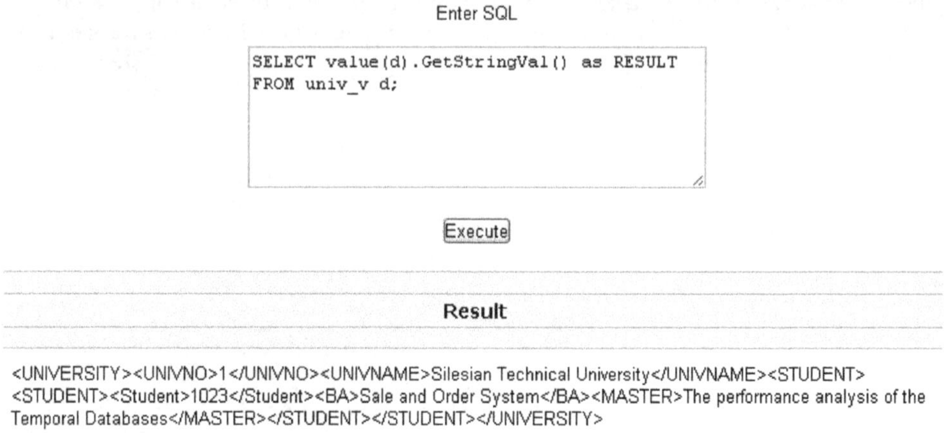

Enter SQL

```
SELECT value(d).GetStringVal() as RESULT
FROM univ_v d;
```

Execute

Result

<UNIVERSITY><UNIVNO>1</UNIVNO><UNIVNAME>Silesian Technical University</UNIVNAME><STUDENT><STUDENT><Student>1023</Student><BA>Sale and Order System</BA><MASTER>The performance analysis of the Temporal Databases</MASTER></STUDENT></STUDENT></UNIVERSITY>

Fig. 23. The XML-formatted result of performing the sample XMLType-based query.

Result

1Silesian Technical University1023Sale and Order SystemThe performance analysis of the Temporal Databases

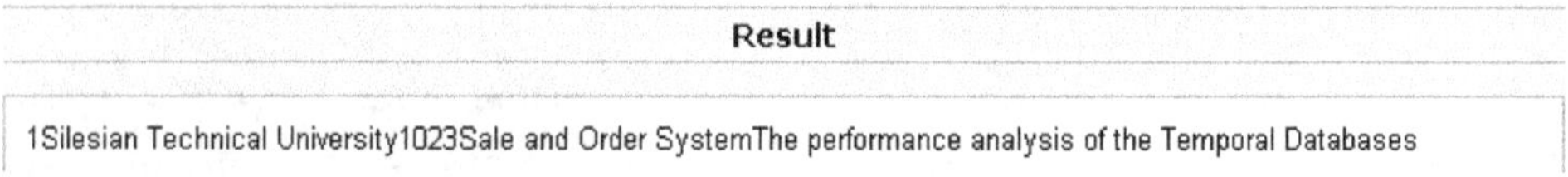

Fig. 24. The result of performing the sample XMLType-based query.

Many other mechanisms, required for manipulating and querying the XMLType tables or views, based on registered XML schemas, were provided to the MOODLE e-learning platform. There are a lot of PHP scripts examples in (PHP Oracle Web Development) that are in fact ready-made solutions. Thus, the numerous functionalities were introduced into the XML module.

Besides, the possibility of formulating a simple XPath queries is provided in a described module. As it is presented in fig. 25, the queried XML document is assumed to be stored in a MOODLE platform server.

In order to provide such functionality, a special PHP function that converts an XML file into an object should be utilized. By the use of:

```
$doc =simplexml_load_file('XML_doc.xml');
```

assignment, all document elements are available. For example, in order to print BA-tagged data, `$doc->student->BA` argument should be used in the *printf* function. To facilitate the algorithm implementation, the document tree hierarchy is stored in a specially created table. Thus, the XPath query realization is reduced to the following steps:

- Check the name of last-written tag.
- Search the auxiliary table to get the level of the tag.
- Convert the well-formed XML document in the given file to an object.
- Loop through the elements at a specified level.
- Print required data in a user's activity window.

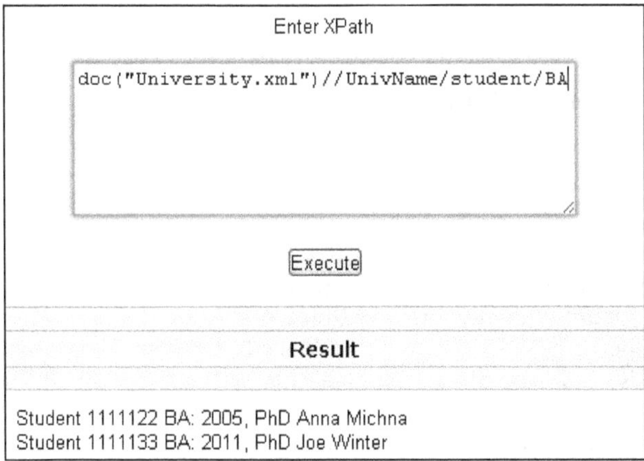

Fig. 25. The result of the sample XPath query.

8. Conclusion

In the chapter the possibility of using e-learning platform as an environment for education of XML language issues has been analyzed. Among them, basic XML structure elements and XML instance analysis were considered. For this purpose appropriate XML module and Synonym block, were created.

The architecture of the module is similar to other built-in modules, but its functionality entailed introducing the specific solutions, suitable for tasks that XML module should implement. Additionally the simple mechanism, determining the number and difficulty of tasks to be solved by given learners, depending on their current progress, was proposed in the developed activity. It is based on numbers of their attempts undertaken to obtain proper task solution. Besides, more advanced XML language issues, directed to the group of participants being at a higher education level, were taken into consideration as well. Thus, retrieving relational data as XML and querying XML data with usage of advanced methods were implemented.

All of the extensions were made using PHP scripts and were tested in the chosen database servers: MySQL, MS SQL Server and Oracle DBMS.

Results of all tests were satisfactory, confirming preliminary assumptions for the possibility of using e-learning MOODLE platform as the environment for interactive teaching of XML language issues. However, there are some limitations in the proposed solution. One of them is the necessity to define the XML elements' attributes as the independent tags in XML instance and cannot be placed within other tags. Besides, there is no possibility to attach externally parsed entities to an XML document. Developed functionality does not cover the subject of XML Queries, either.

Elimination of these limitations as well as evaluation of prepared solutions for wide group of beneficiaries are the first steps of the future work. Next, there is an addition planned to the presented work, extending grader report module with mechanisms assessing solutions of XML tasks. Furthermore, it is worth mentioning that the proposed functionality regards XML language issues but some of its mechanisms are generally enough to be exploited in other areas of education. The lexical analysis and text management (for instance in subject of programming languages) are good examples of such fields.

9. Acknowledgment

Project financed from the funds for learning in years 2010-2012 by a research and development grant number O R00 0113 12.

10. References

Braccini, A.M., Silvestri, C., Za, S., D'Atri, A. (2009). Users' perception of open source e-learning platform. Quality: the case of MOODLE. Available from http://eprints.luiss.it/934/2/Users_perception_of_open_source_e-learning_platform_quality_the_case_of_moodle.pdf

Bray, T., Paoli J., Sperberg-McQueen, C. M. (1998), eds, Extensible Markup Language (XML) 1.0, W3C Recommendation, Available from http://www.w3.org/TR/1998/REC-xml-19980210

Daku, B. (2009) Individualized Laboratory Using Moodle. FIE'09 Proceedings of the 39th IEEE international conference on Frontiers in education conference, ISBN: 978-1-4244-4715-2, NJ USA, 2009.

Dobrzański, L.A., Brom, F., Brytan, Z. (2007). Use of e-learning in teaching fundamentals of materials science. Journal of Achievements in Materials and Manufacturing Engineering, Vol. 24, ISSUE 2, October, 2007.

Harężlak, K., Werner, A. (2009). E-learning Database Course with Usage of Interactive Database Querying. Springer Verlag, *Internet - Technical Development and Applications Series: Advances in Intelligent and Soft Computing*, Vol. 64. Tkacz, E., Kapczynski, A. (Eds.), pp. 81-89, Softcover ISBN: 978-3-642-05018-3, Berlin 2009

Harężlak, K., Werner, A. (2010). Extension of the MOODLE e-learning platform with database management mechanisms. *Proceedings of 3rd Human System Interaction (HSI),* pp. 491-495, ISBN 978-1-4244-7560-5, Digital Object Identifier 10.1109/HSI.2010.5514525, Rzeszów, May, 2010 http://www.w3.org/standards/xml/core

Martin, R. C. (2002).Agile Software Development, Principles, Patterns, and Practices. Prentice Hall Publ. ISBN-10: 0135974445, ISBN-13: 978-0135974445, 2002.

MOODLE Home Page - About MOODLE, Available from http://moodle.org

MOODLE Home Page - Statistics, Available from http://moodle.org/stats/

Nedeva, V. (2005). The possibilities of e-learning, Based on MOODLE software platform. Trakia Journal of Sciences, Vol. 3, No. 7, pp. 12-19. ISSN 1312-1723, 2005. Available from http://tru.uni-sz.bg/tsj/vol3No7_1_files/V.Nedeva.pdf

O'REILLY xml.com, Available from http://www.xml.com/pub/rg/XML_Editors

Rice, F. (2006) Word 2007 XML Format, Microsoft Corporation, Available from http://msdn.microsoft.com/en-us/library/bb266220(v=office.12).aspx

Wasiliev, Y. Building Database-Driven PHP Applications on Oracle XML DB, Available from http://www.oracle.com/technetwork/articles/vasiliev-xmldb-php-094969.html

Wasiliev, Y. PHP Oracle Web Development – Data processing, Security, Caching, XML, Web Services, and AJAX. (2007). PACKT Publishing, Retrieved from http://packtlib.packtpub.com/library/9781847193636/ch08lvl1sec02

Webmaster Tutorial – PHP Tutorial, Available from http://www.webmaster-tutorial.com/tutorial/PHP/XML/1

XML Essentials, Available from http://www.w3.org/standards/xml/core

5

Technological Transparency in the Age of Web 2.0: A Case Study of Interactions in Internet-Based Forums

Kamran Shaikh, Vivek Venkatesh,[1]
Tieja Thomas, Kathryn Urbaniak, Timothy Gallant,[2]
David I. Waddington and Amna Zuberi
Learning for Life Centre, Department of Education, Concordia University, Canada

1. Introduction

Whether computers can be of benefit to the learning process has been a topic of discussion in the realm of educational technology research since the 1950s (Weigel, 2002). Computer technology has promised to revolutionize both teaching and learning in higher education (Slack & Wise, 2005). With the popularization of the Internet in the early 1990s, programs dedicated to the democratization of information technology have assisted the general public to become members of electronic communities (Albernaz, 2002). Online communications were quickly adopted in education - course management systems have long been using bulletin boards and online forums to facilitate various types of interactions, including learner-learner, learner-teacher, teacher-teacher, teacher-content, and learner-content (Shaw & Venkatesh, 2005).

However, in the first decade of the 21st century, with the advent of Web 2.0, the shape of online electronic communities began to change drastically. Online social interactions have seen an exponential growth since the increased adoption of technologies such as wikis and blogs. In this new age of the Web, users are given the power to control what content is displayed on their personal websites, and visitors to these websites are able to provide commentary using media as varied as text, audio and video.

Since 2004, commercial social networking applications such as Facebook, YouTube and Twitter have gained popularity across a variety of users, regardless of gender, culture, geographical regions and age. Facebook alone boasts more than 750 million active users worldwide (as of July 2011), and is ranked as the second most-visited site on the Internet after Google[3]. It is, therefore, rather disheartening to observe how theories of online learning have failed to take into account the paradigm shift we are seeing in the nature of social interactions through the Internet. Furthermore, existing theories have largely failed to account for the role online communities play in building and sustaining specialised forms of

---

[1] Joint first authors

[2] Joint second authors

[3] As ranked by Alexa – The Web Information Company (http://www.alexa.com)

what Lave and Wenger (1991) have dubbed "communities of practice"—namely, a group of people who share an interest, a craft, or a profession.

Theoretical discussions of how the design of online interactions impact learning are scant, at best (McGee, Carmean & Jafari, 2005; Venkatesh, Shaikh & Zuberi, 2010). Part of the problem, we contend, lies in the fact that the pedagogical bases for orchestrating online interactions are based on learning theories and instructional design models derived from face-to-face instruction. This over-reliance on classic theories of learning has led directly to a paucity of research investigating how online learning actually happens "in the wild" (Lave & Wenger, 1991). This holds true both within the educational realm and externally, in the wider Web 2.0 community.

In this chapter, we investigate learning in online forums which are focused on a particular interest, namely, heavy metal music. Even within this highly focused online community of metal fans, the data available for analysis is vast—individual forum members have often posted up to 20,000 times in as little as five years. We therefore decided to focus our analysis on a particular macro-level aspect of the forum: knowledge production processes. In order to understand these processes, we brought to bear a set of ideas about production that were originally espoused by John Dewey (1915). Dewey, in essence, thought that making production processes open and transparent was critical to helping citizens become more effective learners and agents. Applying these ideas to the forums, we theorized that relatively open knowledge production processes would help the heavy metal forum users become more savvy and engaged fans. As we will explain, this hypothesis held true to some extent. Yet our findings also indicated that the positive effects of open, transparent production processes can be mitigated by technocratic interactions between experts and novices.

2. Theoretical framework

2.1 The genesis of technological transparency

In *School and Society*, one of his first significant educational works, John Dewey (1915) emphasized the need for people to understand the basic mechanisms that underpin society. He argued that the rural dwellers of 19th century America, when compared to the inhabitants of Dewey's industrial Chicago, had possessed a better understanding of the technological processes that surrounded them. The inhabitants of rural America, Dewey claimed, understood how things were made, who in their communities was involved in the process, and the implications that this production process had for the lives of workers and consumers. This idea of developing an understanding of how things work is what is referred to as "technological transparency."Dewey thought that knowledge and in-depth understanding of the technologies that underpinned their society would afford citizens the opportunity to intervene in technological processes when necessary and would help them to be aware of how systems, structures or mechanisms around them function (Waddington, 2010). Dewey hoped that the industrial technologies of his day would become *open* to the understanding of citizens, rather than being closed off from their understanding. In this way, citizens would be able to make technologies work for them, rather than simply being shaped by prevailing technologies (Shaikh, Zuberi, Waddington, Thomas & Venkatesh, 2011).

2.2 Open and closed technologies

2.2.1 Defining open and closed technologies

One interesting way, among others, to update Dewey's notion of technological transparency for the contemporary context is to ask about the degree to which today's technologies are transparent and open to our understanding. Thinking along these lines, one can classify technologies along a spectrum from "open" to "closed." Open technologies are technologies that allow the user (a) to understand how the technologies function on both a surface and a deeper level, and (b) to become involved in their overall construction, design, and management. It is this 'openness' that allows for the possibility of agency.

Wikis are one of the best examples of an open Web 2.0 technology—they allow for content to be completely user-generated and allow multiple users to collaborate to create artifacts. Although users do not have complete control of the overall design of the environment, they are the main force behind the development of the objects that populate the environment. If users disagree with specific content on a Wiki, they know that, given the control they may exert over the content in the environment, they have the agency to try to change it.

Closed technologies are those where the end-user is neither encouraged to understand how the technology works, nor participate in its design and evolution. This, from our perspective, results in an indifference towards making changes in the technology. The user accepts it as technology that "just works." The mechanisms necessary for change to occur, whether they are open channels of communication between users and designers or in-depth structural information about the technology, simply do not exist. Closed technologies are, in our current framework, entities where the construction and design choices open to users are limited to non-existent. Some knowingly accept that it cannot be changed and happily use the tool as it was designed, resulting in continued apathy towards promoting change in the technology itself. Facebook is an excellent example of a closed Web 2.0 technology—individual owners can exert a certain amount of control over their profile or 'walls', but the overall design framework is rigid and the functioning of the system is not transparent to the user. This has the advantage of making the technology easy to use in that there are very few decisions for the user to make, but it is unlikely to stimulate interest in the way that the technology itself functions.

2.2.2 The spectrum of openness and knowledge production processes

While the notion of open and closed technologies was originally concerned with individuals understanding how technologies work, it can also be applied to the overall knowledge production process. We hypothesize that when individuals understand the processes at work behind knowledge production, it can have a profound effect in inspiring them to modify or create knowledge of their own. Both open and closed technologies are capable of facilitating the creation of new knowledge; however, they are different with regard to the processes through which new knowledge is produced. Knowledge production technologies like Wikipedia that are open have transformed people's conceptions of the knowledge production process—people have come to see themselves more as participants in the generation and construction of new knowledge. Furthermore, technologies like this have allowed for the valorization of new forms of knowledge (which traditionally may not have been considered worthwhile) and have contested the very nature of knowledge production.

A notable example of technological transparency in the realm of knowledge production is in a class activity we recently designed at Concordia University. Learners enrolled in a graduate course on Online Communities in Concordia's Educational Technology program were required to modify a Wikipedia page detailing the topic of "Community of Practice" (http://en.wikipedia.org/wiki/Community_of_practice). They received minimal instruction regarding the process of knowledge production, were left to consult databases (both online and offline) and were encouraged to develop the artifact as a collective. The information the students posted on Wikipedia was not only vetted by the instructor and their in-class peers, but was also commented upon by reviewers of Wikipedia entries. As is to be expected in a classroom activity, the students were comfortable receiving feedback from their instructor and peers, but they were hesitant and surprised upon realizing that their work was stimulating much discussion by contributors to the Wikipedia page (see a summary of the discussions on http://en.wikipedia.org/wiki/Talk:Community_of_practice). Once the students began interacting with these reviewers—exchanging comments, debating the changes made to their work—they quickly began to realize that their work extended beyond a class assignment. They would often discuss in class what the online community had to say about their Wikipedia entries, and eventually developed a rich understanding of how Wikipedia entries were created and modified.

Through the use of an open technology, the students developed an understanding of the mechanisms involved in creating and modifying knowledge and information; they saw themselves as agents within the knowledge production process. Additionally, the external comments received altered the work significantly—the discussion on their Wikipedia entry led to the students generating content that would not have been created if they had been left to their own devices. Notably, even if a user's contribution is eventually rejected, the decision about the rationale for rejection will usually be relatively democratic and transparent. For example, each Wikipedia entry features a "Discussion" tab on which the edits are discussed, and there is also a "View History" option that allows the user to view how the article has evolved. These options allow both creators and consumers of the article to view which information is contested and to see how the knowledge has accreted (or has, in some cases, disappeared) and been validated over time. This allows the Wikipedia user to see inside knowledge production processes, thereby demystifying it, and this may, consequently, empower the user to become a contributor in his/her own right. In general, we contend that information that is produced through collective processes within open spaces can empower individuals to be both effective users and creators of the knowledge related to the technology in question.

The ability to create new knowledge has also meant a great shift from the traditional knowledge production process. It is no longer strictly hierarchical, where the expert is the sole arbiter of worth and is able to dictate to the novice. In forum technologies (as is the case with Wikipedia), any new information that is brought forward should usually be given some consideration for inclusion in the overall knowledge base. This very shift towards inclusion has changed the foundations of what has been traditionally perceived as knowledge production. Within successful open knowledge production frameworks, building new ideas becomes a participatory endeavor, thereby contributing to the democratization of digital spaces. The knowledge that is produced within open technological frameworks challenges the authority of expert knowledge. Individual expertise is validated and users gain a sense that they have an equal opportunity to be or become an expert and to disseminate their ideas worldwide. However, although open technologies offer learners the arguably beneficial opportunity to be both knowledge users and producers, their design does pose some challenges. For example, the lack of templates and specific guidelines supporting the development of some open designs may challenge their development and long-term survival. MySpace, for example, allowed creators to have complete control over the design of their personalized webspace. Though this may have provided a certain degree of creative license, MySpace decreased in popularity in part because of users' own muddled and complex designs which led to navigation and usability issues (Boyd, in press). In contrast, although it is a more closed technology, Facebook gained popularity through its cleaner, far more structured, less changeable environment.

The empirical research presented in this chapter draws upon data from online bulletin boards and forums, which we situate as being relatively open technologies. Web 2.0 forum technologies afford users an openness that is somewhat less than in the case of Wikis, but is still quite open —the underlying technology is fairly simple, user profiles are extensively customizable and key roles and responsibilities are allocated to users (e.g., moderation). In stark opposition to the Wikipedia example described above, which exemplified a democratic approach to knowledge production, our data and related analyses presented herein show that online forums typify technocratic approaches (Stabile, 1986) to the production and validation of new knowledge. In a technocratic approach, subject-matter expertise trumps other factors (e.g., socio-political) when it comes to decision-making. The research presented in this chapter suggests that online forums are more prone to technocratic styles of knowledge production because of participants' reliance on experts to make meaning from discussions.

3. Methodology & data sources

To better comprehend the nature of online interactions in an era of social computing, we decided to observe thriving, self-selected online forum communities. We employed a qualitative case study of interactions and discussions amongst users of forums related to heavy metal music and culture. Heavy metal music and its fans have been the focus of large-scale sociological research studies that describe the sub-culture from multiple perspectives, including those of music theory and lyrical content (Walser, 1993), as well as its history and tenuous relationship with popular media (Weinstein, 2000). There also exist case studies exploring the effect of heavy metal on the behaviours of adolescent fans (Arnett, 1991, 1993; Giles, 2003; Sibley, 1995), personality distinctions among followers of heavy metal (Hansen & Hansen, 1991; King, 1985), and ethnographic research on face-to-face interactions between members of a community of heavy metal fans (Snell & Hodgetts, 2007). The present research provides empirical analyses of online communities with the express objective of demystifying hierarchies of expertise and analysing how forum members interact to engage in knowledge production processes. We employed a selective sampling strategy of users based on their contributions to two online forums, namely Brave Boards: http://www.bravewords.com/braveboards and Encyclopedia Metallum: http://www.metal-archives.com/, as well as one blog, Blabbermouth: http://www.roadrunnerrecords.com/blabbermouth.net/. See figures 1, 2 and 3 for screen shots of these websites. Users were classified as *super-users*, i.e., individuals who have contributed in excess of 15,000 posts to either of these sites and exhibited high levels of content expertise, or *browsers*, i.e., individuals who primarily used the forums and blogs to seek information, and who typically refrain from posting.

We solicited participation via electronic mail and invited users to individual, hour-long video-recorded interview sessions. Videos contained screen captures of the users interacting within the online forums and blogs, as well as responses to interview questions posed by the research team. A semi-structured interview protocol was employed to elicit self-reflections and users' impressions of the forums. Users' and forum moderators' posts were used as a secondary data source. All data were collected in accordance with Canada's Tri-Council Policy on ethical conduct for research involving human participants.

Register • FAQ • Login

It is currently 02 Aug 2011, 15:22

Board index ‹ Main Forums

All times are UTC - 5 hours

Forum

Forum	Topics	Posts	Last post
The METAL Oracle Metal Talk 24/7 No Rest For The Wicked! Moderators: Metal_King, Nemesis, moshdrum69	328	12167	02 Aug 2011, 15:19 The Devil
The Tavern Talk About Nothin' & Everythin'! Moderators: Metal_King, Nemesis, moshdrum69	335	17649	02 Aug 2011, 15:21 OldManAndChild
Brave Feedback Speak Your Mind! Moderator: BravePilgrim	2	12	02 Aug 2011, 11:00 Rook
Announcements Concert, & 'Zine Promotion - Support The Scene & Plug Your Stuff! Moderators: Metal_King, Nemesis, moshdrum69	163	1808	02 Aug 2011, 15:00 Solarfall
Musicians Forum Information about Musicians, Gear, Promoters, Venues and More In Here Moderators: Metal_King, Nemesis, moshdrum69	40	414	02 Aug 2011, 14:48 OldManAndChild
Hall Of Fame Archive Of Classic Threads From The Members of Our Community	32	5864	09 Mar 2011, 12:57 Carl

Fig. 1. Screen shot of Brave Boards forum home page (http://www.bravewords.com/braveboards).

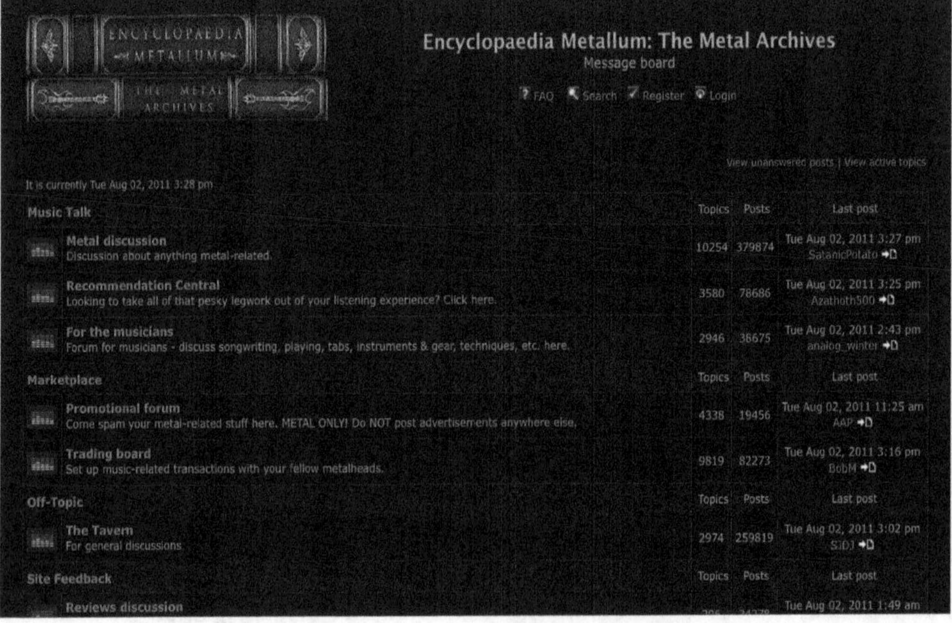

Fig. 2. Screen shot of Encyclopedia Metallum forum home page (http://www.metal-archives.com/board).

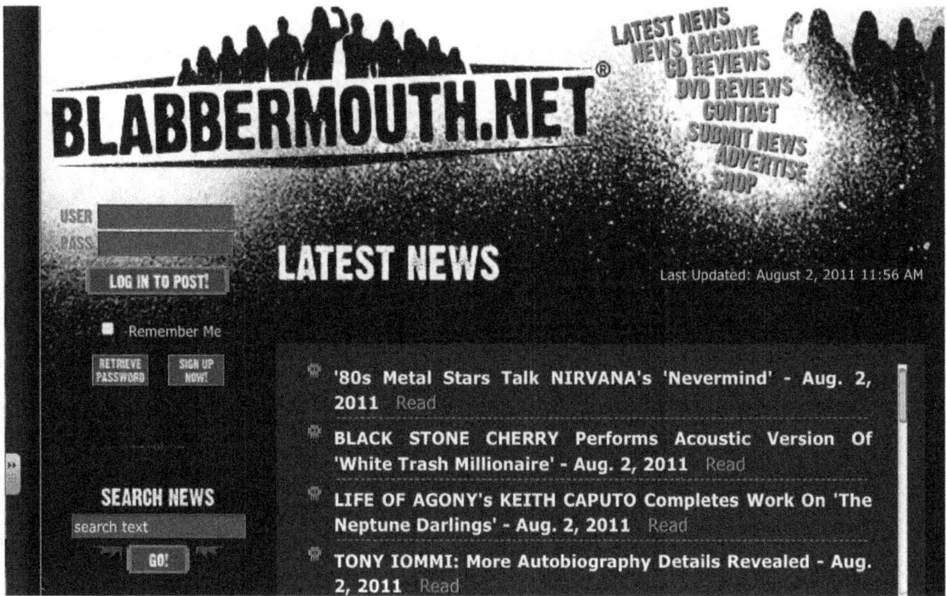

Fig. 3. Screen shot of Blabbermouth home page (http://www.roadrunnerrecords.com/blabbermouth.net).

4. Analysis & discussion

After exploring the postings on Brave Boards, Blabbermouth and Encyclopedia Metallum, we identified three super-users to help describe and validate open and closed knowledge production approaches within the online forums. We then developed predominant data-driven codes which encompassed themes from our theoretical framework of the spectrum of open and closed technologies. These codes, which are described below, include ownership and agency; transparency, democracy and technocracy; technocratic hierarchies of expertise; collaboration and validation; as well as accountability and citizenship.

4.1 Super-user and browser profiles

We explored narrative interview data from three super-users, all of whom agreed to divulge their real names. We also extracted these super-users' relevant posts from the forums to expand upon their interview responses. The prolonged amount of time that super-users have been members of forums, coupled with their extensive interactions within these forums, made their interviews and postings ideal units of analysis.

Our first super-user, Armen, goes by the screen name *icedneonflames* and has been a member of Brave Boards since 2001. Armen has earned *Metal Guru* status after having posted more than 10,000 times. A local musician, Armen originally joined the forum in search of other musicians with whom to have discussions. In the 10 years since Armen joined Brave Boards, he has posted 22,052 times (as of July 29, 2011) and logs in on a daily basis.

Jenny, another *Metal Guru*, and our second super-user goes by the screen name *corvidae*. She has been a member of Brave Boards for close to eight years and has 19,043 posts (as of July 29, 2011). Although she does have a screen name, Jenny does not refrain from using her real name when online. Using the forum to help organize an annual "heavy-metal picnic" at Hyde Park in Toronto, Jenny demonstrates that there is considerable overlap between her online and offline lives.

Our third and final super-user, Ilya, originally joined Encyclopedia Metallum in order to broaden his musical tastes and learn more about heavy metal. Today, Ilya's wide knowledge base of heavy metal music, combined with his knowledge of forums and locating information on the Internet, make him a valuable expert in both the musical genre as well as forum and Internet usage. Ilya tends to log on daily to various forums to read what has been written and to make contributions.

In addition, we include analyses of interviews from two browsers, Derek and Mark (both pseudonyms, as they asked that their identities remain confidential), who typically visit Blabbermouth and Encyclopedia Metallum.

4.2 Ownership and agency

All three super-users highlighted the importance of holding themselves and others personally accountable within the forum. This accountability was sustained through self-policing measures such as addressing hostile (e.g., racist, homophobic) posts, reporting abusive behaviour to forum moderators, and signaling to other users if they post in the wrong section of the forum. During her interview, while browsing Brave Boards Jenny stopped to read a post and remarked, "... this doesn't belong here" and, after scrolling down the page noticed that another user had also pointed this out and indicated where the post should be placed on the forum. The ability to engage with and modify the contents of the forum was critical in developing users' sense of ownership and responsibility towards the forum.

Another device through which these super-users were able to gain a sense of ownership within the forum was through the use of different font colours and emoticons. Jenny stated that "Since I began using the forum I have always written in blue, it's my colour", and she went on to point out some users' unique signatures at the end of their respective posts.

Using various formatting options, Jenny personalised her presence within the forum. In addition, using pictorial representations such as emoticons, Jenny was better able to convey the intended tone of her posts. Additionally, she explained that the use of either full prose or 'text messaging' language influenced the ways in which posts are perceived within the forum:

> "Some people use full sentences, some use text message language [...] it reflects their online personality. If someone uses [full prose], it might seem like too long a post and will be skipped over."

A factor contributing to the ways in which individuals use online forums is the amount of choice they have about how and when they choose to interact. For example, users of the Brave Boards site are free to set their status to either online (visible) or offline (invisible). Jenny argued that appearing 'visible' positively contributes to her forum identity:

> "I'm an open person, I don't care if someone sees I'm online or not. I'm not trying to be anonymous. Others might want to be offline to avoid unwanted contact [and] retain their privacy."

While appearing 'visible' is arguably beneficial, one must consider how giving users a choice about whether or not to appear online affects their agency (Hodkinson, 2007). The option of remaining 'invisible' to Brave Boards participants can afford novice users the opportunity to become "legitimate peripheral participants" (Gannon-Leary & Fontainha,

2007; Lave & Wenger, 1991). This enables users to observe their fellow heavy metal fans' interactions invisibly and derive personal edification from the discussions without the pressure of having to contribute.

Jenny explained that Brave Boards members can choose to sustain public interactions within the forum or they can choose to use the site as a meeting place that leads to more private interactions. Jenny also stated that she knows a lot of the users offline and that the forum is often used as a way of organizing offline activities like going to heavy metal shows. This suggests that providing users with a private email function may serve those who desire more anonymity with a suitable space. It remains important to consider, however, how the provision of a private email function would impact the openness of a given technology. It is conceivable that providing users with a concealed space in which to interact obstructs the transparency of knowledge production in the site.

4.3 Transparency, democracy and technocracy

One of the strengths of open technologies is the level of transparency in terms of communication, administration and functioning of the technology itself. Jenny stated, "... moderators are in another colour so you can easily identify them and can see when they're online so [...] you can go [read their posts] if you need to". Interestingly, while the moderators have ultimate control over the site content, thereby potentially hindering the openness of the knowledge production process, the fact that users could observe the process by which content was removed contributed positively to feelings of openness. This suggests that, similar to the case of Wikipedia, a clear process through which information is generated, contested, deleted, or accepted is crucial to fostering a transparent and democratic environment. It is perhaps this transparent process that encourages users to interact more frequently within structured forums such as Brave Boards. Further, it can be argued that the recognition gained from frequent interactions contributes to both the transparency and appeal of a forum. As Jenny points out,

> "I'm a metal guru [...] it is an automated process that assigns status after a certain number of posts. [Some users] might have been on longer than me, but have posted less and are still at a lower rank."

We observed elements of technocracy when analyzing super-users' interactions with other members. Jenny is active in two of the five Brave Boards feedback threads. These threads exist to enable users to give feedback and provide critiques to the administrators of the forum beyond the simple 'reporting' feature used to flag trolling behaviours and spam. Jenny contributed to a feedback thread on new vertical advertisements on the site. Brave Boards users disliked this format of advertising and although they realized the site does need to make revenue, there was also a sense of futility in resisting the advertisements. Jenny vented:

> "I think it's more the staff not being paid by selling the magazine anymore? Not sure, just speculating ... even if the ads need to be there, why the same ad on both sides? ... And the overlapping is stupid. Sizing needs to be fixed."

Ultimately, the advertisements did remain on the forum but have been configured so they interfere less with the users' experiences. This is an example of "closedness" on the Brave Boards which does not benefit the users or their heavy metal learning experience. The users dislike the ads and find them distracting, but can only avoid them if they use software such as AdBlock or specific browsers which duplicate this functionality.

The other feedback thread Jenny participated in centers around users exerting control over the content posted in a thread. For example, Jenny contributed to a discussion about a user who disliked photo quotes, and who also complained of being unable to delete past posts. In her response to this user, Jenny was critical of his attitude and motive:

> "Why [must you be so] antagonistic? We're a bunch of cool people with a few idiots and trolls. Do you want to be a troll or be a cool guy? It's feedback man, no need to be a douche."

Afterwards, the original poster is told by a couple of moderators that it is possible to delete past posts, and is asked to be more thoughtful about the content of the thread. It is also made clear to the original poster by these moderators that the site is fine as it is:

> "... you have been here 29 days, this version of the board has been active 9 years. If it's not broken, there is no need to fix it. If you really dont like it here, find a new forum."

> "Hey n00b, you dont think in the +9 years this version of the board has been around (or the +12 years that Bravewords has had a forum) that there has never been a Jake E Lee Thread? Well excuse us veterans who may not care to add our two cents again to a post like that unless we are bored or choose not to respond to which Iron Maiden record is the best. We have done it before."

These examples underline the fact that users' contributions are not viewed equally; we explore this inequality in a subsequent section on hierarchies of expertise. Consider also the following example from a thread in the feedback section, by a moderator of Brave Boards called +inertia+, who responds to complaints about the power being exerted by moderators. Below is +inertia+'s response to this criticism:

> "... if you feel strongly enough that I don't deserve to run this place, find me a minimum of 60 users with a post count of 2500 or more that think I'm impartial and "WELL ABOVE (morally speaking) every other poster" and I will gladly step aside. With 3000+ members that's less than 2% of the users."

In his interview, when viewing a forum topic comparing classic heavy metal albums, Armen reinforces the technocracy exerted by super-users regarding the types of knowledge that can be discussed on the forum:

> "... Not this shit again; opinions are not going to change when comparing Iron Maiden to Judas Priest, or [comparing] Megadeth to Metallica ... everyone has seen the classic question posts, so there is nothing new to add."

This can be interpreted as exclusionary since newer members have not been on the site for seven or ten years and do not know that questions about comparisons between genres of metal as propagated by mainstream bands have been addressed extensively on the forum. Other examples that support technocratic distinctions include a quote from Derek, one of the participants classified as a browser, and a veteran of the metal sub-culture, who stated:

> "People get bothered by the post counts. It creates hierarchies. If [one] guy has 200 posts and [another] guy literally has 35,000 posts it is like 'you newbie, why are you saying this, you have no role here."

Derek continues to say that he himself would not give a user with a high post count more credibility, but recognizes that other users might. Jenny confirms Derek's sentiments: "I don't get picked on that much either because of seniority". Armen also spoke of the value placed on users with an elevated status, like Neil Kernon, an award-winning music producer:

> "... [Neil's comments] will be held in more importance...I can't disagree with him... he has a Grammy... people agree with him because he is Neil Kernon."

4.4 Technocratic hierarchies of expertise

The analysis of the interview data with the super-users and their postings within Brave Boards led to the identification of three types of forum users with respect to expertise: the novice user (with little to no expertise), the self-proclaimed expert (a person new to the forum who claims to have extensive knowledge in the subject) and the user-accepted expert (a person who has invested substantial time in contributing to the forum and has demonstrated their knowledge to other users).

Three types of interactions with technocratic dimensions were derived from the varying types of expertise: novice with self-proclaimed expert, novice with user-accepted expert and self-proclaimed expert with user-accepted expert. These three novice-expert interactions are manifested through questions posted on the forum by the novices, which are in turn answered by the experts. In such situations, we remarked that novices do not distinguish between the self-proclaimed experts' and the user-accepted experts' responses, leading to a somewhat blind acceptance of the answer to a query, regardless of its source or validity. The main distinguishing factor is the time invested in the forum, with the user-accepted experts contributing more to discussions within the forum. As a result of prolonged interactions with each other, the user-accepted experts tend to form a smaller clique and act as the forum's experts. When discussing various topics on one forum with another long-time user, super-user Armen simply stated, "[w]e are the experts". This clique of user-accepted experts governs itself and its members interact with each other using language which would otherwise be considered unbecoming. Jenny outlined this attitude of homophily (McPherson, Smith-Lovin & Cook, 2001) while discussing novices and self-proclaimed experts making derogatory remarks to user-accepted experts:

> "It's ok to talk shit and make unacceptable remarks with each other because we know each other [...] but if it's someone who hasn't been around for a while, we won't accept that."

4.5 Collaboration and validation

The transparency of knowledge production processes in online environments has instigated a shift in the traditional knowledge production and dissemination process. One substantial change is that sources can be referenced directly and checked instantaneously. Not surprisingly, all three super-users of the Brave Boards forum cited placing links to other websites on the forum as a common practice. Ilya stated that:

> "Links to YouTube videos of the band will be posted so that you can [check them out] when discussing threads where people are seeking new music to listen to."

By branching off of the site and making links to outside information, users are able to add to, as well as validate, existing information. Armen and Jenny both pointed out that, when presented with questionable information on Brave Boards, they would check another source, like Encyclopedia Metallum. Armen continued, "the post points to information to be checked and [outside sources] can either confirm the information or disprove it".

A number of metal fans use blogs to keep in touch with the happenings and latest developments in the world of heavy metal. Participants such as Derek and Mark contribute to the 'news-worthiness' of blog entries, by rating them on sites like Blabbermouth. Mark talked in depth about Blabbermouth being one of the three sites he checks daily to keep abreast of heavy metal news. Mark noted that Blabbermouth added a way to rate news items and other users' comments by clicking on either an icon of devil horns (like) or a thumbs-down (dislike):

> "What I think is really neat, what they did recently, because I tend to get lazy sometimes, when I want to put a comment down if it is any hassle, like if I try to put it down and it is not going in I won't bother … but I am always logged in anyway … but most of the time it works. But they did just start […] doing for each comment … they have two signs, a devil's sign and a thumbs-down."

4.6 Accountability and citizenship

As discussed, users of Brave Boards highlighted the importance of holding themselves and others personally accountable for their actions within the forum. Implicit in this forum is a culture of practices and ideals, grounded in a technocratic approach that, despite its drawbacks, supports the effective functioning of this collaborative online environment. By adhering to such norms, users share the responsibility for the future of the common space. Moreover, as Armen explained, users work together in order to cultivate a safe and welcoming environment for all members of the community. Armen noted that, when confronted by someone outside of the community, or outside of the clique, the other members will "protect their own". Jenny also stated that, having been a member for such a long time and attaining Metal Guru status, she feels responsible for upholding the norms of the forum like calling out trolls, identifying spam bots, and respecting what she termed the "ebb and flow" of the forum. In the case of individuals who are typically isolated from mainstream society, as heavy metal fans arguably are, the creation and availability of online environments can be particularly beneficial with regards to identity, citizenship, and feelings of belonging (McPherson et al., 2001). The trust that is garnered through positive interactions between users of Brave Boards helps support the creation of a space in which users can build relationships, feel both accepted and respected, as well as find and foster communities in which they belong. An excellent example of the ways in which online forums bolster community cohesion can be found in Jenny's interview. She explained that many relationships cultivated through online forums transfer to offline environments. One example involved her finding a place to stay while abroad at a heavy metal show. When asked if she knew the person Jenny stated that "yes I knew him, online [...] but it was the first time we met [offline]." Further, she recounted the fact that her involvement in the Brave Boards forum has enabled her to spearhead an increasingly popular annual heavy metal picnic, "I host a yearly heavy metal picnic at Hyde Park [...]; lots of people come out [...]; some from the forum."

5. Conclusions

More than 100 years ago, Dewey noted that, in order for students to become critical consumers and producers of knowledge and effective actors in social contexts, they needed to understand how technological processes function. In online forums, we believe that we see an example of a relatively open technological process—a process which, despite technocratic elements, allows knowledge to be created in a reasonably transparent fashion.

Given our analysis of interactions, we believe forums can empower users to think critically and act as agents of knowledge production. It is also possible that this sense of agency will transfer to the overall social context. Though the forums we highlight are not completely open or transparent technologies, we do not foresee this as limiting the production of new knowledge or the interactions between users. Within these online communities, there do exist rules and hierarchies which govern the validation of such knowledge. As seen in our analysis, these rules, which are enforced through an inter-connected and complex network of expert and novice users, are dynamic in nature and constantly evolve with the needs and individual preferences of users.

Our analysis points out that users and creators who are aware of how open knowledge production technologies function can develop substantial new possibilities for agency. They can choose to use the tools to create new knowledge, intervene in existing knowledge production processes, and criticize the means of knowledge production. However, from our analysis, it is clear that even a relatively open system can result in the propagation of technocratic structures. These structures add richness and authority to the discussions and facilitate some types of interaction between experienced users, but they also hinder new users in certain ways. Given the limited scope of our analysis, it is important that further research be conducted into the potential of Internet-based forums to create democratic spaces that promote knowledge production processes. Despite these technocratic structures, the opportunity for new users to enact change and to become prominent members of the community does exist—the very openness and transparency of the community allows them to see a clear path to increased participation and respect within the community.

6. Acknowledgements

This project was made possible through research monies obtained by authors Venkatesh, Waddington and Shaikh from Concordia University's Office of the Vice-President Research and Graduate Studies' Seed Funding program and doctoral bursaries obtained by authors Shaikh and Zuberi from *le fonds québecois de recherche sur la société et la culture*. Portions of the theoretical framework presented in this chapter appear in an article prepared by the authors for the Spring 2011 edition of *Canadian Issues*, published by the Association for Canadian Studies. Special thanks to Blake Judd from Chicago-based extreme metal band Nachtmystium for providing personal insight into how he used MySpace to communicate with fans. We also thank David Perri from Brave Words and Bloody Knuckles, and Rashi Khilnani from Radio Canada International for publicizing our research in popular media outlets, and in the process, helping us recruit participants from the heavy metal community.

7. References

Albernaz, A. (2002). The Internet in Brazil: From digital divide to democracy. *Proceedings of the 14th Annual Conference of the Association of Academic Programs in Latin America and the Caribbean*. Available at: http://www.aaplac.org/library/AlbernazAmi03.pdf

Arnett, J. (1991). Heavy metal music and reckless behavior among adolescents. *Journal of Youth and Adolescence, 20*(6), 573-592.

Arnett, J. (1993). Three profiles of heavy metal fans: A taste for sensation and a subculture of alienation. *Qualitative Sociology, 16*, 423-443.

Boyd, D. (in press). "White Flight in Networked Publics? How Race and Class Shaped American Teen Engagement with MySpace and Facebook." In *Digital Race*

Anthology (L. Nakamura & P. Chow-White, eds.). New York, NY: Routledge. Available at : http://www.danah.org/papers/2009/WhiteFlightDraft3.pdf

Dewey, J. (1915). *The School and Society (2nd edtion)*. Chicago,IL: University of Chicago Press.

Gannon-Leary, P.M. & Fontainha, E. (2007). Communities of practice and virtual learning communities: Benefits, barriers and success factors. *eLearning Papers, 5*. Barcelona, Spain: P.A.U. Education

Giles, D. (2003). *Media psychology*. London, UK: Lawrence Erlbaum Associates.

Hansen, C.H. & Hansen, R.D. (1991). Constructing personality and social reality through music: Individual differences among fans. *Journal of Broadcasting and Electronic Media, 35*(3), 335-351.

Hodkinson, P. (2007), Interactive online journals and individualisation. *New Media and Society, 9* (4), 625-650.

King, P. (1985). Heavy Metal: A new religion. *Journal of the Tennessee Medical Association, 78,* 754–755.

Lave, J. & Wenger, E. (1991). *Situated learning: Legitimate peripheral participation*. Cambridge, UK: Cambridge University Press.

McGee, P. Carmean, C. & Jafari, A. (2005). *Course Management Systems for Learning: Beyond Accidental Pedagogy*. Hershey, PA: Idea Group, Inc.

McPherson, M., Smith-Lovin, L. & Cook, J. M. (2001). Birds of a feather: Homophily in social networks. *Annual Review of Sociology, 27*, 415-444.

Shaikh, K., Zuberi, A., Waddington, D., Thomas, T., & Venkatesh, V. (2011). A manifesto for technological transparency in the age of Web 2.0. *Canadian Issues, Spring 2011,* 87-90.

Shaw S., & Venkatesh, V. (2005). The missing link to enhanced course management systems: Adopting learning content management systems in the educational sphere. In P. McGee, C. Carmean & A. Jafari (Eds.), *Course Management Systems for Learning: Beyond Accidental Pedagogy* (pp. 206 - 231). Hershey, PA: Idea Group, Inc.

Sibley, D. (1995). *Geographies of exclusion: Society and difference in the West*. New York: Routledge.

Slack, J. D., & Wise, J. M. (2005). *Culture and technology: A primer*. New York, NY: Peter Lang Publishing

Stabile, D. R. (1986). Veblen and the political economy of the engineer: The radical thinker and engineering leaders came to technocratic ideas at the same time. *The American Journal of Economics and Sociology, 45* (1), 43-44.

Snell, D. & Hodgetts, D. (2007). Heavy metal, identity and the social negotiation of a community of practice. *Journal of Community and Applied Social Psychology, 17* (6), 430-445

Venkatesh, V., Shaikh, K. & Zuberi, A. (2010). Topic Maps as Indexing Tools in the Educational Sphere: Theoretical Foundations, Review of Empirical Research and Future Challenges. In Perusich, K. (Ed.). *Cognitive Maps* (pp. 1-12). Vienna, Austria: In-Tech.

Waddington, D. I. (2010). Scientific self-defense: Transforming Dewey's idea of technological transparency. *Educational Theory, 60* (5), 621-638.

Walser, R. (1993). *Running with the devil: Power, gender and madness in Heavy Metal music.* Hanover, NH: University Press of New England.

Weigel, V. (2002). *Deep learning for a digital age: Technology's untapped potential to enrich higher education*. San Francisco, CA: Jossey-Bass Publishing.

Weinstein, D. (2000). *Heavy Metal: The Music and its Culture*. Cambridge, MA: DaCapo Press

6

Exploring New Technological Tools for Education: Some Prototypes and Their Pragmatical Classification

Luigia Simona Sica[1], Alessandra Delli Veneri[1] and Orazio Miglino[2]
[1]*NAC (Natural and Artificial Cognition Laboratory), University of Naples "Federico II",*
[2]*LARAL (Laboratory of Autonomous Robotics and Artificial Life), ISTC –CNR, Rome, Italy*

1. Introduction

The aim of this chapter is to introduce at exploring the potential of games in educational sector. More in depth, in this chapter we'll describe: two European projects (*Proactive*[11] and *T3*[1]) with a specific focus on use of technology in formative sector; and a platform (*Eutopia*) experimented in both the projects with which educators can create virtual scenarios where students play a role and simulate a specific situation.

Both *Proactive* and *T3* projects have used an experimental approach in which trainings were implemented in order to test the efficacy of the formation planned.

Preliminary results of the projects will be presented and discussed. The evidence supports the utility of using new technology in non-ordinary contexts, in order to foster learning process.

2. To learn by enjoying oneself

Educational research has generated many methodologies, tools and practices exploiting the potential of technology. Outside the laboratory, however, the advanced techniques employment remains low. Despite technical and methodological progress, the most part of e-learning still consists of video-lessons and page-turning web sites.

The dynamics of teaching/learning through multimedia tools is, instead, an active process that takes into account different general principles of cognitive control (Mayer, 2000): the dual coding (Paivio, 1991); the cognitive load (Chandler & Sweller, 1991); the active processing (Mayer, 2000). This process produces in turn its own specific principles: the integrated mental model (multimedia) rich of clues and recovery (Mayer & Anderson, 1991); the spatial and temporal proximity of stimuli that facilitate learning (Mayer & Anderson, 1992); the relevance or consistency of the material proposed (Harp & Mayer, 1998); the

[1] This project has been funded with support from the European Commission. This publication reflects the views only of the author, and the Commission cannot be held responsible for any use which may be made of the information contained therein.

different ways of transmitting information (Mayer & Moreno, 1998); the customization of the teaching / learning dynamic (Mayer & Gallini, 1990).

The use of computer games to foster learning process is a new input in the didactic world; the interest in exploiting the educational potential of computer games is increasing as instructional games involve a direct focus on the learner's active participation. Alessi (2000) stresses the importance of game-based learning, clarifying that it is a balance between *conceptual* (teaching about) and *procedural* (teaching how to do) knowledge. Computer games address many of the limitations of traditional instructional methods; games have the ability to motivate learning, increase knowledge and skill acquisition and support traditional teaching methods.

Much attention has been given to the so-called serious gaming (the use of commercial or ad hoc games for serious educational purposes) (Ives & Junglas, 2008). The effectiveness of serious games based approach lies in these words by Van Eck: "*The extent to which these games foil expectations (create cognitive disequilibrium), without exceeding the capacity of the player to succeed, largely determines whether they are engaging. Interacting with a game requires a constant cycle of hypothesis formulation, testing, and revision. This process happens rapidly and frequently while the game is played, with immediate feedback. Games that are too easily solved will not be engaging, so good games constantly require input from the learner and provide feedback*" (Van Eck, 2006, 5).

Moreover, games fill up people's large periods of time (adolescents and adults) and promote those levels of attention and concentration that teachers and trainers imagine people should apply within their own learning process. Therefore, what can the educational sector learn and use from these games in order to enhance the learning process by enjoying oneself?

3. Developing digital games for educational goals

The Game-Based Learning (GBL) is the use of digital games with serious goals (i.e. educational objectives) as tools that support learning processes in a significant way. It is also known as educational gaming. Studies in the field of GBL show a clear relation between playing digital games and learning. There are a number of arguments in favour of digital games as learning tools. It is more often argued that they can enhance students' motivation for learning because of their engaging nature. Indeed, digital games can provide challenging experiences that promote the intrinsic satisfaction of the players, keeping them engaged and motivated.

Moreover, players have fun while playing a game because they have to learn it. Indeed, in games, the challenge usually increases as long as the game goes on. Therefore players need to improve their skills and learn new strategies until the game is completed.

Another feature of digital games, that is remarkably aligned to good learning, is that games provide short feedback cycles. This allows players to explore the game environment freely, trying out their hypotheses, learning by trial-and-error and getting immediate information that they can use to redefine wrong assumptions in a risk-free environment. This characteristic is well aligned with educational requirements, given that most educational approaches require the educator to provide students with feedback about their achievements. Therefore, as digital games set the player in a world that is free to explore without requiring the intervention of an instructor, video games are an ideal medium to promote authentic learning and "learning by doing" processes, turning the student into the leader of his / her own learning experience. In this sense digital games can provide meaningful learning experiences by simulating highly interactive scenarios that professionals encounter in real-world settings, where they face open-ended, real-world problems.

In consequence, digital games represent a good medium to promote active learning and improve students' problem-solving skills and not only simple fact memorization. It has been demonstrated that for certain target groups (e.g. school students), they can increase personal fulfillment and lead to higher performance.

For the reasons mentioned above, an increasing number of teachers and trainers recognize the value of digital games in education. Most of the successful Game-Based Learning (GBL) experiences have used mainstream games (e.g. The Sims), usually referred to as "Commercial-Off-The-Shelf" (COTS) games, because they are ready to be used.

Thus, what is the point of creating my own educational games, if there are things out there ready to be used? Creating a game is a time-consuming task, so in an already time-constrained curriculum where educators are usually struggling to achieve the goals defined by educational regulators and institutions the question is "It is worth taking the time?".

There are clear benefits that come from using custom games developed directly by educators instead of using COTS. Indeed, some barriers to the implementation of GBL in formal learning settings have been identified. For example, the lack of integration of most games with the current curriculum and the lack of appropriate assessment frameworks inhibits GBL. Indeed, COTS games are developed to be entertaining, not educative. Games like The Age of EmpiresTM provide contents that are rich and valuable from an educational perspective, but also include errors, misconceptions and inaccuracies to make the games more attractive. This is usually a concern that parents show when they are told that their kids will be using games in the classroom. In addition, COTS games are not always easy to align with current curricula, or do not meet educational standards. Indeed, COTS games can demand last generation computers which are not always present in educational institutions. Or if they exist, educators may not have the adequate privileges or support to install them.

In order to overcome the above mentioned challenges, *ProActive* and *T3* propose a framework in which teachers / trainers would design and implement their own learning games. Or at least, actively contribute to this process.

Indeed, educational games available in the market generally do not meet educators' expectations. Actually the quality of many commercial educational games is low. This could be related to the fact that big gaming companies tend to ignore the educational market because of the difficulties posed by a wide and varied curriculum, a lack of interest on behalf of educational policy makers, the inability of schools to find the sort of money that commercial games tend to require and also the security issues associated with large institutions with small IT budgets.

Thus, educators can profit from developing games *for themselves* that have direct relevance to their teaching objectives / students' profile, and that meet the requirements of their own institutions or educational standards. Nevertheless, the creation of high-quality games is a hard challenge, with multiple approaches and possibilities. Which is the best option for teachers and educators, who may not have an extensive technical background, or a big budget at their disposal to hire a professional development team?

4. Field experiences: "ProActive" and "T3 -Teaching to Teach with Technology" Projects

Two projects funded by the EU Leonardo Da Vinci Life Long Learning Program, "ProActive" (project website: www.proactive-project.eu) and "Teaching to Teach with Technology - T3" (project website: www.t3.unina.it), are designed to validate an innovative teacher/trainer program, demonstrating realistic ways of exploiting advanced techniques within the real constraints facing teachers in their work. Both projects employ a platform for the creation of educational role-playing game called EUTOPIA, that will be better described below.

This game editor is particularly aimed to train and improve soft skills. In addition to the theoretical and technical education, training agencies are also in charge of transferring to students a set of behavioral skills that are a necessary background to deal with professional communities and society. Examples of such skills are the ability to manage emergencies, the ability to negotiate, to take decisions collectively, the attitude to understand others' view points. In general, the teaching of soft skills is primarily linked to experience, where a teacher organizes, supervises and encourages small groups of learners to take part in role playing and simulation.

Most of these techniques for learning soft skills can be transferred in digital platforms and online technologies. There are many different educational games (serious games) in which the player-learner has a specific role and must pursue a goal assigned by the teacher / trainer. Trainers can find games that are dedicated to the transfer of a particular segment of knowledge/skills (closed systems) and platforms that enable teachers and learners to develop and edit their own educational scenarios with specific goals (open systems).

4.1 ProActive Project

ProActive (Fostering Teachers' Creativity through Game-Based Learning) is a two years project in the EU LLL program (Project Number: 505469-LLP-1-2009-1-ES-KA3-KA3MP) which started on January 2010. The project tackles creativity in the context of lifelong learning by stimulating creative teaching practices through the use of different learning metaphors in various educational levels. Through a constructivist approach, the project is creating learning contexts where teachers and trainers can apply creativity in designing their own game-based learning (GBL) scenarios by using digital tools. ProActive offers to teachers and trainers the possibility to use GBL as an innovative and imaginative approach in their teaching practices, in order to enable them to create learning environments interesting and engaging for their students.

In 2009, the European Year of Creativity and Innovation aimed to raise awareness of the importance of creativity and innovation for personal, social and economic development. The initiative addressed a wide spectrum of related themes such as fostering artistic and other forms of creativity through pre-school, primary and secondary education including vocational streams, as well as non-formal and informal education, ICT as media for creative self-expression, and promoting innovation as the route to sustainable development.

More specifically, the main objectives of ProActive are:

1. To stimulate the creativity of teachers / trainers working in LLP sub-programmes, developing a conceptual framework for integrating different learning metaphors;
2. To introduce innovative ICT-based experiences in teaching / training practice, adapting and enhancing the game editors, integrating five learning metaphors;
3. To implement co-design creativity sessions and pilot sites for addressing school, university and vocational education scenarios;
4. To validate the proposed approach as a means of learning and evaluate its impact on teachers' creativity and students' outcomes.

As final results, ProActive will produce guidelines on creativity enhanced by Game-Based Learning and disseminate a database of Game-Based Learning scenarios and related active learning culture within EU education.

The project is carried out by a consortium of six partners from four countries in Europe (as shown in Table 1), covering various education and training systems and learning cultures.

Partner N°	**Acronym**	**Organisation Name**	**City**	**Country**
P1	UB	Universitat de Barcelona	Barcelona	Spain
P2	DPPSS	Sapienza Università di Roma	Roma	Italy
P3	CAST	CAST Limited	Bangor	United Kingdom
P4	UNINA	Università di Napoli Federico II	Naples	Italy
P5	UCM	Universidad Compultense de Madrid	Madrid	Spain
P6	UNIBUC	University of Bucharest	Bucharest	Romania

Table 1.

According to many authors, the educational system in many countries does not promote creative teaching / learning processes (Robinson, 2006; Ferrari et al., 2009). Indeed, formal education does not facilitate creative behaviours and skills from students. Learners most often act as recipient of methods, pedagogies and knowledge (Ferrari, et al. 2009). Teachers tended to give importance to relevance, competence and the need to avoid mistakes (Ferrari, et al, 2009). Indeed, formal education has created a culture that often "*accepts only what is relevant*" (Beghetto, 2007). According to Runco (1999), teachers prefer "*conforming*" and "*considerate*" students. Moreover, Ng and Smith (2004) state that teachers often dislike personality traits associated with creativity, as such persons are often dogmatic and will stand for their own ideas against everything and everyone, are self-confident, ambitious, passionate about their work and have a tough skin.

However, during the last part of the 20th century and early part of the 21st, creativity has been seen to be increasingly significant in education, within cultural policy discussions, starting with the landmark advice of the National Advisory Committee on Creative and

Cultural Education (NACCCE, 1999). Many authors (e.g. Craft, 2005; Sawyer, 2006) suggest that creativity should be an important educational objective: "*in today's knowledge societies, one of the key missions of the schools is to educate for creativity*" (Sawyer, 2006). Current pedagogical discourses attempt to view learners as the centre of teaching and learning processes, with an active role in the production of knowledge and meaning, democratically bringing their expertise, experiences and ideas into the classroom (Williamson & Payton, 2009) and thus stimulating also creativity. Nevertheless, creativity still does not seem to play a central role in the curriculum or learning objectives that teachers are asked to follow in every country (Cachia et al., 2009).

On the basis of Runco (1999), Sharp (2004) and Boghetto (2007), Ferrari et al. (2009) present a model opposing implicit and explicit theories of creativity.

"Implicit theories refer to the tacit and shared knowledge of ordinary people regarding creativity, while explicit theories refer to scientific research findings. This model reflects the change of scope regarding creativity that moves towards a personal approach in which there is a creative potential in all individuals and in different knowledge domains."

ProActive aims at fostering teachers' / trainers' creativity. Thus, the project adopts an approach of personal creativity, in which the creative potential is in all individuals, and can be applied to all domains.

ProActive's psycho-pedagogical framework links the concepts of creativity, Game-Based Learning, game design and the five learning metaphors in an integral whole. Although the term *Game-Based Learning* (GBL) has not been given a precise definition, it has been around for almost two decades. Several authors, such as Prensky, Aldrich, Jenkins or Gee, have been discussing Game-Based Learning definition is and potential in well-known articles and books (Gee, 2003; Prensky, 2001), thus laying the basis of Game-Based Learning concepts. Therefore, we can define Game-Based Learning as *the use of computer or other digital games of any kind as tools that support learning in a meaningful way*. Thus, Game-Based Learning is a trend which analyses the good characteristics of digital games together with their relation with learning, and proposes strategies and paradigms to take advantage of them for education.

For the reasons mentioned above, an increasing number of teachers and trainers recognize the value of digital games in education. However, they are not sure how to bring Game-Based Learning approaches into the field. Indeed, some barriers to the implementation of Game-Based Learning in formal learning settings have been identified within a study conducted by BECTA on COTS (BECTA, 2008).

- The lack of integration of most games with the current curriculum and assessment framework.
- Time constraints.
- Technical and logistical issues (cost, licensing, limitations of school computers, technical support) - Game-Based Learning cannot become part of the fabric of the curriculum without the appropriate technology and technical support, which is challenging in some EU countries.
- Lack of teacher skills.
- Not all learners engage with games and many do not see a link between games and learning.
- Teacher and parent concerns over the content of some games (e-safety).

In order to overcome the above mentioned challenges, ProActive proposes a framework in which teachers / trainers would design their own learning games. Indeed, available market games generally do not match curricular objectives. The big companies tend to ignore the educational market because of the difficulties posed by a wide and varied curriculum, a lack of interest on behalf of educational policy makers, the inability of schools to find the sort of money that commercial games tend to command and also the security issues associated with large institutions with small IT budgets. Thus teachers / trainers may benefit from ProActive, by developing games for themselves that have direct relevance to their teaching objectives.

A constructivist approach to Game-Based Learning is adopted, where teachers and trainers will develop innovative learning artefacts that are interesting and engaging for their students. The game design process will foster educator's creativity. The metaphors of learning will work as guidelines for the project participants in the creation of educational games as they raise awareness and promote reflection on different learning models and guide the game construction. Furthermore, as a result of the situated design process, a creative product will be obtained - a learning artifact (i.e. an educational game), tailored to the learning needs, institutional and curricular constraints and which can be shared with students. Such creative product is pedagogically innovative, useful and adapted to a specific teaching / learning context.

The psycho-pedagogical framework has been be central in several tasks in ProActive. First of all, it provides basis for the organisation of the training and implementation that is taking place in eighteen pilot sites in four European countries (Italy, Romania, Spain and UK). Moreover, training materials for the teachers and trainers are being developed to correspond to the proposed approach. Finally, the ProActive evaluation framework and appropriate evaluation tools are designed as consequence of the elicited methodology.

Traditionally, teachers and trainers used in their practice a dominant learning paradigm: the instructional, thus limiting their creative potential and inhibiting learning. Recent studies instead show that in normal situations learners combine different metaphors to a lesser or greater degree simultaneously: Imitation, Participation, Acquisition, Exercising, and Discovery (Simons, 2003, 2004, 2008). In ProActive we consider that we don't learn in just one way, but in different ways that depend on personal aptitudes, on the situation where learning takes place and on the content to be learnt. The five metaphors learning model (Simons, 2003, 2004, 2008) is a description of different ways of learning in different people, embedded with learning theories. It can be treated as a comprehensive model that comes out by combining some learning models with the theories of change by De Caluwé and Vermaak (1999). The result is a classification of the ways of learning into five groups (one per metaphor), each one representing a preference for learning that is not exclusive. In fact, every person is able to use all metaphors, but each one in a different situation. The core idea is that we don't learn in a sole way, but in different ways that depend on personal aptitudes, on the situation where the learning takes place and on the content to be learnt (Simons & Ruijters, 2004).

Simons (2003) recognizes that we need a language to talk about learning in less educational ways, incorporating implicit, social, collective and dynamic learning and describing different ways of learning besides the traditional perspective on training. The aim of the metaphors is to find an escape from automatic educational thinking when designing workplace learning trajectories.

In fact, although in formal contexts of learning teachers use a sole dominant paradigm, relevant studies show that it is quite different in the ways of learning in everyday contexts. If in formal learning contexts we learn essentially in individual situations from abstract concepts that are separated from the contexts where these concepts will be applied, in everyday life we learn from direct experience using the concept directly in the real situation where they have to be applied in interaction with others.

Simons' work on learning metaphors has been chosen as core psycho-pedagogical model for ProActive since it offers a comprehensive explanation of possible situated learning experiences. The strenghtness of this model in respect of others (Marzano, 2000; Costa & Kallick, 2009) is, in fact, the focus on contextualized educational theories rather then on cognitive instructional paradigms.

Despite this model is a core reference for the ProActive project, it has anyway to be contextualized and adapted to our methodology and purposes. In fact, the metaphor model is quite unrefined and uses the existing literature on learning in not ever clear and compatible ways. Simons' core contribution is that learning can be experienced in different ways, but the metaphors in Simons' work are analyzed basing on organization and professional learning literature, so we have adapted them, as follows, in order to cover also formal educational contexts (schools and universities) and psycho-pedagogical literature.

Our thinking is that everyone can learn in different ways, which depend on the context of learning, the actors involved in the learning process and the artifacts used for learning, etc. Starting from this socio-cultural approach on learning we also claim that artifacts are not neutral: they reflect the psycho-pedagogical model adopted by the artifact designer.

The five metaphors are: acquisition, imitation, experimentation, participation and discovery, and are briefly described below:

1. Acquisition: Regarding the acquisition metaphor, the idea is to transfer information from one who possesses it (the teacher) to another one who acts as a passive receiver (the learner). It doesn't matter who the learner is and how he / she prefers to learn, as learning is always a repetition and a replication of the acquired knowledge, or product of an individual mental activity.
2. Imitation: The imitation metaphor focuses on modeling behaviours by observing others' reactions to events. The leading idea is that vicarious learning experiences can help to shape one's own actions.
3. Experimentation: This metaphor is closely related to "learning by doing" processes. It applies to learning specific activities, complex or dangerous tasks, as it promotes active and contextualized learning processes, mainly related to practical activities and skills (including refining movements). It generally applies to individual practices, but may include some social activities, such as the coordination of teams.
4. Participation: This metaphor focuses on social aspects of learning. Indeed, the content transmitted by the teacher acts as a stimulus for learning, but he / she cannot predict learners' actions (new meanings and learning paths are created).
5. Discovery: Discovery comes from transformative actions through engagement with learning materials and situations, and allows for "incidental" learning experience. Learning by discovery can be individual and / or social; the crucial point is that it creates new contents through an active involvement of the learner.

Taking into account the metaphors in the design phase of the activity can help teachers to increase the pedagogical value of the resulting GBL experience. Besides, thinking about which metaphors they want to use is a way for teachers to escape from the traditional learning model and include innovative and creative teaching practices in their daily strategies.

In order to design meaningful GBL activities, it is important to consider many aspects. Indeed, the game should be perceived as embedded in a learning scenario that takes into account the different parameters of the teaching/learning context. While planning their GBL scenarios, teachers/trainers should take into account the specific characteristics of the learning audience, the specific learning objectives, the evaluation approach, the time-space resources or the technical requirements of the games. Moreover, the step by step organization of the learning activities (i.e. structure of the activities before, during and after the game) should be planned.

Success factors for the construction of a good educational game have been identified. Three different dimensions have been pointed out, namely *gaming aspects, learning aspects* and *technical aspects*.

Within gaming aspects, it is important to take into account that the game should include final objectives, but might also have intermediate / short-term goals in order to facilitate the player in reaching the final ones. The game should be based on clear and consistent rules. Players should strive for continuous improvement. This can be achieved by increasing level of difficulty. However, the level of challenge should not surpass the level of possibilities, in order not to discourage the player. Players should be able to perceive the impact and consequences that their actions have in the game world, in order to be informed about how they are performing, check their progress continuously, and enable them to eventually adjust their actions. Positive feedbacks are often associated with rewards, which help the player in the achievement of the objectives and acts as a mechanism to increase engagement and immersion. The game should be engaging, exciting and interesting for the wider possible number within the target group of students. This is achieved by using game elements like an interesting plot / story, an appealing environment / virtual world, contextualization, challenging goals, etc. The player should feel willing to play the game more than once. It's important to verify that the game includes jokes, humor, or any other elements required to make it more fun. But be aware these elements will not suit every game! (Inaccuracies in content can be dramatic in educational settings).

For what concerns the learning aspects, teachers should consider how well the game fit with their educational objectives. They should also check that the contents, puzzles and language used are adequate for their students, taking into account aspects like age, skills, knowledge level, socio-cultural context, etc. It is highly recommended that teachers provide additional content to students to reinforce learning. It could be provided as additional links, books, reading notes, etc., but also as content that is embedded in the game. These aspects should be considered from the beginning when the learning scenario is being designed. The game should be included in a wider learning scenario which might include other learning activities, such as further discussion / reflection sessions in the classroom, group activities, reports, presentations, homework, etc. The level of challenge of the learning experience should be high enough to keep students engaged but without surpassing their abilities so they do not become frustrated. The game should provide a context in which the level of autonomy of the learner is adequate. Moreover when the GBL scenario is put into practice, it's important to verify if students are really more motivated.

Finally, and considering the technical aspects, the game should be user-friendly and easy to use, so as to allow the player to concentrate on the objectives and not on dealing with a bad interface. The graphics should be appropriate for the target group. For example, cartoon styles are appropriate for kids, while photo-realistic environments are better for teenagers or university students. It is desirable that the game could be reused in different contexts without the need of complex and costly modifications. Besides teachers could be interested in adapting the games produced by other teachers.

Thus, the main goal reached during the ProActive project process, still in progress, has been to involve teachers coming from three different educational setting (school, university and professional organization) and from four different Contries (Spain, Italy, UK and Romania) in the creation of educational scenarios employing digital tools provided by the partnership (Picture 1). One of the game editor is EUTOPIA.

Picture 1. Teachers developing their GBL scenarios

For example one teacher proposed to employ the platform to develop a game whose aim is to train doctors and medical students to introduce, choose and presctipt handicap supports for those people who may need them within their school setting. The game presents moreover an indirect goal: to build a specific knowledge around the handicap supports in order to make the target group more expert about both impairments and technological aids to facilitate learning processes.

Another idea to employ the tool is training young/junior teachers in group dynamics. In particular, teachers should be helped to gain expertise in how to become members of a group in order to facilitate their future students' relationships. The idea is that being part of a community can be considered something to learn.

What comes out from the project activities is that generally, teachers' current practices are based on a quite common employment of ICT tools as a support for learning process. The main goal of every teacher is to interest the students and the idea of joining Proactive project is surely linked to this goal. Teachers also feel important to adapt the educational style to students' actual computer skills and to society change, trying to fill the generational gap on this issue. A strong link between GBL and creativity has been highlighted during the whole activities. Creativity seems enhanced by an innovative way of considering learning processes based on educative serious game. These new tools can improve students' curiosity about the world and facilitate knowledge sharing. Group creativity can be achieved, where everyone joins the everybody's learning process. An interesting difference between *teaching creatively* and *teaching creativity* emerged, where the first refers to a general flexibility within teacher's own approach to learning process, and the second refers to the possibility to teach students how to work in collaborative way, to be open to change towards flexibility and adaptability. In addition, we are talking about teaching through games, giving a good emphasis on the playfulness of the learning dynamics.

In relation to the editor proposed by Proactive, all teachers showed a high level of interest in employing it in their own teaching approach. One of the most important reason is that educational games provide a safe environment where exploring and experimenting knowledge. On the other hand, these tools can enhance both individual and collaborative learning, bringing innovative elements to teachers' teaching styles. These platforms could also help students in their self studying development, thus assuring them a teaching guidance together with the chance to freely produce and build their knowledge. In addition, teachers believed it could be interesting the idea to develop their own editors to support the daily practice. Nevertheless they seemed worried about reaching this specific goal because of their lack of computer skills, expressing the need to be updated and costantly trained.

Eutopia was perceived as a tool to teach and improve relational attitudes (being an on-line role-playing game), thus being employed more in psicosocial subjects like counselling, mediation and negotiation, soft skills training, human resources training (the only exception being a proposal to employ Eutopia also to explore formal knowledge).

4.2 T3 - Teaching to Teach with Technology project

In a recent review-article Selfton-Green (2006) has discussed different definitions of formal and informal learning linked to the context of learning. Both trainers and students have rules, strategies and learning patterns that differ according to age. Therefore, it is crucial to identify strategies of using technology that will be appropriate and consistent with the target of the intervention, in order to produce effective teaching strategies and be able to stimulate a real path of "active processing" of information. In this respect, it is known that the use of serious games is particularly appropriate for young people, but the use of new technologies is difficult in formal learning contexts, with mature individuals accustomed to different types of training.

Against this background, the "Teaching to Teach with Technology (T3)" project designed and validated an innovative teacher/trainer program, demonstrating realistic ways of exploiting advanced techniques within the real constraints facing teachers in their work.

In particular, the "Teaching to Teach with Technology (T3)" project promotes the use of advanced learning technology by:

- university teaching staff in Spain;
- secondary school teachers in UK;
- trainers involved in VET in Italy.

The Project started in December 2009 and was organized into work packages. The milestone of the project were: Needs Analysis; Selection of technologies; Methodology and Learning program; Testing, Trials of the Training Programme, production of guide-lines for games use.

Key features of the program included:

- theoretical classes discussing the features and advantage of the new technologies;
- practical workshops, in which learners (university teaching staff, teachers and trainers) simulate learning sessions and familiarize with technologies;
- project work, in which learners prepare learning projects for use in their own classes, implement the project, and evaluate the results;
- joint assessment of the results by participants in the program.

The final output of the project is a set of freely available tools, designed to encourage the uptake of new learning technologies to employ in universities, schools and professional training.

The principle underlying the definition of learning we have proposed is the classic learning by doing. It's important to underline that before games can take on a meaningful role in formal or informal education, the education sector and the wider public need to better understand the potential and diversity of such 'tools'. In fact, Blunt (2007) advocates that pedagogical methods are typically influenced by the available technologies of the period. Due to the pervasiveness and evolution of technology, students often learn differently from how their educators learnt.

Both psychological and educational literature stressed that the real context, which takes place in the educational relationship, plays a key role in the choice of methods and processes that involve the teaching-learning process. The different learning contexts, in fact, need and use different means of transferring knowledge and they need to be calibrated on partners, setting, and real or virtual places.

For these reasons, T3 project defined different steps of exploring games for educators (for more detailes see www.t3.unina.it). Through the exploration of few steps, the user may initially familiarize with the use of games in education and, then, he can learn to use them in order to increase complexity ranging from a closed mode to an open mode using.

The closed and open system definition aims at representing a training strategy based on instructions, closed systems, or on a more constructivist strategy (open systems). From a technological point of view, the new learning technologies (Miglino, Rega, Nigrelli, 2010) can be distinguished in: closed systems (tools and platforms developed by professionals which deal with a particular subject area and can be used for educational / training purpose), and open systems (tools and platforms that enable teachers to realize learning environments).

The training program proposes three steps (Sica, Nigrelli, Rega, & Miglino, 2011): 1. try sample curriculum; 2. Create your curriculum; 3. Try it in classroom (Fig. 1).

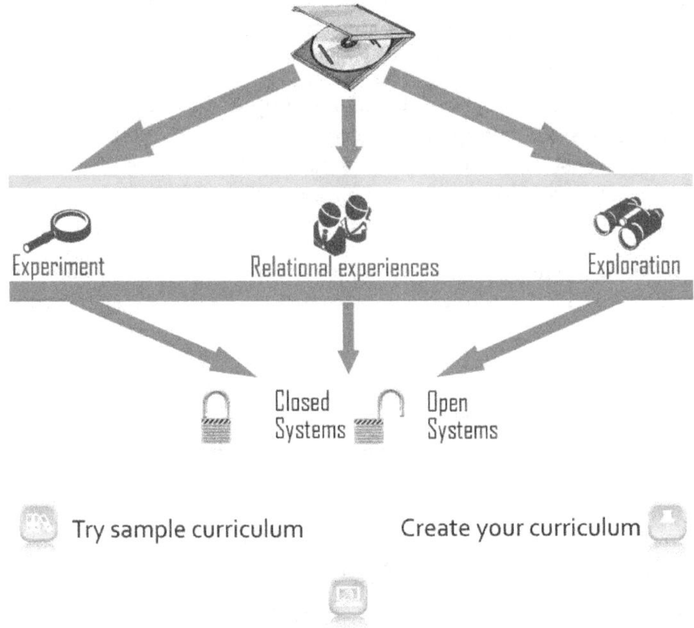

Fig. 1. The training steps of T3 project.

A review of the DGBL (digital game-based learning) literature shows that, in general, educators have adopted three approaches for integrating games into the learning process: students build games from scratch; educators and/or developers build educational games from scratch to teach students; integration of commercial off-the-shelf (COTS) games into the classroom. According to Van Eck (2006), we assume that this approach to DGBL is the most promising in the short term because of its practicality and efficacy and in the long term because of its potential to generate the evidence and support we need to entice game companies to begin developing serious games. This approach involves taking existing games, not necessarily developed as learning games, and using them in the classroom.

The strategies and functions of technology selected were: a. experimenting; b. experiencing soft skills; c. exploring.

a. The "demonstration-experiment" as a teaching strategy is one of the most popular and traditional strategy used by teachers. Perform laboratory experiments is, in fact, the core teaching of many disciplines.
b. "Learning by experience" is a fundamental model and it is referenced in literature pertaining to "the learning organization". This form of learning has the following characteristics: it is an explicit learning focused on the working environment; it is both individual and collective; it is focused not on knowledge, but on skills, attitudes and expertise; the learner has an active role and consciously learns though collaboration with others and under the guidance of experts in safe environments.
c. "exploring" is an innate human propensity to experience the environments in which they are to act. Many educational practices used to explore this tendency to transfer their skills and knowledge. The adventure games are transpositions in technological environment of this type of educational practice.

In light of these considerations, we considered appropriate to calibrate the choice of technologies to be tested taking into account a combination of factors: learning environments, characteristics of the trainers to be trained and subject matter. The learning process is highly dependent on the direct participation within a specific activity. This implies that very little learning is achieved in the traditional sense of the term.

The different learning contexts, as stressed above, need different means of transferring knowledge and they need to be calibrated on: partners, setting, and real or virtual places. Both trainers and students have also rules, strategies and learning patterns that differ according to age (as cognitive and psycho-social development; eg "digital natives" vs. "digital immigrants"). Therefore, it is crucial to identify strategies of using technology that will be appropriate and consistent with the target of the intervention, in order to produce effective teaching strategies and able to stimulate a real path of "active processing" of information.

Figure 2 summarizes the process that led to selection of technologies.

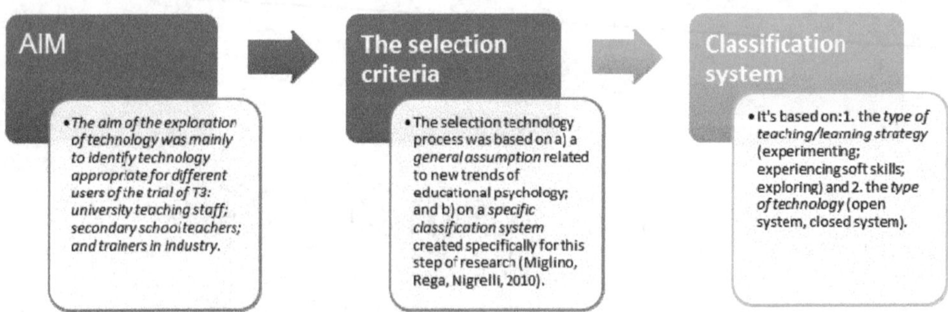

Fig. 2 Step for selection of technologies

Table 2 summarizes the work of classification and identification of learning technologies carried out within the T3 project (Miglino, Rega, & Nigrelli, 2010) and it reports some examples of systems and prototypes that can be used as example of the following categories.

		TYPE OF TEACHING/LEARNING STRATEGY		
		Experimenting	*Experiecing soft skills*	*Exploring*
TYPE OF TECHNOLOGY	*Closed System*	• Avida • BestBot • SimCity • Nerone	• Dread-Ed	• Civilasation • Age of Empires • The Sims
	Open System	• NetLogo • Lego MindStorms	• **Eutopia** • E-circus • Forio	• Anima • E-adventure • QR Code

Table 2. Classification scheme of learning technologies (examples in each category) (Miglino, Rega, & Nigrelli, 2010)

For easier reading of the table 2, Miglino, Rega, and Nigrelli (2010) deepen the description of the technology by splitting the table into three quadrants.

Quadrant 1. Experimenting (Table 3)

Experiments are the core of many disciplines. The design of an experimental session goes in parallel with the assimilation of a body of theory that explains the general generative mechanisms of a given phenomenon. The correct understanding of the theory should lead to a forecast of empirically observable behaviors.

		Type of teaching/learning strategy
		Experiment
Type of technology	Closed System	Avida BestBot SimCity Nerone
	Open System	NetLogo Lego MindStorms

Table 3. Experimenting

This methodology can be applied in different teaching and learning contexts. These software packages fall into the category of closed systems as a focus in the reproduction of a very specific "piece of reality". In addition, to use virtual labs, teachers and students can create their own artificial models of several phenomena. There are programming suites that allow the development of computer simulations (Miglino, Gigliotta, Ponticorvo, & Nolfi, 2007) and physical machines (e.g. robots), even to those people who don't have a sounding background in technical computing.

By using such, so-called, open systems, teachers and students can easily reproduce natural, psychological and social events.

Quadrant 2. Experiecing soft skills (Table 4.)

In addition to the theoretical and technical education, training agencies are also in charge of transferring to students a set of behavioral skills that are a necessary background to deal with professional communities and society. Examples of such skills (commonly referred to as soft skills) are the ability to manage emergencies, the ability to negotiate, to take decisions collectively, the attitude to understand others' view points. In general, the teaching of soft skills is primarily linked to experience, where a teacher organizes, supervises and encourages small groups of learners to take part in role playing and simulation. Es. *Palma* (Gigliotta, Miglino, & Parisi, 2007).

		Teaching/ learning strategy
		Experiecing soft skills
Technology	Closed System	Dread-Ed
		Palma
		Talk To Me
	Open System	Eutopia
		E-circus
		Forio

Table 4. Experiecing soft skills

Most of these techniques for learning soft skills can be transferred in digital platforms and online technologies. There are many different educational games (serious games) in which the player-learner has a particular role and must pursue a goal assigned by the teacher / trainer. Also for this category, trainers can find games that are dedicated to the transfer of a particular segment of knowledge / skills (closed systems) and platforms that enable teachers and learners to develop and edit their own educational scenarios with specific goals (open systems).

Quadrant 3. Exploring (Table 5.)

Basically, learning and exploring can be considered two sides of same coin. Teach and train mean mainly supply schemes (and motivation) to better "travel" in the world where people are living.

Many educational and training practices exploit the exploratory instinct of people to transfer knowledge and skills. Perhaps the best known example of this paradigma is represented by the many versions of the educational treasure hunt.

		Teaching/ learning strategy
		Explore
Technology	Closed System	Civilazation
		Age of Empires
		The Sims
	Open System	Anima
		E-adventure
		QR Code

Table 5. Exploring

According to T3 results, one of the most promising platform in this sense is EUTOPIA.

5. The Platform

EUTOPIA is an online 3D role-playing environment similar to other virtual environments like Second Life™. With this platform educators can create virtual scenarios where students play a role and simulate a specific situation. EUTOPIA can be used to improve negotiating skills and intercultural awareness of professional trainers and staff in contact with the public.

The game development process in EUTOPIA is quite straightforward. Teachers just need to select one of the predefined 3D scenarios (e.g. a city or a meeting room), select the roles that will take part (i.e. define the personality and choose a predefined avatar for each character) and assign them to each participant/student. Then the teacher must set up a virtual session (i.e. simulation) in a server using the created scenario. Participants and teacher join the session and then they interact with each other, following the teacher's plan.

EUTOPIA represents the current development of a previous experience in Information and Communication Technology, SISINE, developed by Natural and Artificial Cognition Laboratory.

SISINE (Miglino *et al.*, 2007) was used to provide innovative training practices and to improve negotiating skills and intercultural awareness of professional trainers, front-office staff and other staff in contact with the public. The training offered focused on the kinds of negotiation workers engage during their everyday professional activities (rather than on classical managerial negotiation). The training methodology was based on a blended strategy combining classroom learning with e-Learning based self-study. Both the classroom learning and the self-study sessions made intensive use of a novel simulation environment. The environment incorporated technologies from Multiplayer Online Role Playing Games (MORPG) (Okamoto *et al.*, 2007). The use of simulation ensured that users can "learn by doing" at home as well in the classroom (Miglino, 2007).

EUTOPIA, in fact, is an on-line platform that allows the production of a particular type of serious game: an educational Multiplayer On-Line Role Playing Games (e-MORPG).

From a formative/teaching side, EUTOPIA has the role to transfer the methodological tradition of the Psychodrama (Moreno, 1946) from the real world to a virtual 3D world.

The platform provides the normal functionality expected by Multiplayer Online Role-Playing Games (Madani & Chohra, 2008), as well as additional functions that allow a trainer to set up games, intervene during game, record specific phases of a game, annotate recordings and discuss them with the players.

Teachers can write scripts for on-line multiplayer games. In designing a multiplayer game they can choose the roles, goals, bodies and personalities of individual players. Once the game is in progress, they can watch what is going on from any viewpoint, intervene at any moment, send messages to players, or activate special "events". When it is over, they can become critics, leading a group discussion and analysing the strategies adopted by the players. This step of debriefing becomes fundamental for the learning process.

As well as preparing scripts for on-line games and assigning characters to users, there are two other ways in which teachers/tutors can intervene in learners' interactions with EUTOPIA. One is to take the role of one of the characters in the simulation. The other is to act as an invisible stage director. In this second role, teachers can: a) invisibly observe the interactions among players; b) access the players' "private characteristics"; c) listen to private messages ("whispers") between players; d) "broadcast" messages visible to all players; e) exchange private messages with a specific user; and f) activate events, changing the course of the simulation.

Learners that play the act reach the virtual stage-set where they can interact each other controlling a virtual alter ego, the avatar (see Fig.3).

Fig. 3. Some avatars

Once logged in, they join a 3D graphical environment in which they are represented by avatars, and can use them to explore the environment. Players communicate via short texts and different forms of paraverbal and non-verbal communication. For instance, they can control how loud they want to speak (shown by the size of characters used in the bubble cartoons) and in what tone of voice (shown by the shape of the bubble). Players can control avatars' gestures and body movements. They can also 'whisper' messages to each other: these are audible only to the other partner in the conversation, and to the tutor. Finally, they can communicate with the tutor to ask for advice or clarification or to raise any other question that concerns them.

In particular, EUTOPIA kit is made up of three software with different functions:

1. Editor - Creation of group sessions and of the elements needed for the training. Editor is used by tutors.
2. Client – Interaction with other users inside the group sessions. Client is divided into:
   - Master for tutors
   - Player for user
3. Viewer – Visualize the previous recorded group interaction sessions, recorder editing and add personal comments. Viewer can be used by users

The environment is represented in 3D graphics allowing participants to move around in the space and to approach other avatars (see Fig. 4).

The first step is to create a storyboard/script which defines the starting point for a story. All scripts are based on a standard structure which determines the way it is stored in the database. Each script has a name (a brief definition which defines the activity), a description of the activity, a story (a detailed, perhaps even quantitative description of the scenario, of the events related to the training session issues, and of possible outcomes), a maximum available time, group goals and success criteria (information about one or more goals common to all participants in the interaction).

Fig. 4. 3D environment

Each script has a "general goal". The success of the training course depends on how far this goal is achieved. Additionally the script describes partial goals for each online session. Of course partial goals are related to the general goal.

The software gives the chance to choose and define the personality of the different characters that will be involved in the session. For each character we can define:

- Features (sex, age, social status).
- Characteristic elements (physical aspect).
- Role in the story.
- Personal story.
- Personality aspects (associated with specific non-verbal communication capabilities).
- Individual goals.

Starting from a script chosen by the tutor, each participant plays the role of one of the characters, associated with an avatar.

Each participant knows the story in which his/her character is involved, knows the goals shared by all participants, knows the goals of his/her character and his/her own individual story (which is not known by the other participants).

During the simulation, the tutor can introduce new elements which may influence the interaction: unforeseen difficulties and new resources. All these events are foreseen in the script, which provides a description of the event and the way it should be presented. The tutor activates events, at what he/she deems to be the most appropriate moment in the simulation. An event could be either a text (letter, fax or document) which appears on the screen, or be represented by an "avatar" character who enters the scene and delivers a message (text and other non-verbal elements).

At the end of the interaction, the tutor watches the simulation recording, notes his/her impressions and conclusions and analyzes the results (if necessary in quantitative terms). It is very important he/she should assess whether group and individual goals have been achieved and to what extent.

The tutor sums up the most important aspects of the session and the way in which the participants have conducted the session. He/she makes it clear whether and to what extent the participants have achieved their individual and group goals. Feedback can be provided immediately after the simulation or in a later meeting. The discussion of the results of the session is conducted in the simulation environment, in free chat mode. During the training experience, players are asked to fill questionnaires on their learning process, in order to give the chance to collect data and analyze the final outcomes.

6. Discussion of results

Results of Proactive and T3 programs are consistent with the literature and they stress the importance of game-based learning, clarifying that it's a balance between conceptual (teaching about) and procedural (teaching how to do) knowledge (Miglino, & Walker, 2010; Sica, Nigrelli, Rega, & Miglino, 2011). In brief, advanced games technologies (computer games, augmented reality, robotics) could address many of the limitations of traditional instructional methods; games have the ability to motivate learning, increase knowledge and skill acquisition and support traditional teaching methods.

In conclusion, the experimental steps of both the projects described leads us to believe that the use of new technologies can also be applied in education. According to scientific literature (Senge, 1990) we could find advantages related to strictly cognitive aspects: the spatial and temporal proximity of stimuli faciliting learning, the relevance or consistency of the material proposed, the different ways of transmitting information, the customization of dynamic teaching / learning. However, we believe that the use of games in education should be preceded by a period of training and familiarization of educators, in order to bridge generational distance in learning modality. Last few generations of adolescents are much more used to frequent on-line platforms, to engage in video-games, compared to teachers met in various training agencies. We think it's useful that teachers are approaching the language of learners, to provide a better educational dialogue.

In this sense, the projects' results are highly encouraging, and T3- program is especially useful in providing a first pragmatic approach to the the use of games in education. Furthermore, Eutopia platform was perceived as a tool to teach and improve relational attitudes, thus being employed more in psicosocial subjects like counselling, mediation and negotiation, soft skills training, human resources training.

7. References

Alessi, S. (2000). *Building versus using simulations.* In J. M. Spector and T. M. Anderson, eds. Integrated and holistic perspectives on learning, instruction and technology: Understanding complexity. Dordrecht: Kluwer.

BECTA (2008). 'Analysis of emerging trends affecting the use of technology in education.' Coventry: BECTA.

Beghetto, R. A. (2007). Does creativity have a place in classroom discussion? Prospective teachers' response preferences. *Thinking Skills and Creativity*, 2, 1-9.

Blunt, R. (2007). *Does Game-Based Learning Work? Results from Three Recent Studies.* Interservice/ Industry Training, Simulation, and Education Conference (I/ITSEC) Papers

Cachia, R., Ferrari, A., Kearney, C., Punie, Y., Van Den Berghe, W., Wastiau, P. (2009). "Creativity in Schools in Europe: A Survey of Teachers". Report JRC55645 of the Joint Research Center of the European Commission. Retrieved July 30th, 2010 from http://ftp.jrc.es/EURdoc/JRC55645_Creativity%20Survey%20Brochure.pdf

Chandler, P. & Sweller, J. (1991). Cognitive load theory and the format of instruction. *Cognition and Instruction*, 8, 293-332.

Costa, A. L., & Kallick, B., (2009). *Habits of Mind Across the Curriculum: Practical and Creative Strategies for Teachers.* Alexandria, VA: Association for Supervision and Curriculum Development.

Craft, A. (2005). *Creativity in schools : tensions and dilemmas.* London: Routledge.

De Caluwé, L. & Vermaak, H. (1999). *Leren veranderen* [learning to change]. Amersfoort: Twynstra Gudde.

Ferrari, A., Cachia, R., Punnie, Y. (2009). JRC Technical Notes - Innovation and Creativity in Education and Training in the EU Member States: Fostering Creative Learning and Supporting Innovative Teaching - *Literature review on Innovation and Creativity in E&T* in the EU Member States (ICEAC) Retrieved July 30th, 2010 from http://ftp.jrc.es/EURdoc/JRC52374_TN.pdf

Gee, J. (2003). *What video games have to teach us about learning and literacy.* New York: Palgrave Macmillan.

Gigliotta, O., Miglino, O. & Parisi, D. (2007). Groups of agents with a leader. *Journal of Artificial Societies and Social Simulation*, 10 (4.1).

Jves, B. And Junglas, I. (2008). Ape Forum: Business Implications Of Virtual Worlds And Serious Games. *Mis Quarterly Executive*, 7(3), Pp. 151-156.

Madani, K. & Chohra, A. (2008). Towards Intelligent Artificial Avatars' Implementation in a Negotiation Training dedicated Multi Player On-line Role playing Game Platform. *International Journal of Computing*, vol.7.

Marzano, R. J. (2000). *Designing a new taxonomy of educational objectives.* Thousand Oaks, CA: Corwin Press.

Mayer, R. E. & Anderson, R. B. (1991). Animations need narrations: An experimental test of a dual-coding hypothesis. *Journal of Educational Psychology*, 83, 484-490.

Mayer, R. E. & Anderson, R. B. (1992). The instructive animation: Helping students build connections between words and pictures in multimedia learning. *Journal of Educational Psychology*, 84, 444-452.

Mayer, R. E. & Gallini, J. K. (1990). When is an illustration worth ten thousand words? *Journal of Educational Psychology*, 82, 715-726.

Mayer, R. E. & Moreno, R. (1998). A split-attention effect in multimedia learning: Evidence for dual information processing systems in working memory. *Journal of Educational Psychology*, 90.

Mayer, R. E. (2001). *Multimedia learning.* New York: Cambridge University Press.

Miglino, O. (2007). The SISINE project: developing an e-learning platform for educational role-playing games, ERCIM NEWS 71, pp. 28.

Miglino, O., Gigliotta, O., Ponticorvo, M. & Nolfi, S (2007). Breedbot: an edutainment rootics system to link digital and real world. In Apollloni B.; Howlett R.J.; Jain L. (Eds). *Knowledge-Based Intelligent Information and Engineering Systems,* pages 74-81. Heidelberg - Germany : Springer

Miglino, O., Di Ferdinando, A., Rega, A. & Benincasa, B. (2007). SISINE: Teaching Negotiation Through A Multiplayer Online Role Playing Game. In D. Remenyi

(Ed.) *Proceedings of the 6th European Conference On E-Learning*, (Pp. 439-448). ISBN: 978-1-905305-57-5. Reading: Academic Conferences Limited.

Miglino, O., Rega, A. & Nigrelli, M. L. (2010). Quali videogiochi possono essere usati a sostegno dei processi di insegnamento/apprendimento. In Atti del VII Convegno dell'Associazione Italiana di Scienze Cognitive

Miglino, O., Walker, R. (2010). Teaching to teach with technology - a project to encourage take-up of advanced technology in education. *Procedia Social and Behavioral Sciences, 2 (2)*, 2492-2496.

Moreno, J. L. (1946). Psychodrama and group psychotherapy. Reading at *American Psychiatric Association Meeting*, Chicago.

NACCCE (1999) "All Our Futures: Creativity, Culture and Education", Report to the Secretary of State for Education and Employment the Secretary of State for Culture, Media and Sport, UK, Retrieved July 30th, 2010 from http://www.cypni.org.uk/downloads/alloutfutures.pdf

Ng, A.K., & Smith, I. (2004). Why is there a Paradox in promoting creativity in the Asian Classroom? In S. Lau, A. N. N. Hui & G. Y. C. Ng (Eds.), Creativity: When east meets west (pp. 87-112): World Scientific Publishing Company.

Okamoto, S., Kamada, M. & Yonekura, T. (2007). A Simple authoring Tool for MORPG on Web. *Institute of Electronics, Information and Communication Engineers Tech. Rep.*, vol. 107, no. 130, MVE2007-30, pp. 43-47.

Paivio, A. (1986). Mental representations: A dual coding approach. Oxford, England: Oxford University Press.

Prensky, M. (2001). *Digital game-based learning*. New York: McGraw-Hill.

Runco, M. A. (1999). *Implicit Theories*. In M. A. Runco & S. R. Pritzker (Eds.), Encyclopedia of creativity (Vol. 2, pp. 27-30). San Diego, California; London: Academic.

Sawyer, R. K. (2006). Educating for innovation. *Thinking Skills and Creativity,* 1, 41–48.

Sefton-Green, J. (2006). *Report 7: Literature Review in Informal Learning with Technology Outside School*. Bristol.

Sharp, C. (2004). Developing Young Children's Creativity: what can we learn from research? *Topic*, 32, 5-12.

Senge M. P. (1990). *The Fifth Discipline: The Art and Practice of the Learning Organization*. New York: Doubleday Currency.

Sica, L.S., Nigrelli, M.L., Rega, A., Miglino, O. (2011). The "Teaching to Teach with Technology" Project: Promoting Advanced Games Technologies in Education. *Proceedings International Conference "The future of Education"*, Firenze, Italy: Simonelli Editore - University Press, vol. 2, 169-173.

Simons, R.J. & Ruijters, M.P.C (2003). *Differing colours of professional learning*. In L. Mason, S. Andreuzza, B. Arfè & L. Del Favero (Eds.), Improving learning, fostering the will to learn. Proceedings Biennial Conference EARLI (pp. 31). Padua, Italy: Cooperativa Libraria Editrice Università di Padova.

Simons, R.J. (2004). Metaphors of learning at work and the role of ICT. Workshop Learning and Technology at Work: London.

Simons, R.J. & Ruijters, M.P.C (2008). Varieties of work-related learning. *International Journal of Educational Research*, 47, 241-251.

Van Eck, R. (2006). Digital Game-Based Learning: It's Not Just the Digital Natives Who Are Restless. *EDUCAUSE Review,* vol. 41, 2, 16–30.

Williamson, B., & Payton, S. (2009) *Curriculum and teaching innovation: Futurlab.* http://www.futurelab.org.uk/resources/documents/handbooks/curriculum_and_teaching_innovation2.pdf

Part 2

E-Learning Assessment

7

E-Learning Evolution and Experiences at the University of Zaragoza

José Luis Alejandre, Ana Allueva, Rafael Tolosana and Raquel Trillo
University of Zaragoza
Spain

1. Introduction

Due to their dynamic and motivating nature, e-Learning tools provide academia with powerful mechanisms to alter the potentially inertial passivity that in-person learning at a physical campus may sometimes bring to students. These tools also try to promote communication and to actively involve students in their learning process. Moreover, they foster interdisciplinary collaboration among academics as well as the dissemination of experiences.

Since its foundation in 1542, the *University of Zaragoza* has been adapting to changes in society and to in-fashion educational practices. During the last decades, the use of emerging technologies such as e-Learning tools have revolutionized the way teaching-learning models had been understood and implemented and they have promoted the Continuous Professional Education (CPE) or Life Long Learning (LLL) and/or the Collaborative Learning (application sharing, discussion threads, etc.) (Perry, 1995). Due to this fact, the *University of Zaragoza* developed its own Virtual Campus, a section in charge of the online offerings of the university where college activities can be completed either partially or wholly online. The Virtual Campus at University of Zaragoza (Spain) is known as "Anillo Digital Docente"[1] (ADD) (*http://add.unizar.es Anillo Digital Docente, Universidad de Zaragoza,* n.d.) and it comprises a number of technical software systems and even hardware devices that support e-Learning, such as Learning Content Management Systems (LCMS) like Moodle (Dougiamas & Taylor, 2003) or Blackboard 9.1 (*http://www.blackboard.com/Platforms/Learn/Overview.aspx BlackBoard e-Learning Platform,* n.d.), and more recently also Clickers and *Opern Course Ware (OCW)*[2] Alternatively, some colleagues at the institution have also been utilizing their own collaborative workspace software systems or groupware such as Basic Support for Cooperative Work (BSCW, also known as Be Smart - Cooperate Worlwide). All of them contribute to create a complete learning management model, which is focused on the learning process rather than on specific technologies.

The aforementioned LCMS support and manage the creation, edition, storing and delivering of e-Learning content and assist with the creation of integral teaching-learning environments (Laviña-Orueta & Mengual-Pavón, 2008). However, as discussed in the 4th

[1] Educational Digital Ring, in English. Website: http://add.unizar.es

[2] A free and open digital publication of university-level educational materials organized as courses installed on `http://ocw.unizar.es`.

Conference on Learning Innovation of the *University of Zaragoza* (Zaragoza, Spain, September 2010), different uses of the LCMS within the institution can be observed:

- a use that exploits LCMS to assist the in-person learning in the physical campus, or even combining on-line learning activities (asynchronous) with in-person learning activities (synchronous) –a learning model that is often known as b-Learning (Wolfe, 2001);
- a use that exploits LCMS to assist the on-line learning courses in a completely asynchronous way.

In this Chapter, we describe the evolution and experiences of the *University of Zaragoza* Virtual Campus, ADD, and we present and analyze official statistics about the courses, number of students and academics that have been involved with e-Learning activities. We highlight the efficient use of these emerging technologies as the foundations of most innovative teaching initiatives. We support the thesis that states that the e-Learning model not only must be technology– and contents– centered, but also oriented to learning quality, processes and contexts. Thus, e-Learning technologies should enrich academics in their role of knowledge builders rather than just merely knowledge providers. In short, we believe that e-Learning promotes an important methodological change where active methodologies go beyond knowledge transmission. In this context, where technology and teaching methodologies co-exist, we present three selected real case studies undertaken in our institution where the role of e-Learning technologies in the development of a number of different methodologies is analyzed. In particular, we analyze the application of e-Learning tools to tutorship, collaborative work and laboratory assessments.

The rest of this chapter is organized as follows: initially, we overview the technological environment of the *University of Zaragoza* in Section 2. After that, we focus on the three selected real cases. The first study case examines the tutorship in the contexts of b-Learning and in-person learning and the technological tools that support the tutorship between academics and students (for more details see Section 3). The second experience is focused on the advantages of collaborative working and the need for adequate technology for implementing this model (for more details see Section 4). In the third case, we highlight the effectiveness of the management of last generation LCMS such as Blackboard 9.1 compared to a number of ad-hoc developed scripting tools in order to automate the assessment of laboratory lessons at a number of courses at the Computer Science Department (for more details see Section 5). Finally, the conclusions and future work are given.

2. Technological environment at the *University of Zaragoza*

A great percentage of the educational activities in the *University of Zaragoza* is supported on Web technological platforms, known as *Learning Management System (LMS)*, used to create, distribute and manage educational material. These platforms are excellent tools in order to facilitate the development of teaching-learning environments as they support the creation and management of a complete educational model. In fact, they provide repositories of materials, communication tools, monitoring and evaluation tools, collaboration systems, management of different roles involved in the teaching-learning activities and different kinds of permissions and licenses, etc.

From our point of view, a virtual learning environment or virtual campus must be considered beyond the idea of simple "distance learning" as it must integrate many factors, such as technology, services, assessment, educational contents and particularly human factors (students, teachers and other staff involved). Moreover, it must be focused on the online learning process and not just on technological aspects. According to this idea, as a starting point we consider the definition of e-Learning from the perspective of quality of learning by García Peñalvo (García-Peñalvo, 2008): Teaching-learning process, aimed at acquiring a set of competencies and skills by the student, characterized by: 1) the use of web-based technologies, 2) the sequencing of a set of structured contents according to predefined and flexible strategies, 3) the interaction with the network of students and tutors, and 4) a set of appropriate assessment mechanisms for both the learning outcomes and the training intervention as a whole, in a collaborative working environment enriched by a set of value-added services that technology can provide to achieve maximum interaction, and where the presence is not immediate but deferred in space and time. García Peñalve considers that this ensures the highest quality in the teaching-learning process.

At the time of writing this chapter (July 2011), the *University of Zaragoza* offers Moodle 1.9, Blackboard CE8 and Blackboard 9.1. Moreover, previous courses in Blackboard CE8 are being migrated to Blackboard 9.1. These platforms host 5,675 online courses which involve 4,056 academics and 64,897 users with the role of student. In Figure 1, we can observe the evolution of the number of courses in the last four years.

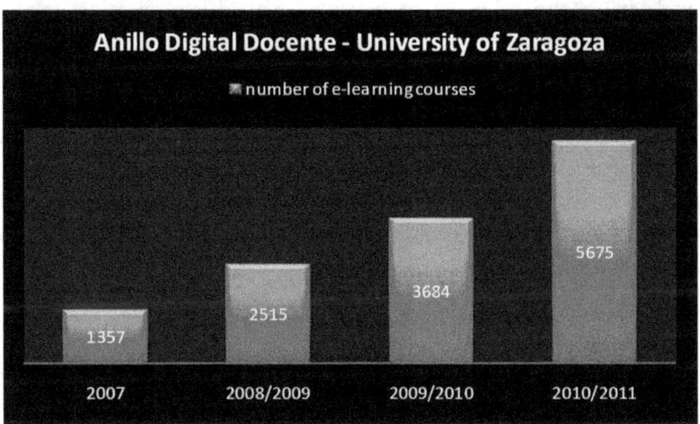

Fig. 1. Evolution of the number of online courses at the University of Zaragoza since 2007

Nevertheless, there exist different uses of these tools in our university. Most courses use them as a support or as a supplement to teaching-learning activities performed in the face-to-face environment. However, there also exists an important percentage of courses where a more advanced model of mixed or hybrid learning called *b-learning* is used. In this case, tools are used to supplement or even to develop the lectures at school. Thus, this model is used to design teaching-learning scenarios including simultaneous synchronous classroom activities and other asynchronous activities commonly used in e-learning. Finally, an increasing percentage of courses are being completely developed in a virtual environment where the teaching-learning model is completely asynchronous, as generally this kind of courses are included in masters and specialized programs where it is very important to leverage the ubiquity in order to create inter-university collaboration with other national and international universities. In this way, a scenario and strategic framework to internationalize our university is being built. However, on this regard, it is important to emphasize that a wide range of academic and legal aspects need to be considered and their complexity increases with the number of countries involved.

In summary, in the University of Zaragoza, the tools are used in teaching-learning activities by considering b-learning methodologies promoting the design of active learning scenarios and collaborative learning. Moreover, this fact also facilitates the continuous assessment and fosters not only the acquisition of specific knowledge, but also the development of attitudes and skills. However, we also find that a great percentage of the students still have a passive attitude towards LMS and that they consider them as mere repositories. This is sometimes aggravated by the limited use of this kind of tools by a number of academics and it must be overcome.

In any case, these tools are a suitable means for selecting teaching-learning resources and encourage interdisciplinarity. Besides, we can affirm that the use of current platforms increases the value of indicators used commonly to evaluate the quality for the integration of methodologies and information and communication technologies, such as active learning, the improvement of student's achievement, the improvement of communication among students and teachers, the promotion of coordination among academics, and the improvement of the quality of the contents.

On the other hand, from the experience of using the different platforms, we know that there are certain shortcomings related to the management of contents to enable, for example, reusing or sharing them collaboratively, especially in the university context. In this sense, *Learning Content Management Systems (LCMS)* are based on a model of content objects or learning objects, which facilitates the management of the repository and the reuse of such objects. Besides, they provide authoring tools or collaborative tools to create them. Moreover, the most modern platforms also incorporate the philosophy of Web 2.0 (Weber & Rech, 2010), as it happens with the latest releases of the platforms currently available at the University of Zaragoza, in particular Blackboard 9.1.

Alternatively, there are specialized platforms such as *Document Management Systems (DMS)* or systems oriented to *Basic Support for Cooperative Work (BSCW)*. In our university, we have the experience of several groups working with BSCW as a platform for collaborative work. The good results obtained with this platform have encouraged its use and demand by other professors. However, currently, in our institution the workload of the collaborative work can only be performed with Blackboard 9.1.

Regarding open educational resources, we consider that it is interesting to distinguish different elements: 1) contents included in courses with open access, 2) open source development tools and open standards, and 3) tools to create flexible licenses that enable flexible reuse of educational activities. At this point, we consider that legal aspects about the access and the distribution of information are essential. Besides, we have to take into account the new formats and interfaces provided by some emerging distribution channels such as university TV channels, iTunes U, youtubeEDU, etc.

Open or free-access projects in the context of e-learning are widely disseminated and they serve as excellent "showcase" for the promotion of educational institutions, and even for the work of their research groups. In our case, they enhance the dissemination primarily among the hispanic-culture institutions. Thus, for example, the University of Zaragoza has recently incorporated to the Open Course Ware Project (OCW).

2.1 The role of information and communication technologies in innovation projects in higher education and e-Learning

The OCW project, like many other educational projects, was born under innovation initiatives by professors and teachers. Nevertheless, the importance and growth of innovation in an educational institution usually depends on a strong institutional support. The University of Zaragoza has been heavily promoting innovation projects in higher education and e-learning by funding them during the last years. This support has led into the creation of innovation groups and interdisciplinary networks oriented to deal with different educational topics among professors specialized in different areas and with different backgrounds. A great percentage of the Innovation Projects are focused on the use of new tools based on Information and Communication Technologies (ICT) but there also exist projects whose research pursues to create models and methodologies for teaching-learning activities with ICT. In the last academic course (2010-2011), 482 innovation projects were developed and 1,237 professors participated in them.

Regarding the efficient use of ICT in a blended learning model, in most innovating initiatives it is agreed that the mere use of a technology does not constitute an innovation process, since the technology by itself is not enough. We think that the use of ICT must mature. The learning scene that is constructed usually starts from a model centered on the materials, which is always possible if an appropriate infrastructure is available. In this process of maturity, this model must be developed considering the applications, platforms, portals, and finally end up in what we could call the service management, which will imply the real and effective implementation of the methodologies.

In consequence, we think that the role of technology in that evolution, and in general in e-learning, must be focused on both the technology and the contents, but oriented towards the quality, the processes, and the learning environments, enriching the role of the academics as facilitators of the learning process to generate (and not only to deliver) new knowledge in a teaching approach based on the student, his/her context, and his/her previous outcomes.

Furthermore, the use of ICT as dynamic and motivating tools succeed in breaking the inertia and the passive attitudes of students, highly increasing their interest in their own activity and education, encouraging their participation, etc. Summing up, ICT are very good instruments to improve the communication in education.

In addition, the use of ICT as a support in this process favors the interdisciplinary and interdepartmental collaboration, motivating our colleagues and improving the dissemination of experiences, in a way that it is possible to share the benefits and the good results obtained, the weak points observed in the development of the activities, and the implementation of the activities.

From all the experiences conducted in our university, we can conclude that ICT are essential to perform the methodological change that is completely introduced with the European Higher Education Area (EHEA), based on the use of active methodologies that go beyond the mere transmission of knowledge. With this approach, traditional classes are reduced by fostering students' participation, the collaborative work, and the tutoring. In this context, the use and diffusion of multimedia materials is encouraged, but tools such as webfolios, chats, blogs, forums, and the Web 2.0 itself, are also of great importance. All these options, platforms and tools favor also the acquisition of competencies. In this sense, a good educational tutorial action for the students is essential.

Nevertheless, we also want to emphasize that, despite all the possibilities offered by ICT tools, current platforms are still frequently used as simple repositories of information. In any case, the cultural level and the computer abilities of students entering the university after leaving the Secondary Education keeps improving, although there is still a need of initiation courses for the acquisition of ICT competencies.

The final efficiency, not only for handling ICT tools, but in all the educational dimension of the repositories of materials, depends on their configuration as reusable learning objects. These objects should follow open standards, that should be easily interchangeable, allowing their use and querying, which could even enable the creation of a common repository of resources. Finally, besides training in the use of tools for educational innovation, in order to enable their effective use in a virtual learning environment both educational and technical support is required, which calls for appropriate funding.

3. Case study 1: Online tools for tutorship in technical and scientific courses

Tutorship is becoming a fundamental role in the context of educational virtual campus of our university, and in general in European Higher Education Space (EES) (Seoane-Pardo et al., 2007). We have a virtual campus and a strong institutional support for the development of high-quality virtual teaching-learning activities. However, in order to be successful, the consideration of human factors on the different on-line strategies is of great importance.

In our educational model, we perform "academic tutorship", which fosters the resolution of students' doubts and questions and allows professors or tutors [3] to monitor and track the evolution of their students and educational activities.

Firstly, we focus our attention on timing, because though the efficient time management and scheduling of the teaching-learning activities of students has not been studied in depth in our university, we firmly believe that it is an essential aspect in the new European Higher Education Space (EES) which we are converging to. In fact, we ask ourselves whether the use of ICT actually affects the workload of our students, and whether it increases/decreases the students' workload. Therefore, we analyze the students' workload and the time they invest in their study and training. Moreover, in our opinion, the influence of a proper student's time management in her/his academic results and how a tutor can help students to organize their activities by means of tutorships should be also analyzed.

Regarding how to measure the students' workload, the unanimous opinion in several forums of our university is that this work should be in charge of the coordinating teams of the different degrees which are institutionalized in our university. In fact, this challenge is being faced nowadays due to the introduction of the new degrees adapted to the European Higher Education Space. It is important to remark that it is easy to talk about perceptions about the relationships between scheduling, timetables, planning, timing, etc. and the use of ICT tools or methodologies. However, conclusions must not be established from only perceptions due to the relevance of this topic. In consequence, we need to quantify the workloads, and develop the methodology, indeed, the measurements can differ among the different areas or subjects.

At this point, we propose a reflection about the concept of timing in higher education spaces by considering timing as the ability to recognize and react immediately to changes and opportunities in the teaching-learning process. We could study how to choose momentum

[3] Generally professors and tutors are the same persons in our institution

for changing or reacting; i.e., how to get a dynamic management of our teaching-learning activities. In this context, we could also reflect upon how to use methodologies such as "Just and Time" with ICT tools. Our conclusions are very diverse, but we agree on that the tutor's role is crucial in this process.

3.1 Experiences with graphic tablets and Wimba tools

Regarding the experiences with ICT tools for academic tutoring, we would like to point out our experience with the use of graphic tablets based on our experience in virtual as well as face-to-face environments.

A graphic tablet, composed by a pen and multi-touch input, provides a new way to work with a computer. Due to its features, in our institution, it has been proven to be a useful complement for other technological systems that can be found in most lecture rooms such as desktop computers, video projectors, etc. During lectures, it increases students' motivation and interest, and fosters active participation. Besides, graphics tablets also are another way for helping students with the use of multimedia materials, educational software, and Web 2.0 (Weber & Rech, 2010) resources during lectures (not necessarily in laboratory sessions). The tablet can replace more powerful hardware such as tablet PC, but its main advantage is its low cost.

Graphics tablets are also used to support the tutorship of on-line technological and scientific courses such as mathematics. In many cases, on-line tutorship for mathematics arises many challenges, for instance the writing of mathematical formulae in the content of messages in an agile way. Moreover, in LCMS of the ADD, graphics tablets can simplify the assessments, as academics can correct the exercises in the device, marking the documents directly in the touch-screen, and they also optimize the use of digital boards of LCMS. During the current course (2010-2011), we have also enriched virtual classrooms with new functionalities for the accomplishment of a complete video conference though the Web. In particular, we have used Wimba Classroom which will be updated to Blackboard Collaborate soon. This tool increases the possibilities for tutoring as it allows us to deliver content, communicate, collaborate, share and interact with on-line participants in real-time by means of text, chat, audio and video. In fact, the tools of Classroom provide students with webcast model or lived broadcast where they have access to professors, course contents, practices, laboratories, etc. beyond the boundaries of the traditional classroom.

In addition to audio and video tools, Wimba Classroom also allows users to use whiteboards to show documents, presentations, images, etc. Moreover, it is also possible to share applications, the desktop, or a particular URL, etc. It also allows users to ask questions to the members in a session and to receive their answers, and to perform surveys and process their answers by displaying statistics. Another interesting option is to record a session to make it available later in our courses in the virtual campus (ADD), or by any other means (MP4 players, iPod, iPhone, etc.). Thus, tutoring sessions can be reused by other students who have the same kind of doubts.

The first experiences with Wimba Classroom for tutorships have shown that it is possible to perform a power online tutoring for all areas of knowledge and that this tools facilitates the establishment of a non-face-to-face tutoring timetable in virtual classrooms. Moreover, it also facilitates collaborative work as for example its "breakout rooms" can be used to divide students into virtual working groups in a classroom.

Another interesting application available on our virtual campus is Wimba Pronto. With this tool, online tutoring can be done by means of an instant messaging platform fully integrated with Blackboard 9.1. The administrative staff creates an account in this tool for each student and professor automacatically when they are admitted in our university, so that they can collaborate among themselves. Moreover, in this way, professors are not in charge of managing contacts (adding and removing their students). The next release of Wimba (Blackboard Collaborate) integrates this functionality with the virtual classroom of Blackboard 9.1 and it will be installed in a short period of time in our university.

In our institution, we have also already tested other instant messaging platforms, such as Microsoft Messenger, but it is difficult to integrate those tools with our virtual campus platforms, because each user has to manage all her/his contacts explicitly. In any case, whatever the tool used, students must be familiarized with the tutorships and tools available to perform them as soon as possible in the courses.

These tools -and in general tools that enable e-Learning tutoring- are considered to foster the involvement and the motivation of the students in the processes of teaching-learning. Moreover, they also promote to receive feedback, and they can be used as a vehicle for teaching-learning activities. Therefore, it is important to establish a set of the best practices for use them in this context.

4. Case study 2: Technological support to collaborative work management

In this section, we present our experiences with the use of the system Basic Support for Cooperative Work (BSCW) (*Web oficial de BSCW. [Available on: http://bscw.fit.fraunhofer.de/] [Last access: 27th July 2011]*, n.d.) for the management of collaborative work at the course "Herramientas Informáticas en Ciencias Experimentales". This is an optional course in the syllabus of the veterinary science degree at the University of Zaragoza. During the last years, the course has received one hundred students per year on average despite its optional choice nature for students. Due to this fact, around one thousand digital documents per course on average are generated as a consequence of the activities that students have to perform individually and cooperatively. This number of documents requires from academics a great effort in order to assess them and provide students with proper feedback. After generating the documents and receiving the feedback, students must do corrections and modify them accordingly to the notes provided by the academics. Thus, the document versioning control, as well as the cooperation with other students (document sharing) is a key aspect.

From our experience, we consider BSCW provides great benefits in the management of these activities, because of its functionality, its easiness of use, its efficiency, its robustness, and its fault tolerance capabilities. Thus, it supports document re-use, document versioning, document access control (with different roles of users such as academics and students and with different levels of sharing). Moreover, BSCW also supports the creation of discussion boards (essential for collaborative work), helps users organize materials and information (by means of repositories), fosters effective communication among users, promotes decision taking, etc. In summary, BSCW assists in the generation of documents in a collaborative way by integrating different functionalities within the same platform (Alejandre-Marco & Allueva-Pinilla, 2007; Alejandre-Marco et al., 2008).

In our case, the installation of the software required to implement this experience was done in Grupo3w server (`http://grupo3w.unizar.es/bscw/`) of the Innovation in Higher

Education group of our university in the course 2006-2007. The administration of such software has also been performed by the staff of that group so far.

4.1 The BSCW platform

The BSCW considered by our group can be used from a public server or installed on a private server under a free-pay license for educational purpose which supports until 1,000 users, and is available on http://bscw.fit.fraunhofer.de. BSCW is a useful tool to manage collaborative work as it is easy to use, efficient and stable and it supports the reuse of documents and their different versions and the establishment of different levels of access permissions for teachers and students to share documents. Besides, it supports the creation of forums and discussion spaces (essential for collaborative work), helps organize materials and information in repositories, enables effective communication means for their users, fosters decision-making, etc. In short, it allows us to integrate several tools under a platform in order to foster the creation of products in a collaborative way. The main features of this platform are:

- Access by means of login and password mechanisms.
- Different levels of access permissions.
- Discussion forums with chronological monitoring of interventions
- Facilities for searching on the Web and on the shared repositories in the tool.
- Conversion among different formats of documents.
- Management of versions of documents.
- Multilingual facilities to customize the interfaces.
- Event services within a robotic system.

Some of the major benefits due to the use of the BSCW platform are:

- Its use is simple, efficient and stable.
- It is an open source software which have been developed under free-pay license for educational purpose.
- It supports the reuse of materials, structures and contents.
- It manages different levels of access permissions to share documents.
- It supports to create forums and discussion spaces for debating.
- It supports to create repositories of materials.
- It supports easy management of people, groups and courses (with different roles)
- It helps to organize the material and information of a course.
- It supports the generation of specific products in collaborative way.
- It facilitates student assessment and evaluation process.
- It supports asynchronous tutoring processes.
- It provides their users with effective communication means.
- It helps foster decision-making.
- It integrates several tools under an unique platform.

A more detailed description of the features of the BSCW platform considered and the benefits that such tool provides us can be found in (*Foro sobre BSCW de RedIRIS. [Available on: http://www.rediris.es/list/info/bscw-es.html] [Last access: 27th July 2011]*, 2011; *OrbiTeam Software GmbH and Co. KG. [Available on: http://www.bscw.de/unternehmen.html] [Last access: 27th July 2011]*, n.d.; *Proyecto ITCOLE–Synergeia-BSCW. [Available on: http://bscl.fit.fraunhofer.de/] [Last access: 27th July 2011]*, n.d.).

4.2 The collaborative work

Collaborative activity developed by students in the course "Herramientas Informáticas en Ciencias Experimentales" was accomplished during the practical sessions even though the students also worked at home in order to develop a final project. In the first session, students organized themselves in working groups. This task was difficult for them because they had to schedule and coordinate different timetables. Besides, they had to register each student in the group in the BSCW platform which requires his/her e-mail address. On the other hand, the platform controls the different shared work spaces by organizing them as folders of a group in an specific course. The folders can contain documents, images, Web links, multimedia objects, discussions, calendars, searches, information about the members of the group, personal Web sites, ...

Practical face-to-face sessions last for two hours and they are distributed along the four months of the course (approximately one session per week). Previous to each practical session, professors provide students with material on the topic to be dealt with, a script for the collaborative work and software to be used by means of the BSCW platform. The collaborative projects defined by professors are about different issues and require different levels of depth.

Each working group must generate one or more documents depicting the work done during their session, being submitted at the end of this. The generated documents must be uploaded in the BSCW platform and can be consulted, discussed and reviewed after the session by the members of the group or the members of the rest of groups. The BSCW platform provides a exhaustive control of the different access and events. Later, these documents are assessed by the professors and sometimes by other groups selected randomly, due to the large amount of information generated.

The final products of each group are uploaded in another repository of the BSCW platform and a forum with different issues is created for each product to discuss about the work done. In addition, face-to-face sessions are scheduled in order to allow each group of students to make a presentation about the work done and share the knowledge and skills acquired during its realization. At this point, it is important to emphasize that along with the realization of the work, students can also have online and face-to-face tutoring sessions. Moreover, their work is evaluated weekly by professors or other working groups by means of BSCW platform (Alejandre-Marco & Allueva-Pinilla, 2007; Alejandre-Marco et al., 2008).

4.3 The methodology for the assessment of the students

Students enrolled in this course can choose between two options to be assessed: 1) evaluation based on a continuous assessment of their works in practical sessions and on the development of a final project; and 2) evaluation based on the mark of two traditional final exams at the end of the course (one exam is a hands on session with the computer and the other consists of a series of development questions). If the student chooses the continuous assessment, we consider four categories in our methodology:

- Evaluation of documents and multimedia material produced in the practice sessions of the course (30% of the final mark).
- Assessment based on other collaborative activities where the student participates in and based on the use of the BSCW platform: how he or she uses the tools for annotating materials, how many times he or she participates in the discussion forums, how many documents of other groups he or she evaluates, etc. (20% of final grade).
- Individual assessment based on the results of four tests about the topics dealt along the course (20% of final grade).
- Evaluation of collaborative working projects developed in his/her group(30% of final mark).

Estimating a final mark for each student that chooses the evaluation based on a continuous assessment is very hard due to the high number of students who often participate in the course and it would not have been possible if we had not had the tools provided by BSCW.

4.4 The document management

All the documents that students generate in all the activities are considered for the continuous assessment. Moreover, the text of the activities, hints, additional information and other documentation that students require for the activities are also considered and hosted in the BSCW platform. In this way, all the digital documents and information generated can be successfully managed by the professors of the course "Herramientas Informáticas en Ciencias Experimentales" of the Veterinary degree at the University of Zaragoza.

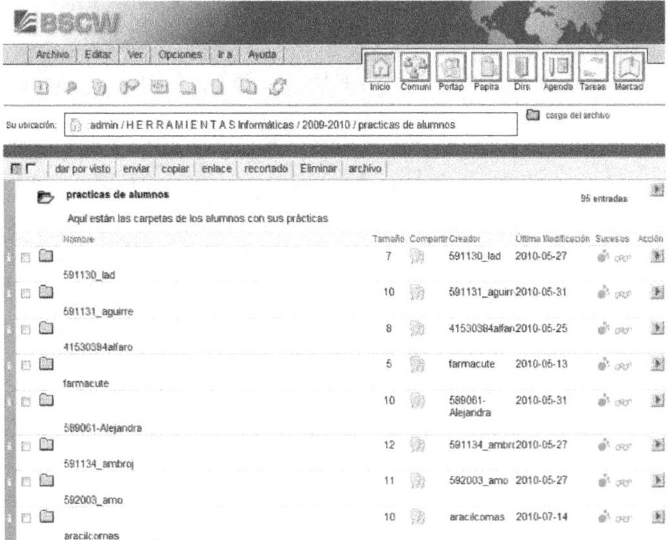

Fig. 2. Working Space

We have to take into account that the overall number of students participating in this course has exceeded 100 on average in the last editions of the course. Due to this fact the number of documents generated is around 1,000 documents per course. Without the support of this content management system, the task would have been really hard and probably impossible.

Fig. 3. Share Folder

Several screenshots where the structure of the course in the BSCW platform during the 2009-2010 course are shown bellow. In the figures, we can appreciate the great amount of material generated by students for their assessment. In Figure 2, we can observe how the folders for each student are organized in the 2009-2010 course (there were 95 students). Moreover, we can also see the size of each folder (number of documents that it contains), being the average value 10.

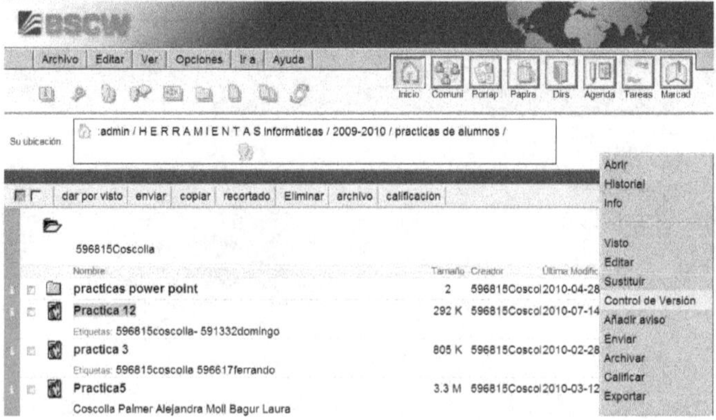

Fig. 4. Versioning Control

In Figure 3, we can observe the option that a user (a student) should use to share his or her folder with others students, forming in that way working groups.

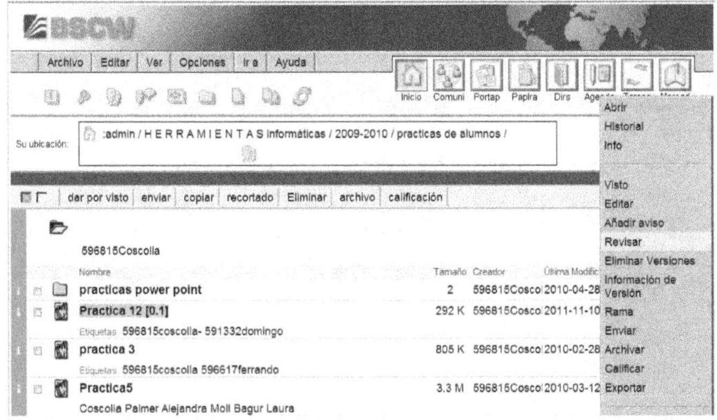

Fig. 5. Review version

The BSCW platform provides us with a complete document management tool which includes document versioning and logging of the different events associated to each document. It supports the monitoring and tracking of the students' evolutions in order to assess their work, and provide them with feedback. In Figures 4, 5 and 6, we can observe how different versions of a document can be generated as well as maintaining its previous versions.

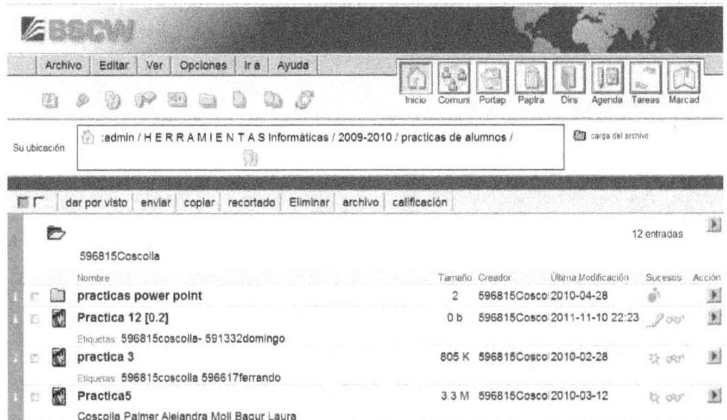

Fig. 6. New version

In Figure 7, we can observe a number of modifications performed to a specific element: which user created it, which users have modified it, cut it, marked it, copied it, etc.

In Figure 8, we can observe the information associated to an event of a specific element: which user read the document, when the document was read (time and date), etc.

5. Case study 3: Assessment of laboratory lessons at programming courses at the Computer Science Department

The Department of Computer Science and Systems Engineering of the University of Zaragoza has currently 220 faculty members, teaching at different engineering degrees as well as in the computer science degree. Around 800 students are taking undergraduate and postgraduate

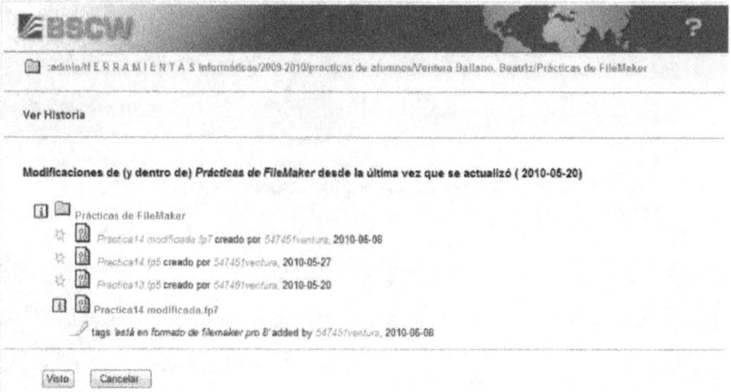

Fig. 7. Log of updations

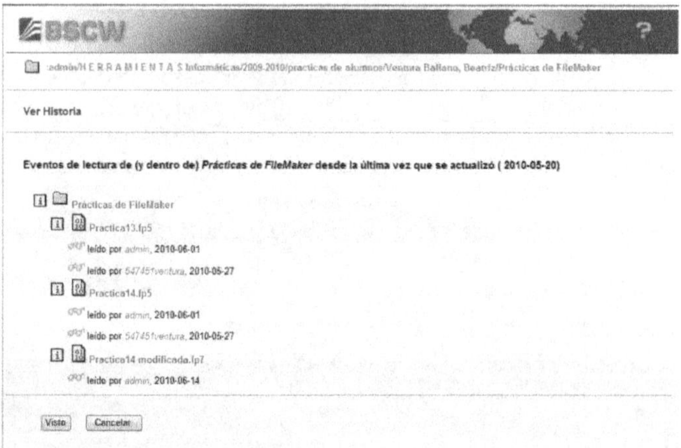

Fig. 8. Log of different events

degree courses taught by this department. Most of these courses comprise practical laboratory sessions where activities related to programming are accomplished.

In general terms, the process cycle for any programming activity can be characterised by the following steps as depicted in Figure 9. In the process, a professor elaborates a programming activity, writes its specification, and disseminates it to the students. Then, the students have to follow the instructions, and as a result implement a computational program: they require a computational environment, which typically consists in an editor, and a compiler. Once, the program required is finished, they have to submit it, this often involves the submission of a set of files. Then, the professor can assess it, this step can be sometimes automated, though this may not be always possible (it will depend on the nature of the activity). Finally, the professor notifies the assessment, and an optional feedback.

A decade ago, the computational environment where the programming laboratory lessons were undertaken was an HP-UX machine with 4 processors and a Solaris operating system –a UNIX based and multi-user environment. Under these circumstances, most of the courses utilized the HP-UX machine itself not only for the development of the lessons, but also

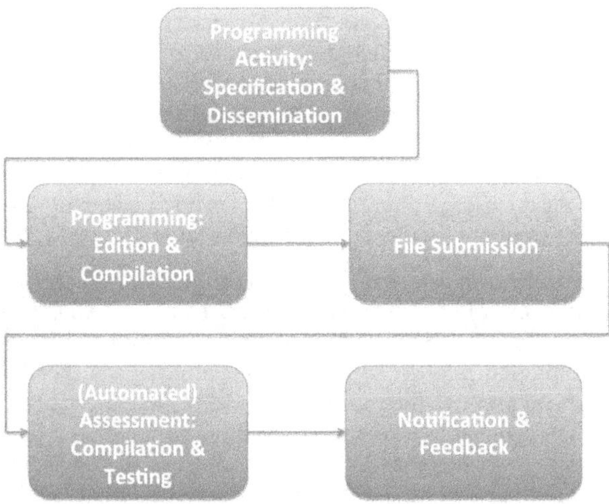

Fig. 9. Process Cycle of a programming activity

Technological Solutions Comparison		
Feature	UNIX-based	LCMS-based
Activity Dissemination	✗	✓
Built-in Edition & Compilation Environment	✓	✗
File Management & Submission	✓	✓
Automated Compilation at the assessment stage	✓	✗
Automated Built-in Assessment & Testing	✓	✗
Assessment Notification	✓	✓
Scalability	✗	✓

Table 1. Comparison between the UNIX-based solution and the LCMS-based solution for the practical lessons in programming courses

for the whole activity process: dissemination, submissions of source files, assessments, and notification. For such a purpose, the technical staff at the Department developed specific UNIX-based scripts for the HP-UX machine that automated some of the steps in the process: the submission of files, the assessment, and the notification. The scripts related to the submission of files were made available to students, and they used them to upload their files. The scripts copied the files in the course disk account in the UNIX machine, and changes their ownership, so that once submitted, the students could only observe their own submissions at the directory (read-only mode), but the academics owned the file and had read and write permissions on it.

Once a submission was done, professors could use other scripts in order to automate as much as possible the assessments: file management, automated compilation, and automated testing when possible. Additionally, by using the operating system mailing service, the assessments were also sent to the students. As a result, there was a set of independent scripts which in co-operation help manage the laboratory activities. With the introduction of new machines, and new operating systems, the ad-hoc traditional solution had limited exportation, and due to its dependence to the operating system, the integration of new functionality, a feature that we can refer to as scalability, for instance, in order to improve communication, is also dependent on the operating system, or to further software development that is not often administratively affordable. Furthermore, the design of the scripts also offered a number of limitations. For example, a submission by a student could only be accomplished once, and in case of mistaken submission, an academic with permissions had to delete the previously submitted file, prior to any other re-submission. This is not a frequent situation for last-year students, but it is rather frequent, however, when first-year students do it.

A more modern approach to tackle this problem is the use of an integrated environment of a LCMS such as the one offered by Blackboard 9.1 at the ADD. The main advantage of such an approach is that LCMS typically integrates a number of other tools, and this characteristic can be exploited in order to improve eventual needs. For instance, in case the development of a practical requires the resolution of many challenges by students, any of the communication tools available at Blackboard could be used for such a purpose. Besides, the Web interface of the system makes it accessible from most of the environments: Blackboard is not constrained to specific operating systems or machines is not needed, a charactersitic which benefits subjects such as introduction to programming in industrial engineering degree where UNIX is not introduced and Windows is the Operating System used. The listing of students is also integrated into the course account in Blackboard, but most importantly, it can be configured in such a way that multiple submissions of a practical exercise are allowed and even the system tracks all of them. Blackboard also integrates the submissions with the qualification centre, so that once an exercise is assessed, then it can be notified to each student in isolation via the Blackboard systems itself.

Table 1 shows all the features described, comparing both technical solutions. The LCMS-based solution does not offer a built-in environment for edition and compilation of source files, and this is something that must be done in the traditional way. Additionally, the assessment may require from professors to download the source files and put them into the computational environment, so that the compilation and testing can be accomplished by professors. In spite of this, however, the usage of a LCMS-based solution has as an advantage that makes it a better solution than the traditional one, which is scalability. Indeed, the usage of LCMS for this activity allows professors to exploit the whole variety of tools that LCMS integrate seamlessly, and that can be utilised in order to improve learning processes –i.e by promoting communication skills, fostering students' participation, etc.

6. Conclusions & future work

In this chapter, we briefly describe the recent eLearning evolution of the University of Zaragoza, and we chose three case studies that highlight how eLearning technologies can help improve learning processes. The first case study describes how to exploit technology for developing on-line tutoring. We propose the use of graphic tablets in order to overcome the challenges that often arises when accomplishing on-line tutorship. For instance, the writing of mathematical formulae in the content of messages in an agile way. In addition to audio and video tools, Wimba Classroom also allows users to use whiteboards to share information. It also allows users to ask questions to the members in a session and to receive their answers, and to perform surveys and process their answers by displaying statistics. Another interesting option is to record sessions and make them subsequently available to the rest of the students. Thus, tutoring sessions can be reused by other students who have the same kind of doubts.

The second case study shows how the BSCW system can be exploited in order to manage collaborative work of a course with a hundred of students in an efficient way. From our experience, we consider BSCW provides great benefits in the management of these activities, because of its functionality, its easiness of use, its efficiency, its robustness, and its fault tolerance capabilities. Thus, it supports document re-use, document versioning, document access control (with different roles of users such as academics and students and with different levels of sharing). Moreover, BSCW also supports the creation of discussion boards (essential for collaborative work), helps users organize materials and information (by means of repositories), fosters effective communication among users, and promotes decision taking.

The third case study describes the experience at activities of programming of computers in practical laboratory courses. Initially, the programming activities were manages by using a set of ad-hoc scripting tools. We emphasize how the use of LCMS such as Blackboard has some disadvantages compared to the traditional ad-hoc approach, since it is not an ad-hoc solution. In contrast, it can exploit all the possibilities of an LCMS, such as the integration of many tools that can help promote learning processes in a better way. In particular, the communication skills during the learning process can be improved better with an LCMS rather than with an ad-hoc solution.

As a future work, it would be interesting to distinguish different roles for professors in an online course. This is technically possible when considering the way in which the platforms that we currently have in our university are configured, with different possible roles for a professor: the designer of the course, the designer of materials, the assistants, the tutors, etc. However, this design is not the usual one in the courses currently implemented in the platforms available in our university, which essentially offer an additional support for face-to-face teaching-learning process. Along the same line, different roles would be considered for a tutor: the academic one, the pedagogical and the personal. Each of these roles would be supported by appropriate ICT tools. There is still much work to do in the area of online academic tutoring, but we think that this is one of the strongest points in this education model, since a good utilization of tutoring for face-to-face students has been proved to be effective for increasing the results of the students.

Besides, if we analyze the strengths of tutoring in the framework of the European Higher Education Space, we find many advantages. For example, we can highlight that it facilitates the competency of the acquisition of a professional language. Regarding the weaknesses, we observe the need and the demand of training for teachers, especially in this case concerning ICT tools that facilitate an online tutoring (e.g., the aforementioned instant messaging applications) and that facilitate providing feedback to the student.

We would also like to emphasize the high workload usually derived from the monitoring and personalized attention in online tutoring models for courses with a large number of students. In our university, there are many courses with more than one hundred students. In the simplest cases where the students basically communicate through email, the number of emails could grow beyond what can be managed if this is not appropriately coordinated with other communication tools such as forums, chat rooms for students, virtual classrooms, etc. Therefore, we insist on the need of training, which should focus on both the tools and the management of online courses, time management, etc.

Finally, our research is focused on comparing these experiences with other technological platforms, so that we can analyze the outcomes of using one or another. In the case of the collaborative work, we also want to test alternative platforms to BSCW such as the new version of platform Blackboard (Blackboard 9.1).

7. References

Alejandre-Marco, J.L. & Allueva-Pinilla, A.I. (2007). Desarrollo de una asignatura en un espacio colaborativo en Red, *1st. International Congress "Innov@ting together". Using New Technologies in educative innovation. Parque Tecnológico Walqa, Huesca, Spain. [Available on http://mediateca.fundacion.telefonica.com/visor.asp?e1293-a6923].*

Alejandre-Marco, J.L., Allueva-Pinilla, A.I. & González-Santos, J.M. (2008). Implementación de un diseño activo y colaborativo de la asignatura Herramientas Informáticas en Ciencias Experimentales mediante la plataforma BSCW, *II Jornadas de Innovación Docente, Tecnologías de la Información y la Comunicación e Investigación Educativa en la Universidad de Zaragoza, Zaragoza, España. [Available on http://ice.unizar.es/uzinnova/jornadas/pdf/101.pdf].*

Dougiamas, M. & Taylor, P. (2003). Moodle: Using learning communities to create an open source course management system, *Proceedings of World Conference on Educational Multimedia, Hypermedia and Telecommunications*, pp. 171–178.

Foro sobre BSCW de RedIRIS. [Available on: http://www.rediris.es/list/info/bscw-es.html] [Last access: 27th July 2011] (2011).

García-Peñalvo, F. J. (2008). Advances in e-learning: Experiences and methodologies, *Technical report*, Hershey, PA, USA: Information Science Reference (formerly Idea Group Reference).

http://add.unizar.es Anillo Digital Docente, Universidad de Zaragoza (n.d.). [Last access 29th August 2011.

http://www.blackboard.com/Platforms/Learn/Overview.aspx BlackBoard e-Learning Platform (n.d.). [Last access: 29th August 2011].

Laviña-Orueta, J. & Mengual-Pavón, L. (dirección y coordinación), (2008). El libro blanco de la universidad digital 2010, *Technical report*, Colección Fundación Telefónica. Editorial Ariel.

OrbiTeam Software GmbH and Co. KG. [Available on: http://www.bscw.de/unternehmen.html] [Last access: 27th July 2011] (n.d.).

Perry, L. (1995). Continuing professional education: luxury or necessity?, *Journal of Advance Nursing 21* pp. 766–771.

Proyecto ITCOLE–Synergeia-BSCW. [Available on: http://bscl.fit.fraunhofer.de/] [Last access: 27th July 2011] (n.d.).

Seoane-Pardo, A. M., García-Carrasco, J. & García-Peñalvo, F. J. G. (2007). La tutoría online como elemento estratégico para una e-formación de calidad, *Teoría de la Educación: Educación y Cultura en la Sociedad de la Información, ISSN 1138-9737. (Ejemplar dedicado a: Tutoría virtual y e-moderación en red)* 8(2): 5–8.

Weber, S. & Rech, J. (2010). *Handbook of Research on Web 2.0, 3.0, and X.0: Technologies, Business, and Social Applications. Editor: San Murugesan*, Vol. ISBN 9781605663845, IGI Global, chapter An Overview and Differentiation of the Evolutionary Steps of the Web X.Y Movement: The Web Before and Beyond 2.0, pp. 12–39.

Web oficial de BSCW. [Available on: http://bscw.fit.fraunhofer.de/] [Last access: 27th July 2011] (n.d.).

Wolfe, C. R. (2001). Learning and teaching on the world wide web, *Technical Report ISBN:0127618910*, Academic Press, In. Orlando.

8

ICTs and Their Applications in Education

Guadalupe Martínez, Ángel Luis Pérez, Mª Isabel Suero and Pedro J. Pardo
University of Extremadura
Spain

1. Introduction

The continuous changes that are occurring in society today because of advances in science and technology require new models and social patterns to be developed and implemented in many fields, a prominent one of which is that of education (Barberá et al., 2008; Coll, 2004; Garrison & Anderson, 2003). We are living in what is often called the Information Age, and which has been evolving into the so-called Knowledge Society. According to Crook (Crook, 1996), education needs to be re-thought in depth to adapt to this new kind of society characterized by knowledge, information, and communication. Indeed, these innovations are already bringing about the birth of a new type of education supported by the widespread diffusion of Information and Communication Technologies (ICTs).

There has been growing research interest in studying the impact of ICTs on educational processes, in parallel with the growing adoption of these technologies at all levels of teaching and learning (Coll et al., 2008). Some authors (Bajarlía & Spiegel, 1997) have noted that students maintain a constant relationship with the technologies that they have grown up with, which allows one to observe the progress of their learning using interactive media, monitoring how, and how much, they learn. In this sense, ICTs in education are seen from two perspectives: learning with them and learning from them (Finol de Govea, 2007). Some authors (Järvelä & Häkkinen, 2002; Kennewell & Beauchamps, 2003; Squires & McDougall, 1994; Tondeur et al., 2007; Twining, 2002) have studied empirically the way in which teachers and students use ICTs in the actual development of the practical work they do in class. This influence of ICTs on education has been investigated by many other authors (Balanskat et al., 2007; Cabero et al., 2003; Cattagni & Farris, 2001; Cebrián, et al., 2007), and indeed is the subject of the work to be described in this chapter which deals with the particular processes of teaching and learning in either purely virtual environments or in presential environments that include new educational materials using ICTs. Some research (Chi et al., 2001; Lehtinen et al., 1999) has focused on such aspects as the teacher's role, the learning undertaken by students in these new environments, or how knowledge is actually constructed using these new virtual tools (Arvaja et al., 2007). Other authors (Beller, 1998) have discussed the importance of integrating ICTs into teaching and learning to make the process more effective. This has led to the emergence of e-learning as an important innovative platform for teaching.

Some research (Yazón et al., 2002) indicates that the use of technology promotes a different way of thinking about teaching and learning provided that it is genuinely student-centred learning, and not treated just as a simple reprise of the "old model" (directed by the teacher) in a new technological environment (Harris, 1999). Others (Coll et al., 2007) note that some authors (Blease & Cohen, 1990; Squires & McDougall, 1994; Twining, 2002) propose directing effort to studying how ICTs are transforming teaching practices.

In recent years, one of the major lines of research has been on how ICTs can be integrated into the teaching and learning process. There have been various studies considering a variety of forms of integration. For some authors (M. Grabe & C. Grabe, 1996), ICT integration should be undertaken as an extension of the traditional teaching process, not as a complete replacement. For others authors (Merrill et al., 1996), for the result to be an enhancement of learning, integration will have to imply a combination of ICTs with traditional teaching procedures, a combination known as "blended learning" or b-learning, designed to move the student to a new level of understanding. According to Gros (Gros, 2000), one form of successfully integrating technology into the curricula is to regularly use ICTs for information, experimenting, simulating, or communicating. This author therefore goes beyond the mere instrumental use of the tool to focus on the content that the students will be taught (Gros, 2000). Other authors have shown the importance of ICTs after assessing the educational possibilities they represent in an objectives-based framework (Reparaz et al., 2000), and accept the need for a change in the roles of both teacher and student (Adell, 1997; Bartolomé, 1996; Cebrián, 1997; Poves, 1997; Reparaz et al., 2000; Roca, 2001; Sánchez, 2000, 2001). While some point out that it is the curriculum which guides the use of ICTs, and not the other way round (Dockstader, 1999), others argue that they should be introduced so as to provoke educational innovation (Dede, 1998; Gros, 2000). For example, both teachers and students are found to be eager to appropriate ICTs into their teaching and learning activities (Area, 2005; Cuban, 2001; Zhao et al., 2002; Zhao & Frank, 2003), facilitating the implementation of innovations.

The use of ICTs allows one to count on a new way to organize, represent, or simulate reality, being effective tools to help achieve a high degree of application of the knowledge acquired in class. Since they allow students to work in collaboration, to use virtual laboratories, display laboratory experiments over the Internet or on their mobiles, they are an excellent resource for learning both concepts and procedures. Indeed, these features make ICTs an especially useful tool for science teaching in general, and physics in particular. For these reasons, the integration of ICTs into science education is emerging as an essential element of the so-called knowledge society. There also stands out the optimal conditions such integration would present for constructivist learning. In recent years, many researchers have explored the role technology can play in constructivist learning, demonstrating that computers provide an appropriate environment for students to express themselves and show that they have acquired new knowledge. From this perspective, technological factors can serve as teaching tools to foster the construction of knowledge (Vélez, 2002).

For Coll (Coll et al., 2007), ICTs reveal their greatest mediating capacity as "psychological instruments" when they are actually used as "cognitive instruments" (Lajoie et al., 1998; Lajoie, 2000; Lajoie & Azevedo, 2006; Salomón et al., 1991) or "tools of the mind" (Jonassen, 1996, 2000), i.e., when they are used so that the student has to establish meaningful connections with the content being studied. However, ICTs are not cognitive tools in themselves. Rather, they are technological tools which, due to the properties of the environments that they make it possible to create, can be used to organize and structure the processes involved in teaching and learning.

In this vein, we believe that ICTs are currently stimulating the emergence of new approaches to the organization of education in the European Higher Education Area

(EHEA) from the standpoints of both research and teaching. For example, one of the most significant current initiatives being developed in almost all areas of study is that of virtual learning platforms or e-learning. To properly implement the teaching process in these new learning environments, one must have appropriate educational materials available that can serve as the fundamental support for the new methods of teaching and learning. These materials themselves can be developed and shared through ICTs.

The work to be presented is centred on the subject of Optoelectronics, a subject that we teach in the second cycle of the degree in Electronics Engineering at the School of Industrial Engineering of the University of Extremadura (Spain). The overall objective was to create educational tools for university education in optoelectronics designed for application on e-learning platforms. Within this overall objective, our aim was to design, prepare, validate, and apply teaching materials from a conceptual, experimental, and didactic perspective.

Figure 1 is a concept map that summarizes the core of this work: the use of ICTs to design and create teaching tools that can be implemented together in the form of a virtual laboratory. With the design and development of such virtual laboratories, students have a system available with which to carry out a study analogous to what could be done with a real system. This has allowed university laboratories to go beyond the physical limits imposed by the traditional means available to them in teaching certain subjects (Aktan et al., 1996; Calvo et al., 2009; Candelas et al., 2004; Domínguez et al., 2005; Dormido, 2004; Guzmán et al., 2005; Laschi & Riccioni, 2008; Riccioni 2010; Salzmann et al., 2000; Yanitelli, 2011).

Specifically, as shown in Figure 1, in the present work:

- We have designed, developed, and validated techniques for structuring information, using for this purpose Concept Maps and the CmapTools software tool to construct, store, and share them. We include learning materials to facilitate the students' learning of the technique of constructing these maps.
- We have studied the latest developments in the field of information communication, such as optical communications, fibre optics, and other optoelectronic devices.
- We have designed, developed, and validated content that can be shared through ICTs. We include learning materials to facilitate the students' construction of new content of this type. This content is as diverse as concept maps, computer simulations (which have evolved from analogue to digital and hyper-realistic), videos of laboratory practicals, multimedia video-tutorials, Web pages, explanations using presentation software, etc.

The originality of our work is that it combines the "hard" science part (such as the study of optical fibres or of the software with which to perform hyper-realistic simulations) with techniques of structuring and organizing information (a part which is more typical of other disciplines closer to the social sciences). The methodology employed in this work is based on the Theory of Meaningful Learning (Ausubel, 1968, 2002) and the Elaboration Theory of Instruction (Reigeluth, 1983) with the modifications put forward by our research group (Pérez et al., 1999, 2004). These theories have guided us in how we design, elaborate, and put into practice a learning process characterized by the use of the new technologies. In section 2 we make our proposal on the theoretical framework used to develop new educational materials that employ ICTs. Subsequently, in Sections 3, 4 and 5 we use this proposal on the development of simulations, instructional videos and concept maps. Finally, in the concluding section we show the results of the application in the classroom of these new educational materials developed, and provide a summary of future work.

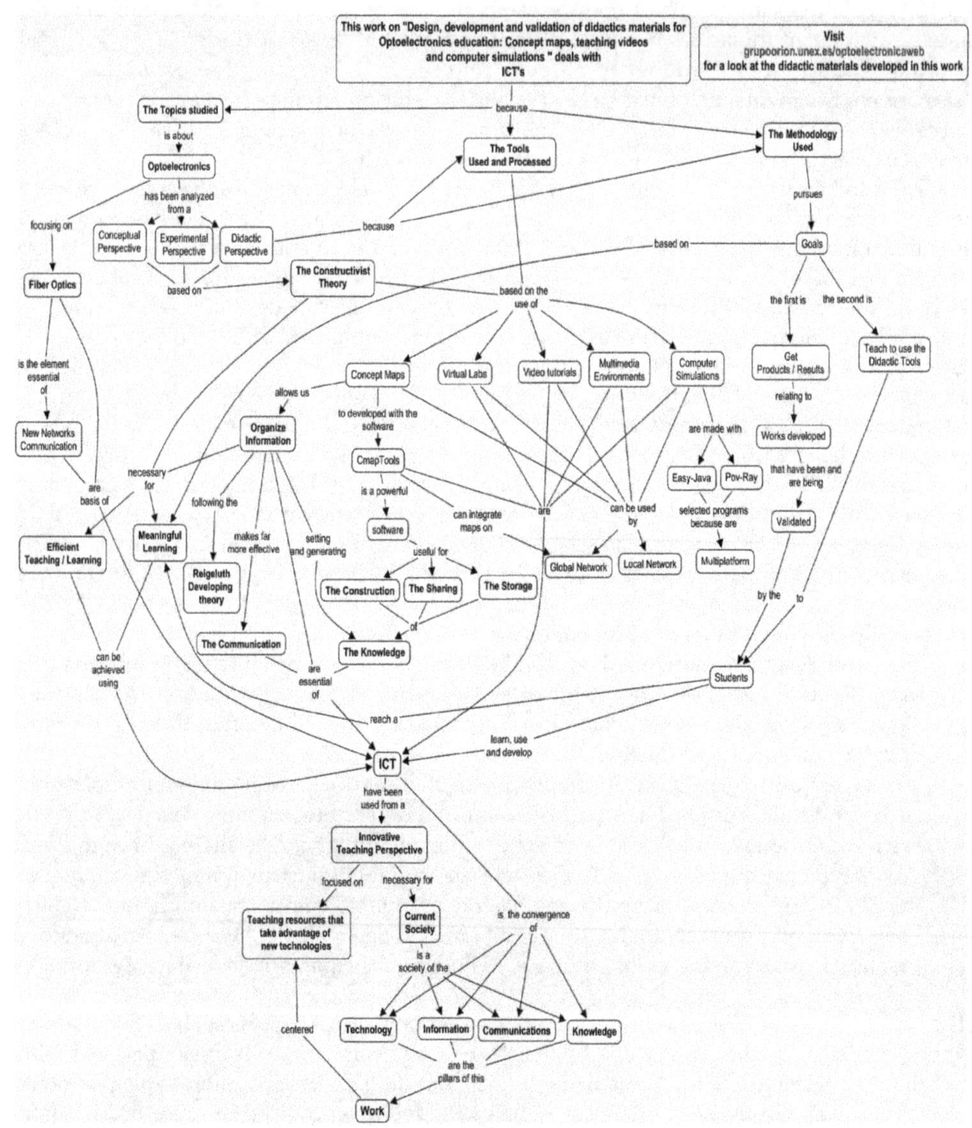

Fig. 1. Concept map showing the focus of our research.

2. ICTs: Use in the elaboration of teaching materials for science education

The teaching materials our research group has elaborated are developed and implemented through ICTs. Theoretically, they are founded on constructivist theories of learning. Each of the educational activities carried out with these materials has specific cognitive demands. Therefore, the learning environment used, such as virtual learning platforms, must provide the students with the appropriate educational tools for these cognitive demands. The cognitive tools that are included in these e-learning or b-learning environments are ICT instruments, aimed at facilitating our students' acquisition of knowledge. Examples are materials used to display, represent, and organize content, fostering the effective transfer of knowledge between teacher and student and among the students themselves.

We have developed various types of educational tools. Some are used to better represent the hierarchy of the content, or the problem or experiment being dealt with in class (e.g., concept maps). A second group help to change the student's mindset by presenting a given physical phenomenon in different situations (for example, as traditional computer simulations and as hyper-realistic simulations). Others (e.g., virtual laboratories, explanatory instructional videos, video-tutorials, etc.) can help bring together in one place the information needed to solve a problem, do some given laboratory practical, or study a particular subject. According to Jonassen (as cited in Reigeluth, 1983), educational tools should be appropriate to the student's learning process, and have to be carefully selected to support the type of procedure needed for each cognitive task.

In teaching science (and physics in particular) as also in other disciplines, ICTs are commonly used to search for and communicate information, or to prepare teaching materials. Beyond this common usage, however, other resources offered by ICTs have proved helpful for science education. For example, Sims (Sims, 2000) notes that interactivity in e-learning is already accepted as implying a certain level of effectiveness and a guarantee of learning. Indeed, this assertion has been basic for us at the time of designing and implementing our computer simulations.

The use of ICTs in a cognitive-constructivist approach to education is the key to a more active, contextualized, authentic, and constructive learning process (Finol de Govea, 2007). Their use in simulating reality can facilitate meaningful learning by bringing the student and the real world closer together.

We consider that it is necessary in the teaching process to transform information into knowledge, e.g., through concept maps. This process requires the content to be selected, structured, and organized, which can be accomplished through virtual learning environments and the use of Internet (Linn, 2002).

Computers today play an important role in acquiring and applying scientific knowledge, thus facilitating science learning. Specifically, to speak of ICTs in teaching or learning demands that particular emphasis be placed on the means and resources needed for the activities, content, and educational objectives of any given topic. It is essential to consider carefully the type of materials that we shall use in our teaching practice to ensure its suitability for the transmission of the information contained in the topic, and its capacity to stimulate the students' mental activity and to connect to their cognitive characteristics.

Thus, in an essentially practical science subject such as optoelectronics, we consider that experimental work is an integral part of its character, so that one needs to implement educational materials that can meet these procedural objectives. For that, we have developed virtual laboratories and instructional videos of laboratory practicals which have provided students and teachers with new teaching models with which they can carry out laboratory experiments in virtual environments. From the perspective of teaching a scientific discipline, we therefore consider it necessary to design and elaborate learning situations in which laboratory practicals receive a specific treatment, and in which ICTs can make a significant contribution to the education of students in that area.

The goal pursued in the present research was to incorporate some of these learning tools into our teaching programs from a pedagogical perspective, and to validate their effectiveness after using them with our students.

Specifically, we propose a teaching model which is in accordance with the theories of cognitive learning. In particular, the teaching methodology of these theories has guided how we design, elaborate, and put into practice a learning process characterized by the use of the new technologies. Each of the teaching material proposals developed in this research will be described individually in the different sections of this chapter.

3. Computer simulations: ICT tools to facilitate meaningful learning

ICTs provide teaching tools that are found to be very effective in the learning process based on virtual platforms. In e-learning, virtual laboratories are particularly useful because of the aid they can provide students when they are carrying out practical activities. According to the UNESCO, a virtual laboratory is defined as a workspace for remote collaboration and experimentation aimed at doing research or similar activities, and at reporting and disseminating the results by means of ICTs (UNESCO, 2000). Some authors (Psillos & Niedderer, 2002) indicate that, by coordinating experimentation activities with simulation, the latter can serve as a cognitive bridge between theory and practice. For others (Marqués, 2000), virtual laboratories are virtual learning environments that take advantage of the capabilities offered by ICTs to create a teaching environment that is free from the constraints of time and space in presential education, capable of ensuring ongoing virtual communication between students and teachers.

Virtual laboratories are based on the simulation of real phenomena. They provide learning environments in which students can construct their own meaningful knowledge that is transferable to other phenomena having the same underlying physical principle. In this sense, simulation is a powerful computer tool of widespread use in all sectors of society, and its definition will naturally depend on the field in which it is applied. In our case, we are interested in the field of education, in which such simulation can be defined as a computer program that reproduces a real phenomenon, but in a simplified form designed to provide specific learning situations (Alessi & Trollip, 1991). Computer simulations that allow interaction on the part of the student can constitute effective virtual laboratories in their process of learning. This is principally because the students can study the actual system and investigate its behaviour in response to changes in some of its parameters by making measurements, etc. In this way, students will not be using the simulation mechanically, but will be immersed in a process oriented to producing meaningful learning through the use of virtual laboratories.

In physics teaching specifically, many authors have highlighted the nature of computer simulations as cognitive tools (Bryan & Slough, 2009; Chang et al., 2008; Finkelstein et al., 2005; Landau, 2006; Naps et al., 2003; Ronen & Eliahu, 2000; Trumper, 2003; Zacharia & Anderson, 2003), since their use is highly beneficial for conceptual development and change, and for understanding many physical phenomena in various areas of study, for example, in mechanics (Gorsky & Finegold, 1992; Tao & Gunstone, 1999), optics (Eylon et al., 1996; Goldberg, 1997; Tao, 2004), or across the curriculum in general (Zacharia & Anderson, 2003).

However, the integration of simulations into the curriculum requires their effectiveness to be evaluated. Specifically, over the course of the last two decades the positive impact of computer simulations has been documented in different stages of the teaching and learning process. Some authors (Snir et al., 1995) affirm that, with computer simulations, the learning process is far more efficient and applicable to problems or situations of the real world. Other studies have shown their benefits for cognitive development, skills, conceptual understanding, etc. (Goldberg & Bendall, 1995; Goodyear et al., 1991; Gorsky & Finegold, 1992; Hewson, 1985; Kaput, 1995; Shin et al., 2003; Tao & Gunstone, 1999; Zacharia & Anderson, 2003). Many of these workers have shown that groups of students who have worked with computer simulations learn more successfully (Baily & Finkelstein, 2009; Finkelstein et al., 2005; Zacharia & Anderson, 2003), although other authors argue that the benefits of learning through simulations are ambiguous (Steinberg, 2000), or that the practices carried out in virtual environments are useful as an educational complement, but cannot replace the real laboratory (Aleksandrov & Nancheva, 2007).

The potential educational value of computer simulations in virtual laboratories lies in their ability to reproduce phenomena with varying degrees of complexity, so that they can be adapted to the students' cognitive level, or to attaining some given educational objective. The ability to interact with the software allows students to modify the conditions of the processes involved, and to analyze the changes they observe. This makes simulation an extremely useful tool in experimental work. Indeed, its possibilities of application seem limitless.

Our research group has a long experience in the development and use of computer simulations, from analogue simulations of more than 25 years ago before the boom in personal computers (Calvo & Pérez, 1983; Pérez et al., 1979a, 1979b; Pérez & Calvo, 1984), to the digital simulations we are working on now. Despite the repeatedly proven teaching effectiveness of simulations, one of the challenges we constantly have to face in developing a simulation is how to adequately reproduce the phenomenon in question. For example, experiments in virtual spaces offer a new approach to presenting the abstract concepts of a real phenomenon. We have often observed that, in the more applied areas of science, some students have serious difficulties in reliably identifying what they observe in the simulated model with reality. In the more theoretical areas, however, it suffices to present purely abstract constructions such as those provided by traditional computer simulations, while in applied areas it is important to include not only the properties characteristic of the basic phenomenon, but also a certain degree of reality in the experiment.

This conflict between the abstract or idealized and the concrete or real has been analyzed by some authors. Goldstone & Son (2005) discusses the trade-off between the advantages of concrete simulations and the benefits of simulations with more idealized models. For Difanzo et al. (1998), a high level of detail by means of realistic representations of objects within the simulation can benefit students in their study of a particular phenomenon by increasing the similarity between the simulation and the real world. Indeed, most research on virtual reality has had the specific purpose of the realistic imitation of real-world phenomena (Grady, 1998). Other authors have argued, however, that relatively simplified and idealized representations are useful for distilling a situation to its essence (Goldstone & Sakamoto, 2003).

Thus, some authors stress the importance of the simplification of reality involved in simulations, of omitting or changing details, since they find the advantage to lie in focusing the students' attention on the development of certain skills (Alessi & Trollit, 1991; M. Grabe & C. Grabe, 1996). But others, taking a constructivist perspective, value the students' opportunity to perform complex tasks in scenarios that simulate real life (García & Gil, 2006; Lajoie & Azevedo, 2006). In this latter case, the simulations reflect the complexity of the real phenomena, allowing the students to develop cognitive skills and re-structure their mental models when they compare the behaviour of the models with reality.

Schematic simulation, for example, is a dynamic, simplified representation of the behaviour of a system. It allows students to manipulate data and examine the consequences, avoiding the confusion and insecurity that would be involved in a complex environment. It can enrich the constructivist approach to learning by enabling students to anchor their cognitive understanding in what they observed through their actions in a given situation (Harper et al., 2000).

While some authors have argued for the benefits of idealization as against the concrete for the acquisition of underlying abstract physical principles, the main objective of our simulations is to fill the gap the student has in realistic situations when faced with observing a real phenomenon after having studied it in a schematic simulation. In this regard, we must distinguish between simulations which "simulate the result", and those which "simulate the experience". Thus, schematic simulations in Java are useful to simulate results. For example, if we remove all the details, and focus schematically on the underlying foundation of the physical phenomenon, one can effectively transfer abstract phenomenon to other scientific fields (Goldstone & Son, 2005). In this regard, we consider that it would be very effective for our students' learning if they could also "simulate the performance of the experience", i.e., if we added to the simulation of the system a realistic visual output of the phenomenon being simulated. In the particular field of our area of education, Optics, the objective of our simulations is to "simulate the experience" - to show students what the abstract phenomenon simulated schematically in Java looks like in reality, creating a hyper-realistic simulation of the phenomenon in its entirety, i.e., the simulated experience.

In our research, we have focused on the development of a virtual environment with computer simulations that have a greater degree of reality than traditional ones. To implement these simulations, we used computer tools designed specifically for scientific environments, and which are freely available and aimed at users who are not programming specialists. Among these tools, we would highlight EJS and POV-Ray, both of free distribution. A common feature of these two environments is that they allow the user to concentrate efforts on the model of the system being studied, and greatly facilitate the entire process of creating the graphical interface and its connection with the model. This is a great advantage in preparing simulations, since one can focus on modeling the phenomenon or system without getting lost in programming the code. With our students, we use EJS which produces Java applets that are easily distributed, and POV-Ray which allows us to complement the Java applets by endowing them with hyper-realism. The result is a virtual learning environment that requires the active involvement of the student, and thus ensures deeper learning.

To summarize the above, interactive simulations facilitate deeper learning of concepts, since it is the students themselves who observe the physical phenomenon and can interact with the model to create mental structures from which to construct their own conceptual models of the phenomenon.

The computer simulations we have implemented form part of a virtual teaching approach using e-learning platforms. Specifically, we use the AVUEX virtual campus of our university with the Moodle platform. These platforms strengthen group work in the form of collaboration between teacher and students and among the students themselves, fostering a constructivist learning environment. Examples of these simulations can be found on our group's website: http://grupoorion.unex.es.

4. Instructional videos: ICT tools to facilitate meaningful learning

The introduction of new virtual platforms with innovative teaching resources into the teaching of experimental sciences is one of the most interesting approaches to teaching today. There are already a great many resources in the fields of engineering education which are related to virtual or remote laboratories (Aktan et al., 1996; Calvo et al., 2009; Candelas et al., 2004; Domínguez et al., 2005; Dormido, 2004; Guzmán et al., 2005; Laschi & Riccioni, 2008; Riccioni 2010; Salzmann et al., 2000; Yanitelli, 2011).

One concern among teachers of all educational levels, including the university level, is to improve education from both a conceptual and a practical point of view. In this line, one of the objectives of the present work has been to organize and elaborate teaching materials designed for both theoretical classes and laboratory practicals, which will motivate the students and promote meaningful learning.

Today, there is increased use of ICTs in teaching scientific and technical subjects, due to the large amount of educational resources that can be elaborated from them. Among these teaching resources, we have noted above the great interest in the use of virtual laboratories, especially in scientific fields such as engineering. Laboratory practicals are a vital educational resource in teaching experimental and technical disciplines, allowing the student to check the degree of assimilation of the theoretical content. However, practical classes sometimes involve a degree of difficulty for students in terms of understanding the experiment. These difficulties may refer either to the physical foundations of the specific laboratory practical involved, or to the functioning of the instruments used.

This work proposed the introduction of ICTs to improve not only the theoretical classes with concept maps or computer simulations, but also laboratory practicals through the design of audiovisual teaching materials dealing with the physical fundamentals and the development of the experiments. Particularly worthy of note among the various means of supporting practical teaching in the laboratory is the use of instructional videos. One can present in them the most interesting and significant aspects of the laboratory practice, adding animations and a multitude of multimedia resources to them to facilitate the teacher's work.

Specifically, we have developed audiovisual materials to support practical work on the subject of Optoelectronics. The virtual laboratories created from the incorporation of these instructional videos have provided a tool that fosters constructivist learning, and hence encourages conceptual change, by means of an organized sequence of proposals for the students to do. These activities stimulate the students to reflect on the information and content they receive.

We believe that the introduction in various formats of audiovisual materials to complement the course's traditional laboratory script can help the student get more out of the laboratory classes, since these materials can provide both theoretical and practical details of the experiments. They can also be a complement to simulation software, as with them the student can see the experimental techniques that are used to study the simulated phenomenon.

Moreover, instructional videos constitute a virtual guide to the experiments that the student will carry out. This is an advantage when there is little laboratory equipment available but various students have to work simultaneously in the laboratory, or when the student is working non-presentially.

Therefore, approaching laboratory practicals sequentially in an instructional video can optimize both the available material resources since not all the groups of students have to use the same material simultaneously, and the available time since it allows the student to carry out more complex experiments or a greater number of them.

In our research, we designed and implemented a teaching innovation project whose aim was either to facilitate the students' preparation prior to their actually doing the laboratory practicals, or for them to carry out those practicals on virtual e-learning and b-learning platforms using the facilities provided by ICTs. In particular, audiovisual material was developed in several formats, and implemented on a Website, covering the content necessary for the study and practical preparation of the subject of Optoelectronics, a subject that we teach in the second cycle of the degree in Electronic Engineering at the School of Industrial Engineering of our University. All of the instructional videos produced have a common structure. They begin with the title of the practical, a brief introduction to put it into the context of the subject, and a description of the basic theoretical concepts related to the experiment they are going to see. The objective proposed by the experiment is indicated, the material used is shown, and then particular emphasis is laid on the steps to follow in doing the experiment. Finally, it is explained how the data should be analyzed and presented.

The methodological approach to the virtual practicals follows the guidelines for the design of virtual learning material proposed by Onrubia (Onrubia, 2005). Specifically, apart from exploiting the technical possibilities offered by ICTs, the materials should also be consistent with two features:

- "Logical meaningfulness": From a constructivist viewpoint, the virtual educational material developed must have a clear organization and structuring of its content. Logical meaningfulness needs to be ensured in the design phase, i.e., with the logical structure of the content. This aspect is taken into account in the organization of the various elements, activities, and sequences that make up the materials being developed.
- "Psychological meaningfulness": The materials should enable the learners to have cognitive elements available that they can relate to the content being studied. Psychological meaningfulness emerges during the students' actual learning process. Therefore, this phase of design will deal with how the material is integrated into our overall teaching methodology, in order to ensure that the students will have developed the cognitive resources needed to assimilate the new content and establish meaningful relationships.

One of the support platforms we use for the instructional videos is the Moodle virtual platform. As indicated by various authors (Coll, 2004; Donnelly, 2005; Mauri et al., 2005; Mauri, 2006; Onrubia, 2005), this can amplify the educational benefits the students obtain from the process, and provides support to them when they are working independently either individually or in groups.

This virtual laboratory in no way means that we are contemplating the disappearance of the real laboratory. Instead our intention is the integration of the two laboratories in our teaching practice. Indeed, it forms part of a teaching methodology which foresees increasing use of a wide range of learning tools that can facilitate successful adaptation to the European Higher Education Area.

Figure 2 shows several screenshots from some instructional videos about optical communications.

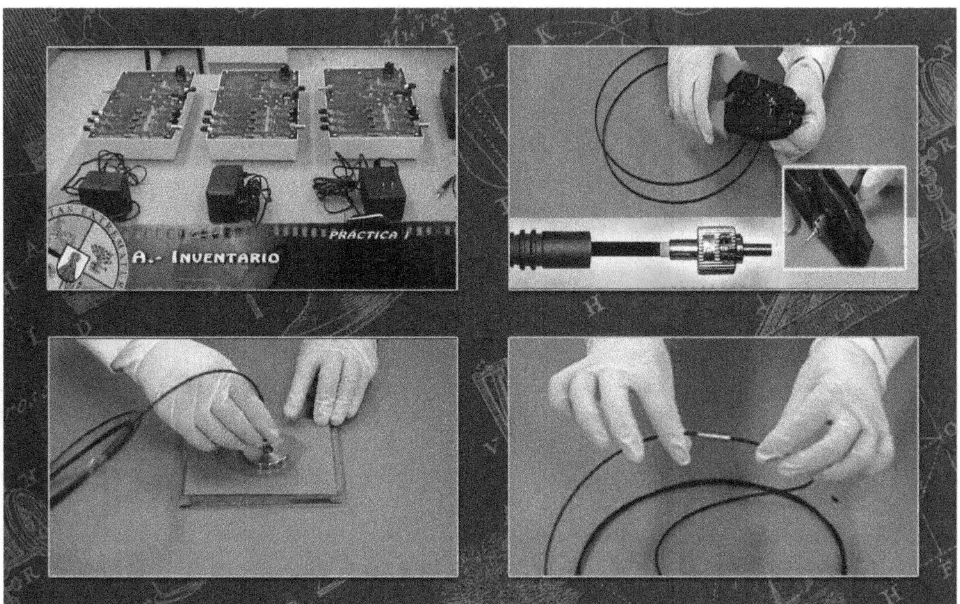

Fig. 2. Some screenshots from the instructional video "Virtual Laboratory on Optical Communications".

The materials developed are available at: http://grupoorion.unex.es.

5. Concept maps: ICT tools to facilitate meaningful learning

In keeping with the purpose of creating learning environments grounded in constructivist theories and meaningful learning (Ausubel, 1968), we apply concept maps (Novak & Gowin, 1984) as a strategy for cognitive organization, and as a visual resource with which to represent a set of conceptual meanings included in a proposition structure. The idea is to display the meaningful relationships between the concepts of the specific content to be taught and the students' knowledge of the subject.

The concept map constitutes an ideal teaching material with which to associate, interrelate, structure, discriminate, describe, and exemplify the content of a subject. To these characteristics, one must add that in recent years the technique has become very popular due to its natural integration with ICTs. In sum, concept maps are today very useful educational tools to help achieve meaningful learning (Ausubel, 1968; Novak & Gowin, 1984; Moreira, 2010).

For scientific subjects in particular, authors such as Novak & Musonda (1991) have pointed out that, in physics teaching, the subject matter may be regarded as "conceptually opaque". I.e., students find it hard to visualize the structure of the concepts involved, and the relationships between them. It is therefore important if that matter is to be learnt meaningfully for it to be presented in a "conceptually transparent" form, i.e., it is necessary to present the topics to students with a clearly related conceptual hierarchy.

The concept map is therefore a tool that is consistent with Novak's educational theory, and part of its usefulness is in detecting and facilitating meaningful learning (Pérez et al., 2004,

2006, 2008, 2010a). The concept map shows schematically an image of a person's knowledge about some particular topic, so that it can also reflect the extent to which that knowledge is the product of a process of meaningful learning. The map shows a series of concepts, organized hierarchically, together with the relationships that are established between them, thus explicitly showing the meanings with which each concept has been endowed.

Concept maps have been used at different educational levels because they allow students to better assimilate the concepts they are learning by a development of new propositions that they integrate into their existing cognitive structure, the result being meaningful learning (Jonassen, 2000; Novak & Gowin, 1984; Okebukola & Jegede, 1988; Roth & Roychoudhury, 1994). In the Theory of Meaningful Learning, the learning process consists of an interaction between the knowledge already existing in the student's cognitive structure and the new knowledge being assimilated. Building on the foundations of this theory, if used to their full potential, concept maps are particularly effective in encouraging meaningful learning, allowing students to construct their knowledge by organizing conceptual content into a hierarchical structure (Novak & Gowin, 1984; Novak & Musonda, 1991; Cifuentes & Hsieh, 2003; Kwon & Cifuentes, 2009; Haugwitz et al., 2010; Pérez et al., 2004, 2006, 2010a).

How the concepts are organized in a concept map (whether more linearly or more differentiated) can indicate the extent to which the creator of the map has learnt more by rote or more in a meaningful form. It is precisely this aspect that makes concept maps such powerful teaching tools. In particular, the meaningfulness of the student's learning will be easily perceptible when its content is organized into an interrelated structure. The elaboration of concept maps allows new information to be organized and related to the already existing cognitive structure, and clearly highlights the establishment of any erroneous relationships or the absence of any relevant concepts. As noted by Novak & Gowin (1984), students will perceive meanings to a greater or lesser extent depending on the new propositional relationships that they have noted and understood. With their use, the learner develops important analytical skills: the selection, organization, and elaboration of knowledge. The tasks involved in their construction and the interpretation of the cognitive structures they contain develop the students' intellectual skills.

Today, thanks to advances in the new technologies, there are many software tools available for the construction of concept maps. Examples are CmapTools, Inspiration, and CMT, inter alia. Various studies have shown the advantages in using such computer programs to facilitate constructing these maps (Alpert & Grueneberg, 2001; Anderson-Inman & Ditson, 1999; Cline et al., 2010; Haugwitz et al., 2010; Kwon & Cifuentes, 2009; Reader & Hammond, 1994).

Our research group uses concept mapping as a working tool in physics teaching (Pérez et al., 2000, 2004, 2006, 2010a, 2010b). For their construction, we chose CmapTools of the IHMC (Institute for Human and Machine Cognition, University of West Florida, Pensacola, FL) (Cañas et al., 2000; Novak & Cañas, 2006). This is a toolkit that facilitates the creation of concept maps on a computer, using applications written in Java. It provides the ability to construct, navigate through, share, and critically negotiate models of knowledge represented as concept maps. It also allows their use in collaborative networks over the Internet, so as to facilitate group work. Thus, CmapTools users constitute a community which shares knowledge and technologies. Projects can be easily shared worldwide thanks to a public server network, accessible from any browser or through the free CmapTools software.

In our research, we have developed concept maps that are models of knowledge for teaching topics of physics, which were subsequently used by our students in validating their educational effectiveness.

The concept maps that we and our students have created (several thousand) are lodged on the Cmap site: "Universidad de Extremadura (España)", and in this way are integrated into the global network of concept maps hosted on Cmap sites, and that is distributed throughout the world. The ideal way to see them is to install the CmapTools software application on the computer, and visit the aforementioned Cmap site. Nevertheless, they can also be seen (with some limitations) at the Web address: http://grupoorion.unex.es:8001.

6. Conclusion

In general, we can say that the educational materials developed in this work have improved the quality of the e-learning of the subject of Optoelectronics, both of the conceptual content through the use of concept maps, and of the procedural content through instructional videos, computer simulations, and virtual laboratories.

The concept maps developed have been validated by comparison with traditional teaching following an experimental design with a control group and an experimental group (Martínez et al., 2010a; Pérez et al., 2010a, 2010b; Suero et al., 2010). A test of knowledge was applied to determine the learning actually achieved by the students of the two groups. The results showed that the concept maps that were constructed had been an effective teaching tool in physics teaching in general, since they helped the students to learn meaningfully the concepts of the topic under study, constituting a useful cognitive strategy for acquiring information in a structured form, and for discovering the meaning of the concepts that were being learnt.

The instructional videos and virtual laboratories mounted on e-learning platforms have been validated through an experimental design with two control groups of students and one experimental group (Martínez et al., 2010b, 2011). The results of different post-tests of knowledge showed these teaching materials to be effective teaching tools in enhancing students' learning. For Optoelectronics in particular, the application of our teaching methodology contributed a clear improvement over the conventional system of teaching the topic. The purpose of using this type of material is their application to e-learning platforms as complements to traditional teaching, and not as replacements for real laboratories where such laboratories are available. Nonetheless, when a real laboratory is unavailable or inaccessible, such materials can of course be very useful indeed. We believe that their ideal use is as a teaching resource that can be used for pre-practical and post-practical study, allowing the acquisition of knowledge to be more efficient. But again, in sum we conclude that, to enhance our students' learning it is important to integrate these materials as complementary methods added to those used in traditional teaching.

With respect to the computer simulations that were developed and implemented in this work, we have demonstrated with our students that this type of computer simulation which we call "hyper-realistic" represents reality with a realism far above that of the usual simulations (Pérez et al., 2011). Specifically, we validated the educational effectiveness of the hyper-realistic virtual environment that we implemented with an experimental design that included a control group of students and an experimental group. The results of the different evaluation tests showed that our simulations resolve some of the weaknesses of the usual computer simulations, such as those deriving from their simplicity and lack of realism of the graphical environment viewed by the student. These simulations offer the student the opportunity to perform Optics practicals at any time. This obviates the problem typical of eminently practical subjects in that the individual work required of the student is usually limited to mere theoretical studies, since the student lacks the appropriate material for additional practice outside the laboratory. Appropriately designed hyper-realistic computer simulations are highly effective teaching tools in certain educational contexts, for example, on e-learning platforms.

The work and the materials that it generated have been and are being used both by our Engineering and Physical Sciences undergraduate students and by our students of various official Master Degree courses that we teach on Physics Education. In addition, teachers of several Latin American universities have told us they are also using them with their students.

We believe that the teaching material we have developed and the form of using it are transferable to other subjects and innovation projects at the university level, which would facilitate future proposals for the use of our materials in other subjects different from those dealt with in this work. Now we have started working on the generation of the videos and simulations described in this work using Stereoscopic-3D technology. To generate photorealistic three-dimensional simulations we are using technology based on ray tracing combined with 3D display technology.

7. Acknowledgment

This research has been partially funded by the European Regional Development Fund through the Regional Government of Extremadura, grant GR10102.

8. References

Adell, J. (1997). Tendencias en educación en la sociedad de las tecnologías de la información. *Edutec. Revista Electrónica de Tecnología Educativa,* Vol. 7, ISSN 1135-9252

Adell, J. (2005). Internet en educación. *Comunicación y Pedagogía,* Vol. 200, pp. 25-28, ISSN 1136-7733

Aktan B., Bohus, C., Crowl, A., & Shor, M. H. (1996). Distance learning applied to control Engineering Laboratories. *IEEE Transactions on Education,* Vol. 39, No. 3, pp. 320-326, ISSN 0018-9359

Aleksandrov, A., & Nancheva, N. (2007). Systems of Teaching Engineering Work on Base of Internet Technologies. *International Journal of Information Technologies and Knowledge,* Vol. 1, pp. 37-44, ISSN 1313-0455

Alessi, S. M., & Trollip, S. R. (Eds.) (1991). *Computer-based instruction: Methods and development (2nd ed.),* Prentice Hall, ISBN 978-0131685925, Englewood Cliffs, NJ

Alpert, S. R., & Grueneberg, K. (2001). Concept mapping with multimedia on the Web. *Journal of Educational Multimedia and Hypermedia,* Vol. 9, No. 4, pp. 313-330, ISSN 1055-8896

Anderson-Inman, L., & Ditson, L. (1999). Computer-based concept mapping: A tool for negotiating meaning. *Learning and Leading with Technology,* Vol. 26, No. 8, pp. 6–13, ISSN 1082-5754

Area, M. (2005). Tecnologías de la información y la comunicación en el sistema escolar. Una revisión de las líneas de investigación. *Revista Electrónica de Investigación y Evaluación Educativa,* Vol. 11, No. 1, pp. 3-25, ISSN 1134-4032

Arvaja, M., Salovaara, H., Häkkinen, P., & Järvelä, S. (2007). Combining individual and group-level perspectives for studying collaborative Knowledge construction in context. *Learning and Instruction*, Vol. 17, No. 4, pp. 448-459, ISSN 0959-4752

Ausubel, D. P. (1968). *Educational psychology: A cognitive view,* Holt McDougal, ISBN 978-0030899515, New York

Ausubel, D.P. (2000). *The acquisition and retention of knowledge: a cognitive view,* Springer, ISBN 978-0792365051, Dordrecht

Baily, C., & Finkelstein, N.D. (2009). Development of quantum perspectives in modern physics, *Physical Review Special Topics - Physics Education Research,* Vol. 5, pp. 010106, ISSN 1554-9178

Bajarlía, G., & Speigel, A. (1997). *Docentes us@ndo Internet*, Ediciones Novedades Educativas, ISBN 978-9879191161, Buenos Aires

Balanskat, A., Blamire, R., & Kefala, S. (2007). Insight: Observatory for new technologies and education. Retrieved on August 1, 2011, Available from http://insight.eun.org/ww/en/pub/insight/misc/specialreports/impact_study.htm

Barberá, E., Mauri, T., & Onrubia, J. (Eds.) (2008). *Cómo valorar la calidad de la enseñanza basada en las TIC: Pautas e instrumentos de Análisis,* Graó, ISBN 978-8478275304, Barcelona

Bartolomé, A. (1996). Preparando para un nuevo modo de conocer, *Edutec. Revista Electrónica de Tecnología Educativa,* Vol. 4, ISSN 1135-9252

Beichner, R., Bernold, L., Burniston, E., Dail, P., Felder, R., Gastineau, J., Gjersten, M., & Risley, J. (1999). Case study of the physics component of an integrated curriculum. *American Journal of Physics,* Vol. 67, No. 7, pp. 16–24, ISSN 0002-9505

Beller, M. O. (1998). The crossroads between lifelong learning nd information technology. A challenge facing leading universities. *Journal of Computer-Mediated Communication,* Vol. 4, No. 2, pp. 9-19, ISSN 1083-6101

Blease, D., & Cohen, L. (1990). *Coping with computers: an ethnographic study in primary classrooms,* Paul Chapman Educational Publishing, ISBN 978-1853960659, London.

Bryan, J.A., & Slough, S.W. (2009). Converging lens simulation design and image predictions. *Physics Education,* Vol. 44, No. 3, pp. 264-275, ISSN 0031-9120

Cabero, J., Castaño, C., Cebreiro, B., Gisbert, M., Martinez, F., Morales, J.A., Prendes, M.P., Romero, R., & Salinas, J. (2003). Las nuevas tecnologías en la actividad universitaria, *Pixel Bit. Revista de Medios y Educación,* Vol. 20, pp. 81-100, ISSN 1133-8482

Calvo, J.L. & Pérez, A.L. (1983). Teaching oscillations with a small computer. *Physics Education,* Vol. 18, No. 4, pp. 172-174, ISSN 0031-9120

Calvo, I., Marcos, M., Orive D., & Sarachaga I. (2009). Building Complex Remote Laboratories. *Computer Applications in Engineering Educations,* Vol. 18, No. 1, pp. 53-66, ISSN 1099-0542

Candelas, F.A., Gil, P., Torres, F., Ortiz, F., Puente, S.T., & Pomares, J. (2004). Virtual remote laboratory for teaching of computer vision and robotic in the University of Alicante. *Proceedings of the IBCE'04, Second IFAC Workshop on Internet Based Control Education,* Grenoble (France), September 2004

Cañas, A. J., Ford, K. M., Coffey, J., Reichherzer, T., Carff, R., Shamma, D., & Breedy, M. (2000). Herramientas para Construir y Compartir Modelos de Conocimiento basados en Mapas Conceptuales. *Revista de Informática Educativa,* Vol. 13, N. 2, pp. 145-158

Cattagni, A., & Farris, E. (2001). Internet Access in US. Public Schools and Classrooms: (1994-2000). USA: National Center for Education Statistics. Retrieved on August 1, 2011, Available from http://nces.ed.gov/pubs2001/2001071.pdf

Cebrián, M., Ruiz, J., & Rodríguez, J. (2007). Estudio del impacto del Proyecto TIC desde la opinión de los docentes y estudiantes en los primeros años de su implantación en los centros públicos de Andalucía. Universidad de Málaga, Grupo de Investigación en Nuevas Tecnologías aplicadas a la Educación.

Cebrián, M. (1997) Nuevas competencias para la formación inicial y permanente del profesorado. *Edutec. Revista Electrónica de Tecnología Educativa,* N° 6, ISSN 1135-9252

Chang, K.E-, Yu-Lung, C., Lin, H-Y., & Sung, Y.T. (2008). Effects of learning support in simulation-based physics learning. *Computers & Education,* Vol. 51, No. 4, pp. 1486-1498, ISSN 0360-1315

Chi, M.T.H., Siler, S., Jeong, H., Amauchi, T., & Hausmann, R.G. (2001). Learning from human tutoring. *Cognitive Science,* Vol. 25, No. 4, pp. 471-533, ISSN 0364-0213

Cifuentes, L., & Hsieh, Y.C. (2003). Visualization for construction of meaning during study time: A quantitative analysis. *International Journal of Instructional Media,* Vol. 30, No. 3, pp. 263-273, ISSN 0092-1815

Cline, B.E., Brewster, C.C., & Fell, R.D. (2010). A rule-based system for automatically evaluating student concept maps. *Source Expert Systems with Applications,* Vol. 37, No. 3, pp. 2282-2291, ISSN 0957-4174

Coll, C. (2004). Psicología de la educación y prácticas educativas mediadas por las tecnologías de la información y la comunicación. Una mirada constructivista. *Sinéctica,* Vol. 25, pp. 1-24 (offprint), ISSN 1665-109X

Coll, C., Mauri, T., & Onrubia, J. (2008). Análisis de los usos reales de las TIC en contextos educativos formales: una aproximación sociocultural. *Revista Electrónica de Investigación Educa*tiva, Vol. 10, No. 1, ISSN 1607-4041

Coll, C., Onrubia, J., & Mauri, T. (2007). Tecnología y prácticas pedagógicas: Las TIC como instrumentos de mediación de la actividad conjunta de profesores y estudiantes. *Anuario de Psicología,* Vol. 38, No. 3, pp. 377- 400, ISSN 0066-5126

Crook, C. (1996). *Computers and the Collaborative Experience of Learning,* Routledge, ISBN 978-0415053600, London

Cuban, L. (2001). *Oversold & Underused. Computers in the Classroom,* Harvard University Press, ISBN 978-0674011090, Cambridge, MA

Dede, C. (Ed.) (1998) *Learning with Technology (1998 ASCD Yearbook),* Association for Supervision & Curriculum Deve, ISBN 978-0871202987, Las Vegas

Difanzo, N., Hantula, D. A., & Bordia, P. (1998). Microworlds for experimental research, Having your (control and collection) cake, and realism too. *Behavioural Research Methods, Instruments, and Computers,* Vol. 30, No. 2, pp. 278–286, ISSN 0743-3808

Dockstader, J. (1999) Teachers of the 21st Century know the what, why, and how of technology integration. *Technological Horizons in Education Journal,* Vol. 26, No. 6, pp. 73-74, ISSN 0192-592X

Domínguez M., Reguera, P. & Fuertes, J.J. (2005). Laboratorio Remoto para la Enseñanza de la Automática en la Universidad de León (España). *Revista Iberoamericana de Automática e Informática Industrial,* Vol. 2, No. 2, pp. 36-45, ISSN 1697-7912

Donnelly, R. (2005). Using technology to support project and problem-based learning, In: *Handbook of Enquiry & Problem Based Learning,* Barreto, T., Maclabhrainn, I., & Fallon, H. (Eds.), pp. 157-177, CELT, ISBN 978-095516980, Galway

Dormido, S. (2004). Control Learning: Present and Future. *Annual Reviews in Control*, Vol. 28, No. 1, pp. 115-136, ISSN 1367-5788

Eylon, B. S., Ronen, M., & Ganiel, U. (1996). Computer simulations as tools for teaching and learning: using a simulation environment in optics. *Journal of Science Education and Technology*, Vol. 5, No. 2, pp. 93–110, ISSN: 1059-0145

Finkelstein, N.D., Adams, W. K., Keller, C. J., Kohl, P. B., Perkins, K. K., Podolefsky, N. S., & Reid, S. (2005). When Learning about the Real World is Better Done Virtually. *Physic review Special Topics - Physics Education Research* Vol. 1, pp. 010103, ISSN 1554-9178

Finol de Govea, A. (2007). Principios Cognitivo-constructivistas en la Aplicación de las Tecnologías de la Información y la Comunicación (TIC) para la Enseñanza-Aprendizaje de Inglés con Propósitos Específicos. *SYNERGIES*, Vol. 3, pp. 38–64, ISSN 1856-035X

García, A., & Gil, M. (2006). Entornos Constructivistas de Aprendizaje Basados en Simulaciones Informática. *Revista Electrónica de Enseñanza de las Ciencias*, Vol. 5, No. 2, pp. 304-322, ISSN 1579-1513

Garrison, D.R., & Anderson, T. (2003). *E-learning in the 21st century: a framework for research and practice*, Routledge, ISBN 978-0415263467, London

Goldberg, F., & Bendall, S. (1995). Making the invisible visible: A teaching/learning environment that builds on a new view of the physics learner. *American Journal of Physics*, Vol. 63, No. 11, pp. 978–991, ISSN 0002-9505

Goldberg, F. (1997). Constructing physics understanding in a computer-supported learning environment. *AIP Conference Proceedings* Vol. 399, pp. 903–911.

Goldstone, R., & Sakamoto, Y. (2003). The transfer of abstract principles governing complex adaptive systems. *Cognitive Psychology*, Vol. 46, No. 4, pp. 414–466, ISSN 0010-0285

Goldstone, R., & Son, J.Y. (2005). The Transfer of Scientific Principles Using Concrete and Idealized Simulations. *The Journal of the Learning Sciences*, Vol. 14, No. 1, pp. 69–110, ISSN 1050-8406

Goodyear, P., Njoo, M., Hijne, H., & Van Berkum, J.J.A. (1991). Learning processes, learner attributes and simulations. *Education & Computing*, Vol. 6, No. 3, pp. 263–304, ISSN 0167-9287

Gorsky, P., & Finegold, M. (1992). Using computer simulations to restructure student's conceptions of force. *Journal of Computers in Mathematics and Science Teaching*, Vol. 11, No. 2, pp. 163-178, ISSN 0731-9258

Grabe, M., & Grabe, C. (1996). *Integrating technology for meaningful learning*, Wadsworth Publishing, ISBN 978-0618637010, Boston

Grady, S.M. (1998). *Virtual reality: Computers mimic the physical world*, Facts on File, ISBN 978-0816036059, New York

Gross, B. (2000). *El ordenador invisible, hacia la apropiación del ordenador en la enseñanza*, Editorial Gedisa, ISBN 978-8474327595, Barcelona

Guzmán J. L., Rodríguez, F., Berenguel, M., & Dormido, S. (2005). Laboratorio virtual para la enseñanza de control climático de invernaderos *Revista iberoamericana de automática e informática industrial*, Vol. 2, No. 2, pp. 82-92, ISSN 1697-7912

Harper, B., Squires, D., & Mcdougall, A. (2000). Constructivist Simulations: A New Design Paradigm. *Journal of Educational Multimedia and Hypermedia*, Vol. 9, No.2, pp. 115-130, ISSN 1055-8896

Harris, M.H. (1999). Is the revolution now over, or has it just begun? A year of the Internet in Higher Education. *The Internet & Higher Education*, Vol. 1, No.4, pp. 243-251, ISSN 1096-7516

Haugwitz, M., Nesbit, J.C., & Sandmann, A. (2010). Cognitive ability and the instructional efficacy of collaborative concept mapping. *Learning and Individual Differences*, Vol. 20, No. 5, pp. 536-543, ISSN 1041-6080

Hewson, P.W. (1985). Diagnosis and remediation of an alternate conception of velocity using a microcomputer program, *American Journal of Physics*, Vol. 53, No. 7, pp. 684–690, ISSN 0002-9505

Järvelä, S., & Häkkinen, P. (2002). Web-based cases in teaching and learning-the quality of discussions and a stage of perspective taking in asynchronous communication. *Interactive Learning Environments*, Vol. 10, No. 1, pp. 1-22, ISSN 1049-4820

Jonassen, D.H. (1996). *Computers in the classroom: Mindtools for critical thinking*, Prentice Hall, ISBN 978-0023611919, Columbus, OH

Jonassen, D.H. (2000). *Computer as mindtools for schools: Engaging critical thinking*, Prentice Hall, ISBN 978-0130807090, Upper Saddle River, NJ

Kaput, J.J. (1995) Creating cyberetic and psychological ramps from the concrete to the abstract: Examples from multiplicate structure, In: *Software goes to schools: Teaching for understanding with new technologies*, D. N. Perkins, J. L. Schwartz, M. M. West, & M. S. Wiske (Eds.), pp. 130–154, Oxford University Press, ISBN 978-0195115772, New York

Kennewell, S., & Beauchamp, G. (2003). The influence of a technology-rich classroom environment on elementary teachers' pedagogy and children's learning. *Proceedings of the IFIP Working Group 3.5. Conference: Young Children and Learning Technologies*, University of Wales Swansea, Parramata (UK), July 2003

Kwon, S.Y., & Cifuentes, L. (2009). The comparative effect of individually-constructed vs. Collaboratively-constructed computer-based concept maps. *Computers & Education* Vol. 52, No. 2, pp. 365–375, ISSN 0360-1315

Lajoie, S.P., Azevedo, R., & Fleiszer, D. (1998). Cognitive tools for assessment and learning in high information flow environment. *Journal of Educational Computing Research*, Vol. 18, No. 3, pp. 205-235, ISSN 0735-6331

Lajoie, S.P. (2000). *Computers as Cognitive Tools, Vol. II: No More Walls*, Routledge, ISBN 978-0805829310, London

Lajoie, S.P., & Azevedo, R. (2006). Teaching and learning in technology-rich environments, In: *Handbook of Educational Psychology*. (2nd ed.), Alexander, P., & Wine, P. (Eds.), pp. 803-821, Lawrence Erlbaum Associates, ISBN 978-0805859713, Mahwah, NJ

Landau, R. (2006). Computational Physics: A Better Model for Physics Education? *Computing in Science & Engineering, Vol.* 8, No. 5, pp. 22-30, ISSN 1521-9615

Laschi, R., & Riccioni, A. (2008). Design and Implementation of a Virtual Lab for Supporting Students in Modeling, Evaluating and Programming Secure Systems, *Proceedings of the 12th International Conference on Interactive Computer-Aided Learning (ICL 2008)*, Villach (Austria), September 2008

Lehtinen, E., Hakkarainen, K., Lipponen, L., Rahikainen, M., & Muukkonen, H. (1999). Computer supported collaborative learning: A review of research and development. *The J.H.G.I. Giesbers Reports on Education, 10*. Retrieved on August 1, 2011, Available from http://www.comlab.hut.fi/opetus/205/etatehtava1.pdf

Linn, M.C. (2002). Promover la educación científica a través de las tecnologías de la información y comunicación (TIC). *Enseñanza de las Ciencias*. Vol. 20, No. 3, pp. 347-355, ISSN 0212-4521

López, M., & Morcillo, J.G. (2007). Las TIC en la enseñanza de la Biología en la educación secundaria: los laboratorios virtuales. *Revista Electrónica de Enseñanza de las Ciencias,* Vol. 6, No. 3, pp. 562-576, ISSN 1579-1513

Marqués, P. (2000). Impacto de las TIC en educación: funciones y limitaciones. *Enciclopedia Virtual de Tecnología Educativa*. Vol. 194, pp. 48-51, ISSN 1133-9926

Martínez, G., Pérez, A. L., Suero, M. I., & Pardo, P. J. (2010a). Comparación del incremento de aprendizaje obtenido al utilizar mapas conceptuales y Cmaptools en el estudio de dos temas diferentes, pero de nivel de contenido conceptual equivalente. *Proceedings of the Fourth International Conference on Concept Mapping,* ISBN 978-9561907058, Viña del Mar (Chile), October 2010

Martínez, G., Pérez, A. L., Suero M. I., Naranjo. F. L., & Pardo, P. J. (2010b). Implementación de un laboratorio virtual de placas solares fotovoltaicas para el desarrollo de prácticas no presenciales. *Proceedings of ticEDUCA2010: Encontro International TIC e Educaçao,* ISBN 978-9899699915, Lisboa (Portugal), November 2010

Martínez, G., Pérez, A. L., Suero M. I., Naranjo. F. L., & Pardo, P. J. (2011). Diseño, elaboración y validación de Videos Didácticos sobre Prácticas de Comunicaciones Ópticas. *Proceedings of the XIX Encuentro Ibérico para la Enseñanza de la Física y XXXIII Reunión Bienal de la RSEF,* Santander (Spain)

Mauri, T., Onrubia, J., Coll, C., & Colomina, R. (2005). La calidad de los contenidos educativos reutilizables: diseño, usabilidad y prácticas de uso. *RED–Revista de Educación a Distancia,* Vol. 2, ISSN 1578-7680

Mauri, T. (2006). Análisis de casos con TIC en la formación inicial del conocimiento profesional experto del profesorado. *Revista Interuniversitaria de Formación de Profesorado,* Vol. 20, No. 3, pp. 219-231, ISSN 1575-0965

Merrill, P., Hammons, K., & Vincent, B. (1996). *Computers in Education (3rd Edition)*, Allyn & Bacon, ISBN 978-0205185177, Boston

Moreira, M.A. (2010). ¿Por qué conceptos? ¿Por qué aprendizaje significativo? ¿Por qué actividades colaborativas? ¿Por qué mapas conceptuales? *Revista Qurriculum,* Vol. 23, pp. 9-23, ISSN 1130-5371

Naps, T. L., Rößling, G., Almstrum, V., & Dann, W. (2003). Exploring the Role of Visualization and Engagement in Computer Science Education. *ACM SIGCSE Bulletin*, Vol. 35, No. 2, pp. 131-152, ISSN 0097-8418

Novak, J.D., & Gowin, D.B. (1984). *Learning how to learn,* Cambridge University Press, ISBN 978-0521319263, London

Novak, J.D., & Musonda, D. (1991). A twelve-year longitudinal study of science concept learning. *American Educational Research Journal*, Vol. 28, No. 1, pp. 117–153, ISSN 0002-8312

Novak, J.D., & Cañas, A.J. (2006). The Theory Underlying Concept Maps and How to Construct Them, Technical Report IHMC CmapTools 2006-01, Florida Institute for Human and Machine Cognition, retrieved on August 1, 2011, Available from: http://cmap.ihmc.us/Publications/ResearchPapers/TheoryUnderlyingConceptMaps.pdf

Okebukola, P.A., & Jegede, O.J. (1988). Cognitive preference and learning mode as determinants of meaningful learning through concept mapping. *Science Education,* Vol. 72, No. 4, pp. 489–500, ISSN 0036-8326

Onrubia, J. (2005). Aprender en entornos virtuales de enseñanza y aprendizaje: actividad conjunta, ayuda pedagógica y construcción del conocimiento" *RED-Revista de Educación a Distancia*, Vol. 2, ISSN 1578-7680

Pérez, A.L.; Peña, J.J.; Mahedero, B. (1979a). Electronic Device of Didactic and Electrometric Interest for the Study of RLC Circuits. *American Journal of Physics*. Vol. 47, No. 2, pp. 178-181, ISSN 0021-8979

Pérez, A.L.; Peña, J.J.; Bueno, M.A.; Vega J.M., & Calvo. J.L. (1979b) Reinforcing the study of impedance. *Physics Education*, Vol. 14, No. 5, pp. 250-252, ISSN 0031-9120

Pérez, A.L. and Calvo, J.L. (1984). A small electronic device for studing chemical kinetics. *Journal of chemical educations*, Vol. 61, No.9, pp. 808-810, ISSN 0021-9584

Pérez, A. L.; Suero, M. I.; Montanero, M., & Montanero, F. M. (1999). Mapas de experto tridimensionales. Aplicaciones al diseño de secuencias instruccionales de física, basadas en la teoría de elaboración, In: *Premios nacionales de investigación educativa*, pp. 93-116, CIDE, ISBN 978-8436932870, Madrid

Pérez, A.L., Suero, M.I., Montanero, F.M., Montanero, M., & Pardo, P.J. (2000): Three-dimensional conceptual maps: an illustration for the logical structure of the content of optic, *Proceedings of the International Conference Physics Teacher Education. Beyond 2000*, ISBN 978- 8469944169, Barcelona (Spain), August 2000

Pérez, A.L., Suero, M.I., Pardo, P.J., & Montanero, M. (2004). Aplicaciones de la teoría de Reigeluth y Stein a la Enseñanza de la Física. Una propuesta basada en la utilización del programa informático Cmaptools. Proceedings of the First Internacional Conference on Concept Mapping, ISBN 978-8497690648, Pamplona (Spain), September 2004

Pérez, A.L., Suero, M.I., Pardo, P.J., & Montanero, M. (2006). Utilización de Cmaptools en la reconstrucción colaborativa de conocimientos sobre la reflexión de la luz. Proceedings of the Second Internacional Conference on Concept Mapping, ISBN 978-9977151482 , San José (Costa Rica), September 2006

Pérez A.L., Suero, M.I., & Pardo, P.J. (2008). Utilización de Cmaps para mejorar los conocimientos relativos a la refracción de la Luz mediante su "Reconstrucción Colaborativa". *Óptica pura y aplicada*, Vol. 41, No. 1, pp. 17-23, ISSN 0030-3917

Pérez, A.L., Suero, M.I., Montanero, M., Pardo, P.J., & Montanero, M. (2010a). Concept maps and conceptual change in physics, In: *Handbook of research on Collaborative learning using concept mapping*, Lupion Torres, P., Cássia Veiga Marriott, R. (Eds.), pp. 325-345, Idea Group Publishing, ISBN 978-1599049939, Hershey

Pérez, A.L., Martínez, G., Suero, M.I., & Pardo, P.J. (2010b). Determinación experimental del incremento de aprendizaje obtenido mediante la utilización de mapas conceptuales y Cmaptools. Comparación de la cantidad de aprendizaje sobre las fibras ópticas conseguido utilizando mapas conceptuales y sin utilizarlos. Proceedings of the Fourth International Conference on Concept Mapping, ISBN 978-9561907058, Viña del Mar (Chile), October 2010

Pérez, A.L., Martínez, G., Suero, M.I., Naranjo, F.L., & Pardo, P.J. (2011). Estudio comparativo de la eficacia de varios entornos de aprendizaje: simulaciones virtuales hiperrealistas, simulaciones esquemáticas y laboratorio tradicional. *Proceedings of the XIX Encuentro Ibérico para la Enseñanza de la Física y XXXIII Reunión Bienal de la RSEF*, Santander (Spain)

Poves, J. (1997). Docencia y aprendizaje en la red: La red de estudiantes de la UAM, *Proceedings of the II Congreso Nacional de Usuarios de Internet e Infovía,* Madrid (Spain), February 1997

Pov-Ray. Persistence Of Vision Raytracer. Retrieved on august 1, 2011, Available from http://www.povray.org/

Psillos, D., & Niedderer, H. (2002). *Teaching and learning in the science laboratory,* Kluwer Academic Publishers, ISBN 978-1402010187, Dordrecht

Reader, W., & Hammond, N. (1994). Computer-based tools to support learning from hypertext: Concept mapping tools and beyond. *Computers & Education,* Vol. 12, No. 1-2, pp. 99–106, ISSN 0360-1315

Reigeluth, C. M. (Ed.) (1983). *Instructional design theories and models: an overwiev of their current status,* Routledge, ISBN 978-0898592757, London

Reparaz, C.H., Sobrino, A., & Mir, J. (2000). Integración curricular de las nuevas tecnologías. Editorial Ariel S.A., ISBN 978-8434428713, Barcelona.

Riccioni, A. (2010). Design, Implementation and Evaluation of a Virtual Laboratory for Computer Engineering Education. *Thesis,(PhD),* Università Degli Studi Di Bologna.

Roca, O. (2001) La autoformación y la formación a distancia: la tecnología de la educación en los procesos de aprendizaje, In: *Para una tecnología educativa,* Sancho, J. (Ed.), pp. 169-192, Horsori Editorial, ISBN 978-8485840311, Barcelona.

Ronen, M., & Eliahu, M. (2000). Simulation - a bridge between theory and reality: the case of electric circuits. *Journal of computer assisted learning,* Vol. 16, No. 1, pp. 14-26, ISSN 0266-4909

Roth, W.M., & Roychoudhury, A. (1994). Science discourse through collaborative concept mapping: new perspectives for the teacher. *International Journal of Science Education,* Vol. 16, No. 4, pp. 437-455, ISSN 0950-0693

Salomon, G., Perkins, D.N., & Globerson, T. (1991). Partners in cognition: Extending human intelligence with intelligent technologies. *Educational Researcher,* Vol. 20, No. 3, pp. 2-9, ISSN 0013-189X

Salzmann, Ch., Gillet, D., & Huguenin, P. (2000). Introduction to Real Time Control using labview with an Application to Distance Learning. *International Journal of Engineering Education,* Vol. 16, No. 3, pp. 255-272, ISSN 0949-149X

Sánchez, J. (2000). *Nuevas tecnologías de la información y comunicación para la construcción del aprender,* Universidad de Chile, ISBN 978-9562888436, Santiago de Chile.

Sánchez, J. (2001). *Aprendizaje visible, tecnología invisible,* Dolmen Ediciones ISBN 978-9562014738, Santiago de Chile

Shin, N., Jonassen, D. H., & McGee S. (2003). *Journal of Research in Science Teaching,* Vol. 40, No. 1, pp. 6–33, ISSN 0022-4308.

Sims, R. (2000). An interactive conundrum: Constructs of interactivity and learning theory. *Australian Journal of Educational Technology,* Vol. 16, No.1, pp. 45-5, ISSN 0814-673X

Snir, J., Smith, C., & Grosslight, L. (1995). Conceptually enhanced simulations: A computer tool for science teaching, In: Software goes to school: *Teaching for understanding with new technologies,* D. N. Perkins, J. L. Schwartz, M. M. West, & M. S. Wiske (Eds.), pp. 106–129, Oxford University Press, ISBN 978-0195115772, New York

Squires, D., & McDougall, S. (1994). Choosing and using educational software: a teacher's guide. Falmer Press, ISBN 978-0750703062, London

Steinberg, R.N. (2000). Computers in teaching science: To simulate or not to simulate? *American Journal of Physics,* Vol. 68, No. 1, pp. 37-41, ISSN 0002-9505

Suero, M.I., Pérez, A.L., Martínez, G. and Pardo, P.J. (2010). Determinación experimental del incremento de aprendizaje obtenido mediante la utilización de mapas conceptuales y Cmaptools. Comparación de la cantidad de aprendizaje obtenido por los alumnos utilizando mapas conceptuales y sin utilizarlos. Proceedings of the Fourth International Conference on Concept Mapping, ISBN 978-9561907058, Viña del Mar (Chile), October 2010

Tao, P., & Gunstone, R. (1999). The process of conceptual change in force and motion during computer-supported physics instruction. *Journal of Research in Science Teaching*, Vol. 36, No. 7, pp. 859–882, ISSN 0022-4308

Tao, P. (2004). Developing understanding of image formation by lenses through collaborative learning mediated by multimedia computer-assisted learning programs. *International Journal of Science Education*, Vol. 26, No. 10, pp. 1171–119, ISSN 0950-0693

Tascón, C. (2002). Principios Psicoinstruccionales de la Formación en la sociedad de la información y la comunicación. Proceedings of the I Congreso Internacional Sociedad de la Información, ISBN 978-8448136039, Las Palmas de Gran Canaria (Spain), February 2002

Tondeur, J., Van Braak, J., & Valcke, M. (2007). Towards a typology of computer use in primary education. *Journal of Computer Assisted Learning*, Vol. 23, No. 3, pp. 197-206, ISSN 0266-4909

Trumper, R. (2003). The physics laboratory – an historical overview and future perspectives. *Science & Education*, Vol. 12, pp. 645-670, ISSN 0926-7220

Twining, P. (2002). Conceptualising computer use in education: Introducing the Computer Practice Framework (CPF). *British Educational Research Journal*, Vol. 28, No. 1, pp. 95-110, ISSN 0141-1926

UNESCO (2000). *Report of the Expert Meeting on Virtual Laboratories*. UNESCO, Paris. Retrieved on August 1, 2011, Available from: http://unesdoc.unesco.org/images/0011/001191/119102eo.pdf

Vélez, G. (2002). *Aprender en la Universidad. La relación del estudiante universitario con el conocimiento*. Universidad Nacional de Río Cuarto, ISBN 978-9506652031, Córdoba

Yanitelli, M.S. (2011). Un cambio significativo en la Enseñanza de las Ciencias. El uso del ordenador en la resolución de situaciones experimentales de Física en el nivel universitario básico. *Thesis (PhD),* Universidad de Burgos.

Yazon, J.M.O., Mayer-Smith, J.A., & Redfield, R.J. (2002). The impact of a web-based genetics course on university students' perspectives on learning a teaching. *Computers & Education,* Vol. 38, No. 1-3, pp. 267-285, ISSN 0360-1315

Zacharia, Z., & Anderson, O. R. (2003). The effects of an interactive computer-based simulation prior to performing a laboratory inquiry-based experiment on students' conceptual understanding of physics. *American Journal of Physics*, Vol. 71, No. 6, pp-618-629, ISSN 0002-9505

Zhao, Y., Pugh, K., Sheldon, S. & Byers, J. L. (2002). Conditions for classroom technology innovations. *Teachers College Record*, Vol. 104, No. 3, pp. 482-515, ISSN 0161-4681

Zhao, Y. & Frank, K. A. (2003). Factors affecting technology uses in schools: an ecological perspective. *American Educational Research Journal*, Vol. 40, No. 4, pp. 807-840, ISSN 0002-8312

Designing an Innovative Training Tool: A Formative E-Assessment System for Project Management

Constanta-Nicoleta Bodea
and Maria-Iuliana Dascalu
Academy of Economic Studies, Bucharest
Romania

1. Introduction

Learning is the only way of developing the necessary competences in the new economy and e-learning is a strategic instrument in this process. E-learning platforms must not be just tools of content distribution of pedagogical resources and not taking into account the real interests of the learners: "...without personalization, e-learning is only ever going to be a generic mass produced experience and will tend towards a model of teaching that makes the computer a virtual lecturer, rather than a virtual personal tutor" (Ashman et al., 2009). In order to correct this drawback of e-learning, coming from the lack of personalization, researchers and educators try to use various methods: evolutionary algorithms, personalized e-testing rules, adaptive feedback or exploiting recommender engines, connected to learning applications. All these methods are briefly described in this paper, in the context of e-assessment in project management (PM) domain. The interest towards the e-assessment services in e-learning environments is explained by the applicability of the e-assessment in various types of education, from formal education, in schools and universities, to work-based education and preparation activities for obtaining professional certifications. The interest for the PM domain is explained by the strategic importance of project, as main form of organization in current economy.

In order to improve learning effectiveness, the formative dimension of e-assessment has been increasingly developed: it isn't regarded only as an evaluation tool, but also as a learning tool. Formative assessment is defined as "an ongoing process of monitoring learners' progresses of knowledge construction" (Hsu et al., 2010) or "the process of seeking and interpreting evidence for use by learners and their teachers to decide where the learners are in their learning, where they need to go and how best to get there" (Assessment Reform Group (ARG), 2002). Its value was greatly appreciated by researchers: formative e-assessment promotes self-reflection and students can take control of their own learning (Pachler et al., 2010). The authors argue that it fills a knowledge gap, that's why formative e-assessment has an important role in learning and training. It is well-used in organizational learning (Bodea & Dascalu, 2010), being known as "assessment for learning" (Birenbaum et al., 2009).

This chapter proposes an adaptive formative e-assessment system, useful in preparing for project management professional certifications. The chapter has several parts. The first one is introductory. In the second part, the authors briefly present a set of formative e-assessment systems used in project management training. In the third part, some theoretical models used in the implementation of the systems are revealed, as well as the state of the art in e-assessment. In the fourth part, the main technical and functional considerations of the developed system are presented. The fifth part consists of the main experimental results. In the sixth and the seventh parts, the future directions and the main conclusions are drawn.

The proposed e-assessment system proved to be an efficient one, from the point of view of its performance and utility. Compared to other e-testing approaches (such as dynamic testing), our solution turned out to be more suitable for large item banks. As a formative learning tool, our solution helped the students to obtain a lower rate of failure and a sharper learning progress curve. There are a few shortcomings of the proposed system, from the point of view of the trainers: they would want to benefit from predefined tests, to add video materials within the solution or to build criteria for rules creation. Still, these improvements can be solved in the feature. The results of the system's evaluation are good enough, that is why one can consider that our e-assessment proposal is an improvement in the area of adaptive e-assessment. Thanks to its formative value, it can be easily used by firms to develop employees' competences.

2. Formative e-assessment in professional training

Without minimizing the importance of practical experience and portfolios, one can state that certifications awarded by well-known professional associations are a proof of professional competences. E-assessment applications are useful tools in the preparation processes for obtaining such certifications. In the field of project management, the Swiss branch of International Project Management Association (IPMA) offers an e-assessment tool, useful to the individuals who are eager to get certified: "X-AM" (http://www.sts.ch/index.php?option= com_content&task=view&id=21&Itemid=42). The users can also see, in addition to navigation buttons and time limits, a navigation table, in the left side of the screen: see Figure 1. The table groups the questions in four categories: the current question, the questions which didn't receive any answers yet, the questions which were answered and the so-called marked questions (to which the user may want to return, as she/he is not sure of the validity of the given answer). Thus, "X-AM" becomes a flexible application, oriented towards the users' needs.

Another useful e-assessment application for project management is the one offered by Queendom (http://www.queendom.com/tests/access_page/index.htm?idRegTest=1130): the application is useful in professional trainings, as it determines the user's profile: whether the user has a suited behavior for projects-based work. The Queendom e-tests resemble to quizzes (see Figure 2): they have 196 questions, graded using a five-point Likert scale (from "Strongly disagree" to "Strongly agree"). Actually, the e-tests check the behavior competences from the IPMA Competences Baseline (International Project Management Association, 2006): the leader competences, the management competences, the interaction or decision competences.

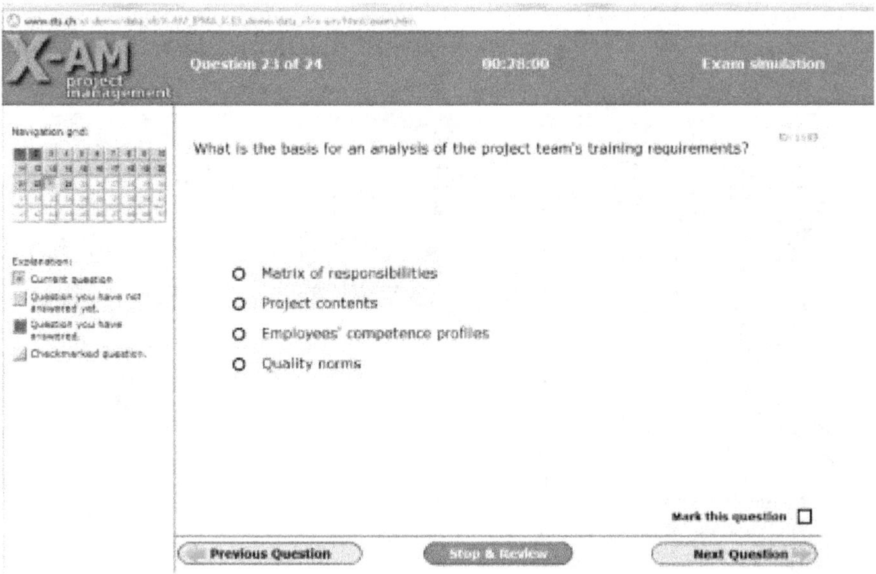

Fig. 1. "X-AM" E-assessment Application

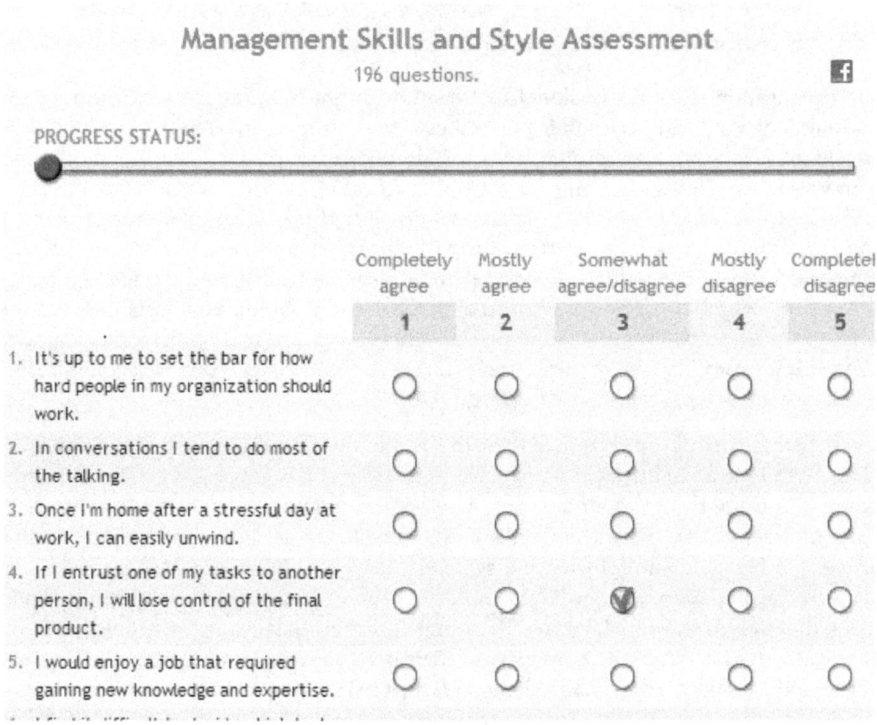

Fig. 2. Queendom E-assessment Application

Another standardized e-assessment system used in business administration and management domains by over 200 000 students is the Graduate Management Admission Test (GMAT): see Figure 3.

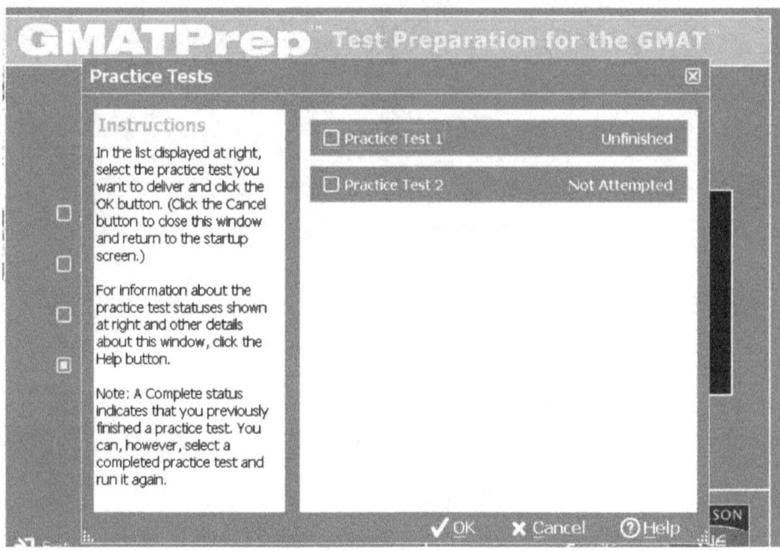

Fig. 3. The E-assessment Application used to Prepare for GMAT Tests

As the preparation for a professional certification might be quite time consuming for an individual engaged in economic activities, the Romanian Association of Project Management offers an e-assessment tool for simulation purposes. This practice complies with the effort of digital economy to raise the accessibility level of information systems: individuals don't have to go the association's office and take a simulation test there; they can do that from anywhere, even from their office. The assessment mechanism offered by the Romanian Association of Project Management benefits from a web service to interrogate the questions' database. The algorithm of building the simulation tests respects some knowledge constraints, bounded to the certification level and a stop criterion, bounded to the questions number in a test. The e-assessment, "CertExam", is available at: http://www.pm.org.ro/certexam/ (see Figure 4).

For e-assessment to be more efficient in the professional training activities, it has to be enriched with formative attributes. Shavelson identifies the following practices in formative assessment: on-the-fly or spontaneous assessment, planned-for-interaction assessment, embedded assessment (Shavelson, 2006). The challenge is to include these formative assessment techniques into information systems. Black and William (2009) pointed a set of activities to be mandatory in order to build a formative e-assessment system: providing feedback that moves learners forward, clarifying and sharing learning intentions and criteria for success, activating students as owners of their own learning or as instructional resources for one another (Black & William, 2009). Wang (2008) completes the list by adding the possibility of repeating the test (correct answers are not immediately given, so that the test can be repeated till all the answers are correct), the possibility of seeing query scores (users are given other users' scores, so that they can compare themselves), applying "all pass and then reward" strategy.

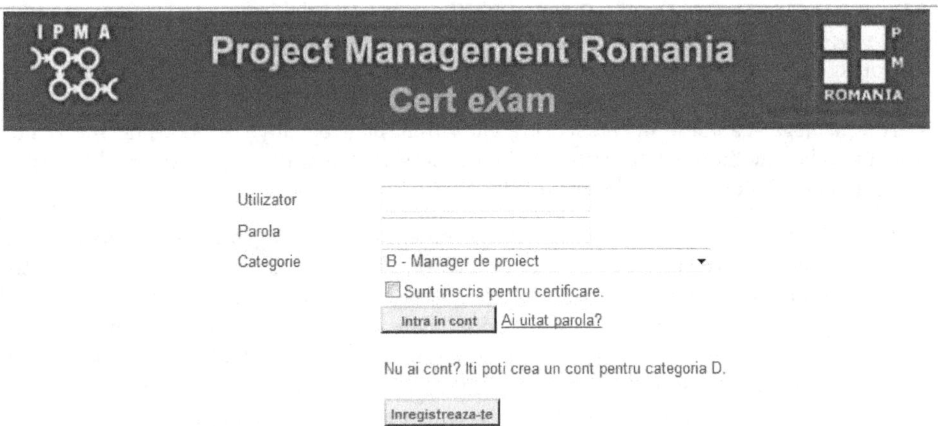

Fig. 4. "CertExam" Application used by the Romanian Association of Project Management

The primary challenge in building a formative assessment application is to really find out what students know, to detect cognitive models used by the students during the representation of the test concepts and apply those models to build computer adaptive tests. Assessment applications have to be tailored not only for students but for teachers and trainers, who use them to create test: each has different priorities, different constraints and different capacity to compromise (for example, some teachers will prefer the test construction to be less flexible, but easier to achieve).

3. Theoretical considerations in building formative e-assessment tasks

According to AL-Smadi & Gütl (2008), the reasons for using e-assessment instead of pen-and-pencil tests are both practical and pedagogical. The practical ones are given by the increase of students' number and, implicitly, of teachers' quantity of work. The e-assessment is meant to resolve the problem of the evaluation of a large number of students in a short period of time. The pedagogical reasons come from the need of systems which evaluate students' knowledge correctly and efficiently. In the past, the purpose of the e-assessment applications was to shorten the time spent by the teachers for evaluation process, but now, the e-assessment applications have new challenges to overcome: the efficient management of questions, the building of intelligent tests, adapted to each user.

The questions' management depends on the type of questions. Open questions are scarcely used in e-assessment, that is why the future discussions will target only the closed questions. The most spread type of question is the multiple-choice question, which is built-up from:

- question root (the question's body);
- pre-built answers, which contain:
    - the key(the correct answers);

- the distractor (the wrong answers).

In order to manage this type of questions, the relation between question and answers has to be treated: each answer has to have a binary value (for example, 1 for correct answers and 0, for the wrong ones). An issue which has to be taken into consideration when building multiple-choice answers is the fact that the correct answer can be guessed. To reduce this risk, Roşca & Cristescu (2004) propose the method of correlated items or the method of inserting a negative value in the scoring algorithm, as a penalty for choosing the wrong answers. The method of correlated items was successfully applied in large-scale experiments, in Taiwan, too (Tam & Lu, 2011).

An interesting approach in questions' management is given by the use of taxonomies, ontologies and semantic graphs. These advanced knowledge structures allow the implementation of advanced techniques for e-assessment. In fact, the competences and concepts from a domain which has to be evaluated through tests are structured in ontologies (Vasconcelos et al., 2009; Schmidt & Kunzmann, 2006; Bodea et al., 2010). Intelligent structures used in questions' management facilitated the development of advanced e-assessment algorithms. The creators of e-assessment applications used, besides the classical linear or dynamic tests, evolutionary algorithms (EAs), rules-based algorithms (RBA), algorithms based on computer adaptive testing (CAT) principle or recommender mechanisms to improve the feedback parts of an e-test.

3.1 Application of evolutionary algorithms

EAs are used in creating pedagogical paths, based on the learners' profile and their learning objectives. Azough, Bellafkih and Bouyakhf (2010) used genetic algorithms to resolve the problem of searching the most optimal path from a starting point, represented by learners' profile, to a final point, represented by learning objectives, while passing through intermediate points, represented by courses. Huang, Huang and Chen (2007) use genetic algorithms for curriculum sequencing, but they don't treat only the content problems, as Azough, Bellafkih and Bouyakhf (2010) do: they also search for the most optimal teaching operation (presentation, example, question or problem). Huang, Huang and Chen (2007) argue that learners' ability should also be studied, when choosing the curriculum, besides considering learners' interests and browsing behaviors.

Particle swarm optimization (PSO) is a very useful EA related technique, with a wide range of applications. Dheeban, Deepak, Dhamodharan and Elias (2010) show that PSO with inertia-coefficient is suitable for improving e-learning courses composition. They also underline that their PSO variant is better than the Basic particle swarm optimization algorithm (BPSO) and experimental results come to strengthen their hypothesis. Wong and Looi (2010) published a detailed study about the application of PSO in the content planning and e-assessment domain. They identified the work of Cheng, Lin and Huang (2009) to be the only known study about a PSO used in an adaptive dynamic question generation system for web-based testing: the key element of their work is the fitness function, which selects a different question on each step in the online test. The fitness function has three parameters: the difficulty level of the question (which has to be as closed as possible to the knowledge level of the user), the question item's relevance (as close as possible to the course content that the instructor wishes to assess the learner on) and the number of times a question is chosen (as low as possible). Cheng, Ling and Huang (2009) compare the PSO search to the exhaustive search and conclude that the first one is more suitable for the large-scale item banks. Chen and Jiang (2007) apply PSO to an assessment paper generation system. According to Wong and Looi (2010), the main difference between an assessment paper generation system and an adaptive dynamic generation system for knowledge assessment is the step in which the PSO is applied: for the first system, the PSO is applied only once, at the beginning of the test, when all the questions are selected; for the second system, the PSO is applied at each test item selection. The PSO fitness function developed by Chen and Jiang (2007) has three sets of control variables: the learning points to cover, the ratios of the questions with different difficulty levels and the total marks of the paper. All these variables are pre-defined by the instructors. Yin, Chang, Hwang, Hwang and Chan (2006) use the same fitness function, but with different variables. Huang (2006) only uses the question difficulty as a function parameter. Wang and Chu (2008) combine a genetic algorithm with their PSO approach. Ho, Yin, Hwang, Shyn and Yean (2009) also use enhanced multi-objective PSO to improve the e-assessment services: they try to solve the problems of multiple assessment criteria and parallel test sheets' composition from large item banks. Their proposed algorithm was compared to a competing genetic algorithm and they proved the superiority of PSO over classical genetic algorithm.

The current study shows another application of PSO to the e-assessment domain. The main purpose of the application is to enhance the formative features of e-assessment, which is not regarded only as a knowledge evaluation instrument, but a knowledge creation one. In order to illustrate the suitability of PSO for resolving the formative e-assessment problem, the applied PSO algorithm is further described. The variables used in the fitness function construction are suitable for a project management certification process. PSO algorithm is a robust stochastic optimization technique, which is inspired from the movement and intelligence of swarms. It uses a number of particles that constitute a group moving around in the search space looking for the best solution. It imitates the bird from a flock which is nearest to the food. All particles have fitness values, evaluated through the fitness function and velocities. The fitness function used for the PSO algorithm applied to project management e-assessment is the following one:

$$Minimize\ f(q) = \begin{cases} |d_q - A| + |d_q - D| + \\ \frac{Exp_q \times CA_q}{ExpMax^2} + \frac{1}{CO_q}, if\ CO_q > 0 \\ |d_q - A| + |d_q - D| + \\ \frac{Exp_q \times CA_q}{ExpMax^2}, if\ CO_q \leq 0 \end{cases} \tag{1}$$

Where

q: the question id
A: ability level of the user, where, $0 \leq A \leq 1$
D: desired difficulty of the e-test, where $D \in \{0, 25;0.50;0.75;1\}$, according to the four certification levels awarded by the International Project Management Association (2006);

d_q: difficulty of the question q, where, where $0 \leq d_q \leq 1$;
ExpMax: the maximum exposure number of a question from the questions pool;

Exp_q: the exposure number for question q, where where $0 \leq Exp_q \leq$ ExpMax;
CA_q: the number of times in which question q has been correctly answered;
CO_q: number of concepts which are verified by the question q, contained by the competences established to be checked by the e-assessment session; the knowledge domain to be checked is divided in competences, which contain concepts;

The PSO algorithm is applied every time a new question is selected. The ability level of the user is updated after each given answer. The parameters from the third term of the fitness function from formula 1 are also changing each step on the way. The test difficulty and the number of concept are established by the trainee (if the session is part of one's preparation process) or by the trainer (if the session is an official step from the certification process). The other elements besides the fitness function are the ones usually used in PSO approaches (Schutte & Groenwold, 2005).

In the PSO algorithm, the goal at each iteration is to find the question having the difficulty level closest to the trainee's ability level and closest to the targeted test difficulty level, being the least exposed so far and checking a large number of concepts from the established learning objectives. The initial ability level of the trainee is established via self-evaluation, a pre-test or uses a default value (taken from a database), as shown in Figure 5.

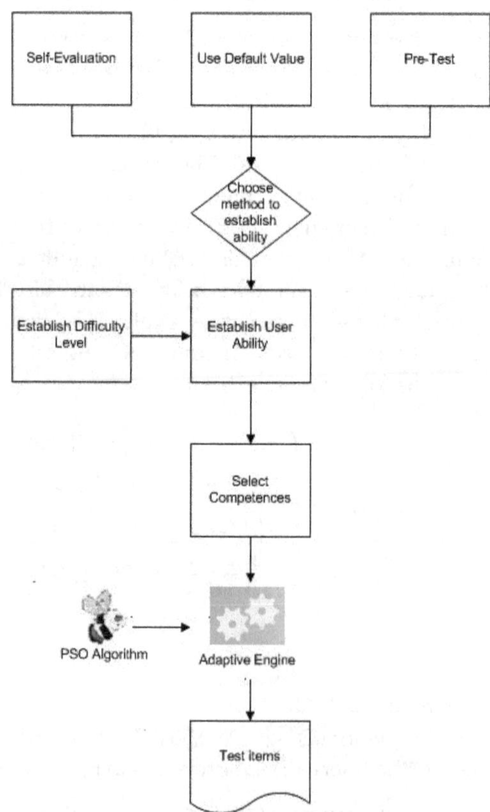

Fig. 5. Workflow of Building Tests with the aid of PSO Algorithm

The prerequisites to access the PSO algorithm are:

- establish difficulty level of the test (for each level, a difficulty value is available: the values are taken by parameter D from formula 1);
- establish the ability level of the user; if the user chooses to self-evaluate himself (inserts his own level), the number is projected to the interval [0,1], to ensure compatibility with the values of the parameter A from formula 1;
- establish the knowledge to be checked by the test; whether the user chooses to step over this stage, all the concepts will be checked; the maximum exposure number of a question from the questions pool: this operation is made by calling the database and it is not visible to the user.

3.2 Application of rules-based algorithms

To allow the creation of electronic formative tests, many researchers have used personalized rules (Lazarinis, Green, & Pearson, 2010; De Bra, Aroyo & Cristea, 2004). Test creators can enter information about assessments. Conditional rules applied in specific points of the e-tests force a new stage progress or a regress to the incorrectly answered questions (Lazarinis, Green, & Pearson, 2010). The application of rule-based tests requires the adoption of an adaptive-test prototype consisting of four parts, according to De Bra, Aroyo & Cristea (2004): the domain model, the user model, the adaptive model and the adaptive engine. Improving formative testing by applying rule-based algorithms further supports the idea that educators, trainers and teachers should be actively involved in improving the students' results, in optimizing the benefits of using e-assessments. National Research Center of assessment, standards and testing students in the U.S. proposes an application so that the teachers can engage in formative testing, in setting the attributes, the context and the type of electronic test answers (Vendlinski, Niemi, Wang, & Monempour, 2008). Although not strictly complying with the four parts proposed by De Bra, Aroyo & Cristea (2004), the application architecture addresses the same principle of separation between questions' management, tests' management or students' management. The application has four modules: Designer, Assembler, Scheduler and Gradebook (Vendlinski, Niemi, Wang, & Monempour, 2008).

The current chapter proposes an RBA (rules-based algorithm) model, where the set of rules for building a test are established by the trainers. Each rule has an initiation point (whether the rule is applied at the beginning of the test or after a certain question), an action (for example, the rule consists in showing only the question of level D) and a set of conditions (for example, the rule is applied if the trainee has previous project management education). The obvious advantage of using rules-based tests is the flexibility offered both to the trainers and the trainees of the system. The tests are adapted to trainees' educational objectives, previous knowledge or courses. In the same time, the trainers gain the possibilities of reflecting on the assessment experiences and offering personalized tests for each student, thus motivating the students and helping them in the learning process.

3.3 Using adaptive feedback and recommendation engines

In the last years, numerous repositories of educational digital resources have been created. These repositories are added to the unclassified resources provided by Internet itself. In this overcrowded space of online educational resources, the e-learning users feel the need of services which can help them identify the proper learning objects. Recommender systems (RS) serve this purpose (Manouselis et al., 2010). A RS guides the user to interesting objects (concepts) in a large space of possible options. In educational area, RS started to spread more and more: some assist students to plan their semester schedule, by checking courses that comply with constraint regulation and with students' preferences (Hsu, 2009), others are used at course ranking (Farzan & Brusilovsky, 2011) or to give proper knowledge to proper members in collaborative team contexts, by respecting role, tasks, members' level of knowledge (Zhen, Huang & Jiang, 2010).

In e-assessment, recommender engines can be used to improve the selection of the tests, taking into account the educational objectives or to optimize the feedback mechanism: each student can receive bibliographical recommendations, according to one's mistakes. RS can be also used by teachers and trainers in selecting the proper questions from a database, like in Cadmus case (Hage & Aimeur, 2005).

The current chapter proposes the use of RS in the feedback module of an e-assessment application. After an e-test is finished, the incorrectly answered questions are analyzed and the concepts which were not understood by the students are extracted. These concepts are mapped to a domain ontology. By using that ontology, a set of lexical instances for each misunderstood concept is obtained and used for internet search. Thus, bibliographical recommendations from the web search are offered to the students.

4. A formative e-assessment system for project management

Taking into account the theoretical considerations in building formative e-assessment tasks, the authors propose a modularized e-assessment system for project management, which uses the Competences Standard of the International Project Management Association (International Project Management Association, 2006). The main purpose of the system was its use in the preparation process for the certification.

4.1 The system architecture and technical details

The architecture of the system is available in Figure 6.

The system has several components, which ensures its flexibility:

- the admin module (offers the possibility to accomplish operations on levels, competences, trainers, users or questions);
- the trainer module (allows the creation of rules-based tests, visualization of previously created tests and visualization of students' information);
- the student module (contains the web application used by the students to resolve online tests, which are created with various adaptation models);
- the web service;
- the business services, which use a domain model, created with nHibernate technology;
- the database, which contains information about questions, tests, simulations, users; the database is relational and is constructed using the IPMA Competences Baseline (International Project Management Association, 2006).

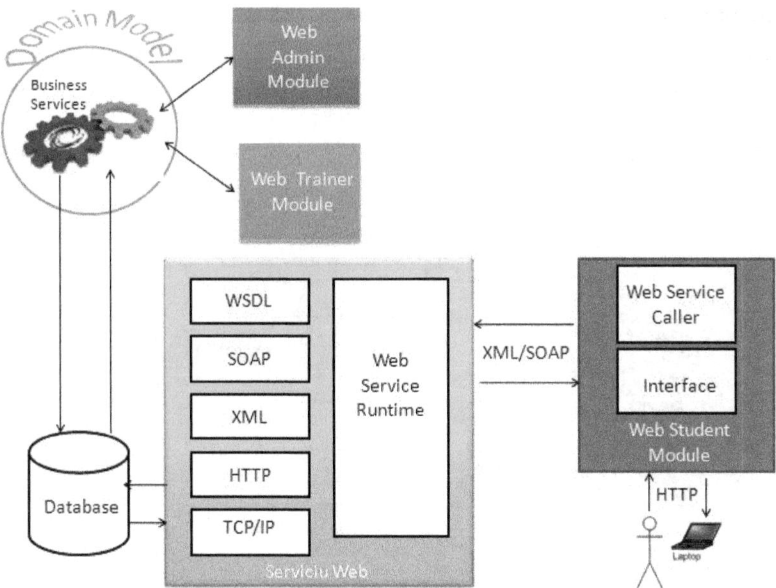

Fig. 6. General Architecture of the Project Management E-assessment System

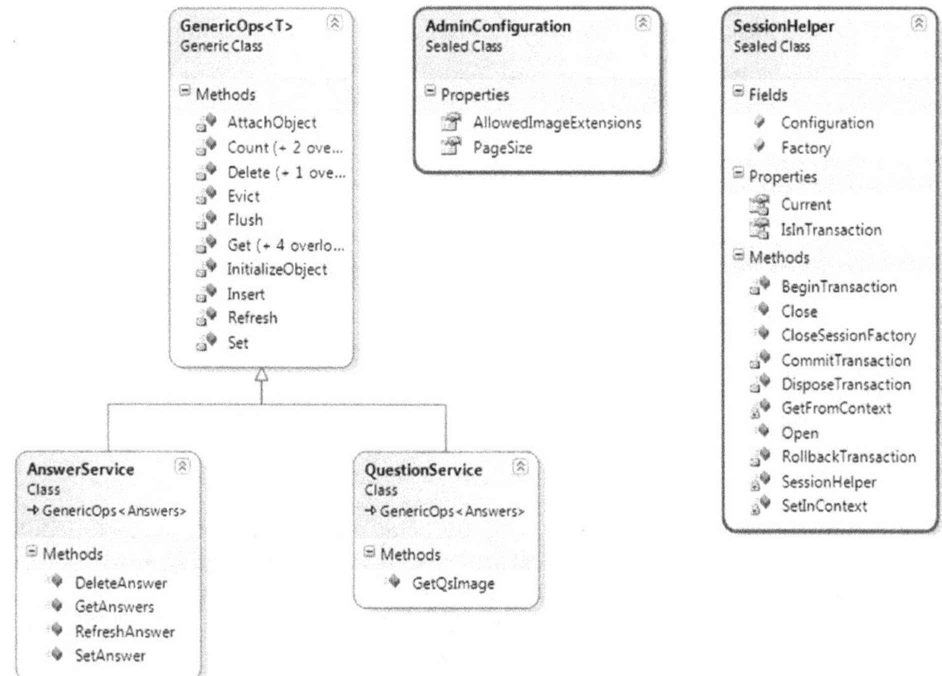

Fig. 7. Excerpt from the Class Diagram of the Business Services

The communication with the database is made in a formal manner:

- the admin and the trainer module communicate with the database via a set of business services (an excerpt from the class diagram of the business services is available Figure 7);
- the student module communicates with the database via the web service, which receives Ajax calls (from Dojo library) (see Figure 8).

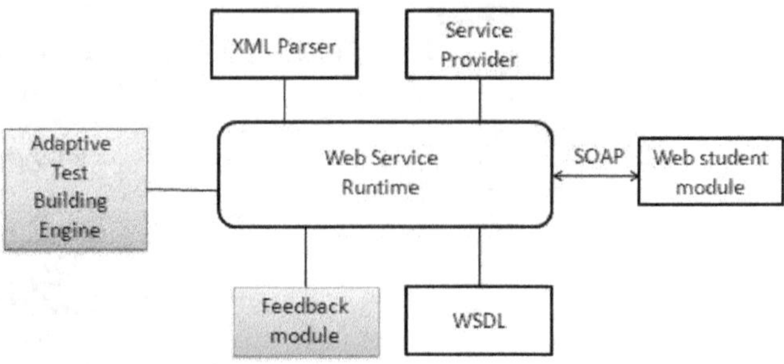

Fig. 8. Web Service Architecture

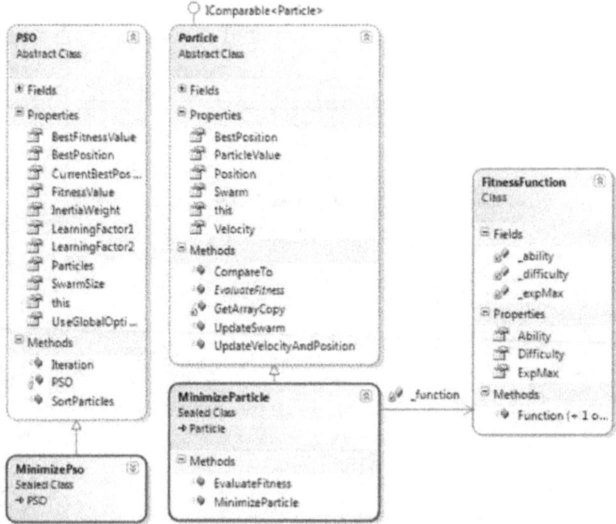

Fig. 9. The Class Diagram of the PSO Algorithm

The solution was developed in C#, the exception being made by the web student module, which was developed in Javascript. The calls to the web service were implemented using the Dojo library. The domain model was created with nHibernate. The formative character of the e-assessment system is given by the adaptive test building engine and the feedback module, from Figure 8. The feedback engine offers the trainees the possibility of revising their mistakes and consulting further web bibliography recommendations, to fill their knowledge gaps. Thus, future learning directions are offered. The adaptive engine contains the PSO algorithm applied to test construction and a rules-based algorithm, where a set of rules for building a test are established via the trainer module. The classes diagram used by the PSO algorithm is shown in Figure 9. Thanks to the use of abstract classes (see class PSO and Particle), the minimizing function can be easily changed. All the parameters which have to be set as prerequisites are fields in FitnessFunction (presented theoretically in formula 1): they are seen as constants by the FitnessFunction.

4.2 The system functionalities

Each module of the e-assessment system has several functionalities. Through the admin module (see the left side of the Figure 10), one can make statistics, edit information about levels, competences, concepts, questions and answers, rules applied in tests, students or simulations. An example of screens form the admin module is available in the right side of the Figure 10: the editing of questions and answers. Each question has attached several multiple-choice answers and one can edit the answers only using a specific question's screen.

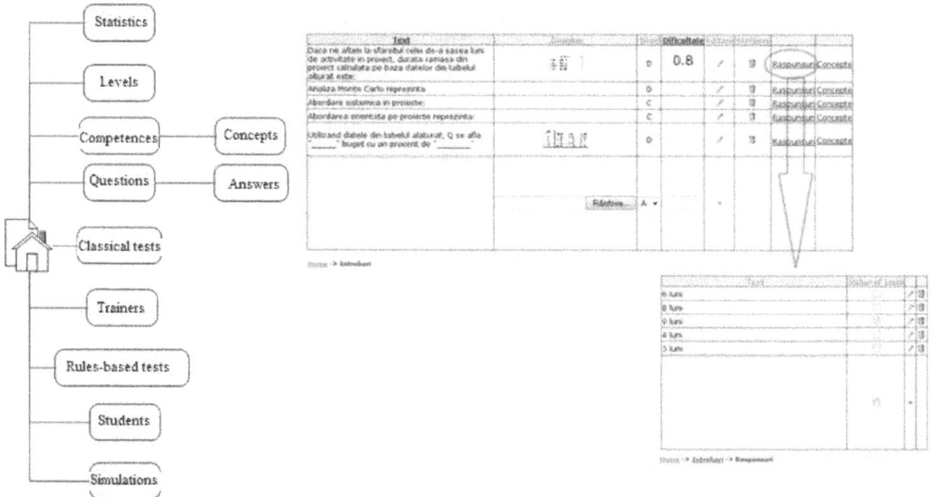

Fig. 10. Functionalities in the Admin Module

The trainer module has the following functionalities: one can view the students (without editing or deleting their information), one can see the rules created by other trainers and create his/her own rules. The trainer's functionalities are available in the upper side of Figure 11 and the rules creation screen in the bottom side of Figure 11.

The web student module has several functionalities (see Figure 12):

- a demo variant of the e-assessment: the same five questions are always offered;
- create new account page: only level D accounts can be created online; the other more featured types of accounts can be obtained only after official registration into the project management certification process, at the Romanian Association of Project Management;
- recover password page: the password is resent via e-mail to the users;

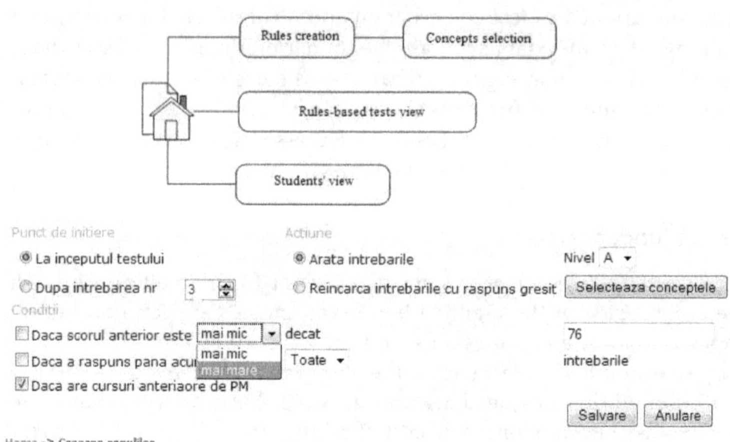

Fig. 11. Functionalities in the Trainer Module

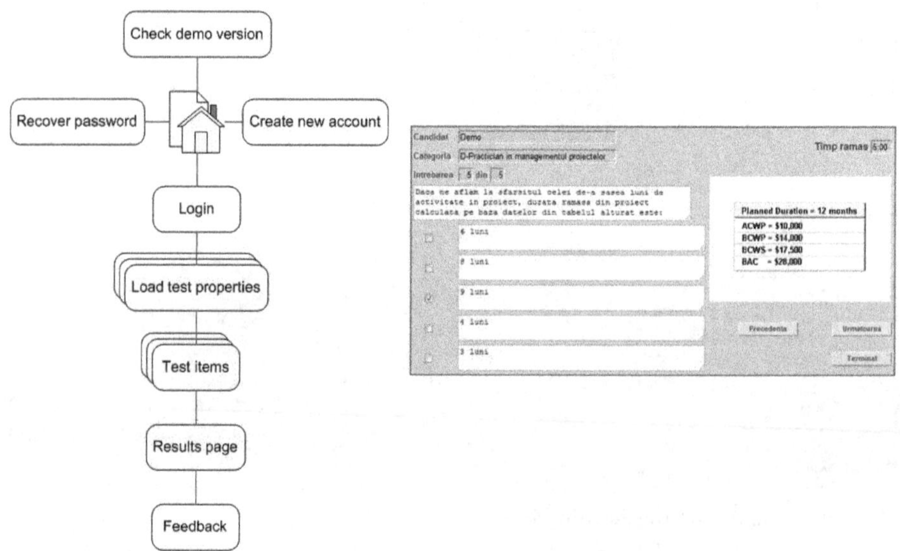

Fig. 12. Functionalities in the Web Student Module

- login page: after inserting the username and password, the trainees have to check whether they are officially registered or not to the certification process (for each case, they have different rights; another important information provided by the trainee is the certification level: A (project director), B (senior project manager), C (project manager) and D (project management associate) (International Project Management Association, 2006); after completing the first step in the login page, the trainee has to provide other useful information (choosing test model, providing necessary information for the chosen test model and so on and so forth): these set of pages help at loading test properties;

- the test item pages contain several graphic elements: the question text, an image (optionally), possible answers, the time frame , navigation buttons (see the right side of Figure 12);
- the results page can be accessed once the test session is over; it contains the final grade, the number of correctly answered questions, the duration of the test and it gives the possibility to access the feedback module;
- the feedback module accesses an educational recommender system engine to provide the trainee further web bibliography for improving one's knowledge.

5. Evaluation of a formative e-assessment system for project management

The e-assessment system was evaluated from two points of view: its performance and its utility. In order to evaluate system performance, the adaptive e-testing was compared to the dynamic e-testing (the questions are randomly selected from the item pool). The utility of the application was evaluated via a short controlled experiment and a questionnaire-based survey.

5.1 Performance evaluation

For evaluating the performance of the e-assessment system, the authors compared the average execution time for selecting one question, in various forms of e-assessment, using item banks of variable dimensions: of 100, 200, 800 and 1600 questions. Also, the number of iterations and the number of particles used by the PSO algorithm was changed. The bigger the size of the item bank is, the more performing the adaptive e-assessment is (see Figure 13). For small item banks, the execution time of an adaptive e-assessment algorithm (PSO for our case) is big, but for large item banks, the execution time is small enough, comparing to other types of algorithms. Also, the execution time for PSO with a lot of iterations and particles is big, but the accuracy of the algorithm is increased.

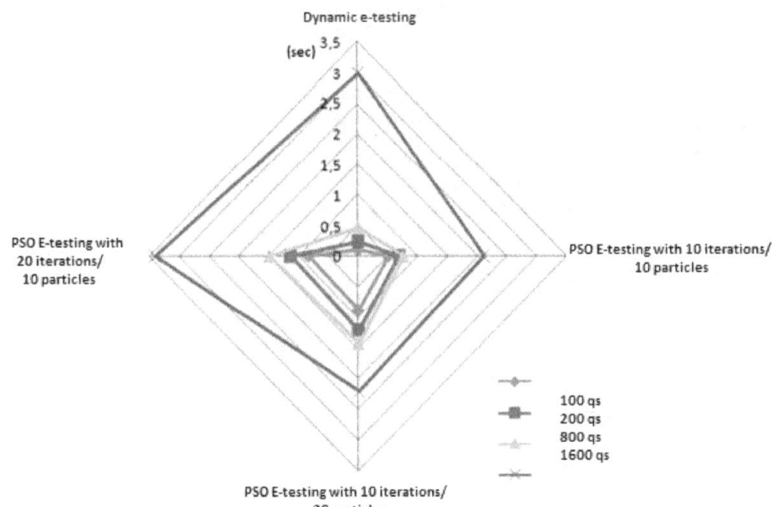

Fig. 13. Average Execution Times for the Selection of One Question, in Various Forms of e-assessment, using Item Banks of Variable Dimensions

5.2 A controlled experiment

The controlled experiment compares the effects of using the proposed e-testing application and the effects of using a classical e-testing application. Two groups of students are used for this purpose, each group having 75 master students. These students were asked to prepare themselves for the certification exam in project management, level D, offered by the Romanian Association of Project Management. Information about the participants to our evaluation study is available in Table 1.

Criterion	Students who used CAT to prepare themselves	Students who didn't use CAT to prepare themselves
Age	under 25: 48 between 25 and 35: 23 over 35: 4	under 25: 44 between 25 and 35: 24 over 35: 7
Previous studies (graduated college)	Technology: 35 Business administration & economics: 32 Other: 8	Technology: 29 Business administration & economics: 30 Other: 16
Hours spent daily in front of a computer	Less than 1 h: 0 Between 1 h and 4 h: 27 Between 4 h and 8 h: 42 Over 8 h: 6	Less than 1 h: 1 Between 1 h and 4 h: 33 Between 4 h and 8 h: 40 Over 8 h: 1

Table 1. Information about the Participants to the Controlled Experiment

All the students passed a diagnostic test, with the same set of questions. The test was a pen-and-pencil test. Then, preparation process for the certification exam started: it has lasted for three months. The first group used the formative e-assessment system three times, during the preparation process. The second group (the control group) used a non-formative system, which had no feedback, adaptive features or recommendation mechanisms. The students from the control group had the possibility to use the non-formative e-assessment system for the same number of times: three times. The two groups didn't know they were using different e-assessment systems. Their results in the preparation process were registered and analyzed. The failure rate was bigger in the controlled group, so the students using the adaptive e-testing were better prepared. Also the progress curve was sharper for the students using the adaptive e-assessment system.

5.3 A Questionnaire-based survey

The questionnaire-based survey focuses on trainers' and trainees' opinions about the utility of the system. The questionnaire contained 10 questions, graded using a 5 points - Likert scale (from "I strongly disagree" to "I strongly agree"). 16 users filled up the questionnaire: 5 tutors (who created rules-based tests) and 11 students. The questions are available in Table 2. When designing the questionnaire, the directives of the Australian Flexible Learning Framework were taken into account: they drew the attention to the the tendency of developers and suppliers of e-assessment applications to be concerned only with the technical aspects of the products, neglecting information about the success and usefulness of products in the learning process *per se* (Australian Flexible Learning Framework, 2011).

All participants agreed that the interface is easy to use, because it is intuitive and it applies the same conventions in all screens. The application is considered quite useful, since it fulfills the established educational objectives and verifies the knowledge gained from assimilation of educational materials provided by the International Project Management Association. Most trainers concluded that the application needs more features: existence of predefined tests, more support to create tests, the possibility to add short videos for the students to be able to react to certain work conduits. Most of the participants agreed that the application was stable; the only problem was the duration of the .NET session, which was too short. This shortcoming was solved by increasing the session duration on the server. The security of the application didn't raise any problems. Most participants consider the feedback to be the most useful feature of the application: 7 out of 11 students strongly agreed on the importance of feedback, 2 agreed and 2 were indifferent. Just 2 out of 11 acknowledge the utility of the adaptive tests: students don't realize that the feedback mechanism is well performing thanks to the adaptive algorithms. This finding can be explained by the fact that technical details are hidden to the students. Most trainers are satisfied with the rules creation interfaces. Just one of them said that he would like to build criteria for rules creation.

Id	Question
Qs1	The interface of the e-assessment solution is attractive and easy to use.
Qs2	The e-assessment application was useful and easily integrated in the educational process.
Qs3	The e-assessment application needs more functionalities.
Qs4	The application stability is satisfacatory.
Qs5	The application security is satisfacatory.
Qs6	If I had the chance, I would choose another e-assessment aplication.
Qs7	(If you are a student) The feedback mechanism is the most important feature of the application.
Qs8	(If you are a student) Applying different adaptivity models in building tests is the most important feature of the application.
Qs9	(If you are a trainer) Test creation is easy to accomplish.
Qs10	(If you are a trainer) Adaptive rules creation is good enough.

Table 2. Questions used at Evaluating the E-assessment System

6. Future directions

As future directions, the following activities are to be followed:

- the optimization of the formative e-testing application;
- spreading of the application in organizations, thus facilitating the development of PM skills.

Regarding the optimization of the formative e-testing application, the fitness function of the PSO approach can be changed, by adding a more accurate description for the fourth term, in which the correlation between the concepts checked by the item tests and the ones established in the learning objectives is depicted. Further experiments are needed, with different learning coefficients for the PSO algorithm and more questions available in the items' pool.

7. Conclusion

The chapter aims at a change of perspective on e-assessment, which is seen not only as a way of knowledge evaluation, but also as a learning instrument, proper for the education of the already employed individuals or for the preparation process for attaining professional certifications. In order to validate this hypothesis, that e-assessment has formative effects, the following methodology was applied: after reviewing the application of e-assessment in professional training, theoretical considerations about building e-assessment systems were drawn, from two points of view: how questions are managed and how tests (sequences of questions) are built. Finally, the implementation of the theoretical considerations was presented within a proposed e-assessment system for project management knowledge. The system was validated though a set of methods: through experiments - for performance and utility validation and through a survey - for utility validation. Positive results were obtained, so a set of best practices can be obtained from the evaluation of the system. In order to build an efficient e-assessment application for PM knowledge, the following strategies are to be applied: the implementation of adaptive algorithms, the exploitation of feedback mechanisms, the implication of teachers/ instructors in the creation of test rules. The evaluation of the system proved its efficiency in professional trainings.

8. References

AL-Smadi, M. & Gütl, C. (2008). Past, Present and Future of e-Assessment: Towards a Flexible e-Assessment System, *Conference ICL 2008*, Villach, Austria, 11/02/2011, Available from: http://www.scribd.com/doc/6947351/Past-Present-and-Future-of-EAssessmentTowards-a-Flexible-EAssessment-System

Ashman, H., Brailsford, T. & Brusilovsky, P. (2009). Personal Services: Debating the Wisdom of Personalisation, *Lecture Notes in Computer Science (5686) - Advances in Web based Learning*, Aachen, August 2009

Assessment Reform Group (ARG) (2002). *Assessment for learning: 10 principles*, Cambridge, UK: University of Cambridge, School of Education

Australian Flexible Learning Framework (2011). Evaluate the Assessment Prrocess, In: *http://designing.flexiblelearning.net.au/assessing/f_evaluate/f020.htm*, March 2011

Azough, S., Bellafkih, M. & Bouyakhf, E. H. (2010). Adaptive E-learning using Genetic Algorithms, *IJCSNS International Journal of Computer Science and Network Security*, Vol. 10, No. 7, pp. 237-277

Biggam, J. (2010). Using Automated Assessment Feedback to Enhance the Quality of Student Learning in Universities: A Case Study, *Technology Enhanced Learning. Quality of Teaching and Educational* Reform, Springer

Birenbaum, M., Kimron, H. Shilton, H. & Shahaf-Barzilay, R. (2009). Cycles of inquiry: Formative assessment in service of learning in classrooms and in school-based professional communities, *Studies in Educational Evaluation* , Vol. 35, pp. 130–149

Black, P. & Wiliam, D. (2009). Developing the theory of formative assessment, *Assessment, Evaluation and Accountability*, Vol. 21, No. 1, 2009, pp. 5-31, doi: 10.1007/s11092-008-9068-5

Bodea, C.-N. & Dascalu, M. (2009). A Parameterized Web-based Testing Model for Project Management, *Lecture Notes in Computer Science (5686) -Advances in Web based Learning, Aachen*, August 2009

Bodea, C.-N. & Dascalu, M. (2010a). Competency-based E-assessment in Project Management and Firm Performance: a Case Study, *Proceedings of the 4th conference on European computing conference* , WSEAS, Bucharest, April 2010

Bodea, C.-N. & Dascalu, M. (2010b). Modeling Project Management Competences: An Ontology-Based Solution for Competency-Based Learning, *Technology Enhanced Learning: Quality of Teaching and Educational Reform, Proceedings of TECH-EDUCATION 2010*, Springer - CCIS 73, Athens, Greece, May 2010

Bodea, C.-N., Dascalu, M .& Coman, M. (2010). Quality of Project Management Education and Training Programmes, *Communications in Computer and Information Science (73) - Technology Enhaced Learning, Quality of Teaching and Educational Reform,* Athens, Greece, May 2010

Bodea, C.N., Niţchi, Ş., Elmas, C., Tănăsescu, A., Dascălu, M.-I. & Mihăilă, A. (2010). Modeling Project Management Competences using an Ontological Approach, *Economic Computation and Economic Cybernetics Studies and Research,* Vol. 44, No. 2, pp. 33-48

Chen, L. & Jiang, W. (2007). The design and implementation of a general examination system, *Computer Engineering and Design*, Vol. 28, No. 17, pp. 4285–4289

Cheng, S.C., Lin, Y.T. & Huang, Y.M. (2009). Dynamic question generation system for web-based testing using particle swarm optimization, *Expert Systems with Applications*, Vol, 36, No. 1, pp. 616–624, doi: 10.1016/j.eswa.2007.09.064

De Bra, P., Aroyo, L. & Cristea , A. (2004). Adaptive web-based educational hypermedia, In *Web dynamics, adaptive to change in content, size, topology and use*, eds. M. Levene, & A. Poulovassilis Springer, pp. 387–410

Dheeban, S.G , Deepak, V., Dhamodharan, L. & Elias, S. (2010). Improved personalized e-course Composition Approach using Modified Particle Swarmn Optimization with Inertia-Coefficient, *International Journal of Computer Applications*, Vol. 1, No. 6, pp. 102-107

Farzan, R. & Brusilovsky, P. (2011). Encouraging user participation in a course recommender system: An impact on user behavior, *Computers in Human Behavior*, Vol. 27, pp. 276–284

Hage, H. &. Aimeur, E. (2005). *Exam Question Recommender System*, Montreal University

Ho, T.F., Yin, P.Y., Hwang, G.J., Shyu, S.J. & Yean, Y.N. (2009). Multi-Objective Parallel Test-Sheet Composition Using Enhanced Particle Swarm Optimization, *Educational Technology & Society*, Vol. 12, No. 4, pp. 193–206

Hsu, J.-L., Chou, H.-W. & Chang, H.-H. (2010). EduMiner: Using text mining for automatic formative assessment, *Expert Systems with Applications*, 2010

Hsu, I.-C. (2009). SXRS: An XLink-based Recommender System using Semantic Web technologies, *Expert Systems with Applications* , Vol. 36, pp. 3795–3804

L. Huang (2006). The application of PSO in intelligent assessment paper generation, *Zhenjiang Institute Journal*, Vol. 19, No. 3, pp. 53–56

Huang, M.-J., Huang, H.-S. & Chen, M.-Y. (2007). Constructing a personalized e-learning system based on genetic algorithm and case-based reasoning approach, *Expert Systems with Applications*, Vol. 33, pp. 551–564, doi: 10.1016/j.eswa.2006.05.019

International Project Management Association (2006). *International Project Management Association Competence Baseline*, Available at: http://www.pm.org.ro/ICB-V-3-0/ICB-V-3-0.pdf

Lazarinis, F., Green, S., Pearson, E. (2010). Creating personalized assessments based on learner knowledge and objectives in a hypermedia Web testing application, *Computers & Education*, Vol. 55, pp. 1732–1743

Manouselis, N., Drachsler, H., Vuorikari, R., Hummel, H. & Koper, R. (2010). Recommender Systems in Technology Enhanced Learning, In: *Recommender Systems Handbook*, eds. F. Ricci, L. Rokach, B. Shapira, P. B. Kantor, Springer, pp. 387-420

Pachler, N., Daly, C., Mor, Y. & Mellar, H. (2010). Formative e-assessment: Practitioner cases, *Computers and Education*, Vol. 54, pp. 715–721

Roşca, I. Gh. & Cristescu, E. (2004). Îmbunatatiri metodologice privind realizarea item-urilor utilizate în evaluarea didactica asistata de calculator, *Informatică Economică*, Vol. 29, No. 129, pp. 33 - 37

Schmidt, A. & Kunzmann, C. (2006). Towards Human Resource Development Ontology for Combining Competence Management and Technology-Enhanced Workplace Learning, *LNCS 4278*, Springer, pp. 1078-1087

Schutte, J. F. & Groenwold, A. (2005). A Study of Global Optimization Using Particle Swarms, *Journal of Global Optimization*, Vol. 31, No. 1, pp. 93 - 108

Shavelson, R.J. (2006). On The Integration Of Formative Assessment In Teaching And Learning with Implications for Teacher Education, *Stanford Education Assessment Laboratory*

Tam, H.P. & Lu, Y.-J. (2011). Developing Assessment for Learning in a Large-Scale Programme, In: *Assessment Reform in Education*, eds Rita Berry & Bob Adamson, Springer, pp. 185 - 196

Vasconcelos, J., Kimble, C., Miranda, H. & Henriques, V. (2009). A Knowledge-engine Architecture for a Competence Management Information System, *UKAIS Conference*, Oxford

Vendlinski, T. P., Niemi, D., Wang, J. & Monempour, S. (2008). Improving Formative Assessment Practice with Educational Information Technology, *Cresst Report 739*, National Center for Research on Evaluation, Standards, and Student Testing, UCLA, University of California, Los Angeles

Wang, T.-H. (2008). Web-based quiz-game-like formative assessment: Development and evaluation, *Computers and Education*, Vol. 51, No. 3, pp. 1247-1263 , doi: 10.1016/j.compedu.2007.11.011

Wang, Q. & Chu, L. (2008). The application of PSO in intelligent assessment paper generation, *Neijiang Technology*, Vol. 1, pp. 134–135

Wong, L.-H. & Looi, C.-K. (2010). Swarm intelligence: new techniques for adaptive systems to provide learning support, *Interactive Learning Environments*, , pp. 1-22, doi: 10.1080/1049482100371468

Yin, P.-Y., Chang, K.-C, Hwang, G.-J., Hwang, G.-H. & Chan, Y. (2006). A particle swarm optimization approach to composing serial test sheets for multiple assessment criteria, *Educational Technology & Society*, Vol. 9, No. 3, pp. 3–15

Zhen, L., Huang, G. Q. & Jiang, Z. (2010). An inner-enterprise knowledge recommender system, *Expert Systems with Applications*, Vol. 37, pp. 1703–1712

10

A Comparative Study Between E-Learning Features

Ajlan S. Al-Ajlan
Information System Management
College of Business and Economics
Qassim University
Kingdom of Saudi Arabia

1. Introduction

Nowadays, there is an increasing demand for methodologies and technologies, especially, for e-learning. E-learning has been defined as interactive learning in which the learning content is available online and provides automatic feedback to the student's learning activities. While recognizing that the world at large will continue to use terminology in different and often ambiguous ways, the term of e-learning is used to refer to the "online" interactions of various kinds that take place between learners and tutors (Dougiamas, 2011; Yuuichi et al., 2006; Tortora, et al., 2002 and Bruce & Curson, 2007).

The main purpose of this chapter is to study, analyze, and explore the right decision when choosing a suitable VLE platform to meet the requirements of Qassim University. It has focused on a comparison between Moodle and other VLE systems, and is based on two kinds of comparison. The first study compared Moodle with nine VLE platforms based on features and capabilities of VLE tools, as in Section 2.1. The second study compared Moodle with other VLE platforms based on the technical aspects of VLEs, as in Section 2.2.

This study has proved that the best platforms are Moodle and Sakai, which have missed just two out of forty features. The second study has strongly recommended choosing Moodle as the optimal VLE platform for Qassim University. The first and second studies have proved that Moodle has the best results. In addition, it has the advantages mentioned in Section 3.3, and we therefore strongly recommend Moodle as the best choice for higher education generally, and for Qassim University in particular.

This chapter is structured as follows. A comparative study between e-learning features is presented in Sections 2, which is the most important section in this chapter. In Section 3, a literature review of Moodle as a selected platform is presented, including the reasons for choosing Moodle together with its limitations, the architecture of Moodle and explains most of its components. Sections 4 and 5 focus on the e-learning tools of Moodle and an assignment activity respectively. Section 6 describes some of the websites that are using Moodle across the world. Finally, the summery of this chapter is in Section 7.

2. Comparative study between e-learning features

An important resource for higher education, especially universities, is VLE, which has been enhancing students' progress with high quality learning around the world. This section will propose a suitable e-learning system to consider it as a specific area of study through a comparative study of the most well-known e-learning systems. It is an important to make a comparison study between VLE products to select the suitable one and test it with our approach and also explore their strengths and limitations. This comparative study is in two phases. The first phase is based on the features and capabilities of VLE tools, and the second is based on the technical aspects of the systems of VLEs.

2.1 Comparative study based on features and capabilities of VLE tools

VLEs have many features and capabilities such as forums, content management, quizzes with different kinds of questions, and a number of activity modules. Moodle has an additional number of contributed modules, including SCORM WebQuest and the Document Management System (Martin, et al., 2004). In this section, we have selected 10 VLE products, including Moodle, to make comparisons between them, and our first comparison is based on the features and capabilities of VLE tools. I am very thankful to the EduTools website (EduTools, 2006), which lists more than 80 VLE products and has performed a comparison of 42 VLE features and capabilities, as in Table 2.

Our comparison focuses on two kinds of products. The first is commercial e-learning systems and comprises Desire2Learn 8.1, ANGEL Learning Management Suite (7.1), TeleTOP Virtual Learning Environment, The Blackboard Learning System (V7) and Scholar360. The second is OSS and comprises LON-CAPA, Sakai 2.3, dotLRN/OpenACS, ATutor 1.5.4 and Moodle 1.8. The comparison has two answers, Y or N. Y means the product has the feature and N means the product does not. Table 4.3 displays information about the ten VLE software packages used in the first comparison. VLE Tools are criteria-based products that enable developers to evaluate and select the best VLE product. No single VLE product can possibly meet all these criteria and may not be the best for interface, technical, functional, or cost reasons. These criteria are described below in Table 2 (Dougiamas, 2011 and Al-Ajlan, et al., 2008).

No	Product	Developer name	Date	URL
1	LON-CAPA	Gerd Kortemeyer	Oct/2006	LON-CAPA Project
2	Desire2Learn 8.1	Desire2Learn Inc.	Oct/2006	Desire2Learn Inc.
3	ANGEL Learning 7.1	ANGEL Learning Inc	Oct/2006	Angel Learning
4	TeleTOP VLE	TeleTop B.V.	Oct/2006	TeleTop
5	Blackboard (V6.2)	BlackBoard	Nov/2006	Blackboard LSE
6	Sakai 2.3	Sakai 2.3	Nov/2006	Sakai
7	dotLRN/OpenACS	dotLRN	Jan/2007	dotlrn.org
8	Scholar360	Scholar360	Jan/2007	www.scholar360.com
9	ATutor 1.5.4	University of Toronto	April/2007	atutor.ca/atutor/index.php
10	Moodle 1.8	Moodlerooms	April/2007	www.Moodle.org

Table 1. General Information about the Selected Products.

VLEs as an e-learning system have many features and capabilities. For simplicity, we have divided these features and capabilities into three phases, which are Learner Tools, Support Tools and Technical Tools, as in Table 4.4. Chapter 3 "Virtual Learning Environments As E-learning Systems" has more details about these tools. Table 2 lists the features and capabilities of VLE tools that we have used in our comparison in this chapter.

1) Learner Tools	2) Support Tools	3) Technical Specifications
1. <u>Communication Tools</u> ▪ Discussion Forums ▪ File Exchange / Internal Email ▪ Online Journal/Notes ▪ Real-time Chat ▪ Video Services / Whiteboard	1. <u>Administration Tools</u> ▪ Authentication ▪ Course Authorization ▪ Registration Integration ▪ Hosted Services	1. <u>Hardware/Software</u> ▪ Client Browser Required ▪ Database Requirements ▪ Server Software ▪ UNIX Server ▪ Windows Server
2. <u>Productivity Tools</u> ▪ Bookmarks ▪ Orientation / Help ▪ Searching Within Course ▪ Calendar / Progress Review ▪ Work Offline/Synchronize	2. <u>Course Delivery Tools</u> ▪ Course Management ▪ Instructor Helpdesk ▪ Online Grading Tools ▪ Student Tracking ▪ Automated Testing and Scoring	2. <u>Pricing/Licensing</u> ▪ Company Profile ▪ Costs ▪ Open Source ▪ Optional Extras ▪ Software Version
3. <u>Student Involvement Tools</u> ▪ Groupwork ▪ Self-assessment ▪ Student Community Building ▪ Student Portfolios	3. <u>Curriculum Design</u> ▪ Accessibility Compliance ▪ Course Templates ▪ Curriculum Management ▪ Customized Look and Feel ▪ Instructional Standards Compliance ▪ Instructional Design Tools ▪ Content Sharing / Reuse	

Table 2. Summaries of the Features and Capabilities of VLE tools.

2.1.1 Learner tools

This phase contains three kinds of tools: Communication Tools, Productivity Tools and Student Involvement Tools. Each Learner Tool has some features and capabilities as in Table 2 above.

These tools contain three kinds of tools, which are Communication Tools, Productivity Tools and Student Involvement Tools. Each kind of Learner Tool contains various features and capabilities, and each product has some of them, as in Table 1.

As we can see in Table 3, the comparison between the VLE products is based on Learner Tools. Four products are shown to be the best with almost the maximum number of features 15 out of 16 features or capabilities of Learner Tools. These products are Moodle, Desire2Learn, ANGEL Learning Management Suite, and Sakai.

As we can see in Table 3, all products have all features and capabilities except Scholar360, TeleTOP Virtual Learning Environment and The Blackboard Learning System (V.7). This means that Moodle and the other remaining products are strong on Learner Tools.

The Learner Tools in Table 3 have many features and capabilities, and to understand what they mean, please visit the EduTools website. We have also listed them in Table 2.

2.1.2 Support tools

These tools contain three kinds of tools: Administration Tools, Course Delivery Tools, and Content Development Tools, and all of these tools have features and capabilities.

As we can see in Table 4, this comparison between the VLE products is based on Support Tools. In this phase, all products have all features and capabilities except Scholar360,

No	1	2	3	4	5	6	7	8	9	10
Name / Product / Tools	LON-CAPA	Desire2Learn 8.1	ANGEL Learning Management Suite	TeleTOP VLE	The Blackboard Learning System	Sakai 2.3	dotLRN/OpenACS	Scholar360	ATutor 1.5.4	Moodle 1.8
1. Learner Tools										
1.1. Communication Tools										
Discussion Forums	Y	Y	Y	Y	Y	Y	Y	Y	Y	Y
Discussion Management	N	Y	Y	Y	Y	Y	Y	Y	Y	Y
File Exchange	Y	Y	Y	Y	Y	Y	Y	Y	Y	Y
Internal Email	Y	Y	Y	Y	Y	Y	Y	Y	Y	Y
Online Journal/Notes	N	Y	Y	N	Y	Y	N	Y	N	Y
Real-time Chat	Y	Y	Y	Y	Y	Y	Y	Y	Y	Y
Video Services	N	N	N	N	N	N	N	N	N	Y
Whiteboard	N	Y	Y	Y	Y	Y	N	N	Y	Y
2. Productivity Tools										
Bookmarks	Y	Y	Y	Y	N	Y	Y	Y	N	N
Calendar / Progress review	Y	Y	Y	Y	Y	Y	Y	Y	Y	Y
Orientation/Help	Y	Y	Y	Y	Y	Y	N	Y	Y	Y
Searching Within Course	Y	Y	Y	Y	Y	Y	Y	N	Y	Y
Work Offline/Synchronize	Y	Y	Y	Y	Y	Y	N	Y	Y	Y
1.3. Student Involvement Tools										
Groupwork	Y	Y	Y	Y	Y	Y	Y	N	Y	Y
Student Community Building	N	Y	Y	Y	Y	Y	Y	Y	Y	Y
Student Portfolios	Y	Y	Y	Y	Y	Y	Y	Y	N	Y
Total Features	16	16	16	16	16	16	16	16	16	16
Total Available Features	11	15	15	14	14	15	11	12	12	15
Total Missing Features	5	1	1	2	2	1	5	4	4	1

Table 3. The Comparison between Selected VLE Products based on Support Tools.

TeleTOP Virtual Learning Environment and The Blackboard Learning System (V.7). This means that Moodle and the other remaining products are strong on Support Tools.
The Support Tools in Table 4 have many features and capabilities, and to understand what they mean, please visit the EduTools. We have also listed them in Table 2.

2.1.3 Technical specifications tools

These tools contain two kinds of tools: Hardware/Software Tools and Pricing/Licensing; all kinds of Technical Specifications Tools have some features and capabilities, as in Table 5. The costs feature is different from other features because if the product has no cost, it means that product has an advantage and we will calculate it as Yes (Y). For example, in Table 5, Moodle has two N and we calculated N of cost as Y, so in the final score Moodle has missed just one feature.

No	1	2	3	4	5	6	7	8	9	10
Product Name / Tools	LON-CAPA	Desire2Learn 8.1	ANGEL Learning Management Suite (7.1)	TeleTOP VLE	The Blackboard Learning System (V 7)	Sakai 2.3	dotLRN/OpenACS	Scholar360	ATutor 1.5.4	Moodle 1.8
2. Support Tools										
2.1. Administration Tools										
➢ Authentication	Y	Y	Y	Y	Y	Y	Y	Y	Y	Y
➢ Course Authorization	Y	Y	Y	Y	Y	Y	Y	Y	Y	Y
➢ Hosted Services	Y	Y	Y	Y	Y	Y	Y	Y	Y	Y
➢ Registration Integration	Y	Y	Y	Y	Y	Y	Y	Y	Y	Y
2.2. Course Delivery Tools										
➢ Test Types	Y	Y	Y	Y	Y	Y	Y	Y	Y	Y
➢ Automated Testing Management	Y	Y	Y	Y	Y	Y	Y	Y	Y	Y
➢ Automated Testing Support	Y	Y	Y	Y	Y	Y	Y	Y	Y	Y
➢ Course Management	Y	Y	Y	Y	Y	Y	Y	Y	Y	Y
➢ Online Grading Tools	Y	Y	Y	Y	Y	Y	Y	Y	Y	Y
➢ Student Tracking	Y	Y	Y	Y	Y	Y	Y	N	Y	Y
2.3. Content Development Tools										
➢ Accessibility Compliance	Y	Y	Y	N	Y	Y	Y	Y	Y	Y
➢ Content Sharing/Reuse	Y	Y	Y	Y	N	Y	Y	Y	Y	Y
➢ Course Templates	Y	Y	Y	Y	Y	Y	Y	Y	Y	Y
➢ Customized Look and Feel	Y	Y	Y	Y	Y	Y	Y	Y	Y	Y
➢ Instructional Design	Y	Y	Y	Y	Y	Y	Y	Y	Y	Y
➢ Instructional Standards Compliance	Y	Y	Y	Y	Y	Y	Y	Y	Y	Y
Total Features	**16**	**16**	**16**	**16**	**16**	**16**	**16**	**16**	**16**	**16**
Total Available Features	**16**	**16**	**16**	**15**	**15**	**16**	**16**	**15**	**16**	**16**
Total Missing Features	**0**	**0**	**0**	**1**	**1**	**0**	**0**	**1**	**0**	**0**

Table 4. The Comparison between Selected VLE Products based on Support Tools.

As we can see in Table 5 below, the comparison between the VLE products is based on Technical Specifications Tools. In this phase, the best product is ATutor 1.5.4, Moodle 1.8, Scholar360 and The Blackboard Learning System, which missed only 1 out of the 8 Technical Specifications Tools. The weakest product is LON-CAPA, which missed 5 out of the 8.

The Technical Specifications in Table 5 have many features and capabilities, and to understand what these features and capabilities mean, please visit the EduTools. We have also listed them in Table 2.

No	1	2	3	4	5	6	7	8	9	10
Tools \ Product Name	LON-CAPA	Desire2Learn 8.1	ANGEL Learning Management Suite (7.1)	TeleTOP VLE	The Blackboard Learning System (V 7)	Sakai 2.3	dotLRN/OpenACS	Scholar360	ATutor 1.5.4	Moodle 1.8
3. Technical Specifications										
3.1. Hardware/Software Tools										
Client Browser Required	N	Y	Y	N	Y	Y	N	Y	Y	Y
Database Requirements	Y	Y	Y	N	Y	Y	Y	Y	Y	Y
Unix Server	Y	N	N	Y	Y	Y	Y	Y	Y	Y
Windows Server	N	Y	Y	Y	Y	Y	Y	Y	Y	Y
3.2. Pricing/Licensing Tools										
Company Profile	N	Y	Y	N	Y	Y	N	Y	Y	N
Costs	N	Y	Y	Y	Y	N	N	Y	N	Y
Open Source	Y	N	N	N	N	Y	Y	N	Y	Y
Optional Extras	N	Y	Y	Y	Y	N	N	Y	Y	Y
Total Features	8	8	8	8	8	8	8	8	8	8
Total Available Features	3	6	6	4	7	6	4	7	8	7
Total Missing Features	5	2	2	4	1	2	4	1	1	1

Table 5. The Comparison between VLE Products based on Technical Specifications Tools.

2.1.4 The final result of the comparison between the ten VLE products

From Table 6 below, we can see the final result of the comparison between the ten VLE products. The best product is Moodle 1.8, which has missed just 2 out of 40 features and capabilities, and the second products are Desire2Learn 8.1, ANGEL Learning Management Suite (7.1) and Sakai 2.3 equally, which have missed 3 out of the 40. Also, Moodle is the best of the OSS products. The weakest product is LON-CAPA, which has missed 10 out of the 40.

No	1	2	3	4	5	6	7	8	9	10
Tools \ Product Name	LON-CAPA	Desire2Learn 8.1	ANGEL Learning Management Suite (7.1)	TeleTOP Virtual Learning Environment	The Blackboard Learning System (V 7)	Sakai 2.3	dotLRN/OpenACS	Scholar360	ATutor 1.5.4	Moodle 1.8
Total Features	40	40	40	40	40	40	40	40	40	40
Total Available Features	30	37	37	33	36	37	31	34	35	38
Total Missing Features	10	3	3	7	4	3	9	6	5	2

Table 6. The Final Result of the Comparison between Ten VLE Products.

We use the GraphPad Prism software to analyse, graph and present scientific data of VLE products because it is a powerful combination of basic biostatistics, curve fitting and scientific graphing in one comprehensive program. More than one hundred scientists in over one hundred countries rely on Prism to analyse, graph and present their scientific data.

Since 1984, created by scientists for scientists, Prism's intuitive programs have provided researchers worldwide with the tools they need to simplify data analysis, statistics and graphing (Jolla, 2008). Figure 1 shows the comparison between the ten products of VLE systems. The total features are 40 but no product has reached this number. In Figure 1, P1, P2 etc mean the VLE product as mentioned in Table 4.8 above respectively.

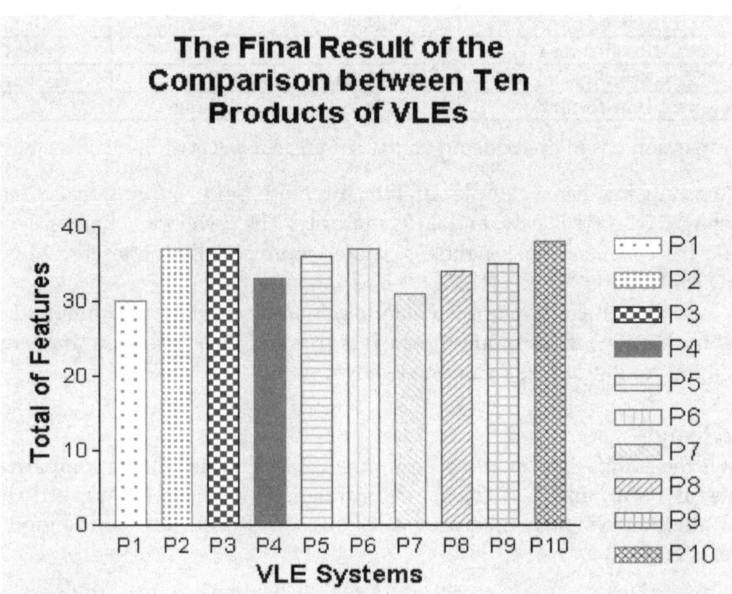

Fig. 1. The Total Features of the Ten VLE Products.

As in Figure 1, the best VLE product is P10 (Moodle 1.8), which has 38 out of 40 features and capabilities, and the weakest is P1 (LON-CAPA), which has 30 out of the 40. P10 (Moodle) has 38 out of the 40 features and capabilities and is the number 1 out of the 10 VLE products. It is number 1 out of the OSS products, which itself has missed just 2 out of the 40 features and capabilities (Al-Ajlan, et al., 2008).

2.2 Comparison based on focusing on the technical aspects of the VLE systems

In this session, the comparison between the systems is based on technical categories. All VLE systems will be compared with the Moodle system as part of our study. As in our literature review, we have selected three studies focusing on this kind of comparison.

2.2.1 First study

As in (Wharekura-tini, et al., 2004) Moodle has limitations, notably it lacks SCORM support, and its roles and permissions system is limited. However, these limitations can be fixed, and are part of the project roadmap in Moodle site.

Table 7 reveals that ATutor, while strong in features and usability, has serious architectural limitations, and although some features in ATutor warrant further investigation, it may be that candidates will opt for Moodle.

Product / Category	ATutor	ILIAS	Moodle
Architecture	Weak	Complex	Good
Implementation	Weak	Complex	Good
Interoperability	Bad	Good	Average
Cost of ownership	Medium	High	Low
Strength of the community	Low	Medium	High
Licensing	GPL	GPL	GPL
Internationalization	Weak	Average	Good
Accessibility	Excellent	Bad	Average
Document transformation	No	Average	No

Table 7. Comparison based on focusing on the technical aspects of the VLE systems.

ILIAS, while promising, has a complex architecture with tight coupling that is hard to work with and debug. The code is new, and lacks maturity. The developer community of ILIAS is small outside the core team. Nevertheless, some features in ILIAS deserve to be reviewed before opting for Moodle.

Moodle has a good architecture, implementation, inter-operability, and internationalization, and also has the strength of the community. It is free and its accessibility is average. On the other hand, it has limitations, as mentioned above.

2.2.2 Second study

Table 8 shows the comparison between 4 products of VLE systems. The comparison is based on categories as (Graf, and List, 2005) determined. This study has proved that Moodle outperforms all other systems and scored 4.467 out of 5. In contrast, Boddington gained the lowest score, at 2.439.

Product / Category	Moodle	Sakai	ATutor	Boddington
Functionality	1.25	.75	.25	.25
Usability	.8	.8	.6	.65
Documentation	.645	.465	.54	.54
Community	.6	.384	.24	.288
Security	.42	.34	.28	.42
Support	.4	.15	.35	.15
Adoption	.352	.336	.208	.336
Total Score (out of 5)	4.467	3.225	2.468	2.439

Table 8. Comparison based on focusing on some Features and Categories of VLEs.

Moodle has nearly the maximum score because it has many of the features expected from an e-learning platform, including forums, resources, quizzes with different kinds of questions, and a number of activity modules. Furthermore, Moodle is very beneficial for language teaching and learning because the interactive tools, such as wiki, discussion forums, and quizzes, can be selectively employed to meet the objectives of the course and to motivate students.

2.2.3 Third study

In (Alvarez, 2008) the study reports that the result of the evaluation shows that Moodle has the best rating in the adaptation category; it can be seen in Table 9 as the best system concerning adaptation issues. It dominates the evaluation by achieving the best value five times. The strengths of Moodle are the realization of communication tools, the creation and administration of learning objects, the comprehensive didactical concepts and the tracking of data. In addition, the outstanding usability of Moodle leads to the maximum evaluation value in the usability category. Concerning the other platforms, ILIAS obtained the best values in the categories for technical aspects, administration, and course management.

<table>
<tr><th colspan="2">Product
Feature</th><th>Adaptability</th><th>Personalization</th><th>Extensibility</th><th>Adaptively</th><th>Ranking</th></tr>
<tr><td>1</td><td>ATutor</td><td>|</td><td>#</td><td>#</td><td>|</td><td>3</td></tr>
<tr><td>2</td><td>Dokeos</td><td>|</td><td>0</td><td>*</td><td>+</td><td>2</td></tr>
<tr><td>3</td><td>dotLRN</td><td>+</td><td>+</td><td>*</td><td>0</td><td>2</td></tr>
<tr><td>4</td><td>ILIAS</td><td>+</td><td>#</td><td>*</td><td>0</td><td>2</td></tr>
<tr><td>5</td><td>LON-CAPA</td><td>+</td><td>#</td><td>#</td><td>|</td><td>2</td></tr>
<tr><td>6</td><td>Moodle</td><td>#</td><td>+</td><td>*</td><td>|</td><td>1</td></tr>
<tr><td>7</td><td>OpenUSS</td><td>#</td><td>#</td><td>#</td><td>0</td><td>2</td></tr>
<tr><td>8</td><td>Sakai</td><td>0</td><td>0</td><td>*</td><td>0</td><td>3</td></tr>
<tr><td>9</td><td>Spaghettilearning</td><td>+</td><td>#</td><td>+</td><td>0</td><td>3</td></tr>
</table>

Table 9. Results of the Adaptation Category.

Moodle has gained the best results, especially in the specific adaptation evaluation as in Table 9. It supports an adaptive feature called "lesson" where learners can be routed automatically through pages depending on the answer to a question after each page. Furthermore, the extensibility is supported very well by a documented API, detailed guidelines, and templates for programming. In addition personalization and adaptability features are present in Moodle (Alvarez, 2008).

2.2.4 Fourth study

In (Cole, 2005), the study reports the percentage of universities that are developing or using e-learning frameworks. The result of e-learning survey conducted the use of web-based learning management systems for higher education. This study discussed with some members of the scientific community on this field in the Department of Computer Science at the University of Oviedo.

As we can see in Figure 2, Moodle is the best product that has 34.55% and the second product is WebCT/Blackboard that has 27.27%. The weakest product is Sakai and dotLRN that have same percentage 10.91%.

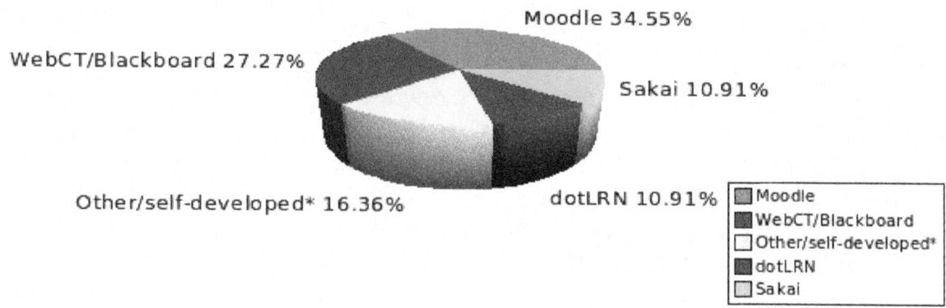

Fig. 2. Chart of use of web-based e-learning systems in Universities.

3. Moodle as a selected platform

According to the comparison study above, we have chosen Moodle as the suitable platform for this project. In this section, we will present the literature on Moodle including its architecture, benefits and limitations and tools, as well as we will mention more reasons for choosing this platform. Moodle is the most user-friendly and flexible free open-source courseware products available all over the world. Moodle is a VLE that lets teachers provide and share documents, assignments, quizzes, forums, chats, etc. with students in an easy-to-learn and user-friendly interface (Dougiamas, 2011; Cole, 2005 and Wharekura-tini, 2004).

Moodle is CMS designed to help educators who want to create quality online courses. It has excellent documentation, strong support for security and administration, and is evolving towards Information Management System/Shareable Content Object Reference Model (IMS/SCORM) standards (Zenha-Rela, et al., 2006 and Cole, 2005). Moodle has a strong development and large user community and users can download and use it on any computer they have at hand (Berry, 2005; Brandl, 2005 and Al-Ajlan, et al., 2008).

3.1 The definition of Moodle

An important feature of the Moodle is the Moodle.org web site, which provides a central point for information, discussion and collaboration among Moodle users, who include system administrators, teachers, researchers, instructional designers and of course, developers. Like Moodle, this site is always evolving to suit the needs of the community. Moodle is now used not only in universities, but also in high schools, primary schools, non-profit organizations, private companies, and by independent teachers and even home-schooling parents. A growing number of people from around the world are contributing to Moodle in different ways (Dougiamas, 2011; Yuuichi et al., 2006, and Dougiamas, 2004).

Moodle is based on Social Constructionist Pedagogy (SCP), which is a learner-oriented philosophy and most VLE modules are based on it. They are largely concerned with how course contents are delivered, in which students are involved in constructing their own knowledge (Graf, et al., 2005 and Cole, 2005). The learner-oriented philosophy of learning is that learners actively construct new knowledge by tinkering and experimenting, and they learn even more by explaining what they have learned to others and by adopting a more subjective stance to the knowledge being created. These ideas run parallel to the way open-source development works, in which the developers also are often users, everyone is free to tinker with the software and code is re-constructed or adapted, peer-reviewed and refined by the means of open discussion (Berry, 2005 and Chavan, et al., 2004).

3.2 The history of Moodle

Moodle was created by Martin Dougiamas while working on a postgraduate degree at the Curtin University of Technology in Australia. In 2002, he was a Webmaster of a university and a system administrator of WebCT installation. He started to develop Moodle to solve some problems with WebCT. The original version was targeted for small classes and a case study, but steadily many features were added by developers and other contributors from all over the world (Martin, et al., 2004; Dougiamas, 2004 and Koh, 2006).

Abhijeet Chavan and Shireen Pavri have said, "Moodle was born out of a need to scratch an itch. Frustrated by proprietary alternatives, Martin, then a PhD candidate in Education with a background in computer science, started Moodle in 1999. In 2002, Version 1.0 was released. Since then, Moodle has continued to evolve at a rapid rate, managed by Martin and propelled by an active world-wide community of users and developers" (Chavan, and Pavri, 2004). The Moodle Company "Moodle.com" has been providing managed hosting and consulting services since 2003. Currently, Moodle has a large and diverse user community with over 1,077,969 users on this site, speaking 86 languages in 212 countries around the world (Al-Ajlan, et al., 2008).

3.3 The reasons for choosing Moodle

OSS is rapidly developing, and new alternatives for non-profit organizations are emerging and maturing. Additionally, open-source learning environments such as Moodle are becoming widely adopted by university and educational institutions. Managing an LMS can be a complex task. Moodle does not hide this complexity and its detailed on-line help, examples and sensible defaults assist users in installing, administering and using the LMS. Moodle allows users to post news items, assignments, electronic journals and resources, and to collect assignments etc. The greatest strength of Moodle is the community that has grown around the project. Both developers and users participate in Moodle's active discussion forums, sharing tips, posting code snippets, helping new users, sharing resources and debating new ideas. Thus, we have chosen the Moodle software to be the area of study and analysis. We want to understand Moodle's environment to explore its functionalities and limitations in order to develop practical examples of the use of VLEs over the world. We list here the most important reasons for choosing this package: (Dougiamas, 2011; Yuuichi et al., 2006; Berry, 2005; Zenha-Rela, et al., 2006; Cole,2005; Dougiamas, 2004; Chavan, et al., 2004; Koh, 2006; Williams et al., 2006; Itmazi, 2005; Shearer, 2003; Wharekura-tini, et al., 2004; MacKenzie, et al., 2006; Chao Su, 2005; Al-Ajlan, et al., 2008 and Massy, 2004).

1. Moodle is OSS, which means users are free to download it, use it, modify it and even distribute it under the terms of GNU;
2. Moodle is CMS & VLE, and lets teachers provide and share documents, graded assignments, quizzes, discussion forums, etc. with their students in an easy-to-learn manner and to create quality online courses;
3. Moodle can be used on almost all servers that can use PHP;
4. The key to Moodle is that has been developed with both pedagogy and technology in mind. One of the main advantages of Moodle over other systems is a strong grounding in social constructionist pedagogy with good educational tools;
5. It works well with languages and is currently being used in 86 languages in 112 countries;
6. Users can download and use Moodle on any computer they have at hand;
7. It has excellent documentation, and strong support for security and administration and easy to upgrade from one version to the next;
8. It has many user-friendly features such as easy installation, customization of options and settings, good support/help and good educational tools;
9. It demonstrates the use of OSS in creating a high quality e-learning environment that incorporates many other subjects;
10. Moodle is the LMS most often recommended of all the OSS packages , as well as being the most popular;
11. The credibility of Moodle is very high. At present, there are 52289 web sites from 193 countries that have registered with it ;

12. The importance of Moodle is its good reputation according to good reports, grade of admission in the community and number of places, existing languages, etc ;
13. Moodle should be able to be used in conjunction with other systems. It keeps all files for one course within a single, normal directory on the server. Administrators allow the provision of seamless forms of file-level access for each teacher, such as SMB, FTP, and so on. Currently, there is work on more features planned for Moodle in future versions, such as export and import data using XML that can be integrated visually into other web sites. In addition, has presented a good solution for this integration, enabling more VLEs to work together by using Web services and related techniques (Al-Ajlan, et al., 2008);
14. Moodle runs without modification on Unix, Linux, Windows, Mac OS X, Netware and any other systems that support PHP;
15. Data is stored in a single database: MySQL or PostgreSQL are best but it also supports Oracle, Access, Interbase, ODBC and others;
16. Some universities integrate Moodle with other VLE products, such as Oxford University which has integrated two OSS learning environments, Bodington VLE and Moodle although they are slightly different to each other.

3.4 The limitations of Moodle

Moodle's low cost, flexibility and ease of use helps bring LMS technology within the reach of those with limited technical and financial resources. Moodle is a fine example of how and why open source works (Williams et al., 2006). On the other hand, Moodle has some disadvantages and we will mention some of them, as follows:

1. OSS is only for IT experts and is too difficult for normal users to install and use; more than 66% users of Moodle have identified themselves as teachers, on-line learning researchers or educational administrators (Chavan, et al., 2004, Koh, 2006);
2. Lack of simple-to-obtain support. The forum has a great deal of information, but nearly all forums are in the English language (Chavan, and Pavri, 2004);
3. It requires that someone on staff takes responsibility for making it work, you cannot just telephone Moodle technical support;
4. Although good with languages, some developments may be needed for vigorous handling of MathML and enhanced tracking features. Still, this program receives a high recommendation (Wharekura-tini, et al., 2004, Koh, 2006);
5. The Moodle website states that the steps required for getting Moodle up and running on a web server are very simple, but in practise this is not the case. There have been many problems that we have had to overcome, which required a technical understanding of the underlying technology and the way it all hangs together (Shearer, 2003);

3.5 The architecture of Moodle

The strength of Moodle is its simple, but solid design and architecture developed by Martin Dougiamas. The architecture of Moodle sets an excellent foundation, following good practices of low coupling and high cohesion, which the other LMSs fail to achieve. This yields a system that is simple, flexible and effective and easily accessible to developers (Dougiamas, 2011). Figure 3 illustrates the architecture of the Moodle site and its components.

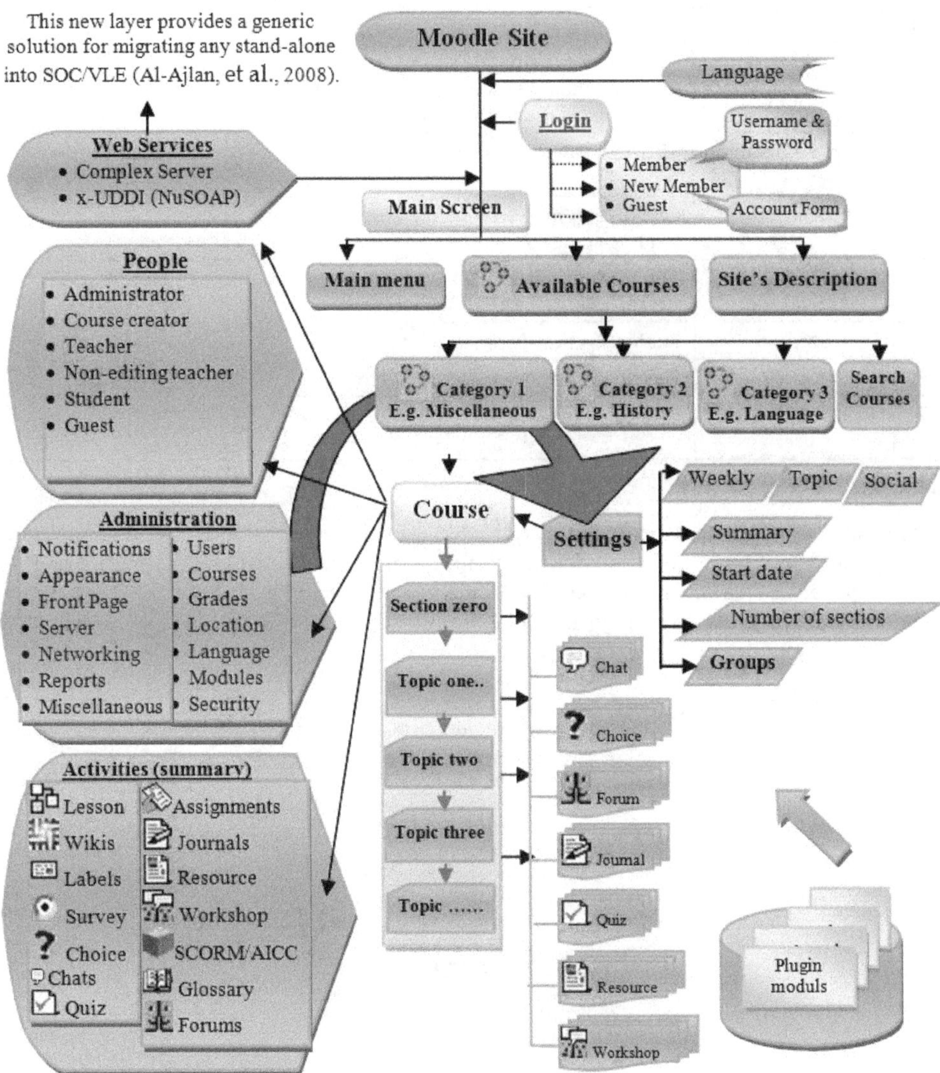

Fig. 3. Architecture of Moodle Sites.

Moodle is a huge VLE software and it is difficult to focus on all parts in this chapter. Therefore, we will focus on the most important components, as in Figure 4.1 above, and these components are:

3.5.1 People

The different kinds of users in any VLE platform and especially in Moodle are described in Table 10. These users need especial authorization depending on their level in Moodle, as in Figure 4. For example, an administrator has the full permission to do anything in the Moodle site and can control users and courses.

No	User	Description
1	Administrator	This kind of user is the most important user and has the full permission to do anything in Moodle, especially in courses. It has the responsibility to manage the site and control all users.
2	Course creator	This user can create new courses and mange them as well as teach these courses.
3	Teacher	Can do anything within a course, including changing the activities and grading students.
4	Non-editing teacher	Can teach in courses and grade students, but may not alter activities.
5	Student	Students generally have fewer privileges within a course.
6	Guest	Has minimal privileges and usually cannot enter text anywhere.
7	Authenticated user	All logged in users.

Table 10. The Users in Moodle Sites.

The authorization for users in Moodle is divided into six levels, as in Figure 4. Every user has some level of permission that Moodle permits, and Figure 4 displays this permission in percentage terms. Administrator has 100% and can do anything in the site. In contrast, Guest has just 10%, such as looking at available courses and sharing in general forums.

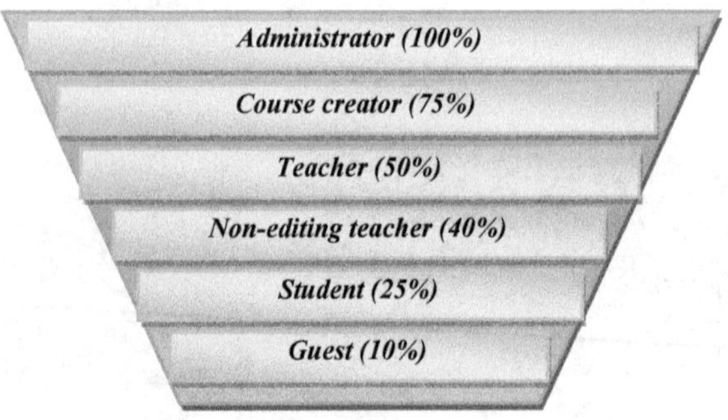

Fig. 4. The level of Authorisation in Moodle Sites.

Figure 5 below shows the users of Moodle in one course at Ajlan's High School. This school has many categories, each with many courses, as in Figure 9. By assigning a role to a user in a context, users are granted the permissions contained in that role for the current context and all lower contexts (site/system, course categories, courses and blocks and activities).

For example, if an administrator grants a student a role in a course, that student will have permission to access that course and all blocks and activities inside it. Their actual permissions may depend on other roles and overrides that have been previously defined. Figure 5 shows the assigned roles of one course in Ajlan's High School, which has 7 kinds of users.

Assign roles

Roles	Description	Users
Administrator	Administrators can usually do anything on the site, in all courses.	1
Course creator	Course creators can create new courses and teach in them.	1
Teacher	Teachers can do anything within a course, including changing the activities and grading students.	2
Non-editing teacher	Non-editing teachers can teach in courses and grade students, but may not alter activities.	0
Student	Students generally have less privileges within a course.	51
Guest	Guests have minimal privileges and usually can not enter text anywhere.	8
Authenticated user	All logged in users.	27

Moodle Docs for this page

You are logged in as Ajlan Suliman Al-Ajlan (Logout)

Fig. 5. The Assign Roles of Users in Ajlan's High School.

3.5.2 Administration

Administration has many tools related to course, as in Figure 6. An administrator can control the course through the administration tools but can only control these tools by the permission granted, as in Figure 6. In our example, all these tools appear for the administrator in the administration site in Ajlan's High School, as in Figure 6.

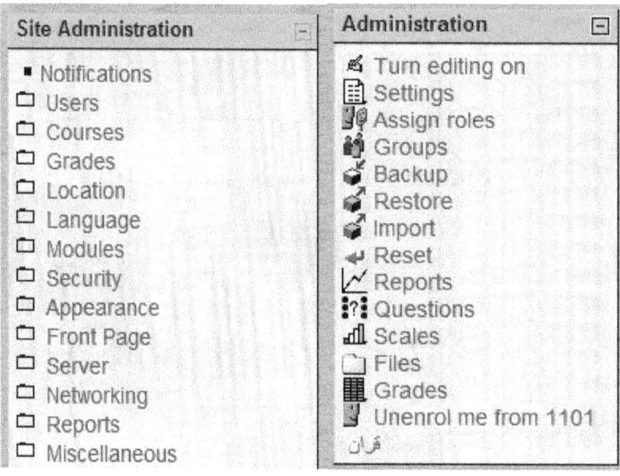

Fig. 6. Tthe Tools of Administration in the Main Screen and Course in Ajlan's High School.

No	Tool	Description
1	Turn editing on	This tool enables the user to open and activate a course.
2	Settings	To create a new course.
3	Assign roles	To add users for the level of authorisation as in Figure 4.2.
4	Groups	The group mode can be defined at two levels: course level and activity level, and each can be sub-divided into three: no groups, separate groups and visible groups.
5	Backup	To save and backup data in user's computer
6	Restore	This allows users to restore files to a course.
7	Import	To upload files that have been saved in a computer with the export feature.
8	Reset	This tool allows users to empty a course of user data, while retaining the activities and other settings.
9	Reports	These are available for each participant and they show their activities in the current course. Teachers always have access to these reports, using the button visible on each persons's profile page. Student access to their own reports is controlled by the teacher via a course setting
10	Questions	Questions five types multiple choice, short answer, true/false, matching and numerical. These questions have an option that is activated by clicking on the checkbox.
11	Scales	Teachers can create new custom scales to be used in a course for any grading activities.
12	Files	To upload files
13	Grades	Many of the activities allow grades to be set. By default, the results of all grades within the course can be seen in the Grades page, available from the main course page.
14	Unenrol me from 1101	This means take a user out of course.

Table 11. The Tools in Administration Form in Course in Moodle Sites.

3.5.3 Activities

Moodle contains a wide range of activity modules, which are activity modules, resource types, and open source and they can be used to build up any type of course. All these activities are under course in the Moodle architecture, as in Figure 3.

3.5.4 Category

This tool enables administrators and teachers to arrange their courses in levels of categories, as in Ajlan's High School in Figure 7. The main category is 'المرحلة الابتدائية' and then the sub-category is 'الصف الاول ابتدائي', which has 7 courses. It is possible to make more than one main category and more than one sub-category.

Course categories

Add new category

Course categories	Courses	Edit	Move category to:
المرحلة الابتدائية	0	X ↓	Top
الصف الاول ابتدائي	7	X ↓	المرحلة الابتدائية
الصف الثاني ابتدائي	7	X ↑ ↓	المرحلة الابتدائية
الصف الثالث ابتدائي	8	X ↑ ↓	المرحلة الابتدائية
الصف الرابع ابتدائي	11	X ↑ ↓	المرحلة الابتدائية
الصف الخامس ابتدائي	12	X ↑ ↓	المرحلة الابتدائية
الصف السادس ابتدائي	12	X ↑	المرحلة الابتدائية
المرحلة المتوسطة	0	X ↑ ↓	Top
الصف الاول المتوسط	13	X ↓	المرحلة المتوسطة
الصف الثاني المتوسط	13	X ↑ ↓	المرحلة المتوسطة
الصف الثالث المتوسط	13	X ↑	المرحلة المتوسطة
المرحلة الثانوية	0	X ↑ ↓	Top
الصف الاول الثانوي	12	X ↓	المرحلة الثانوية

Fig. 7. The Category Tool in Ajlan's High School.

3.5.5 Login

This page enables all users of Moodle to access their account. If the user does not have a username and password, this page enables him/her to register and open an account.

Returning to this web site?

Login here using your username and password
(Cookies must be enabled in your browser)

Username

Password Login

Some courses may allow guest access

Login as a guest

Forgotten your username or password?

Yes, help me log in

You are not logged in. (Login)

Fig. 8. The Login Page in Ajlan's High School.

3.5.6 Main screen

This screen is the main page of the Moodle site, and the administrator can control this page by the Front Page button. This screen has choices that the administrator can offer Moodle's users; options such as site administration, categories, courses, calendar and upcoming events, as well as the option to write an introduction.

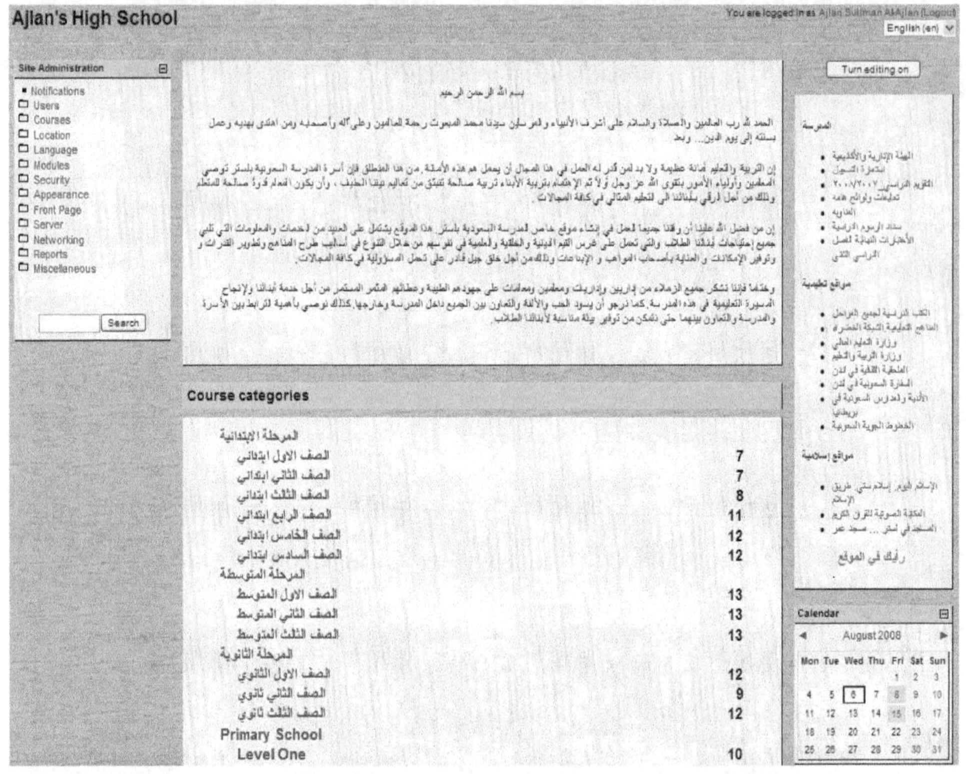

Fig. 9. The Main Screen in Ajlan's High School.

3.5.7 Language

Moodle is an excellent VLE platform for languages; it is being used in over 86 languages in 112 countries around the world. An administrator can control the language by using the Language Button as in the left top in Figure 9. This button has three options: Language Settings, Language Editing and Language Packs. Users can choose the language that best suits their needs by using the selection bottom as in the right top in Figure 9.

3.5.8 Web services

Web services are a new technology and they have made important contributions to knowledge, especially to the e-business field. Therefore, it is important to use this technology in non-profit organizations such as e-learning. Ajlan has succeeded in using Web services together with VLE platforms, by using Moodle as a case study (Al-Ajlan, et al., 2008).

3.6 Virtual learning environment tools of Moodle

VLEs enable teachers to build resources fast and without the need to develop technical skills. VLE tools are criteria-based, and they enable developers to evaluate and select the

most suitable VLE product. No single product can possibly meet all these criteria, and the most suitable within a specific context may not be perfect for interface, technical, functional, or cost reasons. Table 2 describes the tools and features in any VLE product (Britain, et al., 1999; Cheng, et al., 1998; Dougiamas, et al., 2002 and Perrie, 2003):
This section presents the main tools of Moodle, which are activity modules and resource types. The manage activities page enables the administrator to manage Moodle's Tools for the entire site. This includes standard modules and contributed modules that have been added by the site administrator.

3.6.1 Activity modules

Moodle contains a wide range of activity modules that can be used to build up any type of course. They provide a central point for information, discussion and collaboration among Moodle users. The current activates as in version 1.8 are as follows (Dougiamas, 2011):

No	Activity Modules	Description
1	Assignments	The assignment module enables a teacher to allow students to upload and prepare any digital content for grading.
2	Chats	It allows participants to have a real-time synchronous discussion via the web. This is a useful way to get a different understanding of each other and the topic being.
3	Choices	These enable teachers to ask questions, and they specify a choice of multiple responses.
4	Forums	These are where the most discussion takes place between users. Users comfortable with informal communication styles.
5	Glossary	This allows participants to create and maintain a list of definitions, and enables teachers to export entries from one glossary to another within the same course.
6	Journal	This is private between student and teacher and each journal can be directed by an open question. For each particular journal, the whole class can be assessed on one page in one form [20].
7	Labels	It allows users to insert text and graphics among the other activities on the course.
8	Lesson	This delivers content in an interesting and flexible way. It consists of a number of pages; each page normally ends with a question and a number of possible answers.
9	Quizzes	This module allows the teacher to design and set quiz tests, consisting of multiple choices, true/false and short answer questions.
10	Resources	These contain information that the teacher wants to bring into the course.

Table 12. Activity Modules in Moodle Product.

3.6.2 Resource types

Moodle, as any VLE system, supports a range of different resource types that allow users to insert almost any kind of web content into courses, and these resources are under course (Dougiamas, 2011).

No	Resource Types	Description
1	Text Page	This is a simple page written using plain text. A number of formatting types are available to help turn plain text into attractive web pages.
2	HTML Page	It is easy to develop a complete single web page within Moodle, especially when users are using Moodle's WYSIWYG HTML editor.
3	Files and Web Pages	These allow users to link any web page or other file on the public Internet as well as any web page or other file that users have uploaded into the course files area from their own desktop computer.
4	Directory	This can display a whole directory (and its subdirectories) from the course files area. Students can then browse and view all of those files.

Table 13. The number of websites using Moodle in some countries around the world.

4. Websites are using Moodle all over the World

Moodle has a large and diverse user community with over half a million registered users, speaking 86 languages, and currently 53,794 Moodle sites from approximately 112 countries have been registered (Dougiamas, 2011, Brandl, 2005). Table 14 shows 48 countries, chosen from those 112 countries, that have sites and have registered with Moodle.

No	Country	No of Sites	No	Country	No of Sites
1	United States	9530	25	India	384
2	Spain	4800	26	Russian Federation	374
3	Brazil	3751	27	Indonesia	327
4	United Kingdom	3331	28	Venezuela	304
5	Germany	2490	29	New Zealand	282
6	Portugal	1923	30	Sweden	263
7	Australia	1475	31	Turkey	253
8	Canada	1343	32	Malaysia	246
9	Mexico	1306	33	Hungary	234
10	Italy	1219	34	Belgium	200
11	Poland	1020	35	Greece	190
12	Colombia	943	36	South Africa	177
13	Thailand	914	37	Iran	149
14	Taiwan	834	38	Ukraine	134
15	France	795	39	Egypt	120
16	Austria	736	40	Romania	120
17	Netherlands	714	41	Korea	120
18	Chile	706	42	Saudi Arabia	113
19	Japan	692	43	Denmark	109
20	Peru	657	44	Hong Kong	101
21	Argentina	651	45	United Arab Emirates	84
22	Switzerland	542	46	Bulgaria	87
23	Finland	440	47	Morocco	54
24	China	414	48	Lebanon	29

Table 14. The number of websites using Moodle in some countries around the world.

The highest number of sites using Moodle is in the United States (US), where there are more than 9530sites. In Spain, Brazil and the United Kingdom, there are more than 4800, 3751 and 3331 sites respectively that have installed and are using Moodle. In contrast, in Lebanon there are only 29 sites using Moodle. Figure 10 illustrates Moodle on a map of the world. We can see from this map that Moodle is concentrated in Europe and the US.

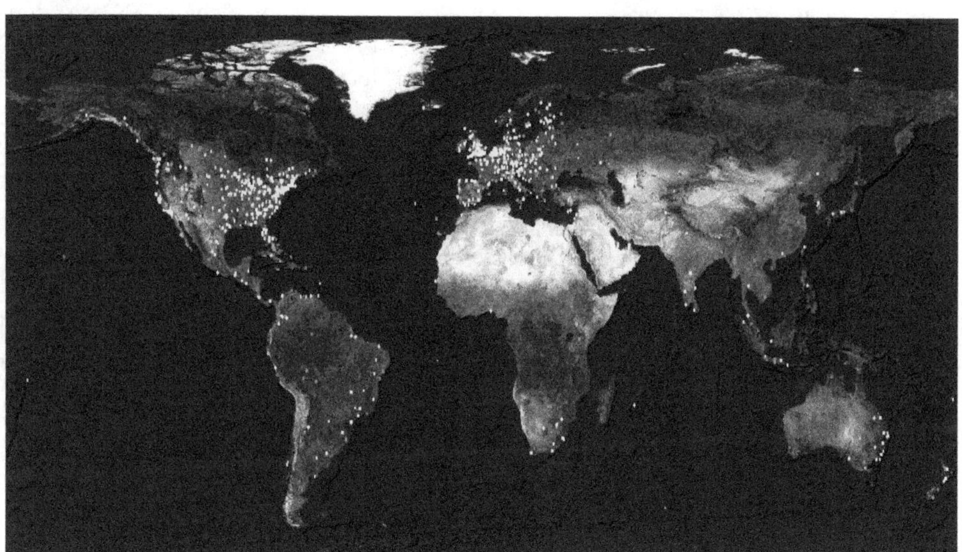

Fig. 10. Moodle Sites that have registered with Moodle across the world.

5. Discussion

This chapter is aimed at taking the right decision when choosing a suitable VLE platform to meet the requirements of Qassim University. This is a large university and needs a strong VLE that meets all its needs. This is an initial study to aid Qassim University in that search for the best VLE system. It has focused on a comparison between Moodle and other VLE systems, and is based on two kinds of comparison. The first phase is based on the features and capabilities of VLE, and the second is based on the technical aspects of the VLE tools.

The first study compared Moodle with nine VLE platforms based on features and capabilities of VLE tools, as in Section 2.1. This study has proved that the best platforms are Moodle and Sakai, which have missed just two out of forty features. The weakest product is Claroline 1.6, which missed 8 out of 40 features. Desire2Learn and ANGEL Learning Management Suite have taken the number two spot equally as they both missed three features. Blackboard Learning System and OLAT are number four equally as they both missed five features and capabilities.

The second study compared Moodle with other VLE platforms based on the technical aspects of VLEs, as in Section 2.2 In general, this study has strongly recommended choosing Moodle as the optimal VLE platform for Qassim University.

The first and second studies have proved that Moodle has the best results. In addition, it has the advantages mentioned in Section 2.1, and we therefore strongly recommend Moodle as the best choice for higher education generally, and for Qassim University in particular.

6. Conclusion

Moodle is a kind of VLE and it is now widely used all over the world by schools, institutes, universities, companies, independent educators, and home schooling parents. It has great potential for creating a successful e-learning experience by providing an abundance of excellent tools that can be used to enhance conventional classroom instruction in any VLE system. Moodle can scale from a single-teacher site to a more than 50-thousand-student University.

This chapter has made a comparative study between Moodle and other VLE systems, and this was based on two kinds of comparison. The first phase was based on the features and capabilities of VLE tools, and the second one was based on the technical aspects of VLE systems. From this study, we aimed to discover the best and most suitable choice of VLE systems that would meet the requirements of Qassim University. In this, our initial assessment, we have succeeded in finding that optimal VLE platform, and it is Moodle.

This chapter has presented the work that has been done to date. The future work is to work hard within Moodle and to test it with a sample by using departments in some colleges at Qassim University in order to discover all possible problems that could occur when using it. Initially, there will be a survey for obtaining information directly from different sources, including participants who are in a position to provide such information. Many variables will be considered at this point and the study will attempt to identify the relationships among such variables.

7. Acknowledgment

The author wishes to acknowledge contributions from many people, including Prof. A. Al-Abdulmunim who is the VP at Qassim University, and Prof. Hindi Al-Hindi who is the Head of Management Information Systems at Qassim University. Also, author is indebted to the Qassim University for its encouragement and financial support.

8. References

Al-Ajlan, A. and Zedan, H. (2008). Why Moodle, Proceedings of 12IEEE International Workshop on Future Trends of Distributed Computing Systems (FTDCS), IEEE Press, Kunming, China, pp. 58–64.

Dougiamas, M. (June 2011). Moodle, 17.06.2011, Available from www.moodle.org.

Yuuichi, S.; Toshihiro, K. ; Seisuke, Y. and Hiroshi, N. (2006). Web-based rapid authoring Tools for LMS quiz creation, Proceedings of 7th International Conference on Information Technology Based Higher Education and Training, (Ultimo, Australia), pp. 617--620, Kumamoto University, IEEE.

Tortora, G. ; Sebillo, M. ; Vitiello, G. and D'Ambrosio, P. (2002). A multilevel Learning management system, Proceedings of the 14th international conference on Software engineering and knowledge engineering, (USA), pp. 541--547, ACM.

Bruce, J. and Curson, N. (2001). UEA Virtual Learning Environnent, UEA, Product evaluation report, Learning Technology Group. 3.05.2011, Available from http://www.uea.ac.uk/ltg/blackboard/VLEreport.pdf.

Berry, M. (2005). An investigation of the effectiveness of moodle in primary education." Deputy Head, St Ives School, Haslemere. 24.04.2011, Available from http://Moodlemoot.org/mod/resource/view.php?id=19.

Massy, J. (2004). Study of the e-Learning suppliers market in europe," Master's thesis, Danish Technological Institute, Heriot-Watt University.

Zenha-Rela, M. and Carvalho, R. (2006). Works in Progress: Self evaluation through monitored peer review using the moodle platform, Proceedings of the 36th Annual Education Conference, (San Diego, CA), pp. 26--27, Univ, IEEE.

Brandl, K. (2005). Are you ready to "Moodle"?, Language Learning & Technology, vol. 9, pp. 16--23, May 2005. University of Washington.

Martin, C. ; Morris-Cotterill, N. and Smith, M. (2004). Open source software for the education market. Eduforge, 14.02.2011, Available from http://eduforge.org.

EduTools, (2006). Course management systems, EduTools, 14.02.2011, Available from http://www.edutools.info/static.jsp?pj8&pageHOME.

Jolla, L. and Motulsky, H. (2008). Graphpad Prism, GraphPad Software, Inc., 7.06.2011, Available from http://www.graphpad.com/prism/Prism.htm.

Wharekura-tini, H. and Aotearoa, K. (2004). Technical Evaluation of Selected Learning Management Systems, Master's thesis, Catalyst IT Limited, Open Polytechnic of New Zealand.

Graf, S. and List, B. (2005). An Evaluation of Open Source E-learning Platforms Stressing Adaptation Issues, Proceedings of the Fifth IEEE International Conference on Advanced Learning Technologies, pp. 163--165, IEEE Computer Society USA.

Alvarez, V. (2008). E-learning Survey, Department of Computer Science at the University of Oviedo, 17.07.2011, Available from http://www.di.uniovi.es/victoralvarez/survey/

Cole, J. (2005). Using MOODLE: Teaching with the Popular Open Source Course Management System, ISBN: 0596008635, O'Reilly.

Dougiamas, M. (2004). Moodle as Virtual Learning Environment for the rest of us, TESL-EJ, vol. 8, pp. 1—8.

Chavan, A. and Pavri, S. (2004). Open-Source Learning Management with Moodle, linux journal, Specialized Systems Consultants.

Koh, K. (2006). Moodle as a Course Management System, eslweb.org, 11.05.2011, Available from http://www.eslweb.org/criticalreviews/moodlem.pdf.

Williams, B. and Dougiamas, M. (2005). Moodle for Teachers. Trainers and Administrators of remote-Learner.net, Creative Commons Non commercial copyright, moodle.org community.

Itmazi, J. (2005). Flexible Learning Management System To Support Learning In The Traditional And Open Universities. Phd program: Advanced methods & technique of software development, Software Engineering Department, Computer Engineering School, Granada University, Granada, Spain.

Shearer, S. (2003). Open source software in education, The Compton School, London.

MacKenzie, J. ; Muirhead, A. and Mann, S. (2006). The use and usefulness of moodle, University of Clasgow, 23.06.2011, Available from http://www.gla.ac.uk/faculties/education/vle/docs/useandusefulness.ppt.

Chao Su, C. (2005). An open source portal for educators, Proceedings of the Fifth IEEE International Conference on Advanced Learning Technologies (ICALT05), vol. 9 of 0-7695-2338, pp. 961--962.

Al-Ajlan, A and Zedan, H. (2008). The Extension of Web Services Architecture to Meet the Technical Requirements of Virtual Learning Environments (Moodle)", Proceedings of ICCES08-IEEE International Conference on Computer Engineering & Systems, IEEE, Cairo, Egypt, pp. 27–32.

Marshall, S. and Noble, H. (2005) Value Added moodle: Experimental integration with the bodington VLE. Learning Technologies Group, Oxford University Computing Services.

Britain, S. and Liber, O. (1999). A Framework for Pedagogical Evaluation of Virtual Learning Environments, JTAP, JISC Technology Applications Programme, University of Wales-Bangor, 1999. 2.05.2011, Available from http://www.leeds.ac.uk/educol/documents/00001237.htm.

Cheng, C. and Yen, J. (1998). Virtual Learning Environment (VLE): a Web-Based Ccollaborative Learning System, Proceedings of the Thirty-First Hawaii International Conference on System Sciences, vol. 1 of 0-8186-8255-8, pp. 480--491, Hong Kong, IEEE.

Dougiamas, M. and Taylor, P. (2002). Interpretive Analysis of an Internet-Based Course Constructed Using a New Courseware Tool Called Moodle, in HERDSA 2002 conference, (Perth, Australia), Curtin University of Technology.

Perrie, Y. (2003). Virtual Learning Environment, The Pharmaceutical Journal, vol. 270, pp. 794--795.

Part 3

New Developments

11

Distributed Intelligent Tutoring System Architectures

Egons Lavendelis
Riga Technical University
Latvia

1. Introduction

Traditional architecture of Intelligent Tutoring Systems (ITSs) does not offer sufficient modularity. There is a lack of open distributed ITS architectures, despite ITSs being systems that may need frequent changes due to the modifications of particular course or adaptation to new courses. The chapter focuses on usage of distributed technologies in development of open ITSs to increase the modularity of the ITSs and facilitate the implementation of needed changes into ITSs. The aim of the chapter is to propose open and highly modular ITS architectures, using two distributed paradigms – intelligent software agents and services.

To realize intelligent tutoring various types of learning materials and problems have to be presented to the learner, moreover it should be done intelligently enough to successfully simulate the human tutor. Thus all known ITSs concentrate on a certain problem domain or course to provide specific functionality for problems and examples of the domain. For example, the system has to be capable to analyse learner's actions during the problem solving. Each new type of problems needs corresponding code to handle it. Problems differ from course to course and may change if the course is changed. As a consequence the functionality of ITS may be modified to adapt to the changes in the course or to a new course. The system should be open for certain types of components handling new types of problems, materials, feedback, etc. The architecture of ITS should support such an openness.

ITSs traditionally have modular architecture consisting of four modules, namely tutoring module, expert module, student diagnosis module and communication module (Grundspenkis & Anohina, 2005). The main principle is to build components using only one type of knowledge (pedagogical knowledge, domain knowledge and knowledge about the learner). As a result, the architecture does not have sufficient modularity for complex ITSs. To facilitate modularity and change management distributed technologies like services and agents are used in ITSs. Well known examples of agent based ITSs are Ines system for nurse education (Hospers et al., 2003), Formal Languages and aUTomata Education system FLUTE (Devedzic et al., 2000), IVET virtual training environment (de Antonio et al, 2005) and WADIES – a Web- and agent-based adaptive learning environment for teaching compilers (Georguli et al., 2003). Grundspenkis and Anohina (2005) have concluded that agent based ITSs mainly implement traditional modules as sets of agents. The authors have defined customizable set of agents that implements the system as a set of distributed components and at the same time maintains the traditional idea of ITS's modules separating different types of knowledge. Nevertheless, there is a need for a distributed architecture, because the set of agents only defines ITS components and does not solve architectural problems of ITSs.

As of author's knowledge no specific service oriented architectures (SOA) for ITS development exist, except the ones presented further in the chapter. The only known distributed ITS architectures are a few multi-agent architectures for ITS development. These architectures mainly consist of agents from the set of agents defined by Grundspenkis and Anohina. The architectures are closed in the sense that system's functionality can not be changed just by adding/removing agents from the system. Examples of such architectures are ABITS (Capuano et al, 2000), IVET (de Antonio et al, 2005) and X-genitor (Triantis & Pintelas, 2004). Several open architectures are proposed to allow adding new student agents and create a learning environment for multiple learners, for example, JADE (Silveira & Vicari, 2002) and two level multi-agent architecture for distance learning environment (Webber & Pesty, 2002). Still, these architectures are open only for new student agents to join the system and are closed for any other types of agents. As a consequence there is a need for architectures enabling usage of all advantages of distributed technologies, including the possibility to change system's functionality by just adding and/or removing distributed components from the system. The chapter describes such ITS architectures. The remainder of the chapter is organized as follows. The Section 2 gives a brief introduction to ITSs by describing the tutoring process carried out by ITSs and presenting the traditional architecture of ITSs. The Section 3 is dedicated to agent based ITSs. It analyses the related work about the agent based ITS architectures and describes open holonic multi-agent ITS architecture. The Section 4 compares intelligent agents to web services. It analyses the lessons learned in the development of holonic multi-agent architecture and possibilities to apply them to SOA. The Section 5 describes service oriented ITS architecture that implements each module as a set of services. The Section 6 proposes hybrid architecture that includes both agents and services. Agents implement higher level deliberative components while services realize lower level reactive components. The Section 7 concludes the chapter.

2. Intelligent tutoring systems

ITSs can be defined as computerized systems used for tutoring and having the following characteristics (Anohina, 2007): (1) they use principles and methods from artificial intelligence (like, knowledge representation, reasoning, natural language processing and machine learning); (2) are adaptive systems that adapt the tutoring process to the characteristics of the learner, so carrying out adaptive or individualized tutoring; (3) simulate human tutor; (4) are based on the cognitive theory. One of the main characteristics of ITSs is that they try to simulate human tutor to implement adaptive tutoring. To cover all activities done by the human tutor the system has to do the following tasks: generate curriculum, provide learning materials and problems for the learner to solve in each topic, evaluate learner's knowledge and give meaningful feedback to the learner to help him/her improve his/her knowledge (Lavendelis, 2009). In adaptive tutoring these activities must be carried out adaptively - each learner should receive individual approach that fits his/her characteristics and/or preferences. Curriculum should be generated to meet the needs of individual learner as well as materials and problems should be adapted to each learner.

Simulation of the human tutor is a complex task for the system. It requires intelligent choices and actions to be made. All actions by the teacher, like creation of the curriculum, choice of the appropriate learning materials or evaluation of the learner's knowledge are complex actions and require intelligence. As a consequence, various intelligent mechanisms are needed for an ITS to simulate such actions. Intelligent mechanisms used to implement adaptive tutoring vary from system to system. Still, the main types of knowledge used in different ITSs are the same. Knowledge about the domain or subject is needed to know what to teach. Knowledge about the learner is needed to know whom to adapt and knowledge about the tutoring process is needed to know how to teach and how to adapt to the learner's characteristics. The goal of ITSs is to use the above-mentioned three types of knowledge to carry out adaptive tutoring. Usually each type of the knowledge is used by different intelligent mechanisms. It is beneficial to define components corresponding to the three main types of knowledge used in ITSs. As a consequence traditional modular ITS architecture consists of three modules, namely, the expert module, the student diagnosis module and the tutoring module, all together named traditional trinity (Grundspenkis & Anohina, 2005). Additionally the communication module is added to manage the user interface, resulting in the modular architecture consisting of 4 modules. The modular architecture is widely used in intelligent tutoring systems, for example, in Ines (Hospers et al, 2003), AlgeBrain (Alpert et al, 1999), FLUTE (Devedzic et al, 2000) and IKAS (Vilkelis et al, 2009) systems. Modules have the following features (Grundspenkis & Anohina, 2005):

- *The expert module* represents the domain expert's knowledge and includes problem solving characteristics. The task of the module is to solve domain problems. It serves as a standard to compare learner's knowledge to.
- *The student diagnosis module* collects information about learner's knowledge and misunderstandings, creating the student model.
- *The tutoring module* holds teaching strategies and instructions to implement tutoring process. The primary tasks of this module are controlling selection, sequencing and presentation of learning material that is most suitable for the learner, determining the type and contents of feedback and help, and answering learners' questions. Strategies contained by the module must be adapted to the needs of each individual learner without any help of humans. The goal of the module is to reduce the gap between learner's knowledge and expert's knowledge as far as possible or in ideal case eliminate the gap completely.
- *The communication module* is the only module interacting with the learner. It has to manage the user interface of the system. It perceives all learners' actions, receives all requests from learners and forwards them to other modules. It is responsible for presentation of all kinds of information (curriculum of the course, materials, problems, feedback, etc.) to the learner, too.

Despite the acceptance of the modular architecture its main drawback is insufficient modularity to build complex adaptive ITSs because the modules have many tasks. Distributed computing technologies, namely, services and agents are used to split the higher level modules into lower level components to increase modularity of ITSs. Moreover, the functionality of ITSs includes many functions and corresponding pieces of code that differ in systems for various courses and even may be needed to change for the same course. Usage of distributed technologies also enables implementation of open ITSs allowing introduction of new functionality without changing existing code. The remainder of the chapter analyses use of the two types of distributed technologies in the architecture of ITSs.

3. Agent based intelligent tutoring systems

Majority of agent based ITSs use the same approach. They implement traditional ITS modules as sets of agents. Popularity of the approach is based on the fact that each module contains functions that can be grouped in logical components. The defined agents correspond to these components. Modules may consist of various numbers of logical components. Each module can be realized as a single agent, a few agents or as a multi-agent system with its own architecture. Still, each module has some basic agents that with needed modifications are used in majority of agent based ITSs. The general set of agents to implement modules of ITS defined by Grundspenkis and Anohina (2005) is the following.

The goal of the *student diagnosis module* is to collect and maintain information about each learner. While part of this information is known before starting the tutoring and does not change during the tutoring process, other parts, like the knowledge level, change during the tutoring process and have to be collected by the agents of the module. Agents have to collect information about the learning process, various characteristics of the learner (emotional, cognitive and character). The following agents are used to collect information (Grundspenkis & Anohina, 2005):

- The knowledge evaluation agent that evaluates the level of the learners' knowledge and skills. Mainly it is done based on learner's results in the tests and problems.
- The psychological agent that collects information about the learner's preferences, learning style and emotions during the learning process.
- The cognitive diagnosis agent determines and registers learner's mistakes. It is also responsible for determining the causes of the learner's mistakes.
- The interaction registering agent registers history of learner's interaction with the system and follows the usage of the system's features. For example, if a learner does not use some important features of the system, the agent may suggest using them.

Agents that build the *pedagogical module* have to create and modify (when needed) the curriculum, provide learning materials, generate problems and provide the feedback to the learner. All these tasks are more or less independent, thus they are assigned to separate agents and the module consists of the following agents (Grundspenkis & Anohina, 2005):

- The curriculum agent that creates, evaluates and modifies the curriculum if needed.
- One or a few teaching strategy agents that implement teaching strategies. These agents provide learning materials in each topic according to the teaching strategy. It is needed to vary teaching strategies, because learners have different learning styles. Some learners prefer to receive an example first while others prefer to read theory and only then receive an example (Bicans et al, 2011).
- The problem generation agent that generates tasks, questions and problems. In the remainder of the paper all tasks, questions and problems given to the learner to evaluate his/her knowledge will be named problems.
- The feedback agent that provides feedback to a learner after he/she has finished the problem solving. The agent is also responsible for providing hints and explanations requested by a learner.

The *expert module* is responsible for solving problems and tasks in the domain taught by the system. This module consists of one or more expert agents that solve problems of the learning course. Usually each expert agent is responsible for problems in one topic or of one type. The *communication module* can be implemented as the interface agent and/or animated pedagogical agent (Grundspenkis & Anohina, 2005). The interface agent is responsible for all tasks concerning the communication with a learner. It is responsible for the whole user interface. This agent may be responsible also for teacher's user interface. Similarly, the animated pedagogical agent is responsible for interactions with a learner. The main difference from the interface agent is that the animated pedagogical agent is two or three dimensional animated person that uses voice, gesture and mimics to interact with the learner. Animated pedagogical agents are made to be perceived as teachers. They make the learning process more interesting to a learner. Additionally to the abovementioned tasks of the communication module, namely, displaying curriculum, providing learning materials, showing the knowledge evaluations and feedback the animated pedagogical agents accomplish one important task of the teacher - they motivate learners to study. The agent achieves it by showing systems emotions, so making the interaction with the ITS more human like. The agents of the communication module are the only agents that communicate with the learner and thus have to carry out all communication tasks. They have to present all information that has been prepared by all other agents of the system like curriculum, learning materials, problems, feedback, etc.). These agents also have to register relevant actions done by the learner and forward them to the agents of other modules that are interested in the corresponding actions. The agents also control the work of all communication devices used to interact with the learner: the user interface, keyboard, mouse as well as various specialized devices like data gloves, video cameras and other equipment of the learning environment (Grundspenkis & Anohina, 2005).

Additionally the set of agents may contain manager agents that coordinate other agents of the set. These agents may be created differently. One manager agent can be created for each module or for a whole system. The Figure 1 depicts the described set of agents. The manager agents are not included in the set, because they can be defined differently. The described set of agents can be customized to meet the functionality of every individual ITS. Some agents can be removed from the set if the system does not need the corresponding functionality. If needed, some additional agents can be added to implement additional functionality that usually is connected with the problem domain, for example, the patient agent in the nurse

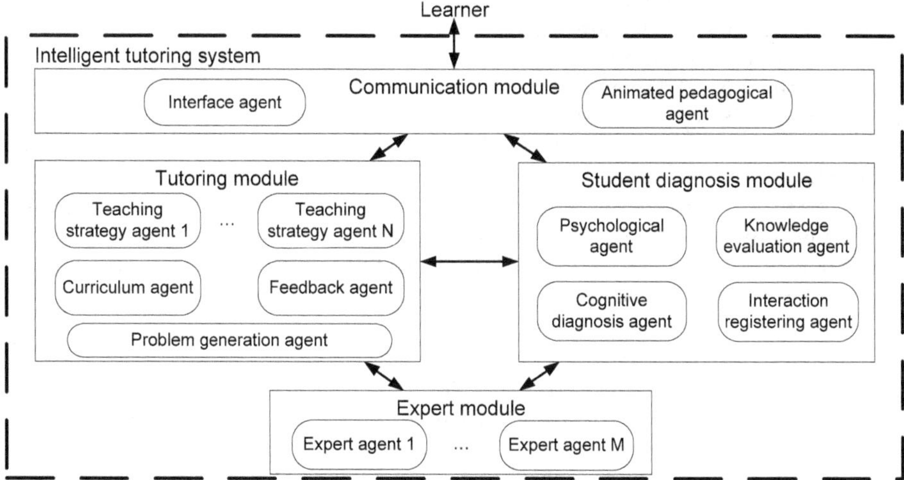

Fig. 1. The set of agents used to implement ITSs (Grundspenkis & Anohina, 2005).

education system Ines (Hospers et al, 2003). The set of agents can be taken as a basis and modified instead of designing the multi agent system from scratch. Nevertheless, implementation of ITSs based on the described set does not eliminate all drawbacks of modular architecture. Firstly, the set of agents does not define interactions among agents. Every agent may interact with any other agent, making the complexity of the interactions grow exponentially if the number of agents grows. Secondly, direct implementation of the set of agents does not ensure openness of the system. Introduction of new functionality into the system is impossible without changing existing components. Thirdly, some agents still are large and have many tasks, reducing modularity of ITSs. Reuse of large-scale agents is complex, too, because agents have many tasks and it is unlikely that there will be two systems that will need all these tasks unchanged. At the same time direct reuse of single task is impossible too, because it is only a part of the component.

A few distributed ITS architectures that facilitate ITS design by providing agents, their tasks and interactions, exist. Majority of them modify or extend the set of agents described above. Examples of such architectures are the multi-agent architecture for distance education systems (Dorca et al, 2003), the IVET architecture (de Antonio et al, 2005), the ABITS architecture (Capuano et al, 2000), the JADE architecture (Silveira & Vicari, 2002) and the X-Genitor framework (Triantis & Pintelas, 2004). Nevertheless, they do not solve the architectural problems in the ITSs. As they are similar to the defined set of agents, they have the same problems with modularity and reuse. Some of the architectures are defined to be open, for new agents of one type. New interface agents can be added to the system to represent new learners. Examples of open architectures in this sense are X-GENITOR and JADE. These open architectures facilitate group learning and collaborative learning in ITSs. Still they are not open for new components that add new functionality to the system without changing existing code. For example, it is not possible to add new agent that is capable to generate new types of problems, but the code of existing problem generation agent has to be changed. Moreover, it has to be analysed how the changes made in the problem generation agent will affect other agents. As a consequence these architectures do not allow benefiting from one of the main advantages of agent technologies - open and distributed computing.

Additionally, existing architectures have the following drawbacks. Agents have many tasks making the development complex. Agents used in ITS are not capable to deal with problems that can be solved by multiple agents, like resolution of various conflicts. Example of such tasks is choice of appropriate learning strategies using various criteria. As a consequence, it can be concluded that known agent based ITS architectures do not take full advantage of the distributed and open nature of multi-agent systems. Thus, there is a need for distributed ITS architectures to enable full usage of all these advantages in ITS development. The remainder of the section presents holonic multi-agent architecture that tries to implement open and highly modular ITSs as well as the MIPITS system (Lavendelis & Grundspenkis, 2010), which is an agent based ITS developed using the described architecture.

3.1 Multi-agent architectures

Small scale multi-agent systems can be developed just by defining agents and specifying interactions among them. This approach starts to fail if the number of agents increases, exponentially increasing the complexity of interactions, because every pair of agents may interact each other. To solve this problem, the concepts of architecture and organization are introduced into the multi-agent systems. Additionally, these concepts are used for agents to create teams and cooperate in problem solving. Two best known multi-agent system architectures are holonic multi-agent systems (Fischer et al, 2003) and multi-multi-agent systems (Nimis & Stockheim, 2004). The idea of *holonic multi-agent systems* is that autonomy of agents is reduced and agents are merged into holons, which appear to outside as a single entity (Fischer et al, 2003). The term "holon" (Greek word "holos" has meaning "whole" and suffix "-on" denotes "part") is adopted from biological system research done by A. Koestler (1967). Holon is a self-organizing structure which consists of substructures and is a part of larger superstructure. In terms of multi-agent systems holon or holonic agent is an agent that consists of other agents named subholons.

In holonic multi-agent systems agents form a hierarchical structure, i.e., each holon can be a part of a higher level holon and consist of lower level holons. It allows adapting the system to the structure of the domain. Hierarchy makes holons suitable for task and result sharing. If the holon has a task assigned to it, the task can be decomposed into some subtasks that are assigned to subholons, which can decompose them into the next level subtasks and so on. If the agent receives a task that it is not able to accomplish it can also find other agents to create a holon with, to accomplish the task together (Fischer et al, 2003).

The autonomy of agents that form a holon is usually reduced by giving one agent (called head or head agent) the privilege to do resource and task allocation in the holon. It can have partial or total control over other agents. Agents that are parts of the holon, but are not head agents are called body of the holon (Gerber et al, 1999). To outside the holon appears as a single entity represented by the head of the holon. The body agents do not communicate outside the holon. So, holons have an interface (head) and they can be developed separately as modules of traditional software engineering. Holons also make change implementation easier, because changes of an agent in one holon directly affect only agents from the same holon. Lavendelis & Grundspenkis (2008) have concluded that ITSs comply well with the main criteria of holonic domains defined by the authors of the holonic approach (Gerber et al, 1999), namely operator abstraction, hierarchical structure, partial decomposability and cooperative system. Thus the holonic multi-agent systems are suitable for ITSs.

The second well-known multi-agent architecture - *multi-multi-agent system* has been developed inside the Agent.Enterprise methodology (Nimis & Stockheim, 2004). The main goal of the project is integration of several multi-agent systems. It is similar to the holonic multi-agent systems in the sense that both architectures propose to create systems that consist of subsystems - holons and multi-agent systems, respectively. Multi-multi-agent systems offer the concept of the gateway agent that accomplishes routing and message conversion between different message formats used in different multi-agent systems. Interactions among agents of various multi-agent systems are enabled. Still, comparing holonic multi-agent systems and multi-multi-agent systems one may conclude that in the context of ITSs there are significant advantages of holonic multi-agent systems. The main of them is that heads of holons unlike the gateway agents can accomplish not only mediator tasks, but also many other tasks. It allows implementing great part of the intelligent mechanisms into the heads of holons. One more important advantage is that holons can be dynamically changed and allow to build open systems. For other advantages of holonic multi-agent systems see (Lavendelis & Grundspenkis, 2011), where it is concluded that the holonic multi agent systems are more suitable for the ITSs and should be used to develop a specific agent based ITS architecture. The next subsection describes such architecture.

3.2 Open holonic multi-agent ITS architecture

Despite the fact that holonic multi-agent systems are suitable for agent based ITS development it is not clear how to use holons in ITSs without any specific architecture. Such architecture is proposed in (Lavendelis & Grundspenkis, 2008). From outside it is a single holon. The only agent that represents the system outside is the interface agent, which implements all interactions with the learner. So, it is the head of the higher level holon and the only agent implementing the communication module. The remaining modules are implemented as subholons and are included in the body of the higher level holon. Each module can be realized as one or more holons. Modules that carry out wide functionality (pedagogical module and student module) are implemented as multiple holons. The functionality of the student module contains the following two groups of functions: learner's knowledge evaluation functions (usually evaluation of the learner's solution) as well as building and maintaining of the student model. Thus the student model is realized as two holonic agents - student modelling and knowledge evaluation agent. The pedagogical module similarly to the above defined set of agents consists of the following holonic agents: the curriculum agent, the teaching strategy agent, the problem generation agent and the feedback agent. The expert module is implemented as a single agent - the expert agent. So, the higher level of the architecture contains 7 body agents (see Figure 2). The higher level agents have the same functionality as the agents from the above defined agent set, except three agents of the student modelling holon are merged into one higher level holon that has all the functionality of the three merged agents. Interactions among the higher level holons are defined in two degrees of detailed elaboration. Firstly the acquaintance diagram is developed showing which holons have any interactions. Secondly, messages sent among agents are defined in the interaction diagrams (Lavendelis, 2009).

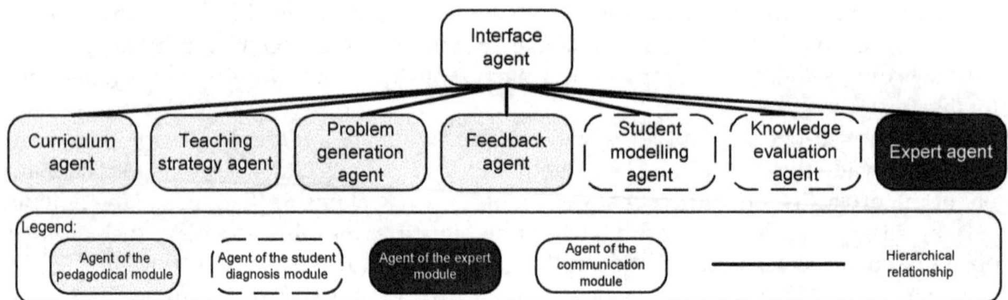

Fig. 2. The higher level of the holonic ITS architecture.

Higher level agents are realized as holons that consist of a single head agent and some subholons (body agents). The head of the holon is responsible for the coordination of all subholons that is done by centralized planning and task allocation to the body agents. The heads use directory facilitator service to find body agents and their capabilities. Heads are responsible for tasks that need one unique performer, like, the head of student modelling agent is responsible for building complete student model and providing it to other agents.

The architecture is open and contains two types of holons: open and closed. Open holons consist of the head and a certain type of body agents, however, the number and exact instances of body agents are not defined during the design of the system and can be freely changed during the maintenance and runtime, so modifying the system's functionality.

Body agents have to register their services at the directory facilitator agent. Heads of open holons use the directory facilitator agent to find actual body agents in open holons. Closed holons consist of agents that are specified during the design and can not be changed during the runtime of the system. Body agents are responsible for certain types of tasks that are subtasks of the holon's tasks. Body agents of closed holons usually carry out principally different tasks. Contrary, body agents of open holons are responsible for different subtypes of one type of tasks. So, it is possible to add a new body agent to an open holon that is responsible for a new subtype of the task. For example, each body agent of an open holon is responsible for generation of one type of problems. New type of problems can be introduced by adding new body agents. Student modelling, curriculum and feedback agents are closed holons, while problem generation, teaching strategy, expert and knowledge evaluation agents are open holons. The interactions in all open holons as well as algorithms used by heads are similar. The main steps carried out to fulfil the task of the holon are the following:

1. The head of the holon receives request to carry out a task. If the task can be done by the head of the holon, it is performed and the result is sent to the requester and the algorithm ends. Otherwise, it continues with the Step 2.
2. The head of the holon queries the directory facilitator agent to find all body agents.
3. If the directory facilitator has found at least one appropriate agent, the head queries the body agents. Depending on the holon only one body agent or all appropriate agents are queried. One agent is queried if only one type of subtasks suites the request. All agents are queried if all types of subtasks suite the request. If no body agents are found a system error is generated.
4. After receiving the request from the head of the holon, body agents carry out the task and send the results to the head.
5. If more than one body agent is queried during the Step 3, the head waits for replies from all of them or until the time-out has occurred. Then, it finds the most appropriate result provided by the body agents. For example, if each body agent has generated a problem of some type, then the head chooses the most appropriate one for the learner.
6. The head forwards either the only result or the result chosen during the Step 5 to the agent that sent the request during the Step 1. The head may also send the result to some other agents, if needed.

Interactions in the closed holons are simpler than in open ones. There is no need to use directory facilitator service, because all body agents and their services are known. After the head of the holon receives the request for some task, it just has to find the corresponding performer for the task. Usually there is only one such performer in closed holons. It might be the head of the holon (usually for global tasks of the holon, like building full student model in the student modelling holon) or any of the body agents. If it is one of the body agents, it is requested to carry out the task and its result is forwarded to the initial requester. Open holons allow addition of new functionality of certain types without changing existing code. It is possible to add new body agents in the open holon and so add new types of subtask that holons are capable to accomplish. For example, each body agent of the problem generation holon generates some type of problems. To add new type of problems to the system, a new body agent is added to the open holon. Still, it is not the only agent that has to be added to the system, to add new type of problems. New body agents must be added to all open holons where each type of problems is treated differently. Such holons are expert agent's holon and knowledge evaluation agent's holon, because each type of problems must be solved and evaluated in different ways. Additionally, all new functionality must be provided to the learner. For, example new type of the problems must be shown to the learner by the interface agent. Thus the functionality of the interface agent should be extendable, too. To achieve it, the conception of hierarchical holonic multi agent systems is extended by implementing the head of the higher level holon (the interface agent) as an open holon. The most common tasks in the user interface are done by the head of the interface agent's holon, while other tasks are done by the body agents. So, a corresponding body agent must be also added to the interface holon to add new type of problems. The whole holonic multi-agent ITS architecture is given in the Figure 3.

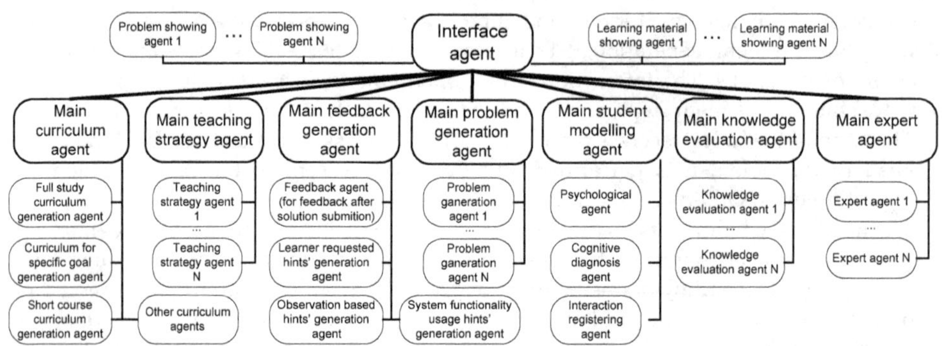

Fig. 3. Holonic ITS architecture (modified from (Lavendelis & Grundspenkis, 2008)).

3.3 Case study – The MIPITS system

The holonic multi-agent ITS architecture is approbated in the case study. An ITS named MIPITS has been developed using the proposed architecture (Lavendelis & Grundspenkis, 2010). The system supports the traditional classroom tutoring for the undergraduate course "Fundamentals of Artificial Intelligence" taught at Riga Technical University, because after attending lectures a learner can repeat the theory given at the lectures using the learning materials provided by the system and assess his/her knowledge with problems provided by the system. After finishing each problem, learner's knowledge is evaluated and he/she receives feedback about his/her solution explaining his/her mistakes. The main focus of the system is on problem solving. The following types of problems are included in the initial version of the system: (1) Different types of tests, including single and multiple choice tests and tests, where a learner has to write the answer by him/herself. (2) Search algorithm problems, where a learner has to do a state space search using the specified algorithm and lists OPEN and CLOSED (Luger, 2005). (3) Two person game problems, where a learner has to apply the MINIMAX algorithm or Alpha-Beta pruning to the given state space (Luger, 2005). The system adapts the problems to the following learner's characteristics. Difficulty level of the problem is adapted to the learner's knowledge level, practicality of the problem and size of the problem are adapted to the corresponding learner's preferences provided by the learner during the registration. Finally, the system follows the types of problems given to the learner and tries to minimize the repetition of problems of the same type.

The adaptation of problems is carried out in the problem generation holon showing that such holons can be efficiently used to implement adaptive tutoring. Previously described general algorithm of the heads of open holons is used to generate the most suitable problem. The suitability of the problems to the learner is measured by calculating the weighted sum of the differences between desired values of criteria and real ones. The problem with the minimal weighted sum is considered to be the most suitable one. The following equation is used to calculate the appropriateness of the problem (Lavendelis & Grundspenkis, 2010):

$$A = -(\left|dif_{pref} - dif_r\right| * c_d + \left|s_{pref} - s_r\right| * c_s + \left|pr_{pref} - pr_r\right| * c_p + f_t * c_f), \text{ where} \quad (1)$$

dif_{pref} - the preferred difficulty of the task;
dif_r - the real difficulty of the task;
c_d - the weight of the difficulty;
s_{pref} - the preferred size of the problem;
s_r - the real size of the problem;
c_s - the weight of the size;
pr_{pref} - the preferred practicality;
pr_r - the real practicality of the problem;
c_p - the weight of the practicality;
f_t - the frequency of problem's type;
c_f - the weight of the frequency.

Weights are determined empirically and are the following: $c_d=2$, $c_s=3$, $c_p=3$, $c_f=6$, because with these weights all criteria have significant impact on the appropriateness.
As the MIPITS system has specific functionality with the main focus on problems, the general architecture is customized to meet the particular requirements of the system. There is only one type of materials in the MIPITS system; thus, there is no need for open holons dealing with the materials. The corresponding agents are implemented as monolith agents instead of holons. The main teaching strategy agent generates all materials and the main interface agent visualizes them in the interface. Similarly, there is only one type of the curriculum and it is not changed after generation. The student modelling and feedback agents also do not have complex functionality in the MIPITS system, thus these agents also are implemented in a monolith way. The agents that deal with the problems are implemented as open holons to allow adding new types of problems. At the initial version of the system agents for the described three types of problems are implemented in each of the open holons, namely, the problem generation, the knowledge evaluation, the expert and the interface holons. For example, the problem generation holon contains the head (the main problem generation agent), the test generation agent, the search algorithm problem generation agent and the game tree problem generation agent. The actual architecture of the system is shown in the Figure 4. The heads of open holons are denoted with grey colour.

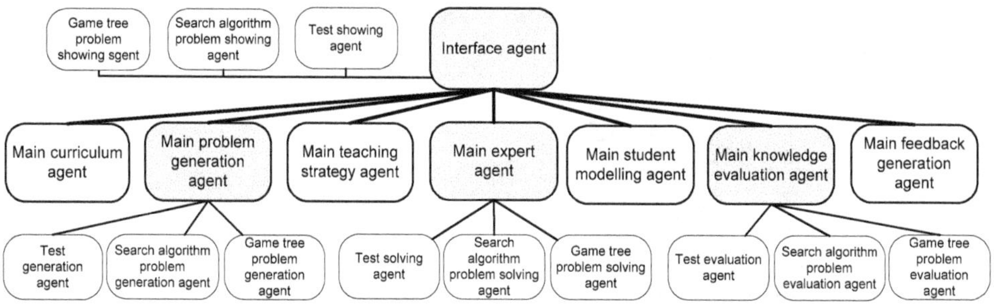

Fig. 4. The architecture of the MIPITS system.

The interface of the MIPITS system consists of two main parts (see Figure 5). The interface is in Latvian, because it is the language of the course. The left side of the main window shows the curriculum. It is shown as a hierarchy. The higher level shows the modules of the course, while lower level shows topics. When the learner chooses the topic to start learning the corresponding learning material is shown in the right side of the interface. The right side is used also to show problems that are given to the learner when he/she submits that he/she has finished the theoretical material and is ready to evaluate his/her knowledge. The layout of the right side differs for various problems. This part of the interface is created and managed by the corresponding body agents of the interface holon. The example of the problem is given in the Figure 5. It is an interface for two-person games algorithm MINI-MAX (Luger, 2005). It is created by the two-person games problem visualization agent. It has typical structure for the problems used in the MIPITS system. The top part of the right side (denoted with 1 in Figure 5) contains the description of the problem and defines what a learner has to do. The middle part (denoted with 2 in Figure 5) contains graphical information. In this case it is the game tree. The bottom part (denoted with 3 in Figure 5) contains controls for student to solve the problem. For the particular type of tasks it contains controls for assigning values to the vertexes in the state space. The student has to show how the hierarchical evaluations of the vertexes change during the execution of the algorithm.

The MIPITS system is open - it can be extended with new types of problems by adding four new body agents to corresponding holons: a problem generation agent, an expert agent, a knowledge evaluation agent and a problem visualisation agent for the particular types of problems. The extendibility of the MIPITS system has been proven by adding new type of problems to already running system without changing existing code. A topic about propositional logic and inference was added (Lavendelis & Grundspenkis, 2011).

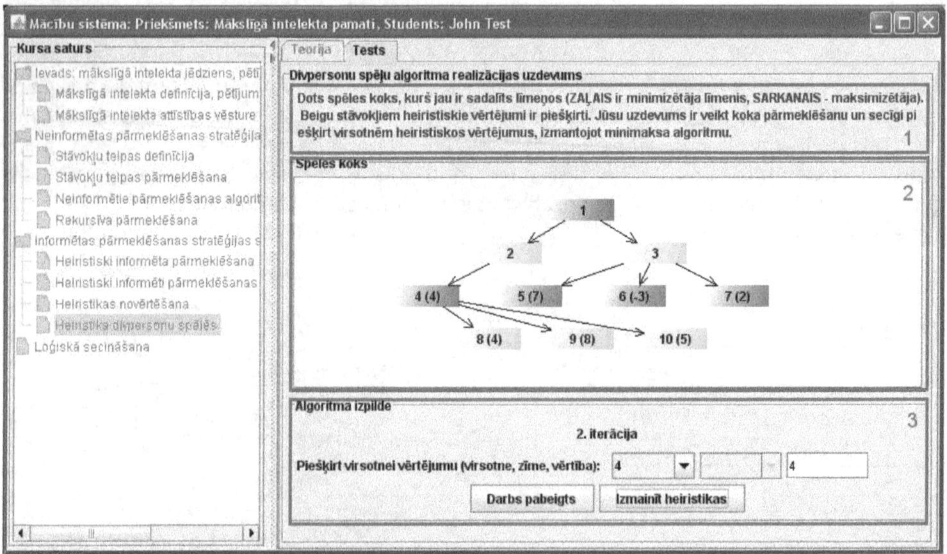

Fig. 5. The user interface of the MIPITS system.

4. Intelligent agents and web services

Despite being two independently developed technologies, services and agents have many similarities, because both of them are based on the principles of distributed computing. Thus it is worth to analyze how the lessons learned from the agent based architectures can be applied to the service oriented ITSs. Lavendelis and Bicans (2011) have indentified the most important similarities between agents and services in the context of ITSs:

- High modularity. Both services and agents offer high modularity, because they support systems that consist of small distributed entities.
- Openness. Both technologies allow dynamical addition of components (agents and services, respectively) to the system, to implement changes into the system. Both technologies offer mechanisms to find newly added components.
- Reactiveness. Reactive agents can be considered as services. For example lower level agents from the holonic agent architecture provide specific service upon request.
- Usage of protocols. Both agents and services use some kind of protocols to interact.

Still agents and services have come from two different fields of research. Intelligent agents have been proposed by artificial intelligence researchers, while services have been introduced by the software engineering specialists. Lavendelis & Bicans (2011) state that there are the following significant differences between agents and services that have to be taken into consideration during the ITS development:

- Reasoning capabilities. Services usually have no reasoning capabilities while agents are considered as reasoning entities.
- Autonomy. Agents are autonomous entities that are capable of proactive actions. Services are strictly reactive and have no autonomy. They are not capable to carry out any goal driven actions.
- Industrial acceptance. At the moment services appear to be industrially accepted and widely used technology. At the same time, agents are mainly used in research projects.
- Complex interaction protocols. Various interaction protocols like negotiations, auctions, etc, can be used in the multi-agent systems to reach agreements and solve problems. Agents have social capabilities to participate in these protocols. Services use simple protocols and have no social capabilities to participate in any complex interactions.

One can conclude that both distributed technologies can be used for ITS development and both of them have their advantages and disadvantages. ITSs contain components that are more suitable to develop as services and components that are more suitable to develop as agents. The main criterion to determine which technology is more suitable is the following. If there is no proactivity one can use services instead of agents to implement components of ITS and benefit from the industrial standards of SOA. Actually, services may be used in the same way as agents to implement modules of ITS. The remainder of the section analyzes how the similarities of the agents and services allow to use the lessons learned in the agent based ITS research in the service oriented ITSs. Additionally, some common principles of software architectures are analysed to include them in the architecture of ITSs.

General software architecture concepts say that the user interface should be separated from the logical part of the system. Usually it is done by creating a layered architecture that also allows separation of components that are dedicated to the repositories (like the learning object repository) and such fundamental technologies like video streaming. So it is beneficial to create a layered architecture that consists of three layers (Lavendelis & Bicans, 2011). *Layer one or the lower layer* contains repositories and fundamental technologies used in the

ITS. *Layer two or the logical layer* is a logical part of the system. It contains all three main modules of the ITS's modular architecture, namely, the student module, the tutoring module and the expert module. *Layer three or the presentation layer* contains all technologies needed to present the contents to the learner. It contains the communication module. The idea of layered architecture complies well with modular and agent oriented architectures. It allows keeping the traditional ITS modules and only separates components working with the repositories. These components usually are completely reactive and have no intelligence. Thus the layered approach allows to separate the intelligent part of the ITS from other parts.

The main lessons learned in the holonic multi-agent ITS architecture are the following. The implementation of the architecture showed that it is beneficial to keep the modules of the traditional ITS architecture and to implement them with distributed components. It allows keeping the main advantage of the modular architecture – the separation of the intelligent mechanisms that work with different types of knowledge. It allows for each component to process only one type of knowledge and abstract from other types. So the modules should be kept in the ITS architecture regardless of the technology used for implementation.

The distributed implementation gave two advantages to the architecture. Firstly, the realization using small-scale components increased the modularity of the system. Secondly, the introduction of holons decreased the coupling of the system, because each body agent is allowed to interact only with agents of the same holon. The head of the holon serves as an interface of the holon. It removed traditional drawback of distributed systems that complexity of interactions increases rapidly if the number of components increases. So, it may be concluded that some forms of organization should be included in distributed architectures. Despite, services do not support such hierarchical structure as holons, the organization and, as a consequence, increased modularity and decreased coupling can be sustained in the service oriented architecture in the following way. One or a few interface services should be introduced in each module. These services would fulfil the role of the heads of the higher level holons. If the higher level components are created the same way as in the holonic architecture, the expert module would have one main service, while the tutoring module, the student module and the communication module would have more than one. The interactions in the system are organized in the following way. The main service receives service requests from other main services. It uses the service registry to find other services (named lower level services) of the module and forwards the request to the appropriate service. The lower level service does its job and returns the result to the main service, which forwards it to the initial requester. So, like in holonic architecture, interactions take place only among main services and between main services and the lower level services of the corresponding module. It decreases the coupling of the system and facilitates its modularity. For example, the main interface service sends the request for problem in a topic to the main problem generation service, which finds the service that can generate a problem in the topic or even the most suitable problem for particular learner.

The holonic architecture implements modules of ITS in an open manner. The implementation of the MIPITS system proved that openness is important feature if the system is modified by adding some new features (Lavendelis & Grundspenkis, 2011). New type of problems that needs completely different processing in all holons was added to the system without changing anything in existing code. Thus, the open implementation of distributed ITSs makes the change implementation and adaptation of the ITS to new course or modifications of the existing course much easier.

Implementation of the multi-agent architecture proved that majority of intelligent adaptation mechanisms are included in the heads of the holons. Heads are not only the mediators, but they make intelligent choices, using different algorithms and reasoning. The heads of the higher level holons are the most important components to provide adaptivity. For example, body agents are capable to generate problems, but the head of the holon chooses the most appropriate problem to the particular learner. The body agents mostly work with repositories. They implement certain actions like extracting or generating materials or problems. So these agents fit more the concept of the service instead of intelligent agents because they are not proactive and execute reactive behaviour by accomplishing some task upon the request of the head of the holon. All proactive and intelligent actions are carried out by the heads of the holon, that fit the logical layer of the general architecture. The body agents on their hand implement the interface between the layers one and two because these agents are used by the agents from the second layer to access the first layer – the repositories.

To conclude, the main advantages of the holonic architecture can be sustained in the service oriented ITS architecture. Still, some features of agent architecture can not be implemented using services. Services do not have built in reasoning mechanisms that are natural to agents. So by implementing components as services the built in intelligent mechanisms are lost and it is not clear how to implement such mechanisms as reasoning inside the services. Potentially this is the main disadvantage in moving from multi-agent to service oriented ITS architecture. If some proactive behaviour is needed, then usage of agents is preferable. Still intelligent mechanisms and proactivity are mostly included in the logical part of the ITS and are rare in other parts. Thus there are components that can be successfully built using services instead of agents. As a consequence there is a point in both pure service oriented ITS architecture and hybrid ITS architecture, where deliberative components are implemented as agents while reactive components are implemented as services. Such architectures are presented in the following two sections.

5. Service oriented intelligent tutoring systems

It has been concluded in previous sections that there are several advantages to implement components of ITSs as services that are better known to software developers than intelligent agents. At the same time the principles of holonic multi-agent ITS architecture can be reused in the service oriented ITSs development. The following ideas have been identified to be adopted from the agent based ITSs and reused in the service oriented ITSs. Firstly, each module is implemented as a set of distributed components. Secondly, only some of the components interact with other components outside the corresponding module to decrease coupling of the system. Thirdly, the ITS is implemented as an open system and new functionality can be added to the system by adding new distributed components, in particular services. The service oriented ITS architecture that realizes all the identified principles is described in the following subsection. The case study of the architecture is given in the section 5.2 by presenting an ITS developed using the architecture.

5.1 Service oriented intelligent tutoring system architecture

The service oriented ITS architecture (Lavendelis & Bicans, 2011) consists of two levels, namely the higher and the lower level. At the higher level of the architecture each module contains one or a few main services that are used from the outside of the module. These services implement interfaces of the modules. At the lower level unlimited number of other services may be included in each module. These services are used only by the main services of the corresponding module. They are not used from the outside of the module. The service oriented ITS architecture implements the main ideas of the layered architecture described in the previous section. Services of the communication module implement the third layer of the layered architecture. All main services of the remaining three modules (the pedagogical module, the expert module and the student diagnosis module) implement the logical part of the system and thus correspond to the second layer. Lastly, all lower level services implement all particular actions with all repositories and with all fundamental technologies like video streaming. Thus these services implement the interface to the third layer of the layered architecture.

Similarly to traditional ITS architectures *the communication module* is the only module interacting with the user. It manages the user interface and has to visualize the curriculum, learning materials, problems and feedback. It receives learner's requests and forwards them to the corresponding services. The module consists of the following higher level services:

- The main interface service, whose role is to register learner's actions and forward them to the corresponding services.
- The main material visualisation service that processes requests to visualize learning materials of different types.
- The main problem visualisation service that similarly to the main material visualisation service processes requests to visualize problems of different types.
- The curriculum visualisation service visualizes the curriculum of the course.
- The feedback visualisation service that has only one function - to give feedback to a learner, when he/she has finished solving the problem or has requested a hint.

To make the architecture open for new types of materials and problems, the communication module contains two types of lower level services that interact only with the corresponding main services. Firstly, the main material visualisation service has one lower level service for each type of materials that is needed to be visualised differently, like video streams and text materials. If new types of materials are introduced in the system, the corresponding lower level service will be added to the module. Secondly, the main problem visualisation service uses the lower level services corresponding to the types of problems used in the system. Thus the main material and problem visualisation services are only mediators - they only have to find appropriate lower level services to visualize materials and problems respectively. Lower level services also have only one task - to visualize the particular type of materials/problems. The higher level services that do not have corresponding lower level services do all tasks by themselves, for example, the curriculum visualisation service is responsible for visualisation of the curriculum. Still, the general architecture can be customized by adding new types of lower level services, if needed. For example, if various types of curriculum are used, corresponding lower level services can be added.

The services of the *pedagogical module* have the same tasks as the module has in the modular architecture. To accomplish them it consists of the following services:

- The curriculum generation service has to provide the curriculum of the course. It may be generated automatically by the service or created by the teacher and stored in the database for the service to read from.
- The main material generation service that is responsible for material generation corresponding to the chosen topic from the curriculum of the course. It uses lower level

services capable to generate particular types of materials. Each type of materials supported by the system has corresponding lower level material generation service. For example, separate lower level material generation services can be created for each of the abovementioned different formats of learning materials.

- The main problem generation service, that is responsible for problem generation. Similarly, to materials, each type of problems has a corresponding lower level service, that generates the corresponding type of problems upon the request of the main service. Such an approach implements similar openness to the multi-agent architecture. The openness of the architecture is further discussed below.
- The feedback generation service, which is responsible for providing feedback to the learner. It receives the knowledge evaluation and creates meaningful feedback that can vary from comments about answer's correctness to detailed explanation of mistakes.

The main material and problem generation services use similar algorithm to carry out interactions during the generation. In fact, majority of the main services use similar algorithm. The following steps are carried out when the main service receives a request to generate a material/problem in the particular topic. The definition of the algorithm will include also actions done by other services to illustrate all interactions:

1. The main service receives generation request.
2. The main service requests student model from the student modelling service described below to know the characteristics of the learner to adapt to.
3. When the main service receives the student model, it queries the service registry to find the corresponding lower level services.
4. If at least one lower level service is found, the request for materials or problems in the certain topic together with needed characteristics is sent to the lower level services.
5. Lower level services create or retrieve from the repository the most suitable materials/problems for the learner's characteristics in the current topic.
6. The lower level services send their results to the main services.
7. The main service receives responses from all services requested before. If more than one service provides a result, the main services chooses the most appropriate result and forwards it to the main interface service and other main services, if needed.

The *expert module* contains only one higher level service named main expert service. It is responsible for solving problems given to the learner. Each type of problems has its own second level service that solves the problem. The main service just has to find the correct second level service. The *student module* contains two higher level services, namely, the main knowledge evaluation service and the main student modelling service. The student modelling service is responsible for collecting information about a learner, his/her actions priorities and knowledge evaluations. It also creates full student model and provides it upon request of other services. The knowledge evaluation service is responsible for evaluating learner's knowledge level by comparing his/her solution of particular problem to the so called system's solution provided by the expert agent.

Similarly to the multi-agent architecture, the service oriented architecture is open in the following sense. New types of materials and problems can be added to the system without changing the code of existing services. Only new services corresponding to the new type of problem or material must be added in each component of the architecture where each type of material/problem is handled by separate service. If any new type of materials is added to the system then two services must be added to the system, namely corresponding lower

level material generation service and lower level material visualisation service. Four new lower level services must be added to introduce new type of problems. Corresponding problem generation service, expert service, knowledge evaluation service and problem visualisation service must be added to the system. The service oriented ITS architecture is given in Figure 6. Besides the described components the figure contains repositories used to store data, but links among services and repositories are omitted to keep the figure readable. The following repositories can be used in the ITS: the student data repository with personal data and student models, the course repository with data about courses and topics, learning material repository and the problem repository (for details, see (Lavendelis & Bicans, 2011).
The described openness is not the only way to customize the architecture. Specific functionality that does not correspond to any of the traditional modules may be needed, Additional separate modules can be created to include such functionalities. For example, teacher's interface is needed in any practically used ITS to modify the course by adding, removing and changing topics, learning materials and problems used in the system. Similarly, to the traditional modules additional ones are implemented as sets of services (Lavendelis & Bicans, 2011).

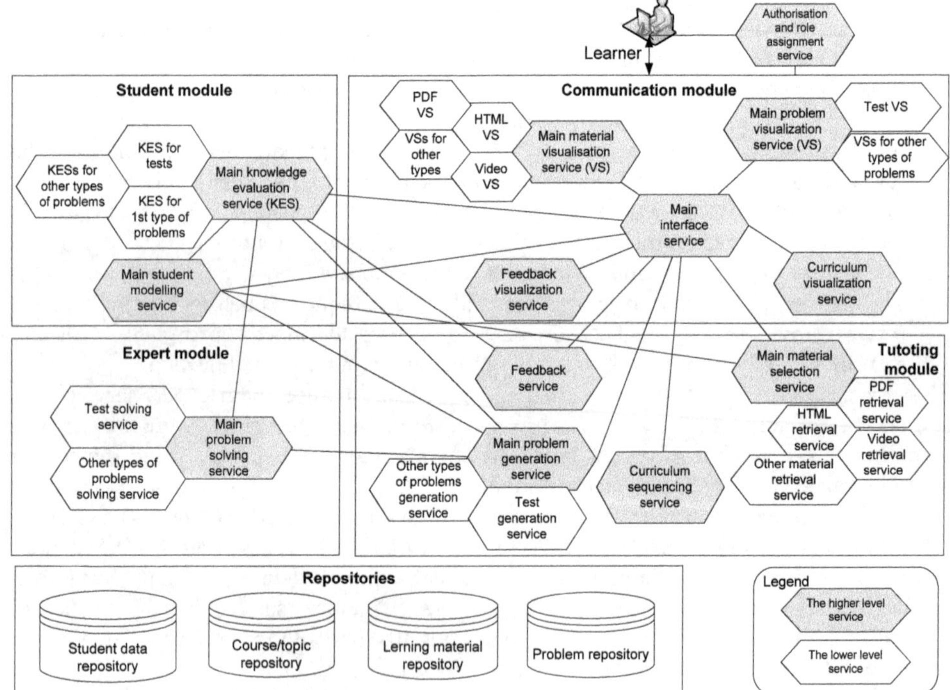

Fig. 6. Service oriented ITS architecture.

5.2 Case study

The described service oriented ITS architecture has been tested during the implementation of the ITS for the graduate course "Artificial Intelligence" taught at Riga Technical

University (Bicans et al, 2011). The course covers general artificial intelligence topics, like agents, planning, ontologies and reasoning. It has video and text learning materials with different levels of granularity. The video LOs are filmed lectures of the course. Materials cover theory, examples and tasks about the topics of the course. The aim of the ITS is to provide out of classroom tutoring, that takes into consideration learning styles of students by presenting a single or a combination of appropriate materials in each topic. The ITS stores and identifies all kinds of LOs describing them with standardized metadata. Links between topics and corresponding learning materials are not stored in the repositories. They are created dynamically. A keyword based algorithm is used to find the materials that can be used at the current topic and select the most suitable materials for the learner's preferences. LOs and topics are described with keywords and if the intersection between the sets of LO's topic's keywords is possible, the LO is considered as linked to the topic. Then only those LOs that match the preferences stored in the student model are selected from the results' set of the first step (Bicans, et al, 2011). Such an approach provides ITS with option to use more LOs from different repositories without manually linking LOs and topics. The curriculum of the course is encoded by a topic map that is a graphical knowledge representation form using topics and associations among them. In the developed ITS a topic map is used to show the hierarchy of the topics, because it visually shows the place of each topic in the course.

The general service oriented ITS architecture is customized during the development of the system to meet its specific needs. The main focus of the developed ITS prototype is on the adaptive LO presentation to learners. Therefore, only corresponding services dealing with LO selection, student model development, tutor's functionality are implemented in the current version of the system. The actual architecture of the ITS is shown in Figure 7. The communication module contains the main interface service and two more higher level services - the topic map viewer service (visualizes curriculum) and the main material visualisation service, which also has two lower level services that visualize both types of

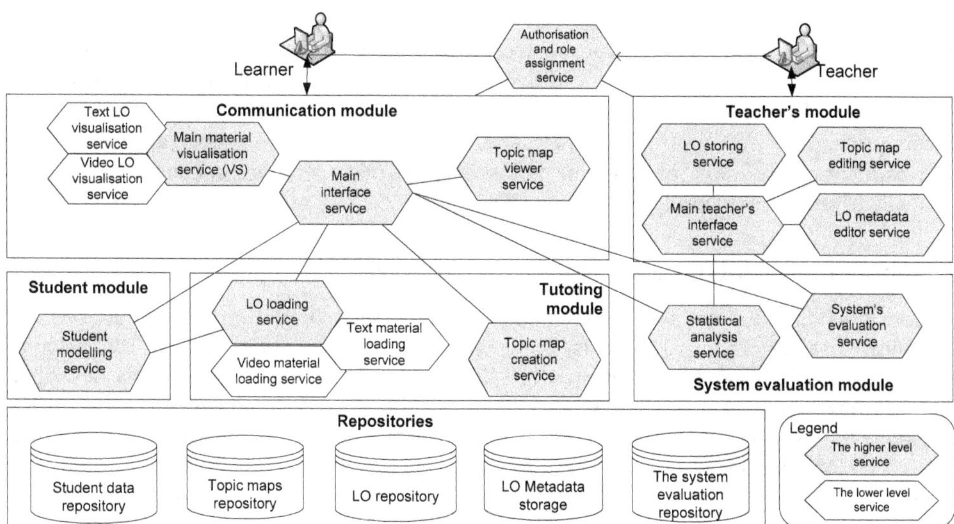

Fig. 7. The actual architecture of the implemented ITS prototype.

LOs used in the system - text and video LOs. The student module just has to maintain static student's profiles. Thus it contains just one service named student modelling service. The tutoring module is implemented using two higher level services, named topic map creation service (curriculum generation service) and LO loading service used to retrieve LOs. It has two lower level services corresponding to both types of LOs. The teacher's module besides the main interface service has services for editing topic maps, as well as for LO metadata editing and LO storing. Finally, the system has one additional module - system evaluation module, whose main task is to collect evaluations of the system provided by the learners.

The user interface of the system is given in Figure 8. The given screenshot is shown to the student when he/she chooses the topic to watch the video about. The menu is in the top left corner of the window (not included in the figure). The centre of the screen is occupied with the video player. One of the main parts of the system is shown in the bottom part of the figure. During the video session the system displays topics that are covered within lecture and related content that corresponds to the selected topic. Also, related topics, lectures and LOs are shown, allowing the learner to navigate to any related topic or material.

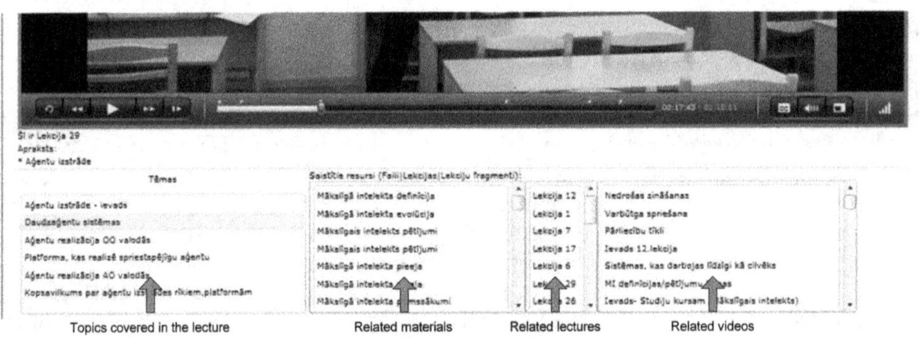

Fig. 8. The user interface of the developed ITS prototype.

The group of 19 students have approbated the developed ITS. They watched videos, red theoretical materials of lectures and explored examples. The feedback showed that granularity of LOs should vary, because some students like LOs with low granularity, while others prefer LOs with high granularity. The videos were used frequently and on average each student viewed 90% of available videos at least once. Another encouraging result is that 90% of students pointed out topic maps as appropriate tool to visualize the curriculum.

6. Hybrid intelligent tutoring system architecture

As concluded above, agents are more suitable to implement some components than services and vice versa for other components. To benefit from the advantages of both technologies hybrid architecture is proposed. It preserves the approach used in the previously described architectures in two senses. Firstly, each module from the traditional ITS architecture is implemented as a set of distributed components. Secondly, the architecture consists of two levels. Still the implementation differs from the previously described architectures. The higher level consists of agents that implement the logical or deliberative part of the system. The agents correspond to the higher level holons of the multi-agent architecture. The lower level of the architecture is mainly implemented as services that carry out simple reactive behaviour upon request like retrieving data from repositories. Agents have the same functions as heads of the holons in the multi-agent architecture - they make all intelligent choices to carry out the tutoring process and use services for particular tasks. Services of the hybrid architecture are used instead of the body agents of the multi-agent architecture. It allows keeping the advantages of both previously described architectures, like openness to new functionality and high modularity. The proposed architecture is presented in the following subsections by specifying agents of each module as well as services used by these agents and, as a consequence, included in the corresponding modules.

6.1 The tutoring module

The tutoring module is responsible for four types of functions, namely, curriculum sequencing, material retrieval or generation, problem generation and providing feedback to the learner after he/she has finished the problem. As a consequence the module contains the following four agents: curriculum agent, teaching strategy agent, problem generation agent and feedback agent. *The curriculum agent* creates the curriculum of the course for each learner. The agent uses topic retrieval service to retrieve topics from the database. The *teaching strategy agent* is responsible for choosing the most suitable material for the learner in each topic from the materials available in the repository. To retrieve materials from the repository it uses services. There is one service for each type of materials used in the system. *The problem generation agent* is responsible for generation of problems that are suitable to the learner's characteristics. The agent gets the student model from the student modelling agent described below. It determines the most suitable type of the problem and calculates parameters like the difficulty level of the problem. The agent uses the problem generation service to generate the problem of the given type with given parameters. *The feedback agent* generates feedback for a learner each time he/she submits his/her solution of the problem. During the creation of the feedback the evaluation of the learner's solution provided by the knowledge evaluation agent is used. Components that implement the tutoring module are shown in Figure 9. Services are shown together with the agent that is using them.

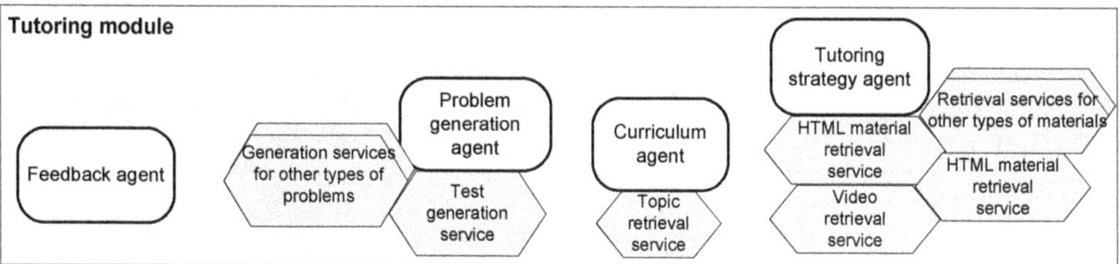

Fig. 9. Components of the tutoring module.

6.2 The communication module

The communication module contains single agent - the interface agent that is responsible for carrying out all interactions with the learner. Firstly, it perceives learner's actions and forwards them to agents of other modules that need information about corresponding actions. Secondly, it is responsible for presenting all information to the learner. It uses services of the module for this purpose. Separate services are created for each type of information given to the learner, namely, materials, problems, curriculum and feedback. To make the architecture open, the additional lower levels of services are introduced in the communication module. The abovementioned services (for example, material visualisation service) are responsible for presentation of all types of the given information (materials). In case such service is implemented as a monolith component, it's code must be changed to support new type of materials. For, example, if there is a need to add an audio material the code of material visualisation service must be changed. Thus such services are implemented only as dispatchers that find the corresponding lower levels service that is capable to visualize the corresponding type of information. The visualisation job is physically done by the lower level service. It allows implementing visualisation of new information just by adding new lower level service, for example, by adding audio material visualisation service. The architecture of the module is given in the Figure 10.

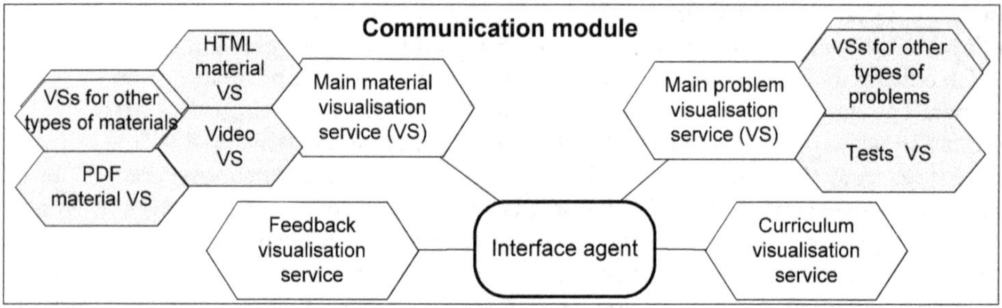

Fig. 10. The architecture of the communication module.

6.3 The expert module

The expert module is implemented identically as in the holonic multi-agent architecture. Both layers of the architecture are implemented as agents, because solving any problem given to the student is a complex task that usually requires some intelligent mechanisms like reasoning which are easier to implement inside agents not services. The higher level of the module's architecture contains only one agent - the expert agent. It receives all requests to solve problems. It finds the corresponding lower level agent and forwards the request to that agent. The lower level consists of agents corresponding to the types of problems used in the system. The architecture of the expert module is depicted in the Figure 11.

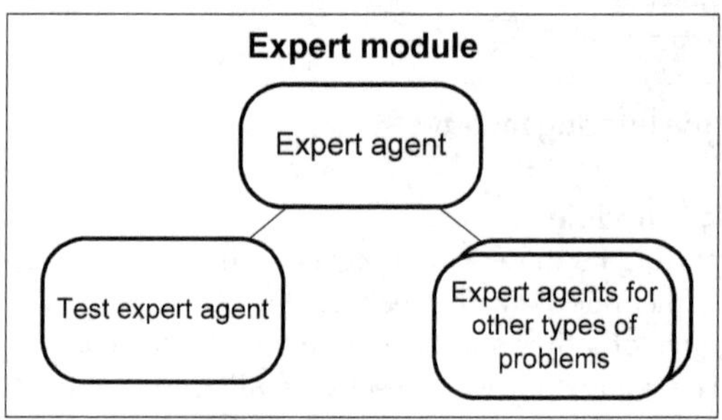

Fig. 11. The expert module's architecture.

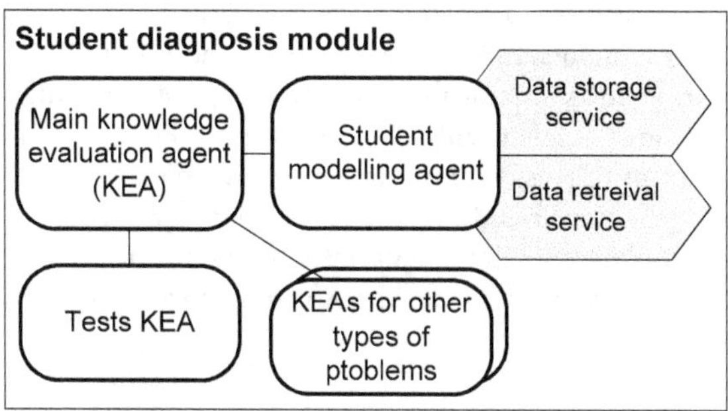

Fig. 12. The student module's architecture.

6.4 The student diagnosis module

The higher level of the student diagnosis module's architecture consists of two agents, namely, student modelling agent and main knowledge evaluation agent. *The student modelling agent* is responsible for creation of the student model and providing it to other agents upon request. The student modelling agent uses data storing and data retrieval services. Data storing service stores facts about the learner (for example, actions done by him/her) upon the request by the agent. The data retrieval service retrieves the stored facts for the agent. The student modelling agent receives all facts about the student, analyzes them and creates the student model. *The knowledge evaluation agent* is responsible for evaluating learner's knowledge in certain topic using the solution of some problem provided by him/her. The knowledge evaluation is done by comparing learner's solution to the correct solution provided by the expert agent. Comparison of two solutions and knowledge evaluation may require complex intelligent mechanisms. Thus, the components of the second level are implemented as agents instead of services. Each type of problems used in the system have corresponding lower level knowledge evaluation agent. The architecture of the student diagnosis module is shown in Figure 12.

6.5 The whole hybrid ITS architecture

The whole hybrid architecture is given in Figure 13 that shows components implementing all four modules. Additionally, interactions among components of different modules are shown. Only agents of the architecture's higher level interact to components of other modules. So, interfaces with other modules are implemented in one or a few agents of each module. The hybrid architecture is open in the similar sense to both above described architectures. Some kinds of new functionality can be added to the system by adding new lower level components and without changing existing components. The most common changes are additions of new types of materials (e.g., audio materials) and new types of problems (e.g., course specific tasks). New type of materials usually needs corresponding functionality like audio streaming to be implemented. New types of problems need the corresponding problem generation, problem solving and knowledge evaluation functionality. To enable easy addition of such functionality the architecture specifies open sets of lower level components corresponding to the functionality that varies from type to type of materials and problems. Open sets are denoted by double boxes in the Figure 13. New components may be added to these sets at any time.

Thus the hybrid architecture preserves the main strengths of the above described service oriented and multi-agent architectures, namely, high modularity and openness for new components. Moreover, it adds significant advantage by implementing each component in suitable technology. The logical layer with all intelligent mechanisms is realized by intelligent agents, while reactive components without any proactive or intelligent actions are realized using simpler technology - services. It removes the main drawbacks of both homogenous architectures. Neither simple components without any intelligent behaviour are implemented as agents, nor are the intelligent mechanisms developed from scratch in the services.

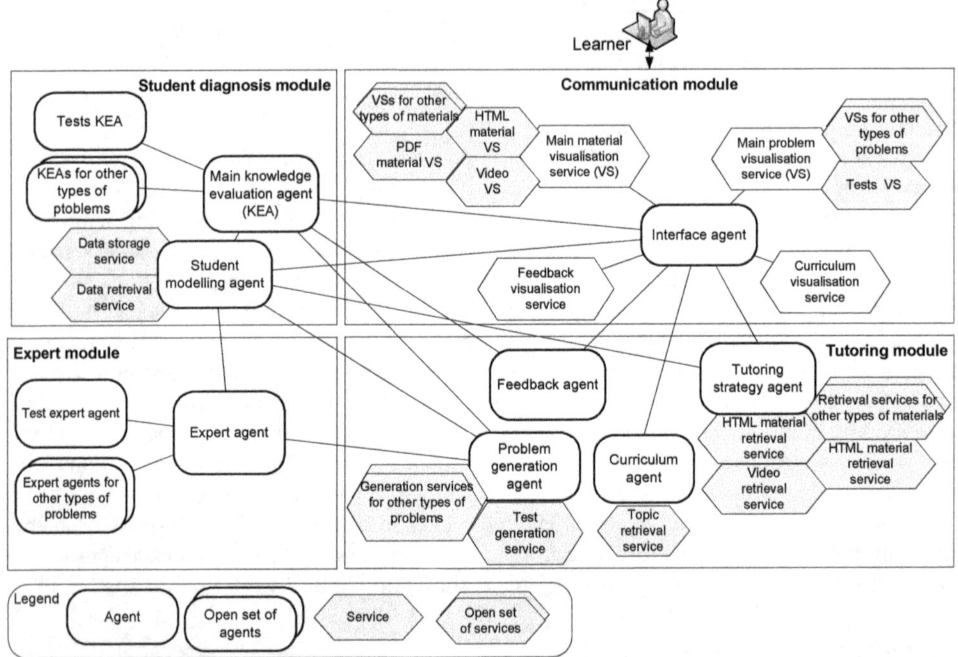

Fig. 13. The hybrid ITS architecture.

7. Conclusion

ITSs based on the traditional architecture have problems with modularity and as a consequence complex development and change implementation, as well as reuse of ITS components is almost impossible. Distributed technologies may be used to eliminate these drawbacks. Still, majority of the known agent based ITSs do not fully use advantages of distributed technologies. They are not open and do not enable reuse of small scale components. To solve these drawbacks three open architectures for ITS development are proposed. The main advantages of the proposed architectures are the following. All of the proposed architectures are open and consist of small-scale components that have one or very few tasks. The openness of the architectures allows creation of systems that are extendable with certain types of functionality by just adding new components and without changing existing code. Such option enables easy adaptation of the ITS's functionality to the changes made in the course as well to any new courses. Usage of small scale components that have only one task means that these components can be reused in any system that needs this task. Additional advantages of the proposed architectures are increased modularity and decreased coupling and as a consequence complexity of interactions achieved by introduction of the organisational principles into the distributed technologies, namely multi-agent systems and service oriented architectures.

Two technologies analyzed in the chapter are similar because of their distributed nature. Therefore the architectures of systems using these technologies should be built using the same principles. Thus the lessons learned in usage of one technology can be used in building systems with another technology. The chapter shows how the lessons learned in agent based ITS development can be used in service oriented ITSs.

Agents and services have significant differences. While agents offer natural implementation of the intelligent mechanisms needed in the logical part of the system, services are easier to implement, and better known for developers. Services also support easy integration of various technologies, like various tools for the user interface of the system, video streaming tools, etc. These characteristics are important for implementation of the lower level components and the user interface. Thus agents are more suitable for some components (more deliberative components), while services are more suitable for other components (more reactive components). That is a reason why in this chapter the multi-agent and the service-oriented architectures are proposed to use as a basis to develop hybrid architecture implementing each component in the technology that fits the nature of the component. The main direction of the future work is to implement the proposed hybrid architecture and test how does it work in the practically implemented prototype of an ITS. Additionally, the possibilities to use hybrid architectures consisting of services and agents to other systems with some reactive and some deliberative components should be analysed.

8. References

Alpert, S.R. Singley, M.K. & Fairweather, P.G. (1999). Deploying Intelligent Tutors on the Web: An Architecture and an Example. *International Journal of Artificial Intelligence in Education, Vol. 10, No. 2,* pp.183-197.

Anohina, A. (2007) *Development of an intelligent supporting system for adaptive tutoring and knowledge assessment.* Doctoral Thesis. -Riga, RTU.

Bicans, J.; Lavendelis, E. & Vanags, M. (2011). Adaptive tutoring by means of student model based learning object selection. *Proceedings of the IADIS International Conference "e-Learning 2011", Rome, Italy, 20 - 23 July 2011, Volume 1,* pp. 251-257.

Capuano, N. et al. (2000). A Multi-Agent Architecture for Intelligent Tutoring. *Presented at the International Conference on Advances in Infrastructure for Electronic Business, Science, and Education on the Internet (SSGRR 2000),* Rome, Italy.

de Antonio, et al. (2005) Intelligent Virtual Environments for Training: An Agent-based Approach. *Proceedings of 4th International Central and Eastern European Conference on Multi-Agent Systems.* Budapest, Hungary, September 15-17.

Capuano, N., et al. (2000). A Multi-Agent Architecture for Intelligent Tutoring. *Proceedings of the International Conference on Advances in Infrastructure for Electronic Business, Science, and Education on the Internet, SSGRR 2000,* L'Aquila, July 31 - August 06.

Devedzic, V. et al. (2000). Teaching Formal Languages by an Intelligent Tutoring System. *In Educational Technology & Society, Vol. 3, No. 2.* pp. 36-49.

Dorça, F.A., Lopes, C.R., Fernández, M.A. (2003). A multiagent architecture for distance education systems. *Proceedings of the 3rd IEEE International Conference on Advanced Learning Technologies, ICALT'03*, p. 368.

Fischer, K., et al. (2003). Holonic Multiagent Systems: A Foundation for the Organisation of Multiagent Systems, *Lecture Notes in Computer Science 2744*, Springer.

Georgouli, K. et al. (2003). A Web Based Tutoring System for Compilers. *Proceedings of the 14th EAEEIE Annual Conference on Innovation in Education for Electrical and Information Engineering (EIE)*, Gdansk, Poland, June 16-18.

Gerber, C.; Siekmann, J. & Vierke, G. (1999). Holonic multi-agent systems, *Technical Report R-99-03, DFKI GmbH.*

Grundspenkis, J. and Anohina, A. (2005). Agents in Intelligent Tutoring Systems: State of the Art. *Scientific Proceedings of Riga Technical University „Computer Science. Applied Computer Systems", 5th series, Vol.22,* Riga, pp.110-121.

Hospers, M. et al. (2003). An Agent-based Intelligent Tutoring System for Nurse Education. *Applications of Intelligent Agents in Health Care* Birkhauser Publishing Ltd, pp. 141-157.

Koestler, A. (1967). *The Ghost in the Machine*. Hutchinson & Co, London.

Lavendelis, E. & Grundspenkis, J. (2008). Open Holonic Multi-Agent Architecture for Intelligent Tutoring System Development. *Proceedings of IADIS International Conference „Intelligent Systems and Agents 2008"*, Amsterdam, The Netherlands, pp. 100-108.

Lavendelis, E. (2009). *Open multi-agent architecture and methodology for intelligent tutoring system development.* Doctoral Thesis. –Riga, RTU. 222 p.

Lavendelis, E. & Grundspenkis, J. (2010). MIPITS - An Agent based Intelligent Tutoring System. *Proceedings of 2nd International Conference on Agents and Artificial Intelligence (ICAART 2010) Vol. 2.*, Valensia, Spain, January, 22-24. pp. 5-13.

Lavendelis, E. and Bicans, J. (2011). Multi-Agent and Service Oriented Architectures for Intelligent Tutoring System Development. *Scientific Journal of Riga Technical University 2011, Series 5, Volume 43*, pp. 27-36.

Lavendelis, E. & Grundspenkis, J. (2011). MASITS Methodology Supported Development of Agent Based Intelligent Tutoring System MIPITS. *Communications in Computer and Information Science. - 129 (3).*, pp 119-132.

Luger, G.F. (2005). *Artificial Intelligence: Structures and Strategies for Complex Problem Solving,* Addison-Wesley, Harlow, England, 903 p.

Nimis, J. & Stockheim, T. (2004). The Agent.Enterprise Multi-Multi-agent System. *Proceedings of the Conference on Agent Technology in Business Applications, Essen, Germany.*

Silveira, R.A. & Vicari, R.M. (2002). Developing Distributed Intelligent Learning Environment with JADE – Java Agents for Distance Education Framework. *ITS 2002, Cerri, S.A., Gouardères, G., Paraguaçu, F. (Eds.), LNCS 2363,* pp. 105–118.

Triantis T. & Pintelas P. (2004). An Integrated Environment for Building Distributed Multi-agent Educational Applications". *AIMSA 2004, LNAI 3192,* pp. 351–360.

Vilkelis, M.; Lukashenko, R. & Anohina, A. (2009). Technical Evolution of the Concept Map Based Intelligent Knowledge Assessment System. *Proceedings of the Workshop on Intelligent Educational Systems and Technology-Enhanced Learning,* September 7, Riga, Latvia, pp. 214-221.

Webber, C. & Pesty, S. (2002). A two-level multi-agent architecture for a distance learning environment. *ITS 2002/Workshop on Architectures and Methodologies for Building Agent-based Learning Environments, E. de Barros Costa,* pp. 26-38.

12

Developing Distributed Repositories of Learning Objects

Salvador Otón, Antonio Ortiz, Luis de-Marcos, Sergio Mazo de Dios, Antonio García, Eva García, José R. Hilera and Roberto Barchino
Computer Science Department, University of Alcala, Technical School of Computer Science Engineering, Alcalá de Henares, Madrid Spain

1. Introduction

A repository or digital storage of educative elements is a collection of resources (learning objects) accessible through a communication network. It is not necessary to have a previous knowledge about the collection containing the structure of the resources or only the metadata describing them, together with a reference to locate it (IMS DRI, 2003).
The aim of a repository is to facilitate the reusability of educational resources, providing access to the stored resources to learning management systems (LMS); learning content management system (LCMS); content portals (for an instance: searching systems of digital libraries, World Wide Web searching, etc.); or any application/software developed to access to learning objects.
Digital repositories, in the broadest sense, are used to store any sort of digital material. However, digital repositories for learning objects are much more complex in terms of what to store and how to do it. The purpose of a digital learning object repository is not just to store and distribute learning objects, but to allow them to be shared by different users and, above all, to make it easier to reuse them in different training activities (figure 1). From the users' point of view, these repositories have the advantage of having access to the content stored in them. To make this possible, the content must be gathered through certain procedures, rules and standards whose implementation is intended to promote the reusability of learning objects. Moreover, the repository itself must follow a series of specifications and standards which enable to browse the content it stores and facilitate interoperability with other repositories.
Most repositories are usually autonomous, that is, they work as portals that can be accessed through a Web-based interface, providing a search mechanism and a list of categories to conduct the search. However, it is becoming increasingly common the possibility of making federated searches in distributed repositories from the original repository.
Some examples of this kind of search can be found in repositories such as those set out in table 1. In this way, it is possible to access to different repositories from the learning management platform, preview their contents and even download and incorporate them into a course.

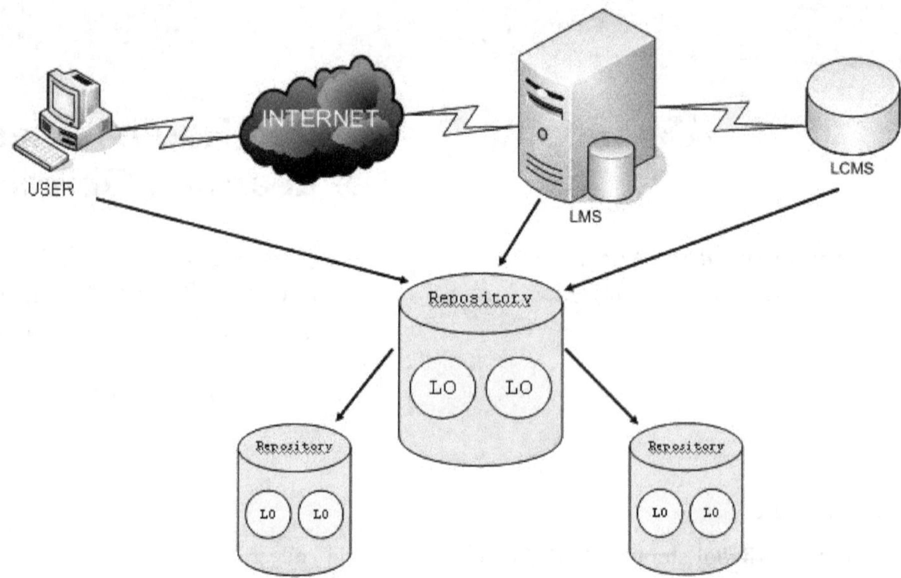

Fig. 1. Learning Objects Repositories.

REPOSITORY	*URL*
Agrega	*http://contenidos.proyectoagrega.es*
Ariadne	*http://www.ariadne-eu.org*
EdNA Online	*http://www.edna.edu.au*
EducaNext	*http://www.educanext.org*
LORNET	*http://www.lornet.org*
MACE	*http://portal.mace-project.eu/*
Merlot	*http://www.merlot.org/*
OER Commons	*http://www.oercommons.org*

Table 1. Public Learning objects repositories.

Therefore, it is now essential that repositories are developed according to standards and specifications that guarantee interoperability with any other repository or search system. In this chapter we present (1) the most important standards and specifications in this area, (2) a service-oriented architecture of a federated repository based on these standards and specifications, and (3) how to develop a federated repository using this SOA architecture. The chapter is structured as follows: section 2 presents the main specifications and standards in the scope of e-learning with an emphasis on those related to construction and management of learning object repositories. Section 3 presents the design of a service-oriented architecture for building a distributed repository of learning objects. Section 4 details how to develop a federated repository using SOAP Web services while section 5 details how to develop a federated repository using RESTful Web services. Finally, section 6 presents our conclusions.

2. Standards and specifications

Nowadays, one of the main problems with e-learning systems is the accessibility, interoperability, durability and reusability of the educational materials. It is necessary that the platforms of e-learning and the author tools are based on standards and specifications and, in addition, all the learning objects are "described" using the same "language". Moreover, it is sure that a learning object will be re-usable, if it is created according to the definition of some standard, and so, the object content must be described through metadata. However, the standards do not provide any guideline of how a learning object can be discovered.

Therefore, the educational content should be:

- Developed as standards.
- Universally discovered.
- Easy to find.
- Independent of metadata format.
- Reusable.
- Independent of the storage platform.
- Integrated in other learning systems.

E-learning systems have made satisfactory progress towards communication through the Internet, either to communicate with users or to intercommunicate with others systems. The main feature of the new e-learning environment is the use of the Web as a single distribution platform. Therefore, e-learning systems provide features which were unknown in the traditional education system, making it possible to solve some deficiencies as the high production and development time costs. However, there is no reusability of the learning objects and software components that compose an e-learning tool.

These problems are summarized by (Koper, 2000) on the following points:

- The increase of the heterogeneous products and the interaction between people and systems, only between people or only between systems.
- The spectacular increase of available information and its dispersion in different systems and applications, which implies the need to communicate the different software products and platforms.
- The distributed e-learning process organization, due to geographic dispersion of the course members.

Therefore, there are different solutions to solve these problems; solutions that try to unify the educational way of creation and the way of integrating platforms and educational repositories, and also the communication of those contents. The solution to these problems is called interoperability.

The IEEE defines interoperability as the ability of two or more systems or components to exchange information and to use the information exchanged. Within the world of e-learning exists a set of standards and specifications (hereinafter "norms") to ensure interoperability between different learning systems and more specifically those related with learning object repositories (Otón S. et al, 2009). These norms enable the exchange of the teaching contents they store and consequently achieve the reuse of those contents in different training projects.

These norms may be classified as follows:

1. Norms geared towards building and defining the learning object itself, that is to say, its content and metadata.

2. Norms geared towards the publication and search for learning objects by making it easier to locate resources in different repositories.
3. Norms designed to assist in the design of repositories whose aim is interoperability and which therefore specify software architecture for their construction.

The majority of the norms belonging to the second and third groups norms are based on Web services and service-oriented architecture (SOA) (W3C, 2004). Web services constitute a reusability mechanism of distributed software components. They can be registered and published in the Web, and they make use of open and standard protocols of Internet, like HTTP, XML, UDDI, SOAP, WSDL and REST, that deal with the interoperability problem among the different technologies and software platforms.

The first group of norms are aimed at the generation, documentation and packaging of learning objects. Its main feature is the description of the object using metadata. The main norm to comply in the description of the metadata of a learning object is LOM (IEEE, 2002). With respect to packaging, we outline the two most used norms today that are SCORM (ADL, 2002) and IMS Common Cartridge (IMS CC, 2008) belonging to a broader standard called Digital Learning Services Standards.

The IMS Common Cartridge (CC) specification proposes a standard way of packaging learning objects and its metadata (making use of the LOM specification). This standard describes the structure of a package, disposing learning resources as a folder tree. Assessments, Question Banks, Discussion Topics, Web content, and many others can be packaged inside a CC cartridge.

CC considers four categories of resources inside a package:

- imsmanifest.xml: A file describing the content of the package. It must be placed at the root directory in the package.
- Web Content: A folder tree which contains digital content resources (Web pages, documents, media files, etc.), Web links and links to other resources inside the package. All resources inside this category must be placed at the Web Content root folder or at one of its subfolders. Only one single Web Content folder can exist inside a package.
- Learning Application Object (LAO): A folder tree with the files (or file references) needed for a learning system to distribute learning object contents. There can be multiple LAOs folders inside a package and each one can contain subfolders.
- Folder: A package may contain folders to group other kinds of resources not considered in the categories defined above.

References between the resources packaged in a cartridge can exist with the following restrictions:

- A Web content resource can reference any other Web content resource, but it can't reference resources outside the Web content folder.
- A LAO resource can reference Web content resources and any other LAO resource inside its folder tree, but it can't reference LAOs outside its folder tree.

One of the basic pillars of interoperability between learning object repositories is the ability to search their contents. Recently, search systems have evolved from only working in one repository to working simultaneously in various distributed repositories; this is known as "federated search". In this kind of search is widespread to use of Web services, so that these services act as intermediaries between different learning objects repository. A proof of this is found in the specification SQI (CEN, 2005). Examples of repositories that implement federated search through SQI can be found in Merlot, Ariadne or GLOBE.

SQI was defined by the CEN (European Committee for Standardization). It forms part of a public initiative known as the CEN/ISSS Learning Technologies Workshop, whose commitment it is to guarantee interoperability between learning object repositories. SQI uses XML as the language for receiving information requests and for returning the results.

SQI specification consists in a definition of a set of methods that a repository should provide, so that remote systems (clients) can query for learning objects stored within the repository. Figure 2 shows how repository A (origin) makes a data request from repository B (destination). For this communication to be possible, it is necessary to use a common query language (based on SQI) which both repositories understand. However, the internal query language of each repository may differ. In this case, a layer (an SQI component) is responsible for making the necessary conversions.

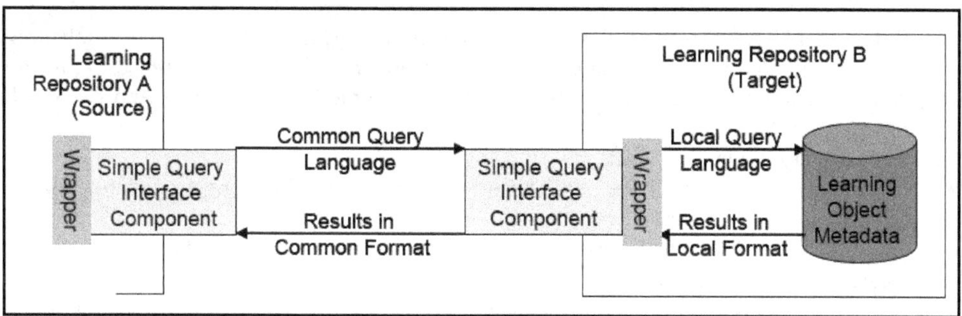

Fig. 2. Communication between two SQI repositories.

SQI identifies thirteen methods to be provided by such systems, these methods are embedded in a Web service that is exposed by the target repository and defined in WSDL files. They are classified in four categories: configuration methods, session management methods and query methods (synchronous and asynchronous).

SPI (Simple Publishing Interface) specification (CEN, 2010), also devised by the CEN, is a protocol for publishing digital objects or their metadata in repositories. It provides a simple protocol which is easy to implement and integrate in already existing systems. His objective is to develop a practical approach towards interoperability between repositories.

SPI makes a distinction between semantic and syntactic interoperability. Syntactic interoperability is the ability of applications to deal with the structure and format of data (for example XML documents). Semantic interoperability refers to the ability of two parties to agree on the meaning of data or methods. When exchanging data, semantic interoperability is achieved when data is interpreted in the same way by all the applications involved.

In a typical SPI scenario, two approaches allow for passing data from a source to a target: "by value" or "by reference". "By value" publishing embeds a learning object, after encoding, into the message that is sent to a target. "By reference" publishing embeds a reference (e.g., a URL) to a learning object to publish into the message that is sent to a target. The model for SPI builds on a separation between data and metadata, the data is a resource (e.g., a learning object) and the metadata is the description of the resource (e.g., using LOM to describe the learning object) (figure 3). Every resource can be described by zero, one, or more metadata instances. A metadata instance must have a metadata identifier that identifies the metadata instance itself, and must have a resource identifier that is equal to the identifier of the resource. The metadata identifier enables distinguishing between multiple metadata instances referring to the same resource. In this model, a metadata instance must be connected to a resource; however the resource may be hosted externally.

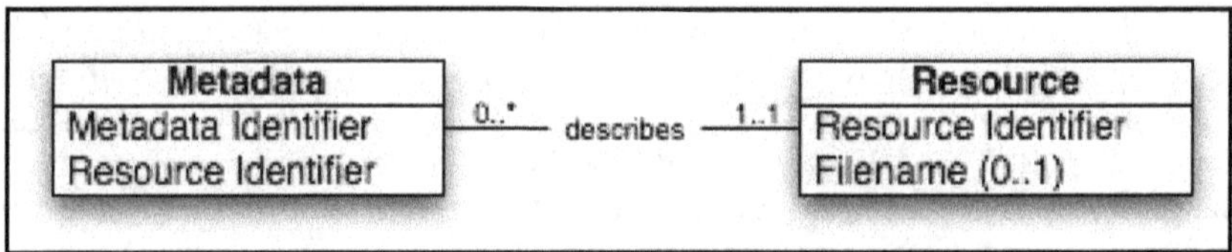

Fig. 3. Resource and Metadata instances in SPI.

The SPI model defines several classes of messages and functional units in a publishing architecture. When binding the specification to a given technology, these concepts are mapped into a concrete specification that can be implemented in a repository and for which conformance can be tested.

SPI defines the following methods:

- Submit/Delete Metadata Record: These are methods for inserting or deleting object descriptions respectively.
- Submit/Delete Resource by value / by reference: These are methods for inserting or deleting resources respectively.
- The SPI model does not include explicit methods for updating resources or metadata instances.

The IMS has also specified a set of services addressed to exchange of information that describes people, groups, memberships, courses and outcomes within the context of learning. That is the IMS Learning Information Services (LIS) specification (IMS LIS, 2010). LIS consists of six services that can either be used individually or in various combinations.

To achieve interoperability across Service Oriented Architectures, IMS has developed the General Web Services (GWS) specification (IMS GWS, 2005). The specification is formed by different profiles focused on addressing, security, attachments and a base profile describing most common problems when Web Services are used. The specification offers solutions to improve those considered by WS-I specifications. LIS is aimed at classic Web Services, i.e., SOAP based Web Services. Other kinds of Web Services such as RESTful Web Services are out of scope.

There is a necessity to create, manage, organize and exchange resource lists (collections of resources and their metadata instances) in distributed learning architectures. IMS Resource Lists Interoperability (RLI) exposes a flexible model (IMS RLI, 2004) that enables resource lists handling between systems that comply with the specification.

In order to exchange vocabulary between the parts of a learning system, the IMS Vocabulary Definitions Exchange (VDEX) defines a grammar for the exchange vocabulary lists (IMS VDEX, 2004). These lists are formed by domain values that are understood by systems involved in the learning architecture.

The IMS Learning Object Discovery and Exchange (LODE) charter (IMS LODE, 2008) is a proposal to achieve easily discoverable and exchangeable learning objects stored in digital repositories. The draft, rather than specify a model, compiles a set of use cases and scenarios which are inside the scope of the research. LODE is focused on Search, Publication, Query

and Metadata. Many of the scenarios considered by LODE are solved in existing specifications, so the final specification of LODE could look like a framework combining e-learning standards to perform discovery and exchange between heterogeneous repositories.
Finally it shall be noted that service-oriented architectures (SOA) are starting to be used massively for building e-learning systems and learning object repositories. We may find a number of interesting norms for the design of these systems to ensure interoperability and to be defined as the architectures of computer systems that support them. The most interesting is IMS Abstract Framework (AF), a framework that covers the entire range of possible e-learning architectures that could be constructed from a set of services based on SOA. It focuses on support for distributed training systems and one of its principles is interoperability. It is also interesting to read "Adoption of Service Oriented Architecture for Enterprise Systems in Education: Recommended Practices" from IMS.
On the other hand we find CORDRA which is one of the most detailed architectures. As an open, standard-based model, it allows to design software systems which are intended for the discovery, sharing and reuse of teaching material through interoperable repositories. Since Ariadne, an architecture has been proposed for repositories which implement SQI-based federated searches.

3. Designing a repository with Service Oriented Architecture

In order to solve interoperability problems it is necessary to define a software architecture which is able to assume certain functions, mainly e-learning systems interoperability (integration) and the reusability of learning objects (Otón S. et al, 2010).
Any developed e-learning architecture should have the following characteristics:

- Open: the goal is to easily create interoperated and connected applications, thus commercial tools from different companies could be assembled into a single global system. To achieve this feature it is necessary to define an architecture following a standard model.
- Scalable: Regardless of the size originally designed of the system, the architecture must be defined to grow in the future. For example: as the educational repositories number increases, the applications in charge of the management must have enough capacity and shall not overload.
- Global: To allow the linguistic and cultural diversity. This is one of the most difficult aims to reach, because most of the applications are designed for an Anglo-Saxon audience: nowadays there are several projects which try to show the same content in different languages depending on the final user.
- Integrated: Not only among the components of the system but among other applications which are not directly related to learning (for example: human resources, financial, knowledge management systems). The final objective is to get the interoperability among all of them.
- Flexible: It is important the ability to implement new solutions without making big changes in the system architecture.

Bellow we present an architecture that solves these problems. From the perspective of interoperability it is based on the main standards and specifications that should be used to guarantee interoperability and reusability of learning objects in repositories. These standards are shown in table 2, arranged by category.

CATEGORY	*SUB-CATEGORY*	*STANDARD*
LEARNING OBJECTS		
	Metadata	*IEEE LOM*
	Packaging	*IMS CC*
	Resources	*IMS RLI*
	Vocabulary	*IMS VDEX*
SEARCHES		
	Interoperability Repositories	*IMS DRI*
	Discovery and Exchange	*IMS LODE*
	Query interoperability	*CEN SQI*
	Publication interoperability	*CEN SPI*
ARCHITECTURES		
	Framework	*IMS AF*
SERVICES		
	Data exchange	*IMS LIS*
	Interoperability	*IMS GWS*

Table 2. Classification of the main standards and specifications related to Learning Objects Repositories.

Web services allow the companies to wrap their business processes publishing them as services; to subscribe to other services and to interchange information among different organizations. Thanks to the maturity achieved by this technology, together with the great expansion it has suffered, its use has gone from being an advantage to be a primary market need.

Web services and SOA architecture constitute a very suitable technology for the implementation of repositories that manage learning objects which are located in different stores of didactic resources, since it offers a clear access to those distributed objects which are in repositories based on different storage and metadata technologies through a single interface.

We suggest a multilayer (or multilevel) architecture, called LORA (Learning Object Reusability Architecture), comprising 3 levels (figure 4). Each of these levels has a fixed role for the correct working of the universal distributed repositories which can be implemented together. These levels are basically fixed by the use of the SQI specification. It is an interface that establishes the search methods that any search system should have (not just in e-learning environments), so that the interoperability of the resulting search system can be guaranteed.

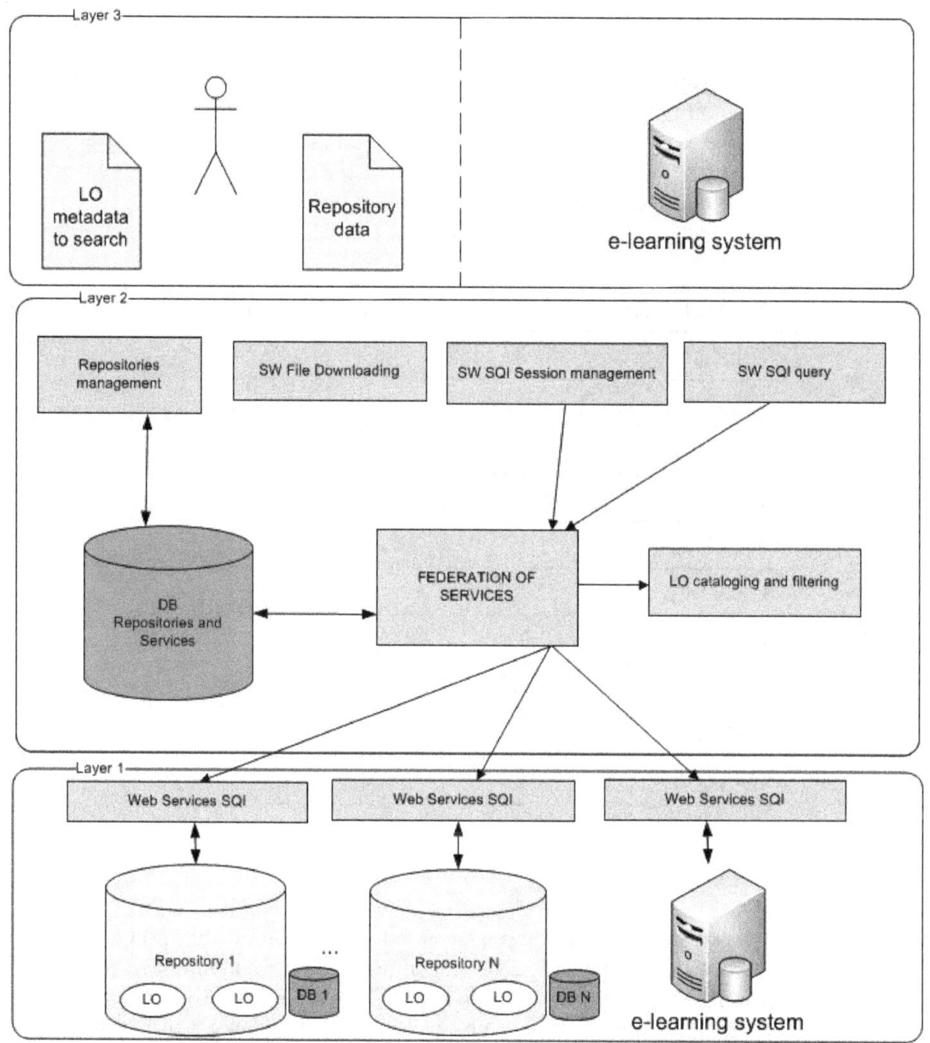

Fig. 4. LORA: A Service Oriented Architecture.

The main features of the architecture are:

- It is a fully interoperable with all other systems and repositories. This not only means that the system can launch searches over other SQI-compliant systems or repositories, but these repositories or systems may also launch searches over LORA-associated repositories. This enables to make content accessibility and reusability as wider and complex as desired.
- It expedites the process of searching learning content. It presents two kinds of searches (which are associated with the implemented PLQL levels-- ProLearn Query Language). This enables a more accurate search level, because the system allows key field-based searches (PLQL level 0) and metadata-based searches (PLQL level 1).

- It is also possible to adapt it to any present or future set of metadata. LORA will only require changing a configuration to virtually adapt the system to any set or subset of metadata. This feature is not available in any other system and it is critical for the system interoperability.

The layers of the LORA system were presented in figure 3. The rest of this section is devoted to describe each of these layers. Standards and/or recommendations employed on each layer are specially highlighted. A summary of them is presented in Table 3.

STANDARD	LAYER 1	LAYER 2	LAYER 3
IEEE LOM	X		
IMS CC	X		
IMS RLI	X		
IMS VDEX	X		
IMS DRI	X	X	X
CEN SQI	X	X	
CEN SPI	X		
IMS AF	X	X	X
IMS LIS	X	X	
IMS GWS	X	X	

Table 3. Standards used by LORA.

The main characteristics of the layers are:

- **Layer 1** comprises all Web services associated to each repository. The IMS GWS (General Web Services) (IMS GWS, 2005) recommendation was employed to build this layer. It determines the way in which Web services are developed and the way in which they interact with each other. These Web services enable the access to learning objects described by the IEEE LOM (Learning Object Metadata) and packaged according to IMS CC (Common Cartridge). In order to access to this data, specifications SQI (Simple Query Interface) and SPI (Simple Publishing Interface) are employed. SQI defines the Web methods to be developed. These methods allow the system to access to the stored learning data. SPI establishes the set of methods to define the way to publish the learning objects in a repository. Moreover, semantic techniques are used to search data. The IMS VDEX (Vocabulary Definition Exchange) (IMS VDEX, 2004) specification has been adopted to tag this metadata and create vocabulary categories. IMS RLI (Resource List Interoperability) (IMS RLI, 2004) is used to arrange, describe and interchange lists of resources included by each learning object. Finally the IMS LIS (Learning Information Services) (IMS LIS, 2010) has been used to make effective every data interchange.

- **Layer 2** comprises the federated search services. They use the services provided by layer 1 to get and handle the data provided by them. Consequently, they also use the SQI specification. Since they are also Web services, they were also developed according to IMS GWS. This layer will also handle all information provided by the repositories, so the use of the IMS LIS specification is also required. In addition to the services requiring SQI methods, another set of services have been developed in order to classify and filter information, and to manage the repositories associated to the search engine. It should also be noted that this layer may be called by other search systems, so it can also be the target of outside calls.
- **Layer 3** corresponds to the presentation layer of the system. All the interfaces that offer access to the system will be found here. Besides, all the aforementioned specifications, IMS DRI (Digital Repositories Interoperability) (IMS DRI, 2003) and IMS AF (Abstract Framework) (IMS AF, 2003) have also been adopted for this layer. IMS DRI defines the features that a repository must offer in order to be interoperable and allow access to its hosted content. IMS AF (Abstract Framework) presents an abstract representation of the set of services that should be used to build an e-learning system in its broader sense, so this specification was the main source to determine the required service.

4. Developing a federated repository with SOAP web services

We have presented an architecture with a clear objective: to enable the universal reusability of learning objects. Besides providing an efficient solution to this problem, we also present an implementation that allows showing all the explained theoretical content. The system developed from the above mentioned architecture has been called LORS (Learning Object Reusability System) and represents a federated repository.

The Java platform has been chosen for the development of the system due to the fact that it is considered as the most currently used. Besides, it is perfectly bounded to the Web development. When SOA architecture is used, the presented system will be completely accessible from any other programming language, platform or system that uses any communication protocol. Also it enables to incorporate new services without affecting the already developed system.

MySQL has been chosen as a database manager for the implementation of this architecture. Also the system led by Glassfish Server, has been chosen as an application server.

In the main user interface of the application (figure 5) they can be seen the two possible actions that will be carried out: federated search and catalogue repositories. It is possible to add new repositories within the repositories management regard for the searches to take effect on them. This is one of the new and most important characteristics this system has, as the interoperability among them is guaranteed when all repositories follow the same search interface. Figure 4 shows how it would be the process of adding new repositories.

The other option offered by the initial website is "search". As it was stated above, the searches done in this system follow the SQI specification; so it is necessary to create a session anonymous or with credentials before starting to look up. There is no user management device in this system, but a SQI management device, so the database table will be directly modified when adding new users.

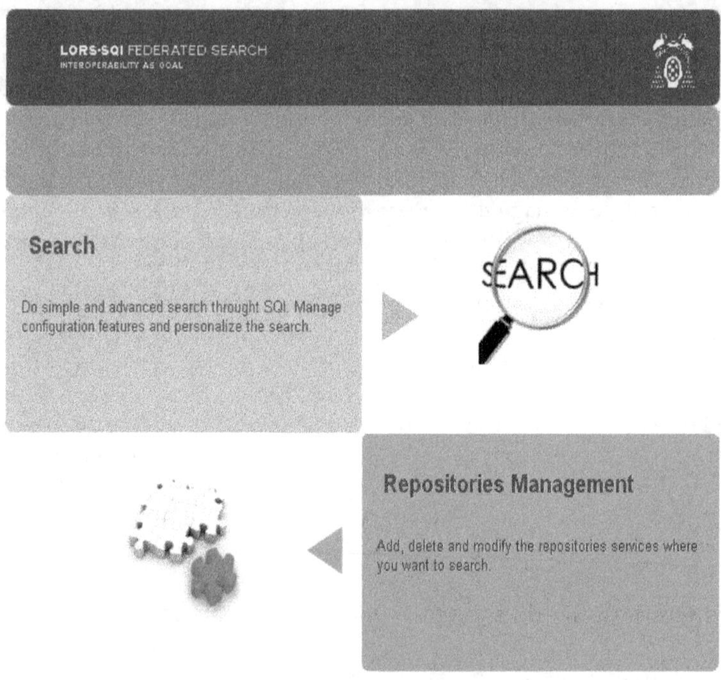

Fig. 5. Main user interface.

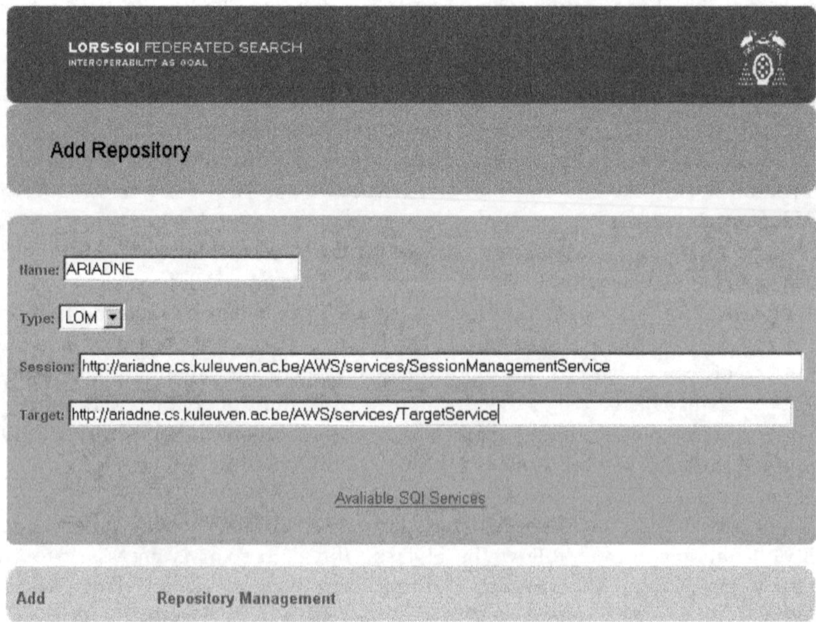

Fig. 6. Adding a new repository to LORS.

Once validated, the same process will be followed for the validation of all repositories registered in LORS; so if we choose to create an anonymous session, it will be created similarly with all repositories LORS has access. Once created the session, the system offers two types of search: simple and advanced.

The advanced search, also called accurate search, offers the possibility of configuring several SQI parameters as the maximum number of results, the size of the result set, or the initial result. As it is an accurate search, it is done based on educational fields. Figure 7 shows how it would be the search interface.

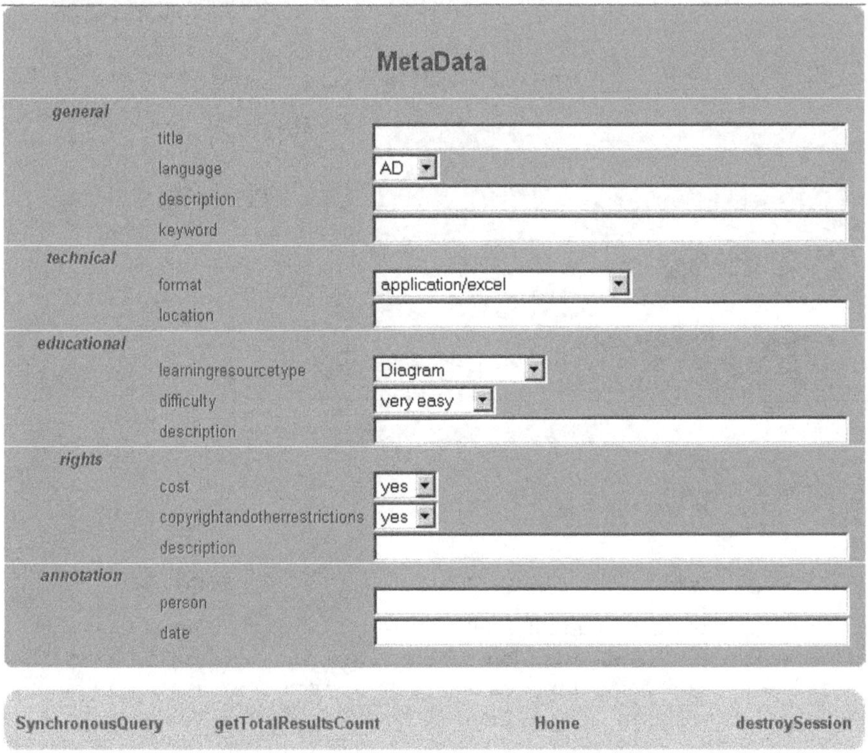

MetaData

general		
	title	
	language	AD
	description	
	keyword	
technical		
	format	application/excel
	location	
educational		
	learningresourcetype	Diagram
	difficulty	very easy
	description	
rights		
	cost	yes
	copyrightandotherrestrictions	yes
	description	
annotation		
	person	
	date	

SynchronousQuery getTotalResultsCount Home destroySession

Fig. 7. Advanced search interface.

In the case of the simple search or inaccurate search, searches are done on the basis of how many times they appear and how relevant they are the terms given in the search statement in the learning objects metadata. As in the previous case, SQI parameters can be established: maximum number of results, size of the result set and the initial result.

Once the search has been done the system will offer an ordered list with all those learning objects fulfilling the specifications set by the user. Figure 8 shows the offered list. Then, the user can download it by clicking the link. One of the main differences of this system is that the repository associated to LORS has an extra service that does not belong to the SQI specification. This way, it is possible to directly download educational material, instead of link to the author's page as other repositories like Ariadne do.

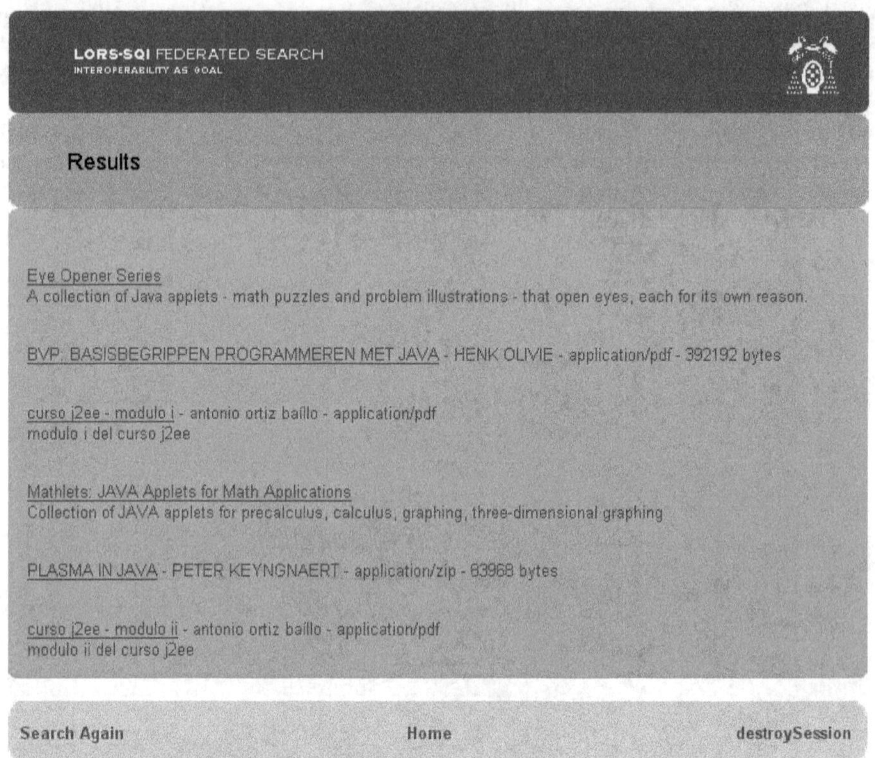

Fig. 8. Obtained results interface.

5. Developing a federated repository with RESTful web services

In the construction of distributed information systems the Web services were widely used but today we can see that the traditional Web services that used technologies based on WSDL and SOAP are being replaced by RESTful Web services. Examples of these transitions can be seeing in Google, Amazon, Flickr, Yahoo and YouTube. All this Web sites had WSDL files to describe their Web services and now they have changed to RESTful Web services.

Representational State Transfer (REST) is an architectural style that induces desirable properties, such as performance, scalability, and modifiability that enable Web services to work best on the Web. In the REST architectural style, data and functionality are considered resources and are accessed using Uniform Resource Identifiers (URIs), typically links on the Web. The resources are acted upon by using a set of simple, well-defined operations. The REST architectural style constrains any architecture to a client/server architecture, and is designed to use a stateless communication protocol, typically HTTP. In the REST architecture style, clients and servers exchange representations of resources by using a standardized interface and protocol. RESTful provides four basic methods for interaction with resources, which are: GET (obtain resources) PUT (introduce a new resource), POST (modify a resource) and DELETE (delete a resource).

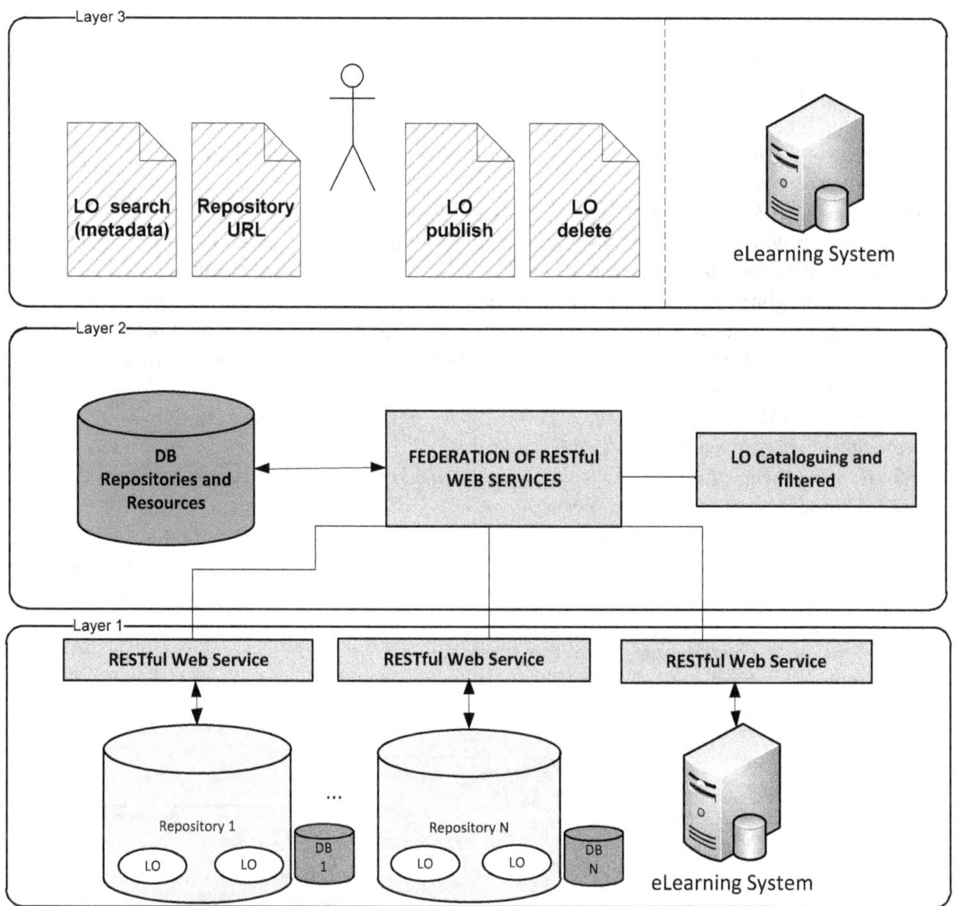

Fig. 9. LORA-REST: A RESTful Service Oriented Architecture.

With the idea of adapting the SQI and SPI specifications to RESTful we have changed and simplify our architecture (figure 9). The main characteristics of the layers are:

- **Layer 1** comprises all RESTful Web services associated to each repository. This RESTful Web services enable access to learning objects described by his metadata. With the GET method, the RESTful Web service enables the system to access to the stored learning data (by its metadata), this method replaces the query SQI methods. With the PUT method, the RESTful Web service enables the system to publish new learning objects in the repository. With the DELETE method, the RESTful Web service enables the system to delete a learning object or his metadata. With the PUT and DELETE methods we complain with the SPI specification.
- **Layer 2** comprises the federated search services. They use the RESTful Web services provided by layer 1 to get and handle the data provided by them. To make a federated search we only need the URL of each repository, and then we use the GET method (with the search criteria of metadata) in the RESTful Web service in each repository and

handle all information provided by the repositories. With the results of each repository the system must classify and filter this information.

- **Layer 3** corresponds to the presentation layer of the system. All the interfaces that offer access to the system will be found here. The system has two primary functions: search learning objects in the federated repositories and add a new repository. If we want comply with the SPI specification we must add two new operations, publish and delete a learning object.

The first step in the design of a system that uses RESTful is to define the data it handles. In the case of repositories of learning objects, data will be as follows. Learning objects are composed of internal elements (resources according to SPI) and metadata describing them. We recommend that the metadata is described using the LOM standard. According to the SPI specification a resource may have 0 or n metadata that describe it. To transfer a resource by reference, its URL must be specified, so the repository will access the address where the resource is in order to include it to the repository.

To adapt the SQI specification to RESTful can perform federated searches in various repositories of learning objects, we only need the URL of the repository in which we want to launch queries. When the user makes a query to one repository it expands this search to the repositories that it has associated. Because we use RESTful, our repository has the role of a client that searches in other repositories. This operation is transparent to the user.

With these requirements we have make a prototype to illustrate how we can develop a RESTful repository. We have designed a database with four tables that represent resources, its metadata, external repositories and external resources. We have transformed these tables in persistent Java classes and from these classes we have developed the RESTful Web services that give access to them. In figure 10 we can see these four persistent classes with his attributes.

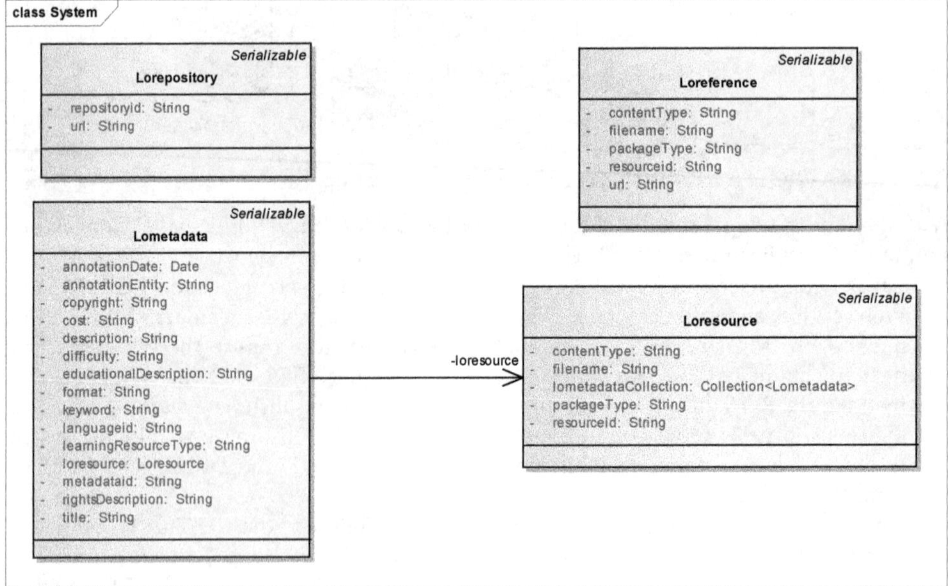

Fig. 10. RESTful prototype data model.

The RESTful Web services for these classes include the methods GET, PUT, POST and DELETE to keep up to date the information in the repository and to comply with the SQI and SPI specifications. We have added a RESTful Web service that enables downloading, inserting and deleting a file associated with a learning object. We have developed the prototype using the NetBeans IDE for the Java programming language as it has useful tools to program and test RESTful Web services.

Figure 11 shows a query to search for metadata records that contain the text "Java" in the "keyword" field of LOM. In this figure we can identify three important areas that are: area 1 is a navigable tree that represents the data of our repository; area 2 allows making queries to the metadata stored in the repository; area 3 shows the results in XML of the query we have made.

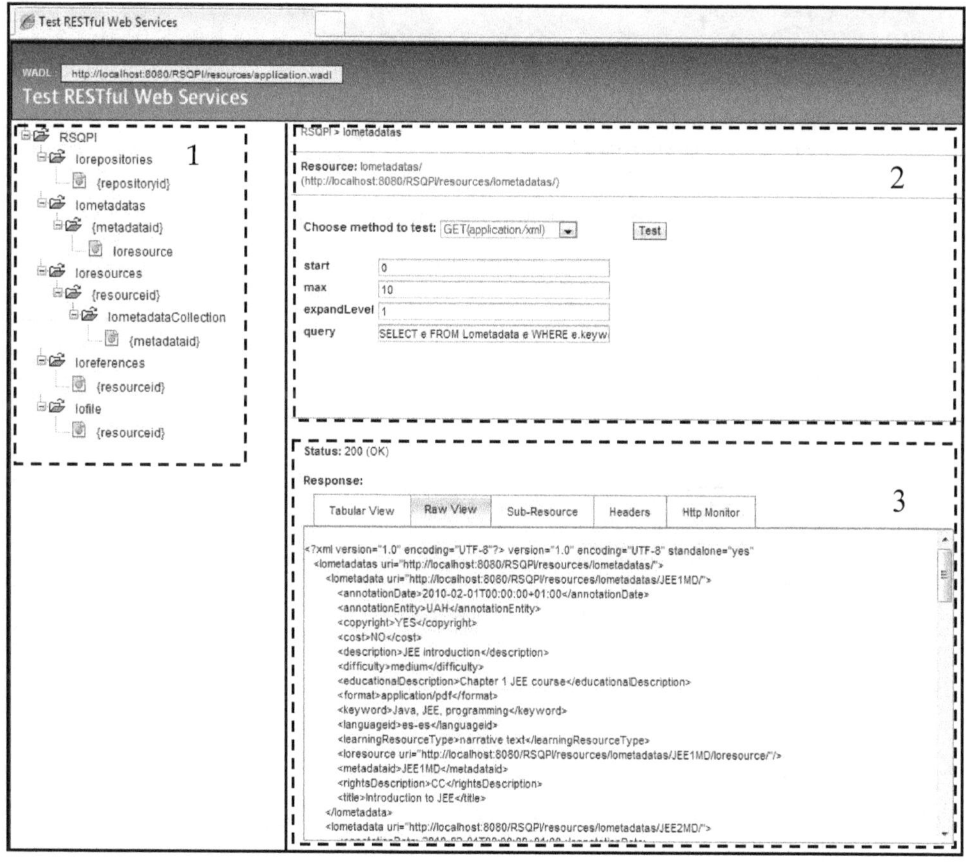

Fig. 11. RESTful metadata query and results.

One important thing to highlight is the possibility of the navigation between our data, for example if we are browsing metadata of one learning object we can access to the resource to which it is associated with. Figures 12 and 13 show this, in figure 12 we are accessing a concrete metadata with the identifier "JEE1MD" and with the URI: "http://localhost:8080/RSQPI/resources/lometadatas/JEE1MD/"; and if we want to access to the resource associated with this metadata (figure 13) we only need its URI, that is: "http://localhost:8080/RSQPI/resources/lometadatas/JEE1MD/loresource/".

http://localhost:8080/RSQPI/resources/lometada...


```xml
<?xml version="1.0" encoding="UTF-8" standalone="yes" ?>
- <lometadata uri="http://localhost:8080/RSQPI/resources/lometadatas/JEE1MD/">
    <annotationDate>2010-02-01T00:00:00+01:00</annotationDate>
    <annotationEntity>UAH</annotationEntity>
    <copyright>YES</copyright>
    <cost>NO</cost>
    <description>JEE introduction</description>
    <difficulty>medium</difficulty>
    <educationalDescription>Chapter 1 JEE course</educationalDescription>
    <format>application/pdf</format>
    <keyword>Java, JEE, programming</keyword>
    <languageid>es-es</languageid>
    <learningResourceType>narrative text</learningResourceType>
    <loresource uri="http://localhost:8080/RSQPI/resources/lometadatas/JEE1MD/loresource/" />
    <metadataid>JEE1MD</metadataid>
    <rightsDescription>CC</rightsDescription>
    <title>Introduction to JEE</title>
  </lometadata>
```


Fig. 12. XML metadata representation.

http://localhost:8080/RSQPI/resources/lometada...


```xml
<?xml version="1.0" encoding="UTF-8" standalone="yes" ?>
- <loresource uri="http://localhost:8080/RSQPI/resources/lometadatas/JEE1MD/loresource/">
    <contentType>application/zip</contentType>
    <filename>JEE1.zip</filename>
  - <lometadataCollection uri="http://localhost:8080/RSQPI/resources/lometadatas/JEE1MD/loresource/lometadataCollection/">
      <lometadata uri="http://localhost:8080/RSQPI/resources/lometadatas/JEE1MD/loresource/lometadataCollection/JEE1MD/" />
    </lometadataCollection>
    <packageType>ADL SCORM</packageType>
    <resourceid>JEE1</resourceid>
  </loresource>
```


Fig. 13. XML resource representation.

In the figure 14 we present a direct access to a file that represents a packaged learning object. In this case the way of accessing the file is via the identifier of a resource, because in the information of a resource we have the "filename" field, so the Web service uses this filename to retrieve the physical file. In this example we are using the URI: "http://localhost:8080/RSQPI/resources/lofile/JEE1/".

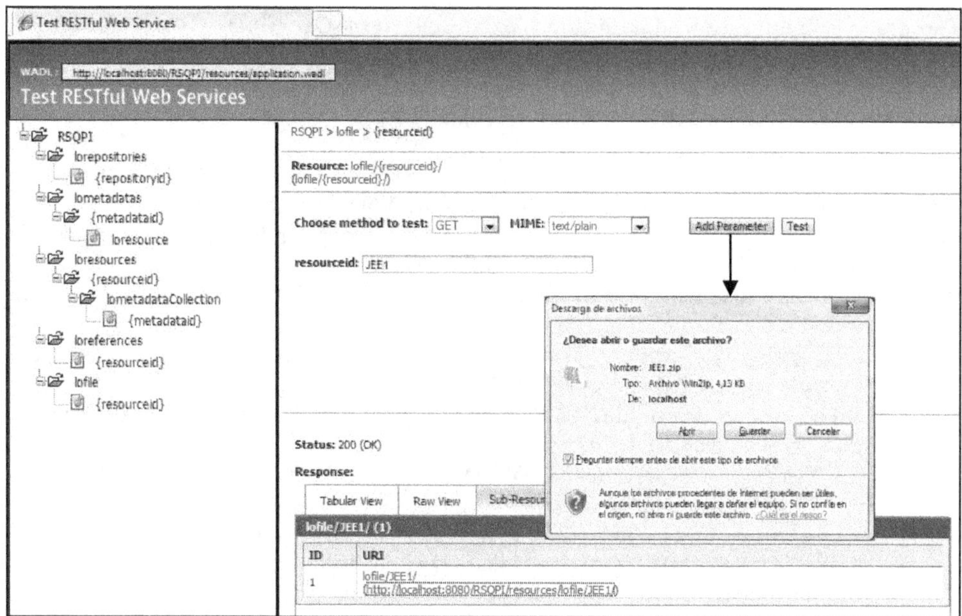

Fig. 14. Retrieving the file of a packaging learning object.

6. Conclusions

When we want to develop an interoperable repository of learning objects we must know the most important specifications and standards in this filed. The vast majority of these norms are based on Web services and SOA, so their knowledge is essential.

As we have seen in the preceding sections, the proliferation of these standards and specifications focused on the interoperability of learning object repositories is very wide-ranging. As a conclusion we can say that the building of a totally interoperable repository of learning objects, which will consequently allow the learning objects it contains to be reused, must comply with a series of very clear norms. In line with the norms set out above, the steps to be followed in order to achieve an interoperable repository may be summarized as follows:

1. A service oriented architecture should be used when analysing and designing the system software that will house it.
2. In order to integrate the repository in a federated search system, the SQI and SPI specifications should be adopted.
3. Steps 1 and 2 complement each other since, as they both use an SOA architecture, it is extremely easy to integrate the services offered by SQI or SPI.
4. Packaging learning objects using specifications like IMS Common Cartridge and describing their metadata will make those objects reusable.

7. References

ADL Advanced Distributed Learning Initiative (2002). *SCORM*. Available from http://www.adlnet.gov/Technologies/scorm/default.aspx

European Committee for Standardization (2005). *SQI: Simple Query Interface*. Available from ftp://ftp.cenorm.be/PUBLIC/CWAs/e-Europe/WS-LT/cwa15454-00-2005-Nov.pdf

European Committee for Standardization (2010). SPI: Simple Publishing Interface. Available from ftp://ftp.cen.eu/CEN/Sectors/TCandWorkshops/Workshops/CWA16097.pdf

IEEE Standards Association (2002). *IEEE 1484.12.1: Learning Object Metadata (LOM)*.

IMS Global Learning Consortium (2003). *IMS Digital Repositories Interoperability*. Available from http://www.imsglobal.org/digitalrepositories/

IMS Global Learning Consortium (2003). *IMS Abstract Framework*. Available from http://www.imsglobal.org/af

IMS Global Learning Consortium (2004). *IMS Resource List Interoperability*. Available from http://www.imsglobal.org/rli

IMS Global Learning Consortium (2004). *IMS Vocabulary Definition Exchange*. Available from http://www.imsglobal.org/vdex

IMS Global Learning Consortium (2005). *IMS General Web Services*. Available from http://www.imsglobal.org/gws

IMS Global Learning Consortium (2007). *IMS Learning Object Discovery and Exchange*. Available from http://www.imsglobal.org/lode.html

IMS Global Learning Consortium (2008). *IMS Common Cartridge*. Available from http://www.imsglobal.org/cc

IMS Global Learning Consortium (2010). *IMS Learning Information Services*. Available from http://www.imsglobal.org/lis

Koper, E. (2000). From change to renewal: Educational technology foundations of electronic learning environments, Open University of Netherlands.

Otón, S., Ortiz, A., Hilera, J.R., Barchino, R., Gutiérrez, J.M., De Marcos, L., Martínez, J.J. & Gutiérrez, J.A. (2009). Requirements to ensure interoperability between learning object repositories, *Proceedings of the EEE2009*, pp. 391 – 396, ISBN: 1-60132-100-7, Las Vegas, Nevada, USA, Jul 13-16, 2009.

Otón, S., Ortiz, A., Hilera, J.R., Barchino, R., Gutiérrez, J.M., Martínez, J.J., Gutiérrez, J.A., de Marcos, L. & Jiménez, M.L. (2010). Service Oriented Architecture for the Implementation of Distributed Repositories of Learning Objects. *International Journal of Innovative Computing Information and Control*, Vol.6, No.3, (March 2010), pp. 843-854, ISSN 1349-4198.

World Wide Web Consortium (2004). *Web Services Architecture*. Available from http://www.w3.org/TR/ws-arch/

13

Collaborative E-Learning: Towards Designing an Innovative Architecture for an Educational Virtual Environment

Michael K. Badawy
Virginia Tech University
USA

1. Introduction

The digital age evolutionary advances have provided humankind with infinite educational opportunities. The greatest challenge to education in a global knowledge society is not how to effectively help learners acquire a well-defined set of knowledge and skills, but, rather, to help them learn how to work innovatively with ideas, and contribute to knowledge creation. Knowledge innovation in e-learning is a process where learners produce new perspectives, find new problem solutions, change the selections of existing knowledge structure and levels, and ultimately create new meaning via interaction and collaboration. A resulting central element is the emergence of new understanding of the original cognition. It follows that knowledge produced through analyzing, synthesizing, and appraising belongs to knowledge of innovation. As an educator, it is the author's conviction that one of the greatest contributions academics can make is to help students develop, and master the competency of "Learning How to Learn".

The utilization of collaborative virtual environments in e-learning is one of the most promising uses of virtual reality technology. Despite the existence of a vast literature covering e-learning system architectures, the author has found that most of the studies are focused on re-creating traditional education, and the use of new technologies serving traditional learning models- rather than an environment giving clear insights into the innovative knowledge generation and articulation. While considerable research has been undertaken in the area of networked virtual environments corresponding to sharing of events, very little research was done on specific services and functionality, (Montoya et al., 2011; Hamalmen, 2011).

In this chapter, e-learning is viewed as an educational paradigm referring to the utilization of web-based technologies to deliver learning activities with the aim of enhancing knowledge and performance. However, current e-learning efforts continue to put heavy emphasis on content delivery and technology (Lin et al. 2010; Chatti et al. 2007). This requires changes of orientation and focus from "content-driven" to "innovative knowledge-driven"; and from "technology-driven" to "learner-driven" e-learning models. This transformation requires creating an e-learning architecture based on knowledge innovation, while providing learners with an innovative learning environment.

This research focuses on exploring, understanding, and developing paths towards a viable framework for collaborative learning in dynamic group environments. Collaborative learning can be defined as a core mechanism embracing a variety of educational approaches to motivate learners to work closely in joint intellectual efforts. Hence, it refers to a situation where a joint solution to a problem is made synchronously and interactively. This means that dialogues will result between collaborating parties in the process of task engagement. This approach yields many positive benefits. This is due to that fact that interactions and deliberations among learners have remarkable beneficial impacts on their learning aptitude (Wolf et al. 2009). The central point here is that, in collaborative learning, participants engage in sharing information, brainstorming, and learning from each other. Therefore, their joint accomplishments would considerably exceed the sum of their individual contributions.

Based on the preceding discussion, the objectives of this chapter can be identified as follows:

- To pinpoint weaknesses in the existing e-learning systems while placing heavy emphasis on content delivery and technology, and explore how the transformation can be made from technology-driven to learner- driven models of e-learning.
- To present the design principles, features, primary aspects, elements, and strategic issues relating to building a collaborative e-learning environment.
- To explore the design and implementation of platforms suitable for educational virtual environments aiming at offering collaborative e-learning services to the users.
- To present a set of action strategies and critical success factors for educational developers to utilize in designing and implementing the proposed innovative architecture for enhancing educational virtual environments.

This chapter has been organized into eight sections. Following this introduction, Section 2 presents a detailed review of the literature providing a critique and an assessment of current e-learning systems. Conceptual definitions along with features of collaborative e-learning (CEL) are discussed in Section 3. Section 4 addresses the question of how the transformation from "Technology-Centric" to "Learner-Centric" models of CEL can be achieved. The design features, elements, and the strategic issues of CEL are discussed in Section 5. Section 6 describes a prototype as a guide towards designing an innovative architecture for an Educational Virtual Environment (EVE). This is accomplished through a presentation of the design principles for virtual spaces for CEL. A set of action strategies and critical success factors that can be utilized by educational developers in designing and implementing an innovative architecture for enhancing educational virtual environments are provided in Section 7. Finally, the conclusions, implications, and future research directions are presented in Section 8.

2. Review of the literature: A critique and an assessment of current e-learning systems

This section focuses on exploring the current status of e-learning systems based on the state of the art and the research literature. In addition, it contrasts "Education" with "Training"; and outlines current approaches to e-learning along with describing a wide range of applications. Finally, a critique and an assessment of e-learning systems are provided.

2.1 Current status of e-learning systems

The rate and speed with which technology development propagation is spreading globally is astounding. Technology permeates every aspect of our lives. The internet has profoundly revolutionized our world. It has increased global connections and competition to an unprecedented level. It has had the greatest impact through the availability of limitless easily accessible information. It is a barrier-free entry to global markets. In fact, it has radically changed the way we live and do business. Recent advances in technology have made learning and training accessible on "anywhere at any time" basis through distributed learning technologies. In such a short time, media literacy has evolved and was transformed into digital media literacy. One such example is how the e-learning approach to education is transforming the global educational system. Hence, e-learning can be defined as: *the delivery of online digital education on demand to learners anywhere* (Afie Badawy, 2009). The vast developments in internet and multimedia technologies are the basic enabler of e-learning with content, consulting, technologies, services, and support being identified as the five key sectors of the e-learning industry (Gierlowski et al. 2009; Nagy.et al; 2005).

Research shows that e-learning comprises all forms of electronically supported learning and teaching. The information and communication systems, whether networked or not, serve as specific media to implement the learning process (Tavangarian et al. 2004). The core point is that the internet, a non-proprietary system, is advancing the creation and delivery of engaging e-learning tools that transcend typical time and space barriers. E-learning is essentially the computer and network-enabled transfer of skills and knowledge. E-learning applications and processes include web-based learning, computer-based learning, virtual classroom opportunities, and digital collaboration. Content is delivered via the internet, intranet/extranet, audio or video tape, satellite TV, and CD-ROM. It can be self-paced or instructor-led and includes media in the form of text, image, animation, streaming video and audio.

E-learning tools refer to the internet-based programs designed for instructional purposes, such as interactive multimedia displays or threaded electronic messaging. Web-based collaborative environments are a special category of e-learning tools which support a group of learners in achieving a common learning goal. A central consideration here is to shift the focus to the question of: how did E-learning technologies emerge and evolve? Conventional e-learning systems were based on instructional packets which were delivered to students using assignments. Evaluations and assessments were undertaken by the instructor. Conversely, the new e-learning places increased emphasis on social learning and use of social software such as blogs, wikis, podcasts, and virtual worlds.

In contrast to the traditional paradigm, e-learning assumes that knowledge (as meaning and understanding) is socially constructed. It follows that learning takes place through conversations about content and grounded interaction about problems and actions. Advocates of social learning claim that one of the best ways to learn something is to try to teach it to others (Seely, et al. 2008). There is also an increased use of virtual classrooms (online presentations delivered live) as an online learning platform and classroom for a diverse set of education providers.

2.2 Education vs. training

Instructional providers along with other E-learning stakeholders in various organizations must now continue leveraging resources for designing and implementing learning and training strategies with the feature of sustained availability "any place any how" to meet the demand and expectations "anytime anywhere". An important issue in defining the domain and boundaries of e-learning is the necessity of differentiating between training and education. We should be cautious not to assume that what works well in education will necessarily work as well in training. While education and training share the psychological constructs of learning, memory, and motivation, fundamental differences exist. These differences relate to the goals, outcomes, and eventual application of the underlying instruction.

It is important to note that learning outcomes are measures of the knowledge gained from an instructional program. Education has been historically concerned with the social and intellectual development of the whole person; there is no upper limit to how elevated a learning outcome should be. A different way of framing the same issue is that while producing an "over educated" student is inconceivable to education providers, the thought of a student being "over trained" can be costly, in terms of time and money, to training providers. In short, it is better to have the prepared student productive on the job- rather than lingering in the classroom. It follows that while knowledge development is the intended outcome in education; skill development is the intended outcome in training.

2.3 Approaches to e-learning

Currently, there is a trend to move towards blended learning services where computer-based activities are integrated with practical or classroom-based situations. Research suggests (Kanev et al., 2009) that different types or forms of e-learning can be considered as a continuum ranging from no use of computers and/or the internet for teaching and learning, through classroom aids, such as making PowerPoint slides available to students through a course website or a learning management system, to laptop programs where students are required to bring and use their laptops as part of a face-to-face class, to hybrid learning, where classroom time is reduced but not eliminated, with more time devoted to on-line learning, which is a form of distance education. This classification refers to web-enhanced, web- supplemented, and web- dependent to reflect increasing intensity of technology utilization. In the above continuum, "blended learning" can cover classroom aids, laptops and hybrid learning, while "distributed learning" can incorporate either hybrid or fully on-line learning.

The above discussion clearly shows that e-learning can describe a wide range of applications. A brief summary of these applications is presented below:

a. Computer-Based Learning (CBL): This refers to the use of computers as a key component of the educational environment. Although CBL can refer to the use of computers in a classroom, the term more broadly refers to a structured environment in which computers are used for teaching purposes.

b. Computer-Based Training (CBT): The term Web-based training (WBT) is often used interchangeably with CBT – the primary difference is the delivery method. While CBT is typically delivered via CD-ROM, WBT is delivered via the internet using a web browser. Note that CBT is a self-based learning activity accessible via a computer or handheld device. It typically presents content in a linear fashion- just like reading an online book or manual. This is why it is often used to teach static processes, such as using software or completing mathematical equations. One advantage is that assessing learning in a CBT usually comes in the form of multiple choice questions, or other assessments that can easily be scored by a computer such as drag-and-drop, radial button, simulation or other interactive means. Assessments are easily scored and recorded via online software, providing immediate end-user feedback and completion status.

   Another advantage is that CBT provides learning incentives beyond traditional learning methodology from textbook, manual, or class-room based instruction. An example is that CBT offers visual learning benefits through animation or video as rich media that can easily be embedded for learning enhancement. A third advantage is that CBT can be easily distributed to a broad audience at a relatively low cost once the initial development is completed. However, CBT poses some learning challenges as well. One drawback is that the creation of effective CBTs requires enormous resources. Typically, the software for developing CBTs (such as Flash or Adobe Director) is often more complex than a subject matter expert or teacher is able to use. Additionally, the lack of human interaction can limit both the type of content that can be delivered, as well as the type of assessment that can be performed.

c. **Computer-Supported Collaborative Learning (CSCL):** Since collaborative learning is the main theme of this chapter, this e-learning modality will be explored in detail later on. It will suffice to assert that CSCL is one of the most promising innovations for improving teaching and learning using modern information and communication technology. While the most recent developments in CSCL have been called E-Learning, the concept of collaborative or group learning - whereby instructional methods are designed to encourage or require students to work together on learning tasks- has existed much longer. However, it is essential to distinguish collaborative learning from the traditional "direct transfer" model in which the instructor is assumed to be the primary provider of knowledge and skills.

d. **Technology-Enhanced Learning (TEL):** The field of TEL applies to the support of any learning activity utilizing technology. While the main concern relates to enhancing efficiency and cost effectiveness, the primary goal is to provide socio-technical innovations for e-learning practices- regarding individuals and organizations regardless of time, place, and pace.

2.4 Shortcomings and weaknesses

2.4.1 The lack of project-based learning

A broad examination of the literature reveals the weaknesses and shortcomings of current e-learning systems (Bouras.et al, 2008; Law and Wong.2003; Monahan. et .al., 2008). There is also evidence that e-learning combines human resources, knowledge, technologies, tools so that learners can effectively hand quickly, accumulate, share, and create new knowledge. Knowledge innovations in e-learning lay their mark on the learning culture which is "learner-centered", project-based, and integrated (Michael Badawy, 2010). This is viewed as a more favorable process for learning and the development of new knowledge. In "project-based" learning, learners take charge of their own learning, taking responsibility for personal understanding, and for the creation of knowledge artifacts. In this project context, the activities and methodologies of approaching projects are "**shared** "at a significant level among the learners. Therefore, learners can better promote knowledge when they address the spontaneous and creative forms that the collaborators use during the course of project completion. This means that the knowledge- creating activities and functions are not "**controlled**".

It is also noteworthy that the existing e-learning system has some inherent weaknesses including the absence of "project-based" learning; and a focus on knowledge acquisition. Additionally, while there is a vast literature about several e-learning system architectures, most of the studies focus on re-creating traditional school education, and the use of new technologies to serve traditional learning models - rather than an environment giving clear insights into the innovative knowledge generation and articulation(Montoya et al., 2011).

2.4.2 Current course and learning management systems are all asynchronous

While current e-learning systems have improved with time, there are still some issues and challenges to be resolved before a truly stimulating and realistic learning experience can be provided on line. Through the use of technologies such as Virtual Reality (VR) and instant communication, students can be more virtually aware of their classmates, and can communicate in real time with them. They can also receive immediate feedback from their instructors, and gain a sense of being present with their peers despite their remote physical locations. These shared virtual environments also facilitate simultaneous viewing of learning materials by the entire class. It also allows them to actively participate in group discussions. Furthermore, the benefits of 3D graphics for education have been explored in the manufacturing industries, urban planning, entertainment, and military operations (Monahan.et.al. 2008; Lin et al; 2010; Montoya et al., 2011; Ryan et.al.2004; Manseur, 2005).

The core point here is that the use of VR and 3D graphics for e-learning has now been extended by the provision of entire VR environments where learning takes place. This highlights a shift in e-learning from the conventional text-based on line learning environment to a more immersive and intuitive one. Since VR is a computer simulation of a natural environment, interaction with a 3D model is more natural than browsing through 2D webpages looking for information (Monahan et al., 2008). These VR environments can support multiple users, further promoting the notion of collaborative learning where students learn together, and often from each other.

Course management tools, such as Blackboard and Scholar, Web Course Tools have been valuable in providing instructors with considerable help in facilitating the management of their online courses. These systems provide students with access to course materials and encourage them to participate in learning activities through the use of on line forums, discussion boards, and text-based chat. While these systems tend to be costly, systems with freely available source code have also been developed (Sung et al. 2009; Monahan et al., 2008). Moodle is such a learning system which is in widespread use. It offers a range of software modules that enable tutors to create on line courses. One area that it attempts to address is the need for pedagogical support. In particular, it promotes the notion of constructionist learning - where a student learns from her/his own experiences, resulting in a student-centered learning environment.

As noted earlier, most of the technologies along with communication methods utilized in current e-learning systems are all asynchronous, and therefore, students cannot receive instant feedback to queries or converse with their peers. This can create collaboration difficulties, and can cause feelings of remoteness for some users. Alternatively, synchronous technologies - such as text and audio communication- bring a real time element into communicating on line and can, therefore, enhance a user's online learning experience.

Specifically, they can help to increase a user's sense of belonging to a supportive learning community (Wolf et al., 2009; McInnerney et al.; 2004). It should also be noted that the presentation of learning content to users in an integrative, interesting, and inspiring manner have great value-added benefits. Text-based learning content often leads to boredom and can prevent students from gaining a clear understanding of the subject matter (Montoya et al., 2011; Lin et al., 2010; Zhang et al., 2004). The presentation of course content through multimedia techniques can be quite engaging to students in their learning activities. Multimedia can also increase their social presence by providing interactive and visually appealing 3D environments where learning and collaboration can take place. The computer often uses this kind of multimedia to create interactive and stimulating game environments, which give users a social presence and an opportunity to collaborate and communicate with others.

2.4.3 The absence or lack of multi-user Virtual Reality (VR) technology

Research shows that a variety of tools and technologies have been developed and used for supporting e-learning communities (Lin et al. 2010; Sung et al., 2009; Hamalamen, 2011; Bouras et.al., 2008). Three components and systems have been identified: the document-focused web-based training tools; the meeting -focused tool (such as video-conferencing tools, Centra symposium…etc.) and the three dimensional (3D)-centered multi-user tools which are based on multi-user Virtual Reality (VR) technology. The first system focuses on the management of documents and on individual learning. The second system- the meeting focused tools-employs the approach of virtually representing the concept of frontal learning-that is the situation of a lecturer sending information to a group of learners, with rather little feedback, and almost no intended horizontal communication among learners. A general problem of these tools is the reduced social connection of the participants. Therefore, in such e-learning sessions, they experience a feeling of alienation.

The third system, VR tools, is focused on having participants experience a sense of interaction with and the existence of other participants. The participants of the 3D virtual session are represented by avatars, which can navigate through 3D environments. They are also able to view the actions of all other participants. In addition, Multi-user Virtual Reality technology tools, when utilized as communication media, offer advantages of creating social presence, thus, enhancing communication and interaction among participants. This is why multi-users of VR technology are used for supporting collaboration.

As noted earlier, current e-learning applications have many limitations that should be addressed and overcome. Essentially, some of the main limitations involve the lack of peer connection and interaction; and the need for flexible available tutorial support. Furthermore, the theoretical advantage of multi-user VR technology is not exploited in an extended manner. It mainly offers text chat communication, and users' representation through avatars. A good example is that advanced communication features, as voice or user gestures, are not commonly utilized.

2.4.4 The need for shifting from "technology-centric and instructor-centric" to "learner-centric" paradigms with a strong focus on constructivism

Recent research studies (Montoya et al., 2011; Wolf et al., 2009; Gierlowski et al., 2009; Kanev et al., 2009; Beetham, 2005) demonstrate that traditional educational instructor -centered approaches need to be replaced with more active instruction. Instead of viewing knowledge as an arbitrary set of facts, knowledge needs to be constructed by the learner so it can be used as a tool for future learning activities. There is an urgent need for shifting the focus of training and education from passive reception of facts to student knowledge transformation wherein an individual constructs new knowledge through interactions and negotiations.

It is essential to underscore the fact that constructivist principles include building on student prior knowledge, making learning relevant and meaningful, giving student's choice and autonomy, and having instructors act as co-learners. In this sense, instructors might design tasks wherein learners solve real world problems, reflect on skills used to manage one's own learning, address misconceptions in their thinking, categorize problems around themes and concepts, and generally take ownership for their own learning.

A significant consideration in this regard is to note that there are two important variations of constructivism - cognitive constructivist and social constructivist. Cognitive constructivists tend to focus on the individual construction of knowledge discovered or built in interaction with the surrounding environment. From this point of view, it is important for educators to foster active learning environments in which learners can individually build knowledge. Essentially, the cognitive constructivist view regards knowledge as internally embodied in the mind of the learner. Unfortunately, individual notions of constructivism often fail to emphasize the dynamic social aspects of learning and cognition- the dialogue, collaboration, negotiation, and questioning of active learning environments.

Conversely, social constructivists view learning as connection with and appropriation from a larger social context. It follows that instructional methods from this latter view focus on dialogue, instructor co-learning, and the joint construction of knowledge. However, these essential features are lacking in the current e-learning paradigm.

As noted earlier, cognitive constructivists focus on making learning more relevant, building on student prior knowledge, and addressing misconceptions. Social constructivists, on the other hand, emphasize human dialogue, interaction, negotiation, and collaboration. It is important to note here that, across both perspectives, constructivist practices emphasize active, generative learning in which instructors continue to perform their critical learning function as learning guides. Note that the focus here is on **"assisting learning", -** not on **"directing and assessing it".**

The impact of using guided or assisted learning - instead of either mechanistic or discovery learning systems- fosters positive effects on learning. In an e-learning environment, such assistance might include questioning, task structuring, coaching, modeling, pushing students to articulate ideas and explore new avenues, and the occasional timely direct instruction. From a social constructivist viewpoint, new learning communities as a consequence can emerge. In summary, in an e-learning environment, the transformation from the current model of "instructor-centric" to "learner-centric" paradigm would have vast positive implications for students, instructors, and educational technology designers.

3. Conceptual definitions and features of Collaborative E-Learning (CEL)

3.1 Definitions

In the collaborative e- learning research literature, there is a broad acceptance of the meaning of CEL (Liang, 2010; Alfonseca et al., 2006; Kreijns et al. 2003; Dillenbourg, 1999). It has been defined as any kind of learning process performed by more than one person that takes place mainly in a Virtual Environment (VE). Another definition is that it is a situation in which two or more people learn or attempt to learn something together. While these definitions can be interpreted differently, the fact remains that they consist of three elements which define the space of what is encountered under the label "CEL": a group of individuals; attempting to learn something; in an interactive joint manner with an element of "togetherness".

As noted earlier, in order to provide e-learning services to the user, the components of the current systems of CEL can be divided up into three different tools: the document-focused web-based training tools; the meeting-focused tools; and the 3-D centered tools. We should keep in mind that several technology tools have accelerated the evolution of e-learning to a more collaborative and team-oriented mode. These tools include chat sessions, application sharing, virtual whiteboards, computer telephony, desktop videoconferencing, asynchronous communication, multi-user simulation environments, and audio graphics (Montoya et al., 2011; Alfonseca et al., 2006). Connections between all these essential elements point to the growing importance of collaboration, reflection, critical thinking, evaluation, and decision-making skills. Undoubtedly, as web technologies surge, skills in discovering, searching, integrating, filtering, and disseminating knowledge will gain more significance.

3.2 Features

The first step for implementing an effective functional e-learning virtual environment is to investigate its main functional features. These functional features should differentiate an e-learning environment from other virtual environments which are designed and implemented for general use (Gierlowski et al., 2009; Bouras et.al, 2008, 2006). Research (Dillenbourg, 1999; Kanev et al. 2009) demonstrates that every virtual environment that integrates the following features can be characterized as a CEL environment:

- Users who have different roles and rights can visit the environment.
- The educational interactions in the environment should change the simple virtual space to communication space. Users should be provided with multiple communication channels, which enable them to interact with each other into the virtual space.
- The environment should be represented by various representation forms, which can range from simple text to 3D worlds.
- The learners in the environment should not be passive, but should be able to interact.
- The system that supports the e-learning environment should be able to integrate various technologies.
- The environment should support various e-learning scenarios.
- The environment should have common features with a physical space.

Another perspective on the CEL features relates to the debate in the literature concerning the differences and commonalities between "collaborative" and "cooperative" leaning. While joining this debate is beyond the scope of this chapter, this author believes that the similarities far outweigh the differences. These similarities have been well articulated by Kreijns et al, 2003, and Lin et al., 2010 which include:

- Learning is active
- The teacher is usually more a facilitator than a "sage on the stage"
- Teaching and learning are shared experiences
- Students participate in small group activities
- Students must take responsibility for learning
- Students are stimulated to reflect on their own assumptions, and thought processes
- Social and team skills are developed through the give-and-take of consensus building

3.3 Why is virtual learning (VR) superior to traditional methods?

There are many areas where VR has been used for supporting education (Sung et al., 2009; Bouras et al., 2008). These include : A. Simulation of complex systems, where the benefit compared to traditional methods is centered on the ability to observe system operations from a variety of perspectives, aided by superior quality visualization and interaction; B. Macroscopic and microscopic visualization, where the benefit compared to traditional methods is the observation of system features that would be either too small or too large to be seen on a normal scale system; and C. Fast and slow time simulation, where the benefit compared to traditional methods is the ability to control timescale in a dynamic event.

Furthermore, compared to traditional methods, there are other significant characteristics of VR that could be leveraged for supporting education including the following (Laister, 2002; Bouras, et al. 2008; Redfern et al., 2002; Seely et al. 2008):

- High levels of interactivity that VR allows: Since most people learn faster by "doing", the VR system provides significantly higher levels of interactivity than other computer-based systems. Similarly, since the interfaces are intuitive and easy to use, the degree of interactivity could be very beneficial.
- Sense of immersion: This is a powerful characteristic, particularly in applications, where the sense of scale is quite important. A good example is that architecture is an area where the sense of scale is required for visualizing the impact of a building design on the external environment and the inhabitants.
- Inherent flexibility/adaptability: The flexibility of the VR system arises from the underlying software nature of the virtual environment. A VR system can be put to many uses by loading different application environments. This means that it is feasible to use a VR system for a wide range of learning applications.

Several propositions have been advanced by researchers relating to the usage of virtual environments in education (Hamalamen, 2011; Bouras et al., 2008; 2006). The following four propositions are germane to our discussion:

- Virtual environments create a feeling of presence by techniques, which shift attention from the real world to the virtual world.
- Virtual environments situate learning in a meaningful context. The environment's "landmarks" play a special role.
- Collaboration is possible and efficient in virtual environments. Moreover, users represented by avatars in the virtual world support the feeling of presence and the joy while learning.
- It is possible to learn by interacting with other students and virtual objects in virtual environments in a way similar to the interaction with real people and objects. This is why it is important to investigate the design principles that should be adopted by educational designers for effectively designing virtual spaces for e-learning.

4. Achieving transformation from "technology-centric" to "learner-centric" models of CEL

4.1 Enhancing CEL through social interaction strategies

Social interaction is a key to collaboration, and collaboration results in social interaction. If there is no social interaction, there would be no real collaboration. Research (Burleson et al., 2011; Kreijn et al., 2003; Beetham, 2005) shows that collaborative learning leads to a deeper level of learning, critical thinking, shared understanding, and long term retention of the learned material. It also provides opportunities for developing social and communication skills, developing positive attitudes towards co-members and learning material, and building social relationships, and group cohesion. These effects are strengthened further when collaborative learning is applied to ill- planned complex tasks embedded in an authentic context. Such conditions also increase the effectiveness of social construction of knowledge, and enable competencies' development.

However, there is agreement in the literature that placing students in groups does not guarantee collaboration (Montoya et al., 2011; Wolf et al., 2009). The incentive to collaborate has to be structured within the groups. A complex of simultaneously applied instructional approaches, reinforcing and/or complementing each other can actually enhance collaborative learning and social interactions among group members. These approaches can result in group members socially interacting in ways that encourage elaboration, questioning, rehearsal, and elicitation. For eliciting social interaction that would enhance collaborative learning, three approaches are proposed by Kreijns, et.al. 2003:

a. The cognitive approach: This approach is aimed at specific activities in the learning task that promote "epistemic fluency"-which is defined as the ability to identify and use different ways of knowing, to understand their different forms of expression and evaluation, and to take perspectives of others who are operating within a different epistemic framework (Morrison et.al. 1996). Note that epistemic fluency can be achieved by applying a set of epistemic tasks within the group learning tasks including describing, explaining, predicting, arguing, critiquing, evaluating, explicating, and defining - all in the context of a discourse.
b. The direct approach: This approach involves the use of specific collaborative techniques that structure a task specific learning activity- such as writing a report. Each specific collaborative technique can be used as a template for adaptation to a slightly different learning activity.
c. The conceptual approach: Centers around the notion of applying a set of conditions that enforce collaboration. It involves tailoring a general conceptual model of collaborative learning to the desired or chosen circumstances that specify the types of collaborate on to be created or enforced (Kreijns et al., 2003). However, conceptual methods cannot be easily learned, but can be used in any subject area, with any student groups, and are highly adaptable to changing conditions. The general dimensions and features of the conceptual approach are outlined below(Gierlowski et al., 2009; Zhou et al., 2008; Monahan et al., 2008; Kreijns et al. 2003; Johnson et al., 1999; Sharan et al., 1992; 1976)
    - Positive interdependence: success can only be achieved through mutual dependency- a team member cannot succeed without other team members.
    - Promotive interaction: Individuals encourage and help each other's efforts in order to achieve the group's goals.
    - Individual accountability: all team members are held accountable for doing their share of the work, and for mastery of all the material to be learned.
    - Interpersonal and small-group skills: Specific skills are needed when learners are learning within a group.
    - Group processing: The group determines which behaviors should continue or change for maximizing success based upon reflection of how the group has performed so far.

4.2 Understanding the foundations and principles of the "learner-centered" paradigm

Fourteen learner-centered psychological principles were developed by The American Psychological Association (1993). These principles have extensive implications and considerable promise for the design of web-based instruction from a learner-centered angle. Based on the extensive research in the field of learning and development, studies address areas such as fostering curiosity and intrinsic motivation, thus, providing learners with choice and personal control, linking new information to old ones in meaningful ways, nurturing social interaction, promoting thinking and reasoning strategies, constructing meaning from information and experience, while considering learners' social and cultural background. These principles are necessary for a successful transformation from "Technology-Centric" to "Learner-Centric" paradigm. Such transformation requires designing a psychologically safe educational environment, electronic mentoring, facilitating learning, and other related tools and strategies.

Educational technologists and instructional designers are strongly advocating the critical need for shifting from instructor-centered to student-centered approaches. A learner-centered pedagogy centers around the notion that students must play an active role in the learning process: participating in determining what to learn, their learning preferences, and what is meaningful to them. The author strongly believes that one of the major benefits of the learner-centered "movement" is to make learning engaging for the learner.

As educators, we should take advantage of online tools in providing our students with opportunities to construct knowledge, actively share and seek information, generate a diverse array of ideas, appreciate multiple perspectives, take ownership in the learning process, engage in social interaction and dialogue, develop multiple modes of representation, and become more self-aware. The core point here is that technology- rich environments can support learner engagement in meaningful contexts, thus, increasing ownership over their own learning. For more information, guidance, and supporting research on learner-centered environments, the reader is referred to: (Hamalamen, 2011; Wolf et al. 2009; Oliver et al., 1999, Chung et.al.1998).

4.3 Training instructors in learning and assuming new roles

The different nature of online teaching calls for a significant change in the training and preparation of instructors to play new roles. Essentially, the role of the faculty member or instructor shifts to facilitator, coach, or mentor who provides leadership and guidance for enhancing student learning. Instructors have multiple roles they can assume on line. These include the roles of a chair, host, lecturer, tutor, facilitator, mediator, mentor, provocateur, observer, participant, co-learner, assistant, and community organizer. Research demonstrates that it might be important for the instructor to act as co-learner or participant in online activities. There is evidence suggesting that the on-line instructor must be flexible in constantly shifting between instructor, facilitator, and consultant roles (Wolf et al., 2009; Alfonseca et al., 2006). For facilitating online collaborative learning, it is also recommended that instructors be patient, flexible, responsive, and clear about expectations and norms for participation.

Research also suggests that categorizing the online acts of instructors into four categories-pedagogical, managerial, technical, and social - would be helpful in understanding the instructor's role in collaborative online environments (Peter et al., 2010; Kirkwood, 2010; Dalziel, 2003; Ashton, et.al.1999). Pedagogical action includes feedback, providing instructions, giving information, offering advice and preferences, summarizing or weaving student comments, and referring to outside resources and experts in the field. In short, the pedagogical role relates to direct instructor involvement in class activities. The second category – online managerial actions- involve overseeing task and course structuring. These include coordinating assignments, discussions, and the overall course organization and management. The third category – technical actions- relate to helping with user or system technology issues. Finally, social actions might include instructor empathy, interpersonal outreach (e.g. welcoming messages, invitations, etc.), discussion of one's own online experiences, and humor. An important research question, in this connection, would be to explore how different technologies and pedagogical strategies change the instructional interaction patterns and help promote community building.

In addition to understanding the roles instructors play, it is also important to reflect and contemplate the question: what do online instructors really do? Research (Peter et al., 2010; Kirkwood, 2010; Peffers et.al. 1999) reveals that online instructors tend to rely on simple tools such as e-mail, static or dynamic syllabi, Web links to course material, posting lecture notes on line, and accepting student work on line. However, most online instructors do not use online chat rooms, multimedia lectures, online examinations, animation, and video streaming. The core point here is that e-learning supports a more social constructive learning environment wherein students negotiate meaning, and are involved in extensive dialogue and interaction.

On the other hand, the role of the instructor, therefore, is in transition from director to facilitator or moderator of learning (Wolf et al., 2009; Selinger, 1999). Furthermore, electronic learners are more autonomous and independent in their own learning than their counterparts in traditional classrooms. E-learners also have greater opportunities for interacting with other learners, their instructor, and outside experts.

One approach to accelerating the transformation from technology-centric to learner-centric paradigm in CEL is to encourage educational technologists and instructional designers to undertake meaningful and credible empirical research explorations and evidence-based work to address three major questions: does CEL increase learning access?; Can it enhance the quality of learning?; and can this be done without additional cost? Clearly, these fundamental questions relate to the substantive dimensions of web-based instruction from the three important perspectives of efficiency, effectiveness, and cost-benefit analysis. Addressing these multi-dimensional issues would go a long way towards understanding the real "value-added" of online learning and its actual contributions.

4.4 Identifying and addressing the pitfalls for social interaction in CEL

There is ample empirical evidence suggesting that cognitive processes necessary for deep learning and information retention occur in dialogues (Van der Linden et al., 2001). However, research on group learning shows that asynchronous distributed learning groups utilizing computer-supported collaborative learning environments often lack the social interaction needed for these dialogues (Montoya et al., 2011; Wolf et al., 2009; Hallett et al, 1997). There are at least two identifiable factors which can be seen as pitfalls to social interaction:

4.4.1 Taking social interaction for granted

It is noteworthy that in a CEL environment, interaction does not just happen, but must be intentionally designed into the instruction. However, most educators take social interaction for granted. The fact remains that social interactions can no more be taken for granted in computer conferences than it can be in face-to-face settings as lecture halls or seminar settings. It follows that the first pitfall refers to taking for granted that social interaction will automatically occur just because technology permits it. Although CEL environments allow a certain degree of social interaction to take place, it is no more a matter of course than it is in face-to-face settings (Peter et al., 2010; Kirkwood, 2010). Therefore, it is prudent to conclude that just providing members of a distributed learning group with more communication media than they already have, neither necessarily fosters nor ensures social interaction. Put differently, availability of communication media is necessary- but not sufficient.

4.4.2 Restricting social interaction to cognitive processes

Research studies (Montoya et al., 2011; and Kreijns et al., 2003) suggest that educators recognizing the first pitfall often tend to limit their actions to the task context which is tightly related to the collaborative execution of learning tasks. In addition, they tend to limit their actions to the educational dimension -where social interaction is solely in service of the cognitive processes or other educational purposes. This, however, might not be enough. Moreover, research findings (Peter et al., 2010; and Kirkwood, 2010) emphasize the need for relationship building and sharing a sense of community and a common goal. Another research finding is that forming a sense of community, where people feel they will be treated sympathetically by their fellows, seems to be a necessary first step for collaborative learning. The fact remains that without a feeling of community, people are on their own, likely to be anxious, defensive, and unwilling to take the risks involved in learning.

It follows that the second pitfall relates to restricting social interaction to the cognitive processes in learning and ignoring or forgetting the importance of the social (psychological) dimension. This dimension concerns social interaction for group forming, group structure, and group dynamics - all of which are essential for building learning communities. This has been characterized in the literature as the "member support and group well-being functions"- which are so important for successful technology-mediated group-work. However, these group well- being functions are often neglected or worse yet, not even considered (Kirkwood, 2010; McConnell, 1994).

5. Design features, primary aspects, elements, and strategic issues of collaborative e-learning

The basic features of the educational virtual environment (EVE) were presented earlier. The balance of this chapter will focus on highlighting efforts geared towards designing an innovative architecture for an educational virtual environment. This discussion will center around three major interrelated issues. First, present the design features, elements, primary aspects, and strategic issues relating to collaborative e-learning environments. Second, discuss the design principles for virtual spaces for collaborative e-learning; Third, present a set of action strategies and critical success factors essential for effective implementation of the design principles, along with an assessment.

5.1 Functional features and primary aspects of a Collaborative Virtual Environment (CVE)

As noted earlier, exploring and investigating its primary functional features is the first step towards designing and implementing a functional and effective e-learning CVE. Several studies in the literature deal with various aspects of these complex issues (Kanev et al., 2009; Calongne, 2007; Bouras.etal.2008; Clark et al., 2006; Dillenbourg, 1999). These functional features should be specific enough in order to differentiate an e-learning environment from other virtual environments. Following Bouras et al. 2008, and Dourish et al. 1996, the design has to deal with some aspects of the "real world", which can be exploited by virtual spaces for collaboration and learning. The real world value of the features listed below is that they provide critical cues. These would allow individuals to organize their behavior accordingly.

Every tool designed for supporting e-collaboration should exploit aspects of space and spatial mechanisms, such as providing identity, orientation, a locus for activity and a mode of control, which can be considered as powerful tools for the design.

CVE designers should include precise tools and take into account specific aspects in order to support the creation of places by the users who would, in turn, be able to create meaning of things in social interactions (Dourish, et al.; 1996; Clark et al. 2006; Bouras et al. 2008). These specific aspects are outlined below:

- **Relational orientation and reciprocity:** The spatial organization of the tools should be the same for all participants. The core point is that since people know that the world is physically structured for others in the same way as it is structured for them, they can use this understanding to orient their own behavior toward other people's use.
- **Proximity and activity:** More or less, people pick up objects that are near, not at a distance; they carry things to view them at close proximity which helps the learners/collaborators to be active and not passive in relating to activities and interacting with other learners.
- **Partitioning:** Resulting from the concept of proximity is the notion of partitioning. Since actions and interactions fall off with distance, this distance can be used for partitioning activities and the level of interaction.
- **Presence, awareness, and support of users' representation:** The sense of ongoing awareness of other people's presence and activity allows learners to structure their own activities, integrate communication and collaboration progressively, seamlessly, and easily. It should be noted that the use of avatars in a virtual environment is key for supporting collaborative e-learning. Additionally, note that the role of the lecturer as a facilitator is supported by the visualization of students represented as avatars in the virtual place (Wolf et al., 2009; Clark.et al.2006). Consequently, the visualization of students in a location helps the lecturer to gather students to specific locations - which provides a context for discourse in the virtual place. In short, it might be useful to represent the users by avatars that can support mimics and gestures, for supporting virtual and social presence, as well as for enhancing the ways of communication among the users with non-verbal communication.

5.2 Fundamental design elements of a collaborative e-learning environment

Research studies by Bouras et. al., 2008 and 2006; Dillenbourg, 1999; and Moshman, 1982 provide an insightful discussion and analysis of additional design elements focused on e-collaboration and e-learning. These are briefly presented below:

- Situated remote communication by supporting multiple communication channels - such as avatar gestures, voice chat, and text chat.
- Remote task collaboration in distributed environments allows users to collaborate on tasks. This design element could be realized by:
    a. Tools such as manipulation of shared objects, brainstorming board tool, locking/unlocking shared objects, user handling, as well as slide presentation and creation.
    b. Supporting users who have different roles and rights when visiting the environment.
- Remote task support: Remote support by other learners, teachers, moderators, and participants. This design element could be realized by uploading material in the virtual space and data sharing.

- Scaffolding tools: Tools such as whiteboard, brainstorming and slide creation can support collaborative scenarios as well as support the learners to undertake tasks in the virtual space. The whiteboard could support the learners in making presentations, while the brainstorming and slide creation could support the exchange and collection of ideas for assigned task.
- Representation of the environment by various representation forms, which can range from simple text to 3D worlds.

5.3 Strategic issues for the design of a collaborative e-learning environment

There are several issues that should be taken into account when using CVEs and developing CVEs in the future (Montoya et al., 2011; Liebregt, 2005, Bouras et al. 2008 and 2006). A brief statement of these issues is presented below:

- Instructors should be able to guide the learners.
- There are requirements for natural communication possibilities including realistic avatars and use of body language.
- It is essential to prevent the users from over-engagement with subtasks - not directly related to the main goal of the CVE.
- It is important to avoid frustration or distraction caused by unnecessarily complex interfaces

Further research problems of computer-mediated group learning could be summarized as follows (Montoya et al., 2011; Kirkwood, 2010; Hsi et al., 1997; Sweller, 1988):

- Reduced social presence-problem of social and cognitive orientation:
  a. Group members tend to feel more as individuals than a group
  b. The problem of "virtual group identity" leads to a depersonalization of group members
  c. Low collaboration takes place
  d. Reduced feeling of togetherness, group identity, and social presence
- Unnecessarily high amount of inessential load:
  a. Split attention effect: separation of related information sources increase extraneous load
  b. Poor use of working-memory capacity due to poor utilization of prior knowledge (rules and causal connections known from reality cannot be used)

The reader is referred to our previous discussion relating to the major pitfalls impeding achievement of the desired social interaction in collaborative e-learning environments.

6. Design principles for virtual spaces for collaborative e-learning: Towards designing an innovative architecture for an Educational Virtual Environment (EVE)

An inclusive set of eight very useful principles to support the design and implementation of desktop collaborative-learning environments were developed by Bouras, et al., 2008. These principles incorporated the resulting incremental developments and advancement of earlier findings and scenarios produced by other researchers such as Osborne, 1963; Aronson et al.; 1978; Lymna, 1981; Young, 1997; Johnson et al., 1998; Millis et al., 1998). A listing of the eight design principles along with a brief discussion are provided below:

Principle 1: Design to support multiple collaborative learning scenarios

Principle 2: Design to maximize the flexibility within a virtual space
Principle 3: Augmenting user's representation and awareness
Principle 4: Design an inclusive, open, and user-centered virtual place
Principle 5: Design a media-learning centric virtual space
Principle 6: Ergonomic design of a virtual place accessible by large audience
Principle 7: Design to reduce the amount of extraneous load of the users
Principle 8: Design a place for many people with different roles

Multiple collaborative tools are designed to support the execution of the different e-learning scenarios such as: brainstorming, roundtable, jigsaw, think pair share, quick-writes, and micro-themes...etc. It is important to recognize that e-learning environments can support many groups of users in a variety of subjects. This means that some scenarios would fit better in certain subjects than in others, for this reason users/instructors should be provided with the capability to choose among various scenarios. Additionally, due to the need for multi-functionality within a collaborative on-line synchronous session, it should be made easy, simple and quick to re-organize the virtual place for a particular activity or scenario. One simple approach is to increase the level of flexibility and divide the virtual environment into smaller areas. Such division would allow for ease of undertaking the specific functions. However, despite its benefits, this approach can result in disorientation and rise of the cognitive load of the users concerning the virtual space operation.

Augmenting the user's representation and awareness underscores the importance of combining gestures, mimics; user representation, audio, video and text chat communication, as well as application sharing, similarly, the virtual objects and media can be integrated. All these key elements would provide users with the capability to share their views with others, and show the objects they are discussing. Awareness of other people and objects is essential for e-learning and helps in focusing on the visualization of others, and the representation of their actions on the objects discussed. But, in order to support as many users as possible, a collaborative virtual space should be accessible as much as possible, and access should remain open and not restricted. Open access is important to guide the moderators, instructors, and the individuals responsible for it. In addition, each part of the technology implementation processes would have to guarantee the continuation and general implementation of the specific technology utilized.

Furthermore, in designing media-learning centric virtual spaces, several guidelines for implementation would have to be followed. Virtual environments require multiple communication channels to be based on the differing needs, and requirements. Many communication channels such as application sharing, message board, voice chat, text chat, etc. should be integrated in the virtual space in order to enhance communication awareness among users. While communication should not be intrusive, users should be able to utilize the right channel for the right task. Equally important is the need for virtual environments to be easily accessible. Furthermore, access to the virtual environment should be user friendly; fast and simple in terms of registration, software download and installation.

It should also be emphasized that reducing the amount of unnecessary load is a very important design principle. The commands of interfaces should be in a graphical user interface fashion, and all functions and tools should be located in the same window. Since the main objective of an e-learning environment is to support the learning process, the operation of the learning environment should be simplified and user friendly. Another key consideration concerns the design of a virtual environment according to the needs of the individual roles. Access tools to support a variety of roles with differing access rights are necessary. Such tools and access rights would support the participant's different roles such as regulating interaction by moderators or instructors, however, these tools may not be available to learners.

7. Action strategies and critical success factors: Implementation of the principles

7.1 Implementation issues

Extensive accounts of the tools and mechanisms for implementation of the design principles discussed above are provided in detail in the literature (Montoya et al., 2011; Lin et al. 2010; Jarczyk, 1992; Bouras et al.2008 ; 2006; 2005;2002). These principles could be implemented in 3D collaborative virtual environments in order to support collaborative e-learning communities. Bouras and his co-authors demonstrated how the principles can be applied using the Educational Virtual Environment (EVE) Training Area tool. This tool can be described as a three-dimensional space where participants – represented by 3D humanoid avatars- can use a variety of e-collaboration tools. In some cases, other tools are used in order to demonstrate different implementations and design approaches.
As discussed earlier, current research on the design of collaborative e-learning virtual environments identified various issues and aspects of such environments. The eight-principles presented above would help designers in creating virtual spaces focused on supporting collaborative e-learning. Despite the usefulness of these design principles, the core question still remains: What is the best practice for transforming them into modeling concepts and specific concrete functional features? It is important to note that in the case of EVE, the first step was to investigate the main functional features. As demonstrated by Bouras et al., 2006, the next step was to create a prototype- which was evaluated by users.
It is not only difficult, but may also be restrictive for educational designers to follow a set of rules for transforming the design principles to functional features. The central issue here is the large set of parameters that need to be taken into account. This includes collaborative e-learning techniques that will be used, user requirements, users' profile, etc. A possible solution to that issue is to use these principles as a guide during a "Design Rationale" process of software engineering. In its simplest, a design rationale is the explicit listing of decisions made during a design process, and the reasons why those decisions were made (Peter et al., 2010; Dalziel, 2003; Ravenscroft et al., 2002; Jarczyk et al., 1992). In short, these principles could be used as criteria to review and select a 3D CVE platform for supporting collaborative e-learning scenarios.

7.2 Evaluation

A usability evaluation of the prototype was undertaken by Bouras, et al. 2006 in order to validate the design of EVE prototype. Research studies (Montoya et al., 2011; Lin et al., 2010; Kirkwood, 2010; Peter et al., 2010; Bouras et al. 2008 and 2006; Dalziel, 2003) suggest that the objectives of the usability evaluation are to: (a) assess usability problems with the EVE interface, and (b) investigate more requirements of the end users in order to improve the functionality of the EVE prototype. These studies report that the general impressions by most of the end users participating in the research were positive.
The concept of EVE prototype has been rated as a promising solution for collaborative e-learning. It was felt that the 3D metaphor of a virtual classroom is a useful approach to support synchronous e-learning, particularly for small groups of learners. Moreover, the

simplification of the user interface using 3D metaphors, the support of different file formats, and the use of audio communication channel are the main factors for the general acceptance. Furthermore, the ease of the user interface utilization of the prototype has been rated as positive. The users indicated that they got along well with the system. However, they stated that the interface of the 2D tools need improvement (e.g., the buttons for the avatar gestures should be replaced by icons). This is in addition to the need for improving the error tolerance of the system.

8. Summary, conclusion, implications, and future research directions

The focus of this chapter has been on exploring and offering a comprehensive paradigm and a conceptual architecture for collaborative e-learning for an educational virtual environment. As a point of departure, the author has started out by portraying the current status of e-learning systems, explaining the evolving role and vision of e-learning. A thorough review of the literature painting a profile of the state of the art has been provided. It has been presented with an eye towards highlighting various approaches to e-learning, along with a critique and an assessment of their shortcomings and weaknesses. This research has revealed that the core weaknesses of current e-learning systems revolve around four major dimensions. These include the lack of project-based learning; current course and learning management systems are all asynchronous; the lack of a multi-user VR technology; and the need for shifting from "technology-centric and instructor-centric" to "learner-centric" paradigms with a strong focus on constructivism.

CEL has been defined as any kind of learning process performed by more than one individual that takes place mainly in a virtual environment. This research helps advance our knowledge and accelerate our understanding of the dynamics of CEL in several ways. First, the criteria, benchmarks, and features of a CEL environment have been refined along with the reasons why VR has been used for supporting education. Second, this research has led to the conclusion that there are significant characteristics of VR which could be leveraged for supporting education. These characteristics along with several research propositions germane to our discussion were examined. Third, a detailed account has been provided representing a pathway consisting of several strategies and mechanisms essential for achieving transformation from "technology-centric" to "learner-centric models of collaborative e-learning". These mechanisms include the critical need for enhancing collaborative e-learning through social interaction strategies; understanding the foundations and principles of the "learner-centered" paradigm; training instructors in learning and assuming new roles; and the necessity for identifying and addressing the pitfalls for social interaction in collaborative e-learning.

Fourth, exploring and investigating CEL primary functional features is the first step towards designing and implementing an effective e-learning collaborative virtual environment. These functional features should be specific enough in order to differentiate an e-learning environment from other virtual environments. The functional features and primary aspects of a collaborative virtual environment have also been presented, along with the fundamental design elements, and the strategic issues to be taken into account in developing collaborative virtual environments in the future. Fifth, a well-designed set of principles for virtual spaces for collaborative e-learning were discussed. Finally, some action strategies and critical success factors concerning the implementation of the design principles have been presented.

Taken collectively, in line with the overall theme of this chapter - crystalizing the multiple dimensions of collaborative e-learning - the path leading towards designing an innovative architecture for an educational virtual environment has been identified.

This research has a number of important implications- which have been discussed throughout the chapter, and thus, there is no need for repeating them here.

This chapter raises a number of research questions and issues to be addressed by scholars and students interested in further exploration of collaborative e-learning. Some of these questions are presented below in a seven-item future research agenda:

- To what extent does collaborative e-learning increase learning access? (efficiency)
- To what extent does it enhance the quality of learning? (effectiveness)
- Are the benefits cost effective? And how can we measure them? (cost-benefit analysis)
- How does collaborative e-learning compare to other technologies in the area of networked virtual dynamic group environments in terms of functionality, outcomes, and administration?
- In addition to the mechanisms and protocols proposed in this chapter, how can social interaction be further enhanced?
- Apart from the methods and protocols presented in this chapter, how can educational designers go about transforming the proposed set of design principles into modeling concepts and specific concrete functional features?
- How would different technologies and pedagogical strategies change the instructional interaction patterns and help promote community building?

9. References

Alfonseca, E.; Martin, E.; Paredes, P.; Carro, R.; Ortigosa, A. (2006). The Impact of Learning Styles on Student Groupings for Collaborative Learning: A Case Study. User Model User- Adap Inter, Vol. 16, pp.377-401.

American Psychological Association. (1993). Learner-Centered Psychological Principles: Guidelines for School Reform and Re-structuring. Washington, DC: American Psychological Association and the Mid-Continent Regioal Educational Laboratory.

Aronson, E.; Blaney, N.; Stephan, C.; Sikes, J.; Snapp, M. (1978). The Jigsaw Classroom. Sage Publications.

Ashton, S.; Roberts, T.; Teles, L. (1999). Investigation of the Role of the Instructor in collaborative online environments. Session presented at the CSCL '99 Conference, Stanford University, CA.

Badawy, Afie (2009). Technology Management Simply Defined: A Tweet Plus Two Characters. Journal of Engineering and Technology Management, Volume 26, Issue 4, December, Pages 219-224.

Badawy, Michael K. (2010). A Research Architecture for Technology Management Education. In H. Bidgoli (Ed.) The Handbook of Technology Management, Core Concepts, Financial Tools and Techniques, Operations and Innovation Management. Vol.1, pp. 3-18. New York: Wiley.

Beetham, H. (2005). E-Learning Research: Emerging Issues?. Research in Learning Technology, Vol. 13, No.1, (March 2005), pp. 81-89.

Bouras, Ch.; Giannaka, E. (2008). Exploiting Virtual Environments to Support Collaborative E-Learning Communities. International Journal of Web-Based Learning and Teaching Technologies, Vol.3. No.2, (April-June 2008), pp.1-22.

Bouras, C.; Tsiatsos, T. (2006). Educational Virtual Environments: Design Rationale and Architecture. Multimedia Tools and Applications, Vol. 29, No.2, pp. 153-173.

Bouras, C.; Tsiatsos, T. (2002). Extending the Limits of CVE to Support Collaborative E-Leaening Scenarios. @nd IEEE International Conference on Advanced Leaening Technologies, Kazan, Russia, September 2002, pp. 420-424

Burleson, W.; Tripathi, P. (2011). Mining Creativity Research to Inform Design Rationale in Open Source Communities. In Human Technology: An Interdisciplinary Journal of Humans in ICT Environments on Creativity and Rationale in Software Design. Agora Center, University of Jyvaskyla.

Calongne, C. (2007). A View from Second Life's Trenches: Are You a Pioneer or a Settler?. Proceedings of the NMC Summer conference, 2007, pp.111-119.

Chatti, M.; Klamma, R.; Jarke, M.; Naeve, A. (2007).The Web 2.0 Driven SECI Model Based Learning Process. Seventh IEEE International Conference on Advanced Learning Technologies, Niigata, pp. 780-782.

Chung, H.; Rodes, P.; Knapczyk, D. (1998). Using Web Conferencing to Promote Ownership in Distance Education coursework, Proceedings of the WebNet 98 World Conference of the WWW, Orlando, Florida, No.IR019242.

Clark,S.; Maher, M. (2006). Collaborative Learning in 3D Virtual Place: Investigating the Role of Place in a Virtual Learning Environment. Journal of Science Education and Technology, Vol. 8, No.1,pp18-31.

Dalziel, J. (2003). Implementing Learning Design: The Learning Activity Management System (LAMS), Unpublished Manuscript,

Dillenbourg, P. (1999). What Do You Mean by Collaborative Learning?. In Dillenbourg (Ed). Collaborative :Cognitive and Computational Approaches. Elsevier, Oxford, pp. 1-19

Dourish, P.; Harrison, S. (1996). Re-Placing Space: The Roles of Place and Space in Collaborative Systems. Proceedings of the ACM Conference on Computer Supported Cooperative Work, pp. 68-85.

Gierlowski, K.; Nowicki, K. (2009). A Novel Architecture for E-Learning Knowledge Assessment Systems. International Journal of Distance Education Technologies, Vol.7, Issue 2, pp. 1-19.

Hallet, K.; Cummings, J. (1997). The Virtual Classroom as Authentic Experience. In Proceedings of The vAnnual Conference on Distance Teaching and Learning, pp.103-107. Madison, Wisconsin: University of Wisconsin-Madison.

Hamalamen, R. (2011). Using a Game Environment to Foster Collaborative Learning: A Design-Based Study. Technology, Pedagogy and Education,Vol.20, No.1, (March 2011, pp. 61-78.

His, S.; Hoadley,C. (1997). Productive Discussion in Science; Gender Equity through Electronic Discourse. Journal of Science Education and Technology, Vo.6, No.1.

Jarczyk, A, Loffler, P.; Shipman, F. (1992). Design Rationale for Software Engineering: A Suevey. 25th Hawaii International Conference on System Sciences, Vol.2, pp. 577-566.

Johnson, D.; Johnson, R. (1999). Learning together and alone: Cooperative, Competitive, and Individualistic Learning (5th ed.), Boston: Allyn & Bacon.

Johnson, D.; Johnson,T.; Smith, k. (1998). Active Learning: Cooperation in the College Classroom. Esina, MN: Interaction Book Company.

Kanev, K.; Kimura, S.; Orr, T. (2009). A Framework for Collaborative Learning in Dynamic Group Environments. International Journal of Distance Education Technologies, Vol.7.Issue 1, pp. 58-77.

Kirkwood, K. (2010) The SNAP Platform: Social Networking for Academic Purposes. Campus wide Information Systems, Vol.27, No.3, pp. 118-126, emerald Group Publishing Limited.

Kreijns, K.; Kirschner, P.; Jochems, W. (2003). Identifying the Pitfalls for Social Interaction in Computer-Supported Collaborative Learning: A Review of the Research. Computers in Human Behavior, Vol.19, pp. 335-353.

Laister, J.; Kober, S. (2002). Social Aspects of Collaborative Learning in Virtual Learning Environments. Proceedings of the Networked Learning 2002 Conference.

Law, N.; Wong, E. (2003). Developmental Trajectory in Knowledge Building: An Investigation. In Wasson, B.; Hoppe, U. Dsigning for Changes. Kluwer Academic Publishers, Dordrecht, pp. 57-66.

Lin, Q.; Zhang, L.; Ding, W.; Wang, W.; Neo, K.; Gay,R. (2010). 3D Collaborative Virtual Environment Based E-Learning Systems. International Journal of Applied Systemic Studies. Vol.3, No.2, pp. 211-226

Liang, J. (2010). A Web-Based Collaborative Design Architecture for Developing Immersive Virtual Reality Driving Platform. International Journal of Computer Integrated Manufacturing, Vol.23, No.10, (October 2010), pp. 876-892.

Liebregt,M. (2005). Collaborative Virtual in Education. Proceedings of the the Second Twente Conference on IT, Enschede, 21 January.

Lymna,F. (1981). The Responsive Classroom Discussion. In Anderson,A. Mainstreaming Digest. College Park. MD; University of Maryland College of Education.

Manseur, R. (2005). Virtual Reality in Science and Engineering Education. Proceedings of the Frontiers in Education Conference.

McConnell,D. (1994) Implementing Computer Supported Coperative Learning. London:Kogan Page. Limited.

McInnerney, J.; Roberts, T. (2004). Online Learning Social Interaction and the Creation of a Sense of Community. Educational Technology and Society, Vol. 7, No.3, pp. 73-81.

Millis, B.; Cottell, P. (1998). Cooperative Learning for Higher Education Faculty. American Council on Education, series on Higher Education. The Oryx Press, Phoenix, AZ.

Monahan,T.; McArdle, G.; Bertolotto, M. (2008). Virtual Reality for Collaborative Learning. Computers & Education, Vol. 50, Issue 4, (May 2008), pp. 1339-1353.

Montoya, M.; Massey, A.; Lockwood, N. (2011). 3D Collaborative Virtual Environments: Exploring the Link between Collaborative Behaviors and Team Performance. Decision Sciences, Vol.42, Issue 2, (May 2011), pp. 451-476.

Morrison, D.; Collins, A. (1996). Epistemic Fluency and Constructivist Learning Experiments. In B. Wilson (Ed.) Constructivist Learning Environments, pp. 107-119. Englewood Cliffs: Educational Technology Press.

Moshman,D. (1982). Exogenous, Endogenous, and Dialectical Constructivism. Development Review, Vol.2, pp.371-384.

Nagy, A. (2005). The Impact of E-Learning, in: Bruck, P.A.; Buchholz, A.; Karssen, Z.; Zerfass, A. (Eds.). E-Content: technologies and Perspectives for the European Market. Berlin: Springer- Verlag, pp. 79-96.

Oliver, R.; McLoughlin, C. (1999). Curriculum and Learning Resources Issues arising from the Use of Web-Based Course Support Systems. International Journal of Educational Telecommunications, Vol. 5, No.4, pp. 419-436.

Osborne, A. (1963). Applied Imagination (3rd ed.). New York: Scribner's

Peffers,K.; Bloom,S. (1999). Internet-Bsed Innovations for Teaching IS Course: The State of Adoption. Journal of Information Technology Theory and Applications, Vol.1, No.1, pp167-172.

Peter, S.; Bacon, E.; Dastbaz, M.(2010). Adaptable, Personalized E-Leaening Incorpration Learning Styles. Campus Wide Information Systems, Vol.27, No.2, , pp.91-100, Emerald Group Publishing Limited.

Ravonscroft, A.; Matheson,M. (2002).Developing and Evaluating Games for Collaborative E-Learning. Journal of Computer Assisted Learning, Vol.18, Issue 1 (March 2002), pp.93-101.

Redfern, S.; Galway, N. (2002).Collaborative Virtual Environments to Support Communication and Community in Internet-Based Distance Education. Journal of Information Technology Education., Vol.1,No.3, pp.201-211.

Ryan, J.; O'Sullivan,C.; Bell,C.; Mooney,R. (2004). A Virtual Reality Electrocardiography Teaschnig Tool. Proceedings of the Second International Conference in Biomedical Engineering, pp. 250-253.

Seely Brown, J.; Adler, R. P. (2008). Minds on Fire: Open Education, the Long Tail, and Learning 2.0. Educause Review, January/February 2008, pp. 16-32.

Selinger,M. (1999). The Role of the Techer/Moderator in Virtual Learning Environments. Unpiblished Manuscript, University of Warwick,UK.

Sharan, S.; Sharan, Y. (1976). Small Group Teaching. Englewood Cliffs, NJ: Educational Technology Publications.

Sharan, Y.: Sharan, S. (1992). Expanding Cooperative Learning through Group Investigation. New York: Columbia University.

Sung, R.; Ritchie, J.; Robinson, G.; Day, P.; Corney, J.; Lim, T. (2009). Automated Design Process Modeling and Analysis Using Immersive Virtual Reality. Computer-Aided Design, Vol.41, Issue 12, (December 2009), pp. 1082-1094.

Sweller, j. (1988). Cognitive Load During Problem Solving: Effects on Learning. Cognitive Science, Vol. 12, No. 29, pp. 257-285.

Tavangarian, D.; Leypold, M.; Nolting, K.; Roser, M. (2004). Is E-Learning the Solution for Individual Learning?, Journal of E-Learning, Vol.12, No.4, pp. 15-24.

Van der Linden., Renshaw (Eds.). (2001).Dialogic Learning. Dordrecht: Kluwer Academic Publishers.

Wolf, B.; Burleson, W.; Arroyo, I. ; Dragon, T.; Cooper, D.; Picard, W. (2009). Affect-Aware Tutors: Recognizing and Responding to Student Affect. International Journal of Learning Technology, Vol.4, No.3/4 (November 2009), pp. 68-81.

Young, A. (1997). Mentoring, Modeling, Moitoring, Motivating: Response to Students' Ungraded Writing as Academic Conversation. In Sorcinelli, M.; Elbow,P. (Eds). WEriting to Learn: Strategies for Assigning and Responding to Writing Across Disciplines.

Zhang, J.; Zhao, L.; Nunamaker, J. (2004). Can E-Learning Replace Classroom Learning?. Communication of the ACM, Vol.47, No. 5, pp. 74-79.

Zhou, D.; Zhang, Z.; Zhong, S.; Xie, P. (2008).The Design of Software Architecture for E-Learning Platforms. In Pan, Z. (Ed), Edutainment, LNCS, pp. 32-40.

14

Bio-Inspired E-Learning Systems – A Simulation Case: English Language Teaching

Moise Gabriela, Netedu Loredana and Toader Florentina Alina
Petroleum-Gas University of Ploiesti
Romania

1. Introduction

The objectives of using new computing techniques in e-learning systems are defined by the necessity of teaching according to the individual needs of the students, to whom education should provide different e-contents, pedagogical paths and interaction manners.

As nowadays e-learning systems are too rigid, there have been numerous attempts to develop really adaptable e-learning systems (Paramythis & Loidl-Reisinger, 2004) (Brusilovsky & Nijhavan, 2002). This implies hard work and teams formed of specialists from diverse fields: instructional, computer science, teaching area experts and important financial and time resources. The main factor that affects the functionality of e-learning systems is the human being, an instable factor, and, therefore the instructional objectives depend on an instable and unpredictable factor.

As a result, an e-learning system has to be prepared to deal with any learning situation. Building an e-learning system efficient for any learning context is possible only on the condition of using new computing techniques. In the field of online instruction, the part called machine's intelligence has a primordial role. The machine's intelligence derived from sophisticated software programme having the following features: adaptability, flexibility, reactivity, autonomy, collaboration and reasoning capacity.

Intelligent Tutoring System and Adaptive Hypermedia System are the main types of e-learning systems that provide instruction according to the parameters of the instructional process. These parameters characterize the actors of the instructional process and the environment and are included in the components of an e-learning system: expert model, learner model, instructional model and interface model (Phobun & Vicheanpanya, 2010)

An adaptive system is a system that changes its behaviour according to the environment's changes in order to reach certain goals. An intelligent e-learning system is an adaptive, complex system. The complexity of the system is due to the different interactions between its component parts and to the nature of these interactions: human-machine, human-human via machine and machine-machine. To confer the system self-learning capacity, the usage of artificial intelligence is imperative.

In (Ruiz et al., 2008), the authors present two types of e-learning systems which adapt taking into account the learning styles of the learners:

"1. Systems that use learning styles to guide the design of the educational contents. These systems are based on offering the users the type of materials that are preferred by individuals classified in their specific learning style.

2. Systems that use learning styles to guide the adaptation of the structure of the contents to the mental processes of each individual (particular styles of thinking, perceiving or remembering) that falls in a certain category."

The adaptation property of the e-learning systems presented in (Ruiz et al., 2008) is reached using a set of rules or using objects with a certain format adequate for each instructional situation.

Learner's classification, considering his/her individual learning style is used in the software system for online learning proposed in (Moise, 2007), called iLearning. The system is based on shaping a course by means of conceptual maps. Each node of the conceptual maps contains pedagogical resources in different formats and structures according to the learning styles of each student. The implementation of an iLearning system on a computer is realised using intelligent agents technology.

The system described in (Tzouveli et al., 2008) offers a flexible solution capable to adapt to learners' preferences using e-questionnaires to establish automatically learners' profile.

The problems of adaptation and flexibility of the e-learning systems are difficult, as the main actors are complex and unpredictable. In order to solve such problems, the researchers ask for new computing techniques.

Bio-computing techniques simulate biological mechanisms and are used in solving the most difficult problems. The purpose of this chapter is to present e-learning systems architectures based on new computing techniques, namely neural networks and swarm intelligence techniques.

Artificial neural networks techniques are inspired by the activity of the human brain and swarm intelligence techniques are inspired by insects' behaviour. The authors selected these artificial life techniques in order to solve the problems related to collective and individual intelligences, collective and individual behaviours, collective and individual knowledge. The expected results are: a higher level of students participation in the instructional process, a better internalisation of rules and contents, more numerous and diverse types of interaction, a higher level of motivation and self-esteem. The expected results respond to cognitive, psychological and instructional demands.

2. Theoretical background

In this section, there are presented two bio-inspired techniques, namely neural networks and swarm intelligence, techniques that may be successfully used in designing adaptable e-learning systems.

Bio-inspired techniques, unlike conventional intelligent techniques, use algorithms that enable them to learn by themselves, without further human intervention.

2.1 Neural networks

Neural networks are structures inspired from neuron circuits of the nervous systems and they are composed of interconnected computing units. Each neuron sends and receives impulses from other neurons and these changes are modelled as data changes. The main element of a neural network is the artificial neuron. Some indexes of neural networks development are the following: Warren McCulloch and Walter Pitts proposed the model in 1943 and it has still remained the fundamental unit of most of the neural networks. (McCulloch and Pitts, 1943) In 1958, Frank Rosenblatt added the learning abilities and developed the model of perceptron. (Rosenblatt, 1958) In 1986, David Rumelhart, Geoffrey

Hinton and Ronald Williams defined a training algorithm for neural networks. (Rumelhart, Hinton, Williams, 1985) The diagram of a neuron with d inputs and one output is presented in figure 1.

The main elements of a neural network that affects the functionality of the network are: the structure, the learning technique and the transfer function that reflects the way how the input is transferred to the output.

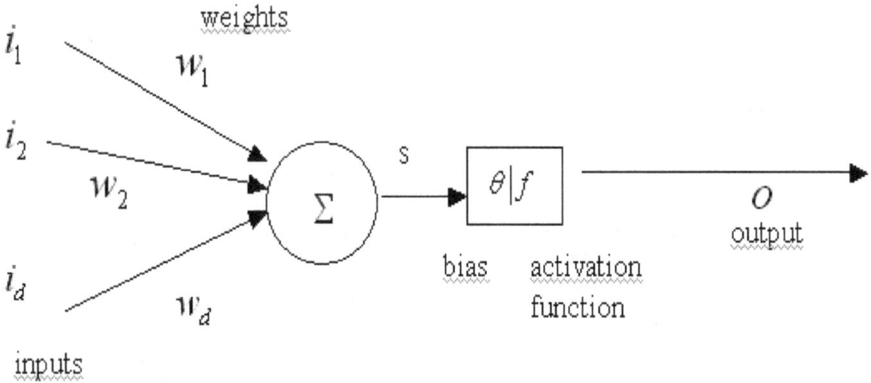

Fig. 1. Neuron with d inputs and one output.

Each input has associated a synaptic weight, noted with w. This weight determines the effect of a certain input on the activation level of the neuron. The balanced sum of the inputs $\sum_{j=1}^{d} w_j i_j$ (called net input) defines the activation of the neuron. The net input value is based on all input connections.

The net input can be calculated using the euclidian distance: $\sqrt{\sum_{j=1}^{d} \left(w_j - i_j\right)^2}$

The function f represents the activation (or transfer) function and θ represents the bias. The output (o) is calculated using the following formula.

$$o = f\left(\sum_{j=1}^{d} i_d w_d - \theta\right) \tag{1}$$

The most used forms of the activation function are presented in the formulas 2-6.

- step function

$$f(s) = \begin{cases} 0, s \leq 0 \\ 1, s > 0 \end{cases} \tag{2}$$

- signum function (used by Warren McCulloch and Walter Pitts)

$$f(s)=\begin{cases}-1, s\le 0\\ 1, s>0\end{cases} \tag{3}$$

- linear function

$$f(s)=s \tag{4}$$

- sigmoid function

$$f(s)=\frac{1}{1+e^{-ks}}, k>0 \tag{5}$$

- generalized sigmoid function

$$f(s)=\frac{1}{1+a*e^{-bs}}, b>0 \tag{6}$$

There are two fundamental structures for the neural networks: the feedforward neural network and the neural network with reaction. In the model proposed by Moise (Moise, 2010), it is used a feedforward neural network with a topology on levels, according to the geometrical positions of the neural units (figure 2).
The model of a feedforward neural network with one input layer (with d units), one hidden layer (with p units), one output layer (with n units) and a linear activation function is described in formulas 7-8 (figura 2).

$$\begin{aligned}
z_1 &= f(net_1-\theta_1)=f\left(\sum_{j=1}^{d} w_{1j}*i_j-\theta_1\right)= \\
&= w_{11}*i_1+\ldots+w_{1d}*i_d-\theta_1 \\
&\ldots \\
z_p &= f(net_p-\theta_p)=f\left(\sum_{j=1}^{d} w_{pj}*i_j-\theta_p\right)= \\
&= w_{p1}*i_1+\ldots+w_{pd}*i_d-\theta_p
\end{aligned} \tag{7}$$

$$\begin{aligned}
o_1 &= f'(net'_1-\theta'_1)=f\left(\sum_{j=1}^{r} v_{1j}*z_j-\theta'_1\right)= \\
&= v_{11}*z_1+\ldots+v_{1p}*z_p-\theta'_1 \\
&\ldots \\
o_r &= f'(net'_r-\theta'_r)=f'\left(\sum_{j=1}^{r} v_{rj}*z_j-\theta'_r\right)= \\
&= v_{r1}*z_2+\ldots+v_{rp}*z_p-\theta'_r
\end{aligned} \tag{8}$$

In the formulas 7-8, we considered that $f(net)=f'(net\ )=net$.

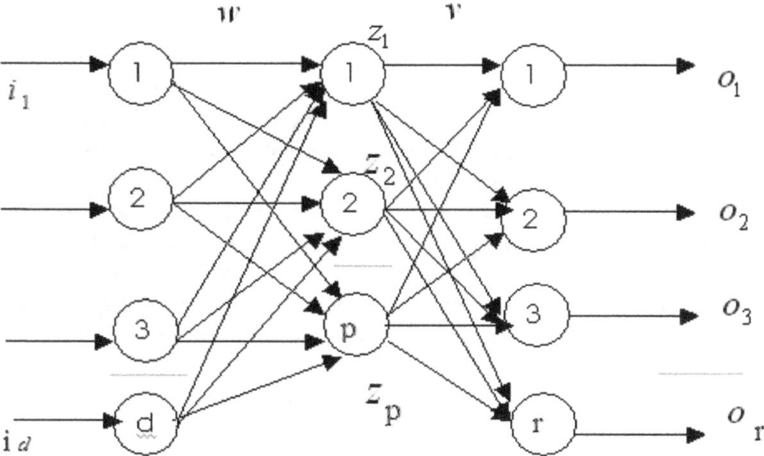

Fig. 2. The Architecture of a neural network to adaptable e-learning system.

The positive weights determine the excitatory connections and the negative weights determine the inhibitory connections. The weights 0 denote the absence of connection between two neurons. The higher the absolute value of the weights ($w_{j,i}$) is, the stronger the influence of the neuron i on the neuron j is stronger.
The neural networks are information processing adaptive systems. The most important quality of a neural network is its learning capacity. According to the received information, learning can be supervised or unsupervised. The supervised learning uses a training dataset, pairs of inputs and correct outputs. The algorithm used in the model of the e-learning system is the backpropagation algorithm and it works as follows: it computes the error as the difference between the desired output and the current output. The error is delivered back to the input of the neural network (Freeman, J. A., Skapura, 1991).
The performance function can be as in formula 9.

$$\sum_{j=1}^{r}\left(d_j^{(m)} - o_j^{(m)}\right)^2 \text{ or } \sum_{l=1}^{e}\sum_{j=1}^{r}\left(d_j^{(m)} - o_j^{(m)}\right)^2 \tag{9}$$

Where e represents the number of pairs (inputs, desired outputs), which form the training set.
The learning process of the neural network consists of two phases: one phase of learning and one phase of testing.
More details about the theory of a neural network can be found in (Freeman, J. A., Skapura, 1991).

The weights' set that minimizes the error is the solution to the problem. Training of the neural network can be realized till the error decreases to an acceptable value or till reaches a maxim predefined epochs.

2.2 Swarm intelligence

It is known that classic optimization algorithms do not offer an efficient manner of solving involved large scale combinatorial and highly non-linear problems. The main characteristics of these classic algorithms are that they are characterized by an accentuated inflexibility concerning the need to adapt the algorithm to the proposed problem (Chan & Tiwari, 2007). So a set of assumptions is made and their truthfulness is not always easy to prove and it can easily affect the quality of the returned solution.

In this context, the development of nature-inspired algorithms is well motivated and it proposes a new perspective in solving these categories of problems by providing in most cases a better solution comparative to the classical optimization algorithms.

A branch of these nature-inspired algorithms is known as Swarm Intelligence and includes algorithms as Particle Swarm Optimization, Ant Colony Optimization, Artificial Bee Colony, and so one.

Swarm Intelligence was defined in 1989 by Gerardi Beni and Jing Wang as the collective behaviour of decentralized and self-organized systems. Swarm Intelligence Systems are composed of a population consisting in simple agents that interact locally with one another and with the environment by following simple rules (Chan & Tiwari, 2007). The agents' behaviour is defined by a certain degree of randomness and their social interactions are inspired by nature. Swarm Intelligence techniques are based on applying behavioural response to the environmental state, which serves as a work state memory and do not depend on specific agents.

In 1994 Mark Millonas mentioned the five basic principles of swarm intelligence (Stanarevic & Bacanin, 2011):

- The proximity's principle - each individual is able to memorize space and time computations;
- The quality's principle - each individual is able to respond to the quality of the environmental factors;
- The diverse response's principle - each individual "should not commit its activities along excessively narrow channels".
- The stability's principle - the changes considering the individuals behaviour should not be influenced by the environment changes;
- The adaptability's principle -individuals behaviour can be changed when it's worth his computational price.

General Assignment Problem is represented by the necessity of assigning with a minimum cost a set of tasks to a set of agents with limited capacity. Each task can be assigned to single agents and uses certain of this agents' resource.

This study aims to propose a solution for a General Assignment Problem using a Swarm Intelligence technique, represented by *Artificial Bee Colony* algorithm.

Artificial Bee Colony represents a Swarm Intelligence technique that tries to model the natural behaviour of real honey bees in food foraging. By performing the waggle dance during the food procuring the bees can successfully share information about the direction and the distance of food and also about the amount of nectar available at the indicated location (Chan & Tiwari, 2007).

The studies considering bee comportment shows that the waggle dance contains a series of information about the food source: the direction of the bees' body indicates the direction of the food in relation to the sun, the waggles intensity is proportional to the distance to the food location and the dance length indicates the amount of nectar available at the food source.

In 1996 Yonezawa and Kikuchi developed an algorithm after closely observing the foraging behavior of honey bees and indicated the importance of group intelligence (Yonezawa & Kikuchi, 1996). The proposed algorithm highlights the fact that the results obtained by simulating an artificial systems including two bees are superior to the results obtained by simulating an artificial systems including a single honey bee.

In 2005 Karaboga proposed a new perspective by simulating the foraging behaviour for solving multi-dimensional and multi-model optimization problems, called Artificial Bee Colony (Karaboga, 2005).

The artificial bee population consists of three groups of bees (Chan & Tiwari, 2007):

- Employed bees - they are assigned to a specific food location; when the amount of nectar on this area goes to zero, they become scouts;
- Onlookers - considering the waggle dance performed by the employed bees, they choose one of the food locations described by this dance; the probability of choosing a location increase proportionally with the amount of nectar available there;
- Scouts - they navigate through the search area without any assistance in order to find new food locations.

The ABC algorithm is based on representing the possible solution to the optimization problem as the position of the food source, while the amount of food corresponds to the solution quality. In these conditions, the number of the employed bees or onlookers bees is equal to the number of solutions in the population.

The main steps of this algorithm are (Stanarevic & Bacanin, 2011):

- Send the employed bees into the search space and determine the nectar amounts available;
- Calculate the probability values of the preferred sources for the onlooker bees
- Stop the searching process on the location abandoned by bees;
- Randomly send the scoots into the search area in order to find new food sources;
- Memorize the location of the best food sources find so far.

The Artificial Bee Colony algorithm used in General Assignment Problem is presented in schema from figure 3.

The variables used in problem codification are:

- EmployedBeeNumber = the initial number of employed bees;
- OnlookesBeesNumber = the initial number of employed bees;
- MaximimIterationNumber = the maximum accepted iteration number;
- fiti= the fitness value corresponding to the i bee;
- EmplBeei=Employed Bee number i;
- OnlkBeei =Onlooker Bee number i;
- i_Neighbour= neighbor corresponding to the I bee;
- pi=the probability of the Onlooker bee to choose the location of the EmplBeei
- SN=Scout Number

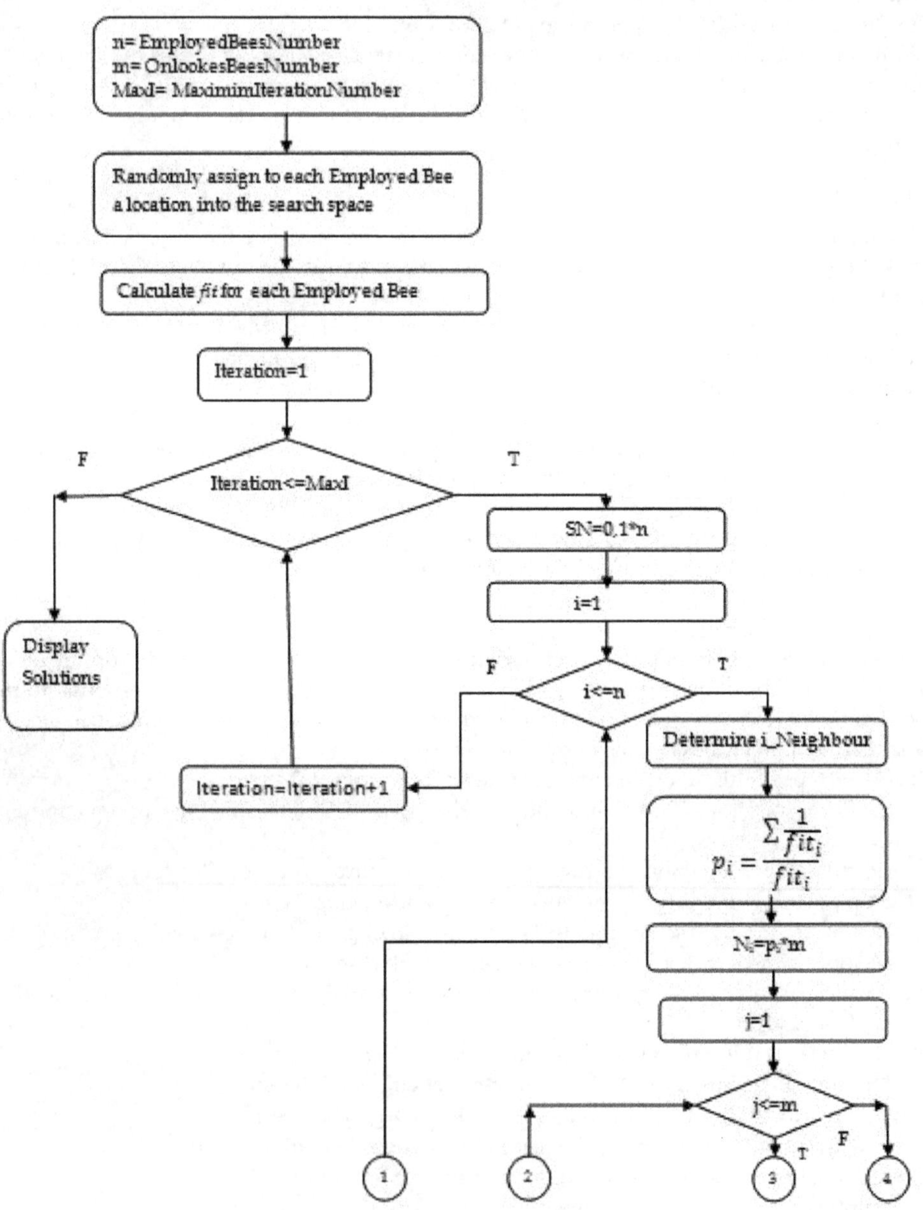

Fig. 3. (Continued)

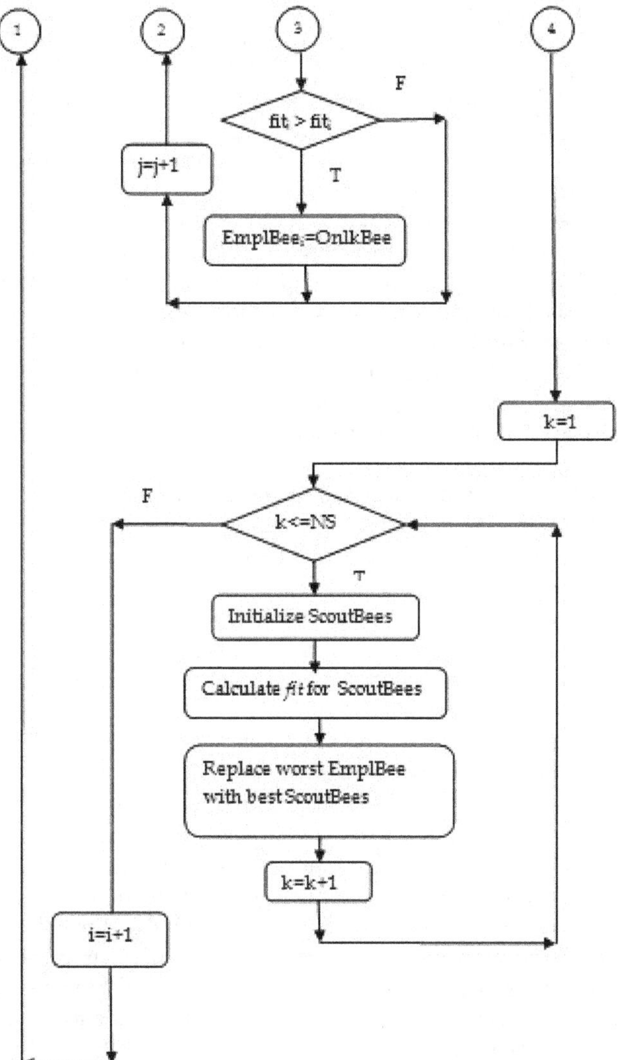

Fig. 3. The Schema of the Artificial Bee Colony Algorithm.

The authors consider that the problems related to the learning process are difficult problems, non-determinist, so, in this chapter there is presented an approach based on neural networks and swarm intelligence in order to model the learning process into an adaptable and flexible e-learning system.

3. Neural networks and swarm intelligence based e-learning systems

Mota (Mota, 2008) uses the neural networks to design two types of adaptability in an e-learning system: adaptive presentation and adaptive navigation. (http://paginas.fe.up.pt/

~prodei/DSIE08/papers/35.pdf) The student model is defined considering Kolb learning styles inventory: Reflector, Theorist, Pragmatist and Activist student. The adaptation strategy uses SCORM 1.3 learning objects. The architecture proposed by Mota in (Mota, 2008) contains a Multilayer Perceptron trained with back propagation learning algorithm. The neural network is integrated in an intelligent unit, called CeLIP - Cesae eLearning Intelligent Player. Learners will have associated suitable learning objects according to their learning styles, user preferences and performance.

In (Seridi-Bouchelaghem, Sari, Sellami, 2005), there are used two neural networks: the former to select the appropriate basic units ("a basic unit is a multi-media document having intrinsically a teaching quality, i.e. which can be used within the framework of the knowledge transmission") for the learner and the latter neural network is used when the learners do not pass the post-test and select base units having reinforcing roles.

An Artificial Neural Net model is used in (Seridi, H., Sari T., Sellami, M., 2006) in order to select in an adaptive way the learning basic unit. Viewing the problem of adaptive course generation upon learners' profiles as a classification problem, the authors propose two neural networks:

The former neural network is used to select the adequate learning material in the first stage of learning and has the following properties:

- each neuron in the output layer is assigned to a learning material, referred as a basic unit in (Seridi, H., Sari T., Sellami, M., 2006);
- each neuron in the input layer represents the concepts related to the learning goal of the course;
- the hidden layer is used to computation and the number of neurons of the hidden layer is modified manually in the training stage.

The latter neural network is used in the reinforcement stage in the cases in which learners do not pass the test after the concepts training:

- The input of this network represents a grade of concepts' understanding by the learners;
- The output layer is defined by the basic units having the reinforcing role.

The algorithm used for neural network's training is backpropagation.

The system proposed initially in the paper (Moise, 2010) and further extended in this chapter uses a conceptual map based representation of an electronic course, the ABC algorithm to initial assign Learning Units (containing different teaching models for the same concepts, theory etc.) and a neural network based intelligent engine to adjust the unfolding of the learning-teaching process to the learner's needs.

An electronic course can be modelled using a conceptual map with k nodes (figure 4) (Moise, Dumitrescu, 2003; Moise, Ionita, 2008)

Each node has associated more learning units (for a node i, we note the number of pedagogical resources with nLU_i). The maxim number of combination is $\prod_{i=1}^{k} nLU_i$, so the teaching models are less than $\prod_{i=1}^{k} nLU_i$. A learning unit (LU) consists in pedagogical resources and a teaching model. So, a node can be taught in different way using different learning units.

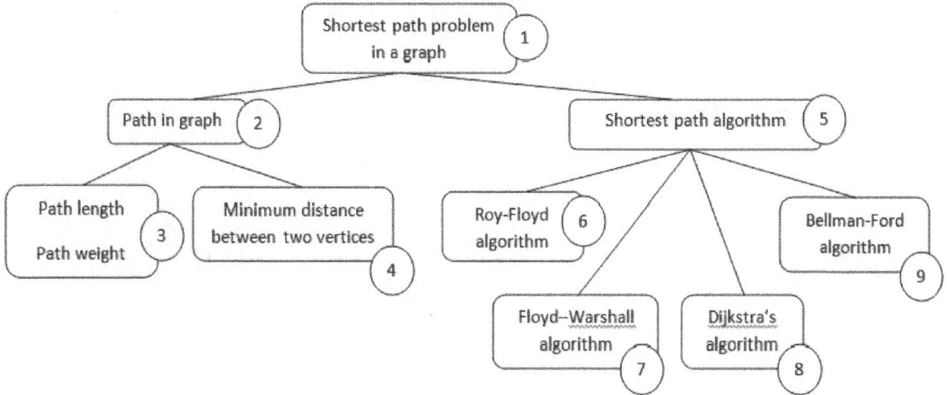

Fig. 4. Conceptual Map of an Electronical Course.

The problem of a right association between learners and learning units is solved in two phases:

1. Initial assignment between learners and LU using ABC algorithm;
2. Adaptation of the pedagogical path to each learner, by using neural network.

Phase 1

General Assignment Problem is represented by the necessity of assigning with a minimum cost a set of tasks to a set of agents with limited capacity. Each task can be assigned to single agents and uses certain of this agents' resource.

These types of problems are common for the computer and communications area, vehicle routing, group technology, scheduling, etc.

This study aims to propose a solution for a General Assignment Problem using a Swarm Intelligence technique, represented by Artificial Bee Colony.

The proposed problem can be described as follows: a set of learners $\{L_1, L_2, \ldots L_n\}$ subscribe to attend a series of e-learning courses. In order to obtain information about the student's experience, about his learning skills and his preferences, an e-questionnaire is completed at the moment of the platform registration. Taking into account this information a learners' profile is associated to each candidate. On the e-learning platform there are a set of Learning Units for each e-course $\{LU_1, LU_2, \ldots LU_k\}$ and the purpose is to assign each student to a proper Learning Unit in order to maximize students' performance.

The bees will represent the Learning Units and the constraints associated regard the number of students that can simultaneously access a specific LU and the fact that one student can only access a single Learning Unit at the time.

The search space is represented by the learners. When a learner has assigned a Learning Unit, a fitness function is calculated considering the learners' profile and the Learning Unit characteristics and the value of this fitness function needs to be maximized. Learners' profile is defined using the instruction context (Moise, 2007):

- Mental context (MC) includes: general abilities and knowledge, the intelligence of the student, mental structure and the capacity of the learner to learn, understand and practice the material.
- Social context (SC) includes the familiar context, familiar stress, friends view.

- Technological context (TC) refers to course structure, format, informational technology, technological equipment.
- Knowledge context (KC) refers on previous knowledge, past experience related on the topic presented in course.
- Emotional context (EC) refers to the motivation, interest and goals of the students.
- Classroom context (CC) includes teaching methods, the structure of students (age, gender, ethnical structure, etc.)

The fitness function can be established defining for each parameter of instruction context a values scale. An example of the fitness function is presented in formula 10.

$$f_{ij} = \frac{E\_Q_{ij} + E_{ij}}{O_j} \tag{10}$$

Where E_Q_{ij} represents a value that indicates the level of knowledge that the learner i has in the Learning Unit j area, E_{ij} represents the student's experience in that area and O_j represents the occupancy degree of the considered learning unit.

Phase 2

The implementation of the adaptability property of the system is realised using a neural network, which has the goal to provide for each learner the proper teaching model. The neural network is trained, therefore an input vector involves a certain output. We define a value for acceptable error and we note it with ε .

We choose the structure of the neural network consisting of an input layer, a hidden layer and output layer and the standard connection (all neighbour layers are connected) (schema from figure 2). The input layer has a number of units equal with the number of inputs. The input vector is defined by values which state the instruction context (MC, SC, TC, KC, CC, EC) (Moise, 2007)

Each context factor is defined by a set of parameters. Generalizing, the input vector is defined as in 11.

$$\begin{pmatrix} mc_1, mc_2, \ldots, sc_1, sc_2, \ldots, tc_1, tc_2, \ldots, \\ kc_1, kc_2, \ldots, ec_1, ec_2, \ldots cc_1, cc_2, \ldots \end{pmatrix}$$

$$MC \quad SC \quad TC \tag{11}$$

$$KC \qquad EC \quad CC$$

The output layer has more units (corresponding to the teaching models which conduct to maximal performance). The desired goal is to associate to each instruction context the proper model teaching. The number of units from the hidden layer can be chosen using a heuristic method or one can adjust it during the folding of the teaching process in order to increase the complexity of the network.

For instance, if we consider a neural network with d inputs and r outputs, we can select $\sqrt{d * r}$ hidden units.

The neural network has to resolve the following problem: the association of an instruction context sacred to a learner with a teaching model obtained through the composition of the teaching models of each node from the conceptual map. Often, the architecture of the neural network remains fix and the values of weights are changed.

Schema of using the neural network in the instructional adaptive system is presented in figure 5. We suppose that there are four teaching models (TM).

$\begin{pmatrix}1\\0\\0\\0\end{pmatrix}$ - TM no.1 $\begin{pmatrix}0\\1\\0\\0\end{pmatrix}$ - TM no. 2 $\begin{pmatrix}0\\0\\1\\0\end{pmatrix}$ -TM no. 3 $\begin{pmatrix}0\\0\\0\\1\end{pmatrix}$ - TM no. 4

The inputs have the following forms:

$\begin{pmatrix}i_1\\i_2\\\dots\\i_d\end{pmatrix}$, where $i_k \in \{0,1\}$. For instance $\begin{pmatrix}1\\0\\0\end{pmatrix}$ represents the visual learning style, $\begin{pmatrix}0\\1\\0\end{pmatrix}$ auditory learning style, $\begin{pmatrix}0\\0\\1\end{pmatrix}$ kinesthetic learning style,

The training set contains p pairs $\{knowninput, desiredoutput\}$, hereupon we add perturbed inputs.

$$H = \left\{ \left(\begin{pmatrix}1\\0\\0\\\dots\\0\end{pmatrix}, \begin{pmatrix}1\\0\\0\\0\end{pmatrix} \right), \left(\begin{pmatrix}0\\1\\0\\\dots\\0\end{pmatrix}, \begin{pmatrix}0\\1\\0\\0\end{pmatrix} \right), \left(\begin{pmatrix}0\\0\\1\\\dots\\0\end{pmatrix}, \begin{pmatrix}0\\0\\1\\0\end{pmatrix} \right), \dots, \left(\begin{pmatrix}0\\0\\0\\\dots\\1\end{pmatrix}, \begin{pmatrix}0\\0\\0\\1\end{pmatrix} \right) \right\}$$

The error associated to the training set computed according to the formula 12.

$$E = \frac{1}{2}\sum_{i=1}^{4}(t_i - o_i)^2 \tag{12}$$

where o_i is the current output and
t_i is the desired output
The output of the neural network is computed as in formula 13.

$$o_1 = f\left(\sum_{i=0}^{3} v_{i1} * z_i\right), \tag{13}$$

where $z_i = f\left(\sum_{j=0}^{d} w_{j1} * x_j\right)$ for $i = 1,2,3$ and $z_0 = -1$

$x_0 = -1$ and x_j are binary vectors

If $d = 3$, then the number of the hidden units is 3.
In order to adjust the weights, we use the backpropagation algorithm to train neural network presented in figure 5.

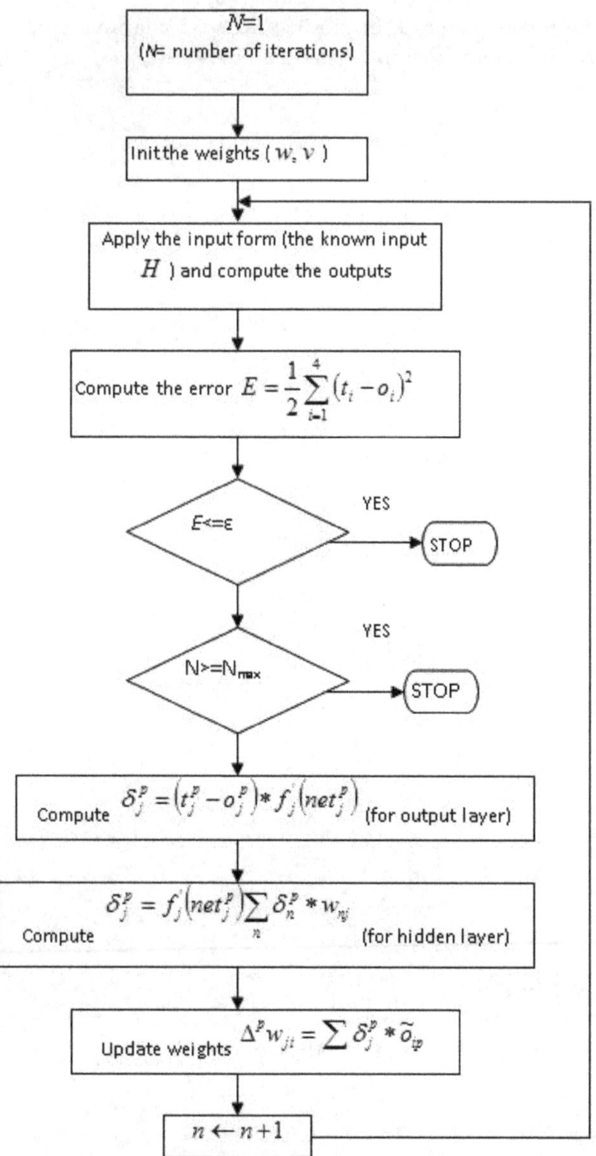

Fig. 5. The Backpropagation Algorithm.

4. Use of new computing techniques in learning English as a foreign language

Learning is an inner capacity of the living beings, which, due to new computing techniques, namely bio-computing ones, has transgressed ontological borders and has become a capacity of artificial intelligence systems as well. In acquiring a foreign/second language (L2), learning "can be broadly defined as the internalization of rules and formulas which are then used to communicate in the L2." (Ellis, 1996) In this sense, language learning is considered synonymous with language acquisition. However, Krashen (Krashen, 1981) makes a clear distinction between the two terms, referring to learning as a process of developing conscious or metalingual knowledge through formal study, whereas acquisition implies spontaneous rule internalization, similar with "picking up". New technologies should take into consideration both capacities, as natural, spontaneous acquisition and formal study alike are essential in one's personal development of communicative skills.

When defining second language acquisition (SLA), Rod Ellis makes no distinction between learning and acquisition, in that he refers to SLA as "subconscious or conscious processes by which a language, other than the mother tongue, is learned in a natural or a tutored setting. It covers the development of phonology, lexis, grammar, and pragmatic knowledge." (Ellis, 1996) The traditional study of foreign languages was limited mostly to the internalization of morphosyntactic rules and vocabulary in a rather decontextualised, memory-based manner. Technology development, and as a result, permanent access to up-to-date information, as well as intercultural direct contacts established in an increasingly globalized work and education market, have facilitated and changed the way a foreign language is perceived and learned. There is an astonishing number of youngsters and grown-ups in nowadays society who, according to Krashen terminology, acquire or "pick up" rather than learn a second language, without any tutoring, textbooks or methodologies, forced by new social and work market conditions.

The present analysis will focus on learning English as a tutored, formal activity within the Practical Course classes of the Romanian-English Specialization (day classes and Distance Education forms), functioning within the Petroleum-Gas University of Ploieşti. Practical Course of English is an obligatory subject and it is allocated 4 hours (in the 1st year) and 3 hours per week, respectively (in the 2nd and the 3rd years) throughout the 3-year curricula of this specialization.

The authors aim at highlighting the advantages of using e-learning within foreign language classes, both in Distance Education and day classes, and the changes that the use of e-learning triggers in the process of SLA. Aspects to be discussed in this respect are: the new roles of the participants in education, types of interaction, e-course generation and navigation, use of technology in ELT (namely ProLang phonetic laboratory, as interactive equipment available within University of Ploieşti).

The authors consider learning a collaborative accomplishment of an individual's, in that he/ she receives language inputs, practices and internalizes them in order to finally produce and transmit language outputs in the form of oral or written communication. The traditional emitter of the language inputs used to be the teacher, so formal study was a face-to-face collaboration of students and their teacher, supported or mediated by different types of educational material. Besides Teacher-Student and/or Student-Student interaction, in the last decades, there have manifested new types of interaction, namely Student-Machine, Teacher-Machine and Machine-Machine. The increasing implementation and use of artificial life techniques allow a shift in the perception of computers, from mere equipment to valuable partners and participants in education, language learning included.

Learning by means of electronic devices has already proven its advantages, when used in the process of SLA: endless opportunities for up-to-date information and immediate access to primary and secondary sources (books, textbooks, dictionaries, encyclopaedias etc), exploring both virtual and real linguistic contexts otherwise unavailable in the class, receiving foreign language inputs from native speakers, with different accents, rhythms or register styles, the possibility of synchronous and asynchronous communication with students' peers or teachers, a reduced level of anxiety for less confident students, flexible and adaptive contents custom-made for students' individual pace, needs and personal learning styles, the possibility of immediate evaluation of their performance, developing computing skills of both students and teachers, a higher level of motivation and involvement, as students make use in their education of familiar facilities: e-mail, Internet navigation, forums and other types of group works, Internet Relay Chat, learning media such as texts, graphics, stills, animated images, real-life or education-targeted film etc.

As a result, the foreign language teacher stops being the only provider of accurate language or the primary source of comprehensible linguistic items in terms of pronunciation, vocabulary, morphology, syntax or pragmatics. Students and teacher alike take new roles within e-learning based activities, different from traditional education. Although the teacher continues to be the organizer, tutor, controller and assessor of the learning process, his or her magister position is not as obvious as in the traditional, face to face education. Students feel more independent, relaxed and confident in what seems to be a learner-driven lesson, within which the teacher behaves more like a silent observer and assessor or like an equal participant in group activities. Computer techniques mediation allows varied interaction, which, according to Julien Edge, presents several advantages in foreign language teaching and learning: "a change of interaction brings a change of focus of attention, which helps keep people interested; in pairs and groups, there is opportunity for more individuals to use the language; students perform differently away from the pressure of teacher and whole-class attention; students learn to be more self-reliant"(Edge, 1993). This medium will also enable students to repeat a word, stop, go forwards and backwards in the course at an individual pace, without disturbing the rest of the class.

If advantages of using new technology and computing techniques are not to be questioned and discussed any further, these complex, adaptive and flexible systems of e-learning pose various challenges as well. Besides the financial issue and the computer literacy required, a major challenge is that of e-course generation. First, an electronic practical course of English is to meet the demands of any course, in that it should observe the syllabus of the subject, establish realistic objectives and appropriate teaching strategies, choose contents and support materials that appeal to students' areas of interest and consider their level, establish and announce the modality and frequency of evaluation. In the case discussed, most of the 1st year university students at the Romanian-English specialization are intermediate and upper-intermediate (8 years of English, on average), their major issues being grammar and reluctance to speak in front of the class. Evaluation consists of three tests per semester, in which both receptive and productive skills are being assessed.

Considering the fact that the 1st year students form a heterogeneous group, in terms of linguistic competence and computer literacy, an e-course of English should be organized in coherent, still flexible and adaptive modules, with user-friendly layout and tools, and nodes that associate various pedagogical resources. A focus on functions (introducing oneself, inviting, asking for information, apologizing and so forth) and themes (Family, Travelling, Education, Hobbies) would be useful in organizing and ordering contents, as it provides a natural context for vocabulary acquisition and grammar rules internalization.

Each unit is to offer visual and audio support, to consider the four basic skills and to be learner-oriented, in that the student may have the possibility to choose tools and different levels of language (Phonetics, Vocabulary, Morphology and Syntax) depending on his/ her individual needs and knowledge. In terms of Swarm Intelligence technique, students become decentralized and self-organized agents that interact with one another and the teacher, respectively, and with the multimedia environment in order to solve multi-leveled problems. Still, there will be common objectives and a unique evaluation at the end of each unit.

Learning a foreign language resembles neural activity as well, in that it implies the existence of linguistic inputs and outputs. Rod Ellis defines input as "the language to which the learner is exposed to. It can be spoken or written" and it "serves as the data which the learner must use to determine the rules of the target language" (Ellis, 1996) Depending on students' background, knowledge and communication skills, as well as on the appropriateness of the e-course organization of contents, input may be comprehensible or incomprehensible, case in which the course should be adjusted. In 1983, Krashen and Terrell formulated the input hypothesis, which states the following: "in order for acquirers to progress to the next stage in the acquisition of the target language, they need to understand input language that includes a structure that is part of the next stage." Krashen synthesizes this with the formula "I +1", where "I" represents the input, and "I +1" - the input that contains structure slightly above the current level of the learner. The output is the language produced by the learner, both in its spoken and written form, and, depending on the student's actual progress and level of rules internalization, the output may be in its turn comprehensible or incomprehensible to the others. In the latter situation, he/she should return to the linguistic level or the thematic unit of the course that posed the problem, or, if there are more students in this situation, the e-course should be readjusted.

In current foreign language teaching and learning, the most common and popular technology continues to be audio devices, as they are affordable and require no particular educational environment. Video devices prove also useful in SLA, as they support the development of the receptive skills, by adding to sound images which provide natural and synaesthetic communication contexts, thus facilitating acquisition. Dictionaries and online encyclopaedias are currently available on mobile telephones that tend to become an integrated part not only of a student's everyday life but also of his/her formal education. Multimedia computers, either as stand-alones or within networks, combine the above-mentioned advantages of technology in a compact form and at increasingly accessible price. A complex, interactive equipment is currently used within Practical Course classes at Petroleum-Gas University, namely ProLang laboratory. The model PL 28 consists of 28 students units, fixed on furniture, 28 student headsets with microphones, 1 console and 1 headset with microphone for the teacher, 1 ProLang software and 1 mounting kit. The teacher console is commanded by a microcomputer that incorporates microphone mixers and internal amplifiers, and allows students simultaneous individual activity, as well as independently working of 4 groups. Student units dispose of a "rising hand" button that may improve T-S interaction and eliminate some students' reluctance of speaking in front of the class. The equipment allows varied, simultaneous activities: listening, conversation, repetition, group discussion and simultaneous translation, fact that keeps the learner's interest and attention throughout the class, by making him/her an active participant in foreign language learning. ProLang provides also tools for recording and archiving, which allows self-evaluation and progress tracking. As foreign language teachers are currently making use of different materials in order to meet the 1st year students' individual needs, the design of an adaptive, flexible, new computing techniques-based e-course would ease both teaching and learning in that it might resolve the challenge of working with extremely heterogeneous groups, in terms of communication skills, learning styles, aptitudes and background.

Simulation case: English Language Teaching

Target group: the 1st year students (a group of 28 students).

5 teaching methods:

1. Listening;
2. Conversation;
3. Repetition;
4. Group Discussion;
5. Simultaneous translation.

Instruction context:

1. students' background (knowledge context);
2. knowledge skills (mental context);
3. communication skills (mental context);
4. teaching method (classroom context);
5. ProLang lab (technological context).

Learning units are grouped according to levels of language:

1. Phonetics;
2. Vocabulary;
3. Morphology;
4. Syntax.

The steps needed to design the e-learning system are:

i. There is built the Conceptual Map of the Practical English Course (Figure 6).
ii. Students attend an e-Questionnaires to establish the instruction context.

Each variable of the instruction context receives a value (numerical or Boolean).

1. Students' background receives one of the values: intermediate (0) and upper-intermediate (1).
2. Knowledge skills receive one of the values: absence (0) and existence (1).
3. Communication skills receive one of the values: absence (0) and existence (1).
4. Teaching method receive one of the values: Listening (1), Conversation (2), Repetition (3), Group Discussion (4), Simultaneous translation (5).
5. ProLang lab one of the values: absence (0) and existence (1).

iii. There is realised an initial assignment between learners and LU using ABC algorithm. The fitness function is established experimentally. The occupancy degree of each learning unit is 28. The fitness function can have a mathematical form or can be as a set of rule of form presented in 14.

If (condition)
Then (consequent)
Else (alternative)
End If (14)

iv. Adaptation of the pedagogical path to each learner using neural network.

The neural network is built according the model presented above and in paper from the reference (Moise, 2010).

The neural network resolves the problem of the association of an instruction context (each student is described according to the instruction context) to a learning unit.

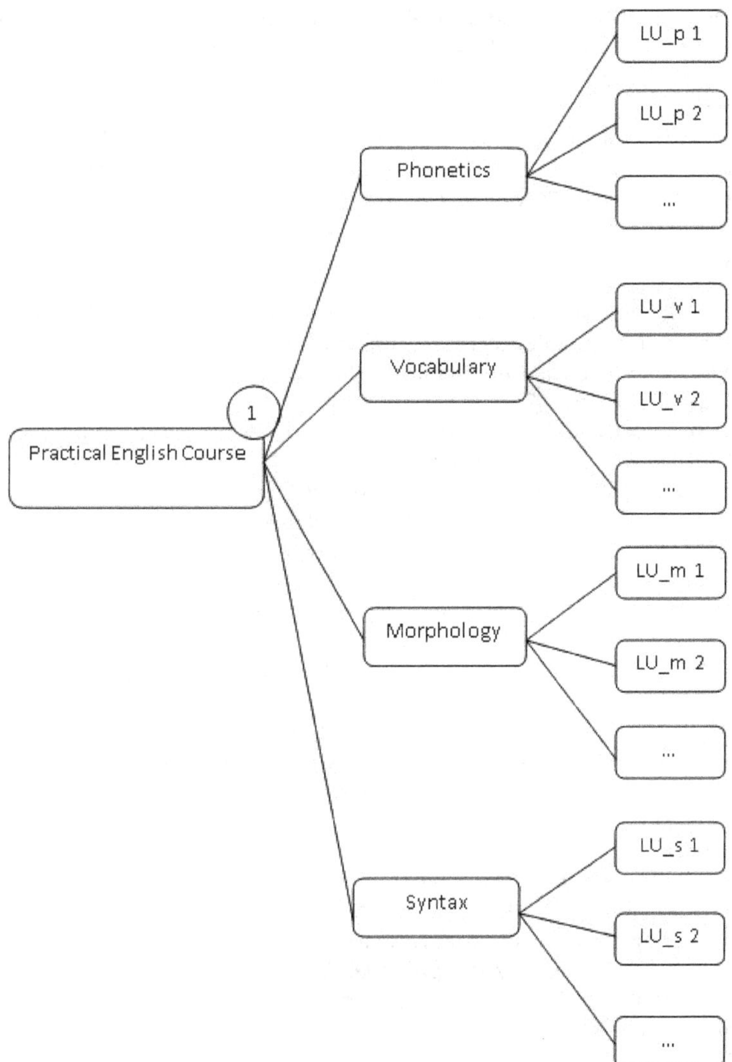

Fig. 6. Conceptual Map of Practical English Course.

5. Conclusion

The proposed e-learning system is avant-garde in the purpose of the e-learning system development trends. The tendency is to replace human teacher, so there are necessary sophisticated techniques to obtain good performance in the conditions of a learner control or machine control in the e-learning system. The techniques are inspired from the living world and have been successfully applied in different types of systems, including e-learning systems. Starting from the theoretical background of the e-learning processes, namely instructional systems, communications and computers theories, the approaches presented in this chapter are relatively new and difficult to implement. As main drawbacks, we mention: heterogeneous teams of experts (IT and specialization experts), initial long time and high costs for developing such systems, lack of computer literacy for some of the students and teachers involved.

The authors consider this chapter as a possible start point for interested teams of e-learning systems developers, in that future preoccupation in this area is to find IT experts willing to implement these techniques in valuable systems.

6. References

Brusilovsky, P. & Nijhavan, H. (2002). A Framework for Adaptive E-Learning Based on Distributed Re-usable Learning Activities, *Proceedings of World Conference on E-Learning in Corporate, Government, Healthcare, and Higher Education,* 1-880094-46-0 , Canada, October, 2002

Cerghit, I. (2006). *Metode de învățământ (our translation: Methods used in education),* Polirom, ISBN: 973-46-0175-X, Iaşi, Romania

Chan, F.T.S., Tiwari, M.K. (Ed(s).). (2007). *Swarm Intelligence Focus on Ant and Particle Swarm Optimization*, ISBN 978-3-902613-09-7, Available from: http://www.intechopen.com/books/show/title/swarm_intelligence_focus_on_ant_and_particle_swarm_optimization

Dorigo, S. (2004). *Ant Colony Optimization,* MIT Press, ISBN 0-262-04219-3, United States of America

Edge, J. (1993). *Essentials of English Language Teaching,* Longman, ISBN: 0-582-02565-6, Singapore

Ellis, R. (1996). *Understanding Second Language Acquisition,* Oxford University Press, UK

Freeman, J. A., Skapura, D., M. (March 1991). *Neural Networks Algorithms, Applications and Programming Techniques*, Addison-Wesley Publishing Company, 0201513765, USA

Harmer, J. (1995). *The Practice of English Language Teaching,* Longman, ISBN: 0582-04656-4, Malaysia

Karaboga, D. (2005). An Idea Based on Honey Bee Swarm for Numerical Optimization, Technical Report TR06, Erciyes University, Engineering Faculty, Computer Engineering Department Turkey, Available from: http://mf.erciyes.edu.tr/abc/pub/tr06_2005.pdf

Kennedy, J., Russell, C. (2001). *Swarm Intelligence,* Academic Press, ISBN 1-55860-595-9, United States of America

Krashen, S. D., Terrell T. D. (1983). *The Natural Approach: Language Acquisition in the Classroom*, Oxford University Press, UK

McCulloch, W., S., Pitts, W. (1943). A logical calculus of the ideas immanent in nervous activity, *Bulletin of Mathematical Biophysics*, Vol. 5, pp. 115-133, 0007-4985

Moise, G. (2007). A Rules Based on Context Methodology to Build the Pedagogical Resources, *Proceedings of the 2nd International Conference on Virtual Learning,* ISBN 973-737-218-2 978-973-737-380-9, Romania, 2007

Moise, G. (2007). A Rules Based on Context Methodology to Build the Pedagogical Resources, *Proceedings of the 2nd International Conference on Virtual Learning*, 978-973-737-380-9, Romania, 2007

Moise, G. (2007). A Software System for Online Learning Applied in the Field of Computer Science, *International Journal of Computers, Communications & Control*, Vol. II, No. 1, (January-March 2007), pp. 84-93, 1841 - 9836

Moise, G. (2010). Usage of the Artificial Neural Networks in the Intelligent Tutoring System, (2010), *Proceedings of The 5th International Conference on Virtual Learning*, ISSN 1844-8933, Romania, 2010, Available from: http://www.icvl.eu/2010/disc/icvl/index.htm.

Moise, G., Dumitrescu, S. (2003). Applications of visual knowledge representation in instruction models, *Proceeding of Sixth Computer Based Learning in Science*, 9963-8525-1-3, Cyprus, July, 2003

Moise, G., Ioniţă L. (2008). Educational Semantic Networks and Their Applications, Science and Technology in the Context of Sustainable Development, *Bulletin of PG University of Ploiesti*, MIF, Vol. LX, No. 2, pp. 77-86, 1224-4899

Mota, J. (2008). Using Learning Styles and Neural Networks as an Approach to eLearning Content and Layout Adaptation, In : *Doctoral Symposium on Informatics Engineering* 2008, July 2011, Available from: http://paginas.fe.up.pt/~prodei/DSIE08/papers/35.pdf

Nwana, H. S. (1990), Intelligent Tutoring Systems: an overview, *Artificial Intelligence Review*, Vol. 4, (1990), pp. 251-277, 0269-2821

Paramythis, A. and Loidl-Reisinger, S. (2004). Adaptive Learning Environments and eLearning Standards, *Electronic Jornal of e-Learning*, Vol. 2, No.1, pp. 181–194, 1479-4403

Phobun, P., Vicheanpanya, J. (2010). Adaptive intelligent tutoring systems for e-learning systems. *Procedia Social and Behavioral Sciences*, Vol. 2, No. 2, (2010), pp. 4064–4069, 1877-0428

Richards, J. C., Rodgers, T. S. (1991). *Approaches and Methods in Language Teaching. A Description and Analysis*, Cambridge University Press, ISBN: 0-521-31255-8 (paperback), USA

Rosenblatt, F. (1958). The Perceptron: A Probabilistic Model for Information Storage and Organization in the Brain, Cornell Aeronautical Laboratory, *Psychological Review*, Vol. 65, No. 6, (1958), pp. 386-408, 0033-295X

Ruiz, M. P., Díaz, M, J. F., Soler, F. O., Pérez, J. R. P. (2008). Adaptation in current e-learning systems, *Computer Standards & Interfaces*, Vol.30, No. 30, (January 2008), pp 62–70, 0920-5489

Rumelhart, D. E., Hinton, G. E., Williams, R. J. (1986). Learning Internal Representations by Error Propagation, In *Parallel Distributed Processing* Vol 1, ed. Rumelhart, D. E. and J. L. McClelland, pp. 318-362. Cambridge, MA: MIT Press

Seridi, H., Sari T., Sellami, M. (2006). Adaptive Instructional Planning Using Neural Networks in Intelligent Learning Systems, *The International Arab Journal of Information Technology*, Vol. 3, No. 3, (July 2006), pp. 183-192, 1683-3198

Seridi-Bouchelaghem, H., Sari, T., Sellami, M. (2005). A neural Network for Generating Adaptive Lessons, *Journal of Computer Science*, Vol. 1, No.2, (2005), pp. 232-243, 1549-3636

Sleeman, D., & Brown, J. S. (1982). *Introduction: Intelligent Tutoring Systems*. In D. Sleeman & J. S. Brown (Eds.), Intelligent Tutoring Systems, New York: Academic Press, 1-11, 0126486816, USA

Stanarevic, N., Tuba, M., Bacanin, N. (2011). Modified artificial bee colony algorithm for constrained problems optimization, *International Journal Of Mathematical Models And Methods In Applied Sciences*, Issue 3, Volume 5, pp. 644-651

Tzouveli, P., Mylonas, P., Kollias, S. (2008). An intelligent e-learning system based on learner profiling and learning resources adaptation, *Computers & Education*, Vol. 51, No. 1, (August 2008), pp. 224–238, 0360-1315

Wenger, E. (1987). *Artificial intelligence and tutoring systems: computational and cognitive approaches to the communication of knowledge*, Morgan Kaufmann Publishers Inc., San Francisco, CA, 0-934613-26-5, USA.

Yonezawa Y., Kikuchi T. (1996), Ecological Algorithm for Optimal Ordering Used by Collective Honey Bee Behavior, *Proceedings of the Seventh International Symposium on Micro Machine and Human Science*, ISBN 0-7803-3596-1, Nagoya , Japan, 02 Oct 1996 - 04 Oct 1996

*** ProLang - The digital phonetic lab, July 2011, Available from: http://www.quartzmatrix.ro

15

Creation of E-Learning Systems by Applying Model-Based Instructional System Development Environment and Platform Independent Models

Habib M. Fardoun and Daniyal M. Alghazzawi
King Abdulaziz University (KAU), Jeddah, Saudi Arabia

1. Introduction

The design and implementation of e-Learning platforms is essential for the development and future of information and communication technologies in knowledge management in the teaching/learning process. Universities and companies require a methodology for developing versatile and flexible e-Learning applications that are, at the same time, capable of storing the large volumes of information required by these educational processes and efficiently conveying this information to their users. This situation is a catalyst revealing the vital need for the efficient and timely development of a teaching/learning process based on e-Learning platforms that takes into account the needs of the student/teacher and achieves optimum quality. To achieve this goal a methodology is required that standardizes the conception, design and implementation of this type of systems based on the creation of basic artefacts that can be used equally well across the different platforms developed. The methodology proposed should be based on a systematic approach for the development of e-Learning systems considering systematic methods coming from both e-Learning and software development communities, involving a series of stages each containing work flows and phases and a set of artefacts (cards, reports, templates, etc.) that can form the basis of the design and development of any e-Learning platform. By doing so, we aim at the development of, what we have named, a Model-Based Instructional System Development Environment (Mb-ISDE), to include e-Learning development in the current trends of model-based software development.
In this chapter, our interest is focus on platform-independent models useful for e-Learning development and concretely on the Task & Domain models, these models will be analyzed in detail and how we they are used for the development e-Learning systems following a model-based instructional system development.
Our proposal, Model-Based Instructional System Design Environment contains several and different models and these models can be divided and classified into different ways based on multiple criteria.
Currently, creating product software, and e-Learning software is not an exception, comes with a lot of compatibility issues. Existing application landscapes within e-Learning consist of a lot of different applications, facilities, operating systems, programming languages, etc. In an ideal scenario new software build in such a context is compatible with all existing and future systems. Users of professional software shouldn't have to deal with compatibility issues. However, there are simply too many platforms in existence, and too many conflicting

implementation requirements, to ever agree on a single choice in any of these fields. The solution of the current software engineering proposals is Model-Driven Development (MDD) (OMG, 2003).

The Model-Driven Development specifies three models on a system, a computation independent model; a platform independent model and a platform specific model (see Fig. 1).

1. The computation independent model (CIM) focuses on the on the environment of the system, and the requirements for the system. The details of the structure and processing of the system are hidden or as yet undetermined.
2. The platform independent model (PIM) focuses on the operation of a system while hiding the details necessary for a particular platform. A platform independent model shows that part of the complete specification that does not change from one platform to another. The Platform Independent Model can be compared to the ontological system notion. Ontology is independent implementation by definition.
3. The platform specific model (PSM) combines the platform independent model with an additional focus on the detail of the use of a specific platform by a system.

Fig. 1. User interface Platform models.

In this chapter we will treat the PIM models and in especially the Task and Domain models inside of this platform. Previous models are usually stored in an XML-based when a user interfaces description language is used, for instance UsiXML. Our main goal is that our domain model will contain references and learning objects. In the other side, our task model will represent those tasks the user will be allowed to perform by using the user interface, and the temporal constraints between these tasks. Under these considerations, in this chapter, we introduce the task and domain model of our Mb-ISDE process. These units allow the construction of e-Learning systems by defining and relating these user tasks and domain objects to presentation and dialog interface models.

In an e-Learning environment many different activities or tasks can be carried out. In this context, a task model is often defined as a description of an interactive task to be performed by the learners of an e-Learning application through the e-Learning application's user interface. In this kind of applications there are tasks performed by a single user, but there also some tasks carried out in collaboration. Therefore, a task model is required with collaborative tasks support. In these collaborative environments activities include coordination, cooperation, collaboration and communication tasks. In our proposal we are using ConcurTaskTrees (Paternò F. , 2002) and CUA (Pinelle, Gutwin, & Greenberg, 2004) notations in order to support the specification of e-Learning and groupware tasks. While CTT is enough for regular tasks specification, it is complemented with CUA to include this collaborative tasks requirements specification. Our eLearniXML notation includes all these task requirements as all the cooperative and communicative task requirements presentation necessary for covering an e-Learning system use.

So, our task model proposal is inspired notations and standards already available, where specific needs and constraint s imposed by e-Learning systems have been identified. Thus,

the proposed task model is based on notations as ConcurTaskTrees (Paternò F., 2002), UML and description languages recent user interfaces using CTT notation, such as (UsiXML) and FlowiXML (Guerrero García, Vanderdonckt, & González Calleros, 2008).
In a similar way, our domain model, which traditionally accompanies the proposals to develop user interfaces based on models, is syntactic and semantic. Learning objects and relationships among them will be treated in this chapter. But domain model is not useful for that, domain model is also useful for specify additional featured elements of e-Learning (see Fig. 2).

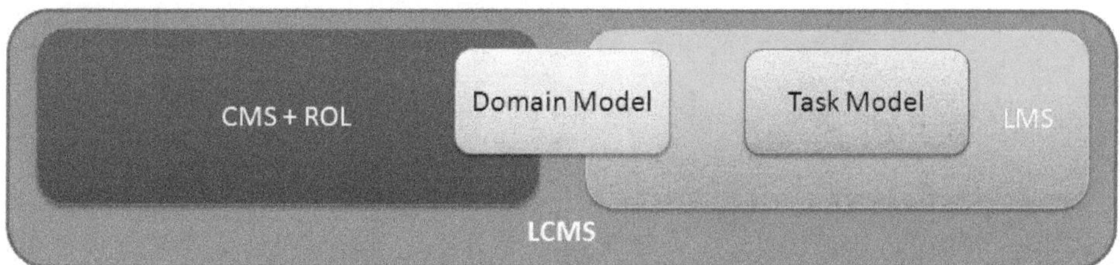

Fig. 2. Task and domain models position for developing an e-Learning system, (Fardoun, 2009).

2. Task model

A task model is a key model when a software product is developed. Using a model-driven technique for development, it is possible to provide important elements of our software product from a task model. Meaningful examples of it can be shown in (Limbourg, Vanderdonckt, Michotte, Bouillon, & López Jaquero, 2005; UsiXML).
In an e-Learning system the task model does not lose magnitude and, as for any other highly interactive systems, the task model is very important. With it we can specify the different tasks associated with teaching and learning process, highlighting those operations that teachers and students make.
Complexity of task model specification is even more intense when a collaborative system is specified and developed. This fact becomes more evident if we consider the new teaching and learning techniques CATs (Johnson, Johnson, & Smith, 1991; Heller, Keith, & Anderson, 1992; Aronson, Blaney, Stephan, Sikes, & Snapp, 1978).
To carry out our contribution first we review the available task analysis and modelling notations. In this sense, the best positioned notation is the ConcurTaskTrees (Mori, Paternò, & Santoro, 2002), we found that this notation is one of the most promising notations, even though, from our point of view it presents some limitation to model collaborative tasks, and in the other side it does not present any limitation for modelling cooperative tasks. In addition, this notation is widespread in the interaction field and has a well-established track record. The problem that we identified is that the temporal operators are not always sufficient to specify when a task starts or finishes.
We will return to this point in a later section to describe this limitation with more detail. In addition, traditional task model notations are not completely intuitive (see Fig. 3) for a novice people in general, for non-familiarities with it. And others problems can be mentioned too, for instant scalability or collaborative facilities are weak points.
Based on this context, we finished identifying and introducing a new notation. That notation was a Gantt chart-based notation (Maylor H., 2001; Wilson J. M., 2003). This notation is

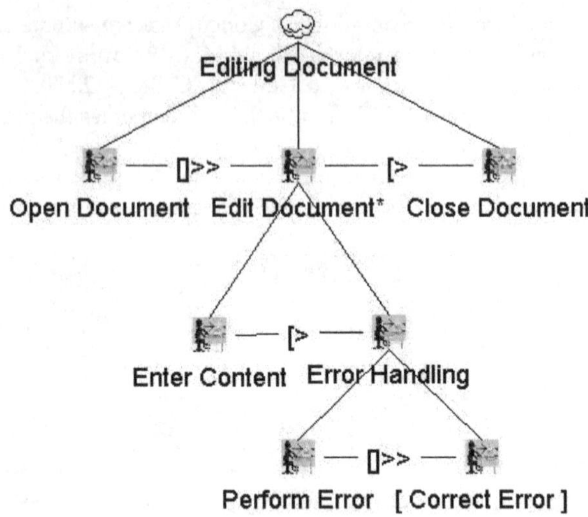

Fig. 3. A task model sample with Concur Task Tree notation.

identified like suitable for task model specification because it is intuitive, easy of understand, easy of learn, scalable, flexible, and it is possible to specify collaborative and cooperative tasks.

In our eLearniXML notation (see Fig. 4) we can represent, as in a CTT specification, concurrent and sequential tasks and there is also an immediate feedback according to their

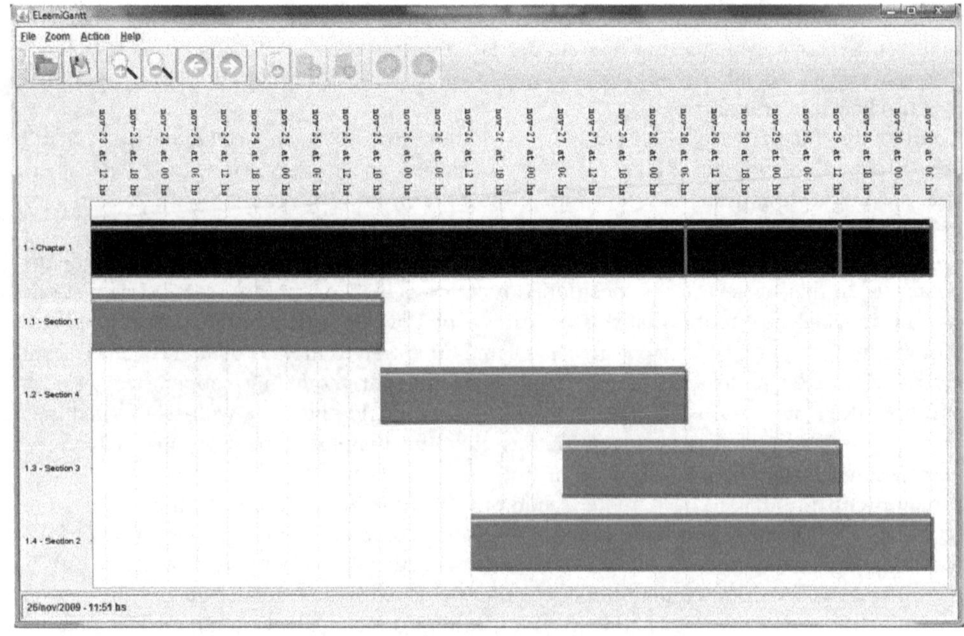

Fig. 4. Sample of eLearniXML Task-Oriented notation.

development, from the start till the end of the tasks. This aspect is mainly interesting to us for the development and specification of software products of e-Learning systems, where without becoming interactive systems with critical characteristics when considering the time, this element is essential.

With this task model, eLearniXML is an effective notation for planning and scheduling operations involving a minimum of dependencies and interrelationships among the activities. The technique is best applied to activities for which time durations is necessary to estimate, since there is no provision for treatment of uncertainty. On the other hand, eLearniXML tasks are easy to construct and understand, even though they may contain a great amount of information. In general, the tasks are easily maintained provided the task requirements are somewhat static.

So, the advantages of using our task model for e-Learning systems versus other task notation, such as CTT or CUA: Collaboration Usability Analysis (Pinelle, Gutwin, & Greenberg, 2004) notations are gathered as follows:

1. **Clarity, easy to understand:** one of the biggest benefits of the eLearniXML task is the notation ability to boil down multiple tasks and timelines into a single document. Stakeholders throughout an organization can easily understand where teams are in a process while grasping the ways in which independent elements come together toward lesson and activities completion.
2. **Learn-ability:** self-understanding of the use of the notation. ELearniXML has the capability of to enable end users (Teachers and Students) to learn how to use it. This advantage is considered as an aspect of usability, and is of major concern in the design of complex applications.
3. **Communication:** teachers by using eLearniXML notation replace meetings and enhance other status updates. Simply clarifying task positions offers an easy, visual method to help teachers understand activities progress.
4. **Motivation:** teachers become more effective when faced with a form of external motivation. ELearniXML notation offer teachers the ability to focus work at the front of a task/activity timeline, or at the tail end of a task segment. Both types of team members can find eLearniXML notations meaningful as they plug their own work habits into the overall e-Lesson schedule.
5. **Coordination:** the benefits of the eLearniXML notation include the ability to sequence activities for the management of e-Lessons and its resources by teachers. Teachers can even use combinations of tasks to break down e-Lessons into more manageable sets of activities.
6. **Creativity:** sometimes, a lack of time or resources forces teachers to find creative solutions. Seeing how individual activities intertwine on eLearniXML notation often encourages new partnerships and collaborations that might not have evolved under traditional activities.
7. **Time Management:** teachers regard scheduling as one of the major benefits of eLearniXML notation in a creative environment over the other notations. Helping teachers to understand the overall impact of the lessons delays can foster stronger collaboration while encouraging better activities organization.
8. **Flexibility:** the facility to issue new tasks notation, with eLearniXML, as the teacher's e-Lesson evolves lets him react to unexpected changes in the e-Lessons scope or timeline. While revising his e-Lesson schedule offering him a realistic view of an e-Lesson can help teachers recover from setbacks or adjust to other changes.

9. **Manageability:** the benefits of eLearniXML notation include externalizing assignments. By visualizing all of the tasks of an activity and all the activities of an e-Lesson, so teachers can make more focused, effective decisions about the used resources and timetables.
10. **Efficiency:** another one of the benefits of eLearniXML notation is the ability for teachers to leverage each other's deadlines for maximum efficiency. For instance, while one teacher waits on the outcome of three other tasks before starting a crucial piece of the activity, he or she can perform other e-Lesson tasks. Visualizing resource usage during e-Lessons allows teachers to make better use of students, teaching, and teaching techniques.

After showing the benefits of using eLearniXML notation, the way in which it represents its tasks process, we shall start to present the task model description.

2.1 Describing our proposal of task model

Our task model offers visual facilities related to temporal and spatiotemporal relationships. The first one is inspired on temporal operators of CTT. In our Mb-ISDE, task models are indispensable models in order to achieve quality characteristics, since the task model allows for the specification of the tasks to be performed though the user interface.

Normally, a learning process incorporates the following functionality: (1) establishing the objectives for the learning process, (2) finding and revising instructional material, (3) assessing student's level of knowledge, (4) assigning appropriate material to students, (5) review students' progress and intervening when necessary and (6) write reports of the results of the learning process. We organize these functionalities into three sets of mechanisms: communication, for instance, contact with the teacher, discussion group, debate or interest group, coordination; for instance, agenda, news, exam or work, and cooperation; for instance, slides, recorded presentation, bibliography, demonstration, or co-authorship. In order to specify our task models we identified different kinds of tasks and modifiers. These tasks are depicted in Table 1, these tasks types, temporal constraints, have taken inspiration from the CTT task model notations. And at Fig. 2 where some these tasks can be done asynchronous while some others are synchronous. There are different examples of the modifiers that we consider when a task model is specified.

Task	Description
	Abstract tasks which require complex activities whose performance cannot be univocally allocated, for example, a learning process.
	User tasks which are performed by the user, for instance, thinking or reasoning by the learner.
	Application tasks which are completely executed by the software product, for instance showing learning objects or a lesson.
	Interaction tasks. These tasks are performed by the user interacting with a computer, for instance, seeing a presentation, hearing a recorded presentation or reading bibliography.

Table 1. Types of tasks of ConcurTaskTrees used in our task model proposal.

Tasks	Descrption
	Group tasks which are performed by several users with different roles without technology support. For instance a debate, discussion or tutorial activities.
	Cooperation tasks. Tasks executed by several users interacting between them with technology support synchronous or asynchronously. In these tasks we can know who did what and how. This can be especially interesting when a task is done by a group of learners.
	Collaboration tasks which are tasks performed by several users. These users work together and it is not important to know who does what. A focus group, brainstorming sessions or a class session is examples of this kind of tasks.

Table 2. New types of tasks used in our notation.

2.2 Integration of our task model and Mb-ISDE

As reflected above in our models of tasks for each task, we specify three elements to answer following questions:

1. Who is or who are the actors involved in each task?
2. What do those involved actors use in carrying out the task?, and
3. What is the temporal and spatiotemporal relationship do the tasks have among themselves?

Depending on the task, the involved actors in each task are shown in Table 3.

Icon	Name	Description
	Teacher	It represents the person on charge of teaching. He/she is responsible for leading the process of teaching and learning, as he must plan, organize, regulate, control and correct the student's learning and his/her own activity. Teachers must be in constant interaction and communication with his students. He/she corresponds with the task of providing resources and plan activities that contribute to the educational process.
	Student	It represents the final destinatary of the teaching process. He/she can use different resources. With this user we symbolize an individual student activity.
	Group of Students	It represents a group of students working together to achieve a shared goal. A student can belong to various groups of students.
	Application	It represents activities that are carried out automatically and in parallel with the educational process.

Table 3. eLearniXML task model actors.

2.3 Task model operators

In addition to the various stakeholders presented in our task model, we have also worked on the identification of temporal and spatiotemporal operators while developing our task models. To make this work we initially start adapting the defined operators with CTT, but we observed certain limitations on these operators, because in our scenarios sometimes appear more demanding or space-time precision. Spatiotemporal operators that we consider today are reflected in Table 4 and Table 5 and are inspired by (Allen, 1983). In next tables temporal and spatiotemporal operators are reflected.

Icon	Name	Description
Temporal Operators		
T1 ||| T2	Concurrence	Tasks may occur in any order without constraints
T1 [] T2	Choice	Choice from a set of tasks.
T1 >> T2	Enabling	Task T1 enables the occurrence of T2
T1 []>> T2	Enabling with information passing	Task T1 enables the occurrence of T2 passing it information.
T1 [> T2	Disabling	The task T1 is definitively deactivated once task T2 starts.
T1 |> T2	Suspend/Resume	Task T2 interrupts task T1. When task T2 ends, task T1 can resume its execution.
T^*	Iteration	The task T1 is executing continually
T^i	Finite iteration	The task T1 is executing (i) times
[T]	Optional execution	The task execution is optional

Table 4. Temporal operators defined at eLearniXML.

In any case, our proposal of temporal and spatiotemporal operators don't present those symbols associated in Table 4 nor in Table 5, because it has a graphical presentation which at the same time, our specification is purely visual and only it takes a textual representation when it is stored (see Fig. 4) where it made a reference to the start and end times for each task.

We also want to emphasize that in order to maximize the scalability and legibility of our proposed notation we have incorporated the fragment notion (item inspired by the fragments defined in UML 2.0 (OMG, 2004) to develop sequence diagrams). Its use is useful for us to draw a frame around the relationship between tasks by providing them with its operator (temporal or spatiotemporal) and to modulate the specification, i.e., we can name a part of a specification and reuse it in another moment making reference to the awarded designation.

Icon	Name	Description
Spatiotemporal Operators		
T1 .= T2	Start to start	Task T1 starts at the same time as Task T2
T1 =. T2	Finish to finish	Task T1 ends at the same time as Task T2
T1 =.. T2	Finish to start	Task T1 finishes at the same time as Task T2 starts
T1 ..= T2	Start to finish	Task T1 starts at the same time as Task T2 finishes

Table 5. Space-time operators defined at eLearniXML.

Another characteristic of the eLearniXML notation is that it could be presented by two different ways: user-oriented and task-oriented. The first type of presentation is used to have a more detailed view of the users and the tasks they are performing along a space of time. While the second type of presentations gives a detailed view of the users and the used resources of each task.

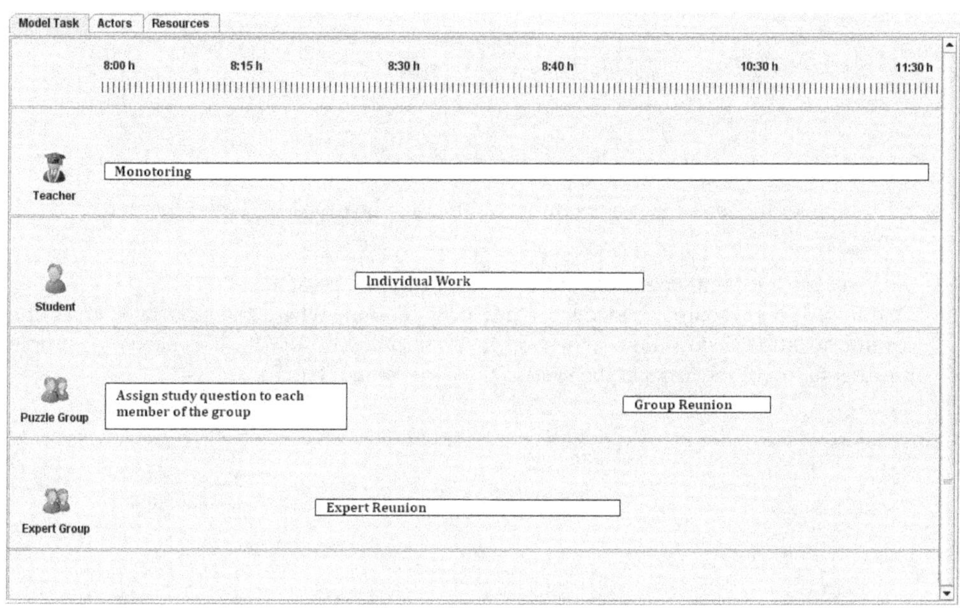

Fig. 5. Example of the use of the time-space operators defined in eLearniXML. User-Oriented notation.

To demonstrate the use of the operators we use and the utility of the fragments, next we depict a series of examples demonstrating its use (see Fig. 5 and Fig. 6).These examples are presented with the both type of the notation.

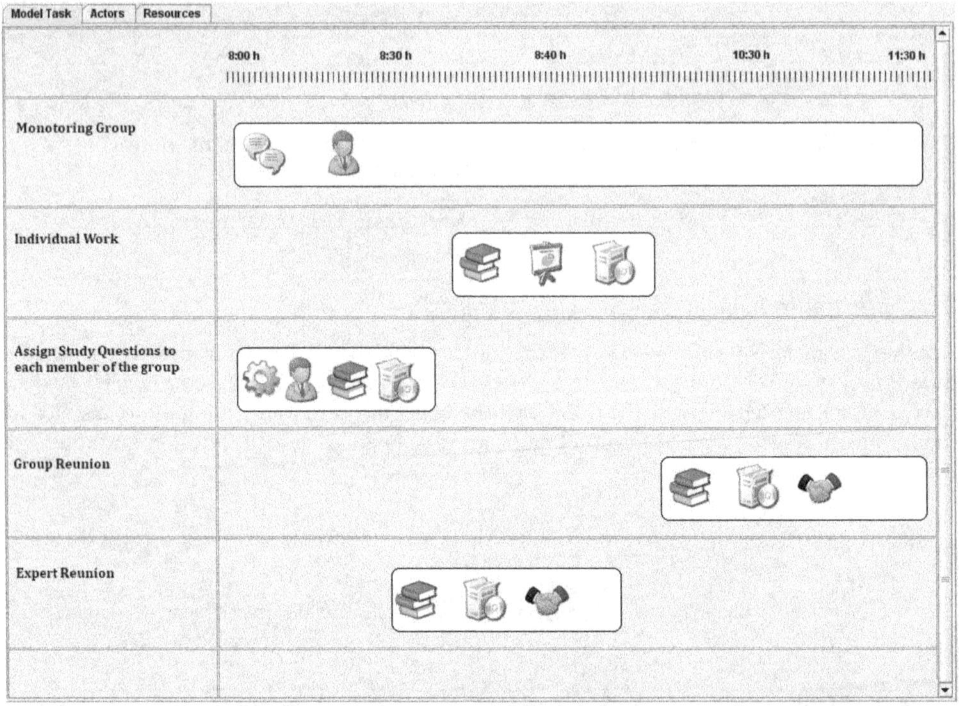

Fig. 6. Example of the use of some operators defined in eLearniXML. Task-Oriented notation.

Next some of the temporal operators of the eLearniXML are presented.

1. Enabling: it represents a sequence work presentation, where the first task gives the control to the second task when it finishes and so on. It just needs a simple representation of the tasks in the system to be presented, Fig. 7.

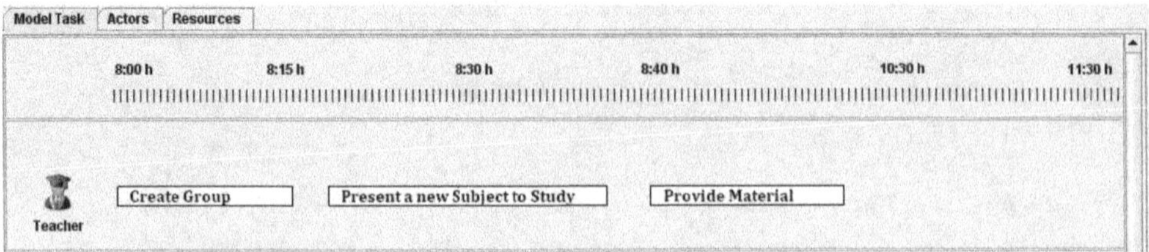

Fig. 7. Enabling temporal operator presented by eLearniXML notation.

2. Concurrence: the tasks may be happen in any order without limitations. This operator is presented between different or same actors of the system and it presentation is simple, Fig. 8.

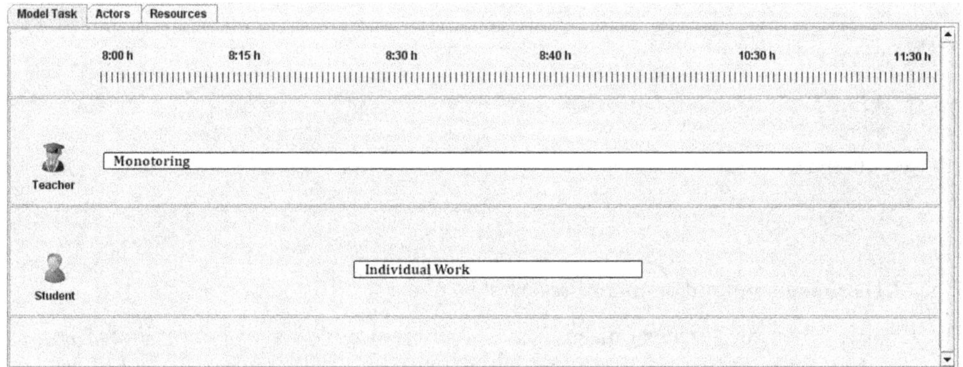

Fig. 8. Concurrence temporal operator presented by eLearniXML notation.

3. Suspend / Resume: the "Assist Team-mates in Learning Material" task interrupts the box that includes the current teacher and student tasks. Once this task is finish both actors can continue with their interrupted tasks. This is a complex operator and it is represented in the aspect of a box limiting the tasks to be interrupted. It can include tasks of several actors at the same time, Fig. 9.

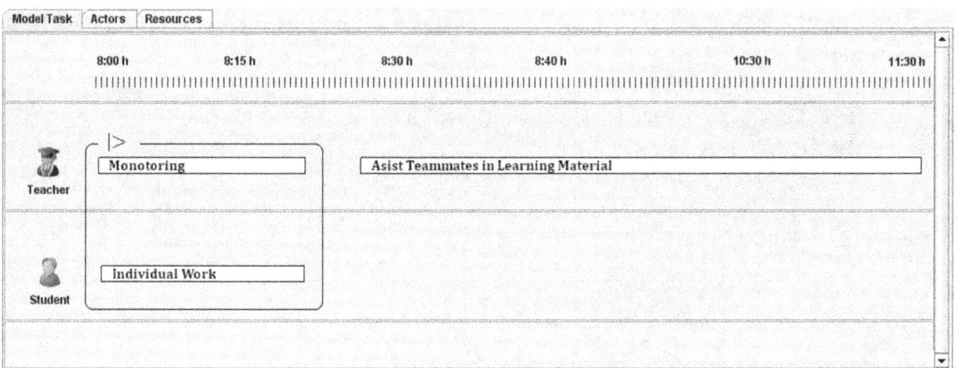

Fig. 9. Suspend/Resume temporal operator presented by eLearniXML notation.

4. Disabling: the "Present a new concept to study" task interrupts the box that includes the current teacher and student tasks. This task is presented with a box including all the related tasks, Fig. 10.

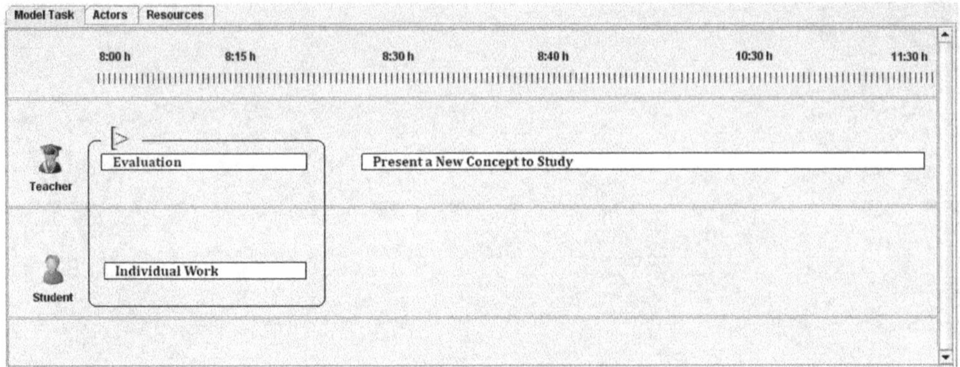

Fig. 10. Disabling temporal operator presented by eLearniXML notation.

5. Choice: When the teacher finishes his task "Present a New Concept to Study" he can select the task "Evaluation" included in the box before continuing with the last task, or he can just jump to the last task without passing the second one, Fig. 11.

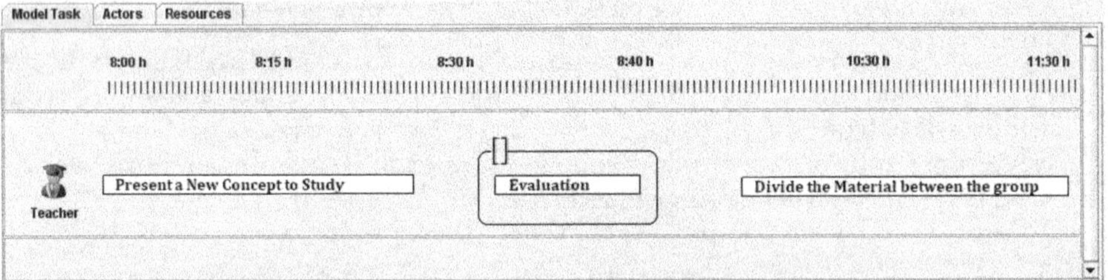

Fig. 11. Choice temporal operator presented by eLearniXML notation.

6. Iteration: the task is executed many times as it is indicated. This task is represented by a box, Fig. 12.

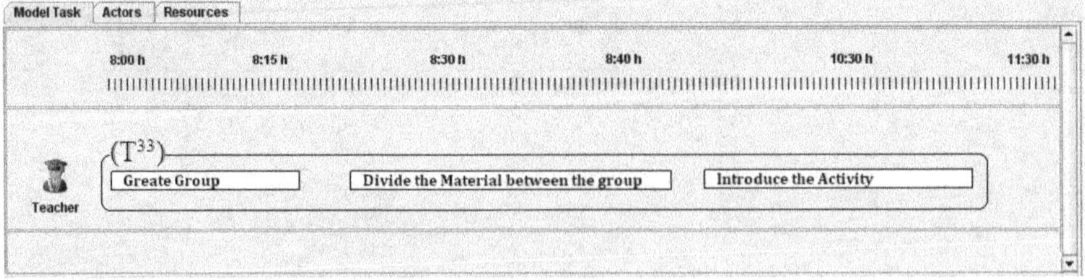

Fig. 12. Iteration temporal operator presented by eLearniXML notation.

2.4 Task model diagram

As we said the task model diagram plays an important role because it represents the logical activities that should support users to interact correctly, with the eLearniXML application, and reach their aim. Knowing the necessary tasks to goal attainment is fundamental to the design process; we create the necessary background, to obtain a complete interactive system.

And, finally, we have achieved that our task model, represents the intersection between user interface design and more systematic approaches by providing here a means of representing and manipulating an abstraction of activities that should be performed to reach user goals. As we extend our task diagram from the CTT ones, tasks here are also described with a name, and a type. Task type here has more aspects it can be: abstract, one of the defined users (teachers, students), group (group of students, group of student/s and teacher/s) interaction, application, cooperation and collaboration. A user task refers to a cognitive action like taking a decision, or acquiring information. User tasks are useful to predict a task execution time. An interaction task involves an active interaction of the user with the application (e.g., selecting student, browsing an exam). An application task is an action that is performed by the system (e.g., displaying an exam, auto-evaluate students work, creating homogenous/heterogeneous groups). An abstract task is an intermediary construct allowing a grouping of tasks of different types; these grouped tasks can be saved and reused in the future by the user. A class diagram associated to our proposed task diagram is depicted in Fig. 13.

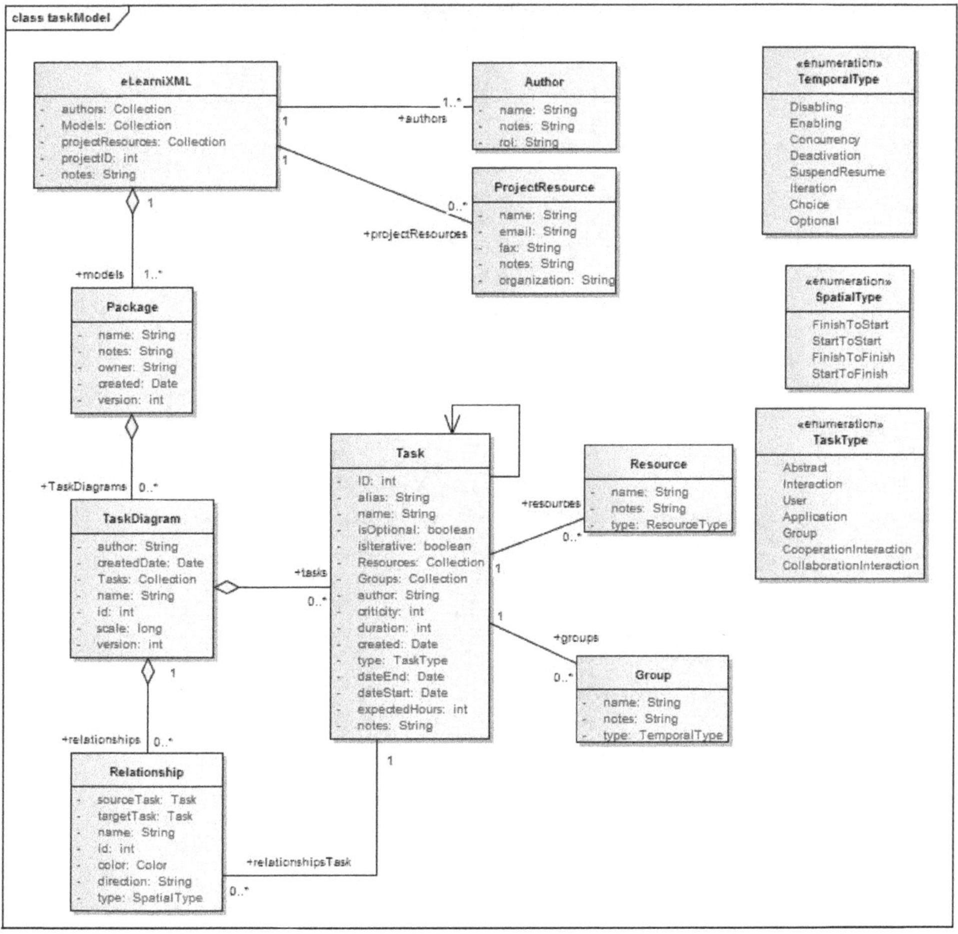

Fig. 13. ELearniXML task model.

1. Decomposition enables representing the hierarchical structure of a task tree, (idem to the CTT notation).
2. Temporal allows specifying a temporal relationship between sibling tasks of a task tree. The only difference this type of relationship has with the CTT one is that, all the undeterministic choices have been deleted. The temporal operators, presented in Table 4 are used here.
3. Spatiotemporal operators allow specifying a spatiotemporal relationship between tasks of a task model. The spatiotemporal operators presented in Table 5 are used here.

Elements	Description
eLearniXML	The eLearniXML package contains the high level e-Learning system objects and entry point into the model itself using the Models collection and the other system level collections.
Package	A Package element corresponds to a set of models in the eLearniXML. It is a common ground in our task model. Every model is stored and organized into packages.
TaskDiagram	A TaskDiagram contains a collection of task and relationships (spatiotemporal).
Relationship	A relationship object represents the various kinds of links between tasks. It is accessed from either the source or target task, using the spatiotemporal operator collection.
Task	The Task entity contains information about a task and its associated extended properties such as grouping and resources. A task is the basic item in a task model. Abstract, user, interaction, group, application, collaboration and cooperative are all different types of task elements.
Resource	A resource is a named person/object with timing constraints and percent complete indicators. Use this entity to manage the work associated with delivering a task.
Group	A collection of tasks (*fragments*). This is commonly used for establish temporal relationships.
Author	An Author object represents a named model author. Accessed using the eLearniXML Authors collection.
ProjectResource	A Project Resource is a named person who is available to work on the current project in any capacity. Accessed using the eLearniXML Resources collection.

Table 6. Definition of eLearniXML task model elements.

2.5 ELearniXML task model analysis

The task model is the particularly relevant model when we treat with model-based development, for example when a user interface is developed. Using this model it is possible to specify what can be done with the software, whatever the task is. In our case, applications should provide flexible educational opportunities where new possibilities to build group works between teachers and students are possible and without involving, for example, teachers don't need to know specific programming languages to get their own ways of working.

As mentioned before the objective we pursue with the chosen graphical notation for modelling tasks in an e-Learning system is to contribute to its acceptance by potential users. This graphical notation allows a user to model the planning of tasks necessary for the completion of a project. Given the relative ease of reading this type of notations, the tool that uses this diagram thus becomes a tool for the teacher/s that lets him make a graph of the class/course/model progress, but it is also a good way of communication between the different involved members in the project.

The type of notation we choose to work with has a number of advantages over other notations and to make this analysis systematically, we collect the different faces that a Strengths, Weaknesses, Opportunities, and Threats "SWOT" (Hill & Westbrook, 1997) analysis provides on our decision.

Table 7 has identified the advantages and disadvantages of our proposal. As a first step here in this example we have only identified the limitation that the specification achieved by using the eLearniXML notation can not specify how to perform the tasks. As positive aspects there is the proposed scalable feature, a characteristic that is often ascribed to the ConcurTaskTrees notation. Moreover, from the user's point of view (external source) the use of this notation facilitates directly the use of a tool that makes use of this notation by the potential users of our proposal.

	Positive	Negative
Internal Source	- It can be generative - Is scalable - Can be used throughout the entire cycle of teaching and learning - Supports concurrency - Supports sequential	- Do not specify how to perform tasks
External Source	- Easy Learning - Easy to understand - Easy to use - There are so many available tools	- Have not been identified

Table 7. Strengths, Weaknesses, Opportunities, and Threats analysis of our election.

3. Domain model

Another important model for e-Learning systems development is the domain model. It is useful for to provide a repository of learning objects (LO), e.g. a software system which stores educational resources and their metadata, and provides some kind of interface for accessing and retrieving them. As the domain model is a representation of the objects in a domain and their interrelationships. Therefore, in the domain model we should find not only the Learning Objects, but also, with what would be most important, this model should provide their associated semantics (Baker, 2006). With this information it is possible to support the educational content recovery effort and access.

The amount of educational content available in digital form necessitates the use of models that facilitate the creation, interoperability and distribution of such content through the most common means of communication, the Web. As in any other area of computing (and what is not computer), standardization facilitates the integration of heterogeneous elements and avoids as much as headaches for users. In the case of e-Learning standardization allows us to work with different suppliers or sources of content and tools, promotes reuse, etc. by saving costs and time, for both suppliers and customers content. Thus, and as discussed in the task model section, our first steps to make a reasonable proposal of our domain model became available is by identifying the relation between to identify since our standards and proposals related to e-Learning refers. In this sense we identified several e-Learning standards, developed by different organizations. Among them include the following:

1. AICC developed by the U.S. aviation industry,
2. IEEE LTSC, Institute of Electronic and Computer Engineering
3. IMS Global Learning Consortium
4. SCORM ®, which is the most widespread. Therefore, this standard required a greater level of depth.

Our basic goal in the domain model is to improve instructional planning practices for presentation of Learning Objects (LOs) by using course sequencing technique of ITS and adaptation techniques of AHS (Hatzilygeroudis, Prentzas, & Garofalakis, 2005). The LO is one of the main research topics in the e-Learning. Especially, researchers pay attention the reusability and granularity issues of LOs and instructional quality of LOs. In order to address these issues, we advocate the idea that user interface design and development for knowledge based systems and most other types of applications are resource-consuming activity.

3.1 Analysis and diagram of ELearniXML domain model

The following diagram (see Fig. 14) provides a high level overview of the eLearniXML for accessing, manipulating, modifying and creating domain models. The top level object is, in a similar way in task model, the eLearniXML, which contains collections for a variety of e-Learning level objects, as well as the main domain model collection that provides access to the learning objects and relationships between them.

Next, elements and descriptions of eLearniXML domain model, shown in Fig. 14, are documented in Table 8. This specification of the domain model has a common structure with previous task model diagram. So, common entities can be identified, for instance eLearniXML or Package. All diagram, task and models are structured with packages entities.

In our specification, relationships among learning objects are identified also. In the domain model two types of relationships and groupings are documented: semantic and domain. In the first group of relationships learning objects can be linked by using semantic relationships, e.g: antonymy, homonym, etc. On the other side, domain relationships are associated to syntactic relationships: aggregation, association, etc. These relationships are documented in Table 9.

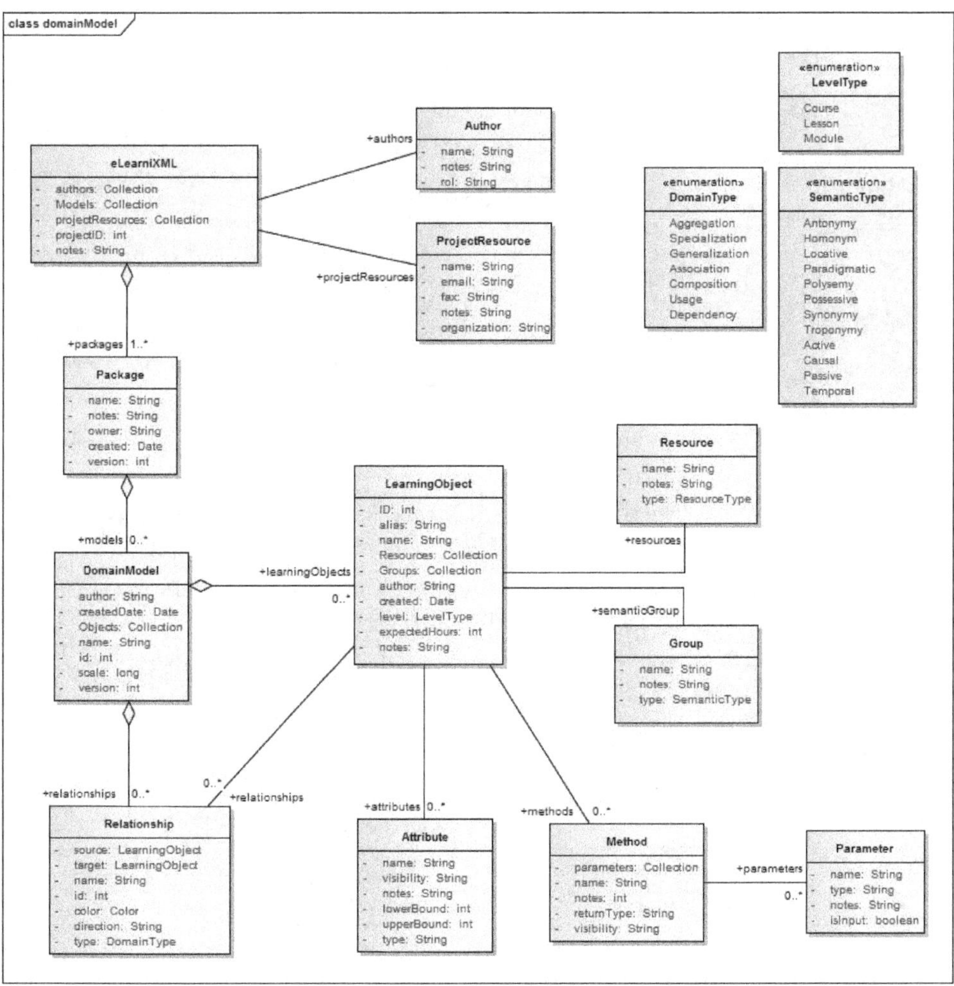

Fig. 14. Domain Model specification in eLearniXML.

Elements	Description
eLearniXML	The eLearniXML package contains the high level e-Learning system objects and entry point into the model itself using the Models collection and the other system level collections.
Package	A Package element corresponds to a set of models (task and domain) in the eLearniXML. It is a common ground in our domain model. Every model is stored and organized into packages.
DomainDiagram	A DomainDiagram contains a collection of learning objects and relationships (domain relationships).
Relationship	A relationship object represents the various kinds of links between learning objects. It is accessed from either the source or target object, using the domain type relationships (e.g.: aggregation, specialization, generalization, association, etc.).
LearningObject	The LearningObject entity contains information about a learning object and its associated extended properties such as grouping and resources. A learning object is the basic item in a domain model..
Resource	A resource is a named person/object with timing constraints and percent complete indicators.
Group	A collection of tasks (*fragments*). This is commonly used for establish semantic relationships among learning objects.
Author	An Author object represents a named model author. Accessed using the eLearniXML Authors collection.
ProjectResource	A Project Resource is a named person who is available to work on the current project in any capacity.

Table 8. Element descriptions in eLearniXML domain model.

Relationships	Description
Active	A semantic between two concepts, one of which expresses the performance of an operation or process affecting the other.
Antonymy	A semantic relation between two concepts, one of which is the opposite of B; e.g. cold is the opposite of warm
Associative	A domain relation which is defined psychologically: that (some) people associate concepts (A is mentally associated with B by somebody). Often are associative relations just unspecified relations.
Causal	A semantic relation between two concepts, where a concept A is the cause of other concept B. For example: Scurvy is caused by lack of vitamin C

Relationships	Description
Homonym	A semantic relation between two concepts, two concepts, A and B, are expressed by the same symbol. Example: Both a financial institution and a edge of a river are expressed by the word bank (the word has two senses).
Specialization | Generalization	These two domain relationships designate the relations between a general concept and individual instances of that concept. A is an example of B. Example: Copenhagen is an instance of the general concept 'capital'.
Locative	A semantic relation between two concepts, in which a concept indicates a location of a thing designated by another concept. A is located in B; example: Minorities in Denmark.
Aggregation | Composition	These two domain relationships designate the relations between the whole and its parts (A is part of B) A metonym is the name of a constituent part of, the substance of, or a member of something. Metonymy is opposite to homonymy (B has A as part of itself). (A is narrower than B; B is broader than A).
Passive	A temporal relation between two concepts, one of which is affected by or subjected to an operation or process expressed by the other.
Paradigmatic	A semantic relation between two concepts that is considered to be either fixed by nature, self-evident, or established by convention. Examples: mother / child; fat /obesity; a state /its capital city
Polysemy	A semantic relation between two concepts, a polysemous (or polysemantic) word is a word that has several sub-senses which are related with one another. (A1, A2 and A3 shares the same expression)
Possessive	A semantic relation between two concepts, a relation between a possessor and what is possessed.
Association	A domain relation where a concept A is semantically related to another term.
Synonymy	A denotes the same as B; A is equivalent with B.
Temporal	A semantic relation in whom a concept indicates a time or period of an event designated by another concept. Example: Second World War, 1939-1945.
Troponymy	A semantic relation where the relation of being a manner of does something (or sense 2: "the place names of a region or a language considered collectively").

Table 9. Types of relationships in domain models of eLearniXML.

4. Analyses and diagram of ELearniXML domain model

In order to present the actors in a clear way as the tasks and relationships among them, we will present an example which makes use of them. Our example will be related to the new techniques of teaching and learning. Among the different existing methodological proposals.
In this section, we will use the puzzle of Aronson (Aronson, Blaney, Stephan, Sikes, & Snapp, 1978; Heller, Keith, & Anderson, 1992) serves to illustrate the use of our proposal. This proposal deference this methodological strategy of other proposals, of group work, is the emphasis with which it is raised in the positive dependence among its members so that the value of an individual action is linked to the group result. For that, the interactions between group members are structured into two types of functions: (1) the investigation of isolated sub-subjects; (2) the re-composition of the full subject. Schematically, the steps of the development of Aronson puzzle are as follows:
The idea of puzzle activity is to organize the class into groups called puzzle teams. Each of the components of the equipment selected and responsible for a different part of the task, thus establishing a new integrated team called research group composed of each of those members of the puzzles teams that have chosen the same part of the task. Once the sub-group members of the research group developed the task, they return to their puzzle group to expose and receive information from the rest of their colleagues, so that the whole work will depend on the mutual cooperation and responsibility among members of puzzle groups.
One of the issues raised by the puzzle of Aronson is the need to redefine the role of teachers. The related tasks to this teaching technique and apprentice are described below and shown at Fig. 15 and Fig. 16:

1. Selecting the puzzle group members: the teams are not formed randomly, teachers may use different criteria and this activity will be supported by the technology.
2. Suggest the subject to work: it must be a subject that can be divided into many parts as the number of the members of the puzzle, considering that each of these parties have a similar specific weight, so that there are no inequalities among members of the group puzzle. This activity is made by the teacher or the puzzle group members by the authorization of the teacher. If the group members are physically distributed, their activity also will be supported by technology (communication and coordination mechanisms).

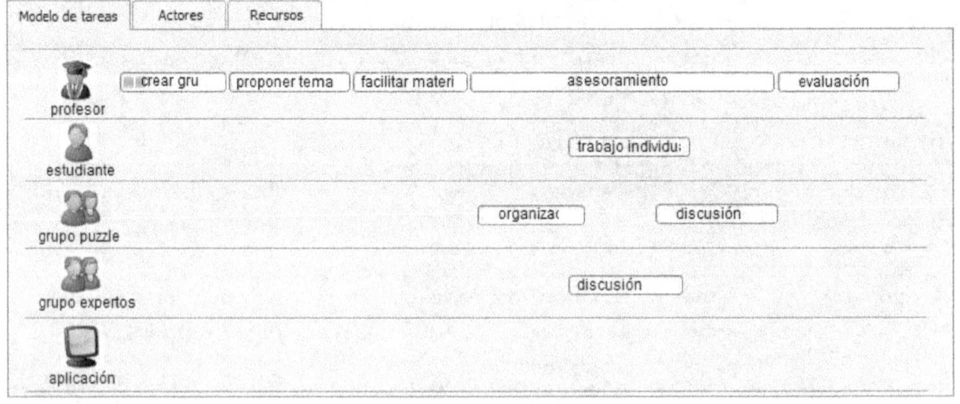

Fig. 15. Part of the tasks planning of a puzzle activity modelled with eLearniXML notation.

3. Provide the necessary material: it should be clear the distribution of the subjects allocated to each research group, so that each member of the puzzle group may elect a part. Teachers should also provide guidance on where or how to find the information that every one of the research group's needs, such as materials or bibliographic work close to the subject.

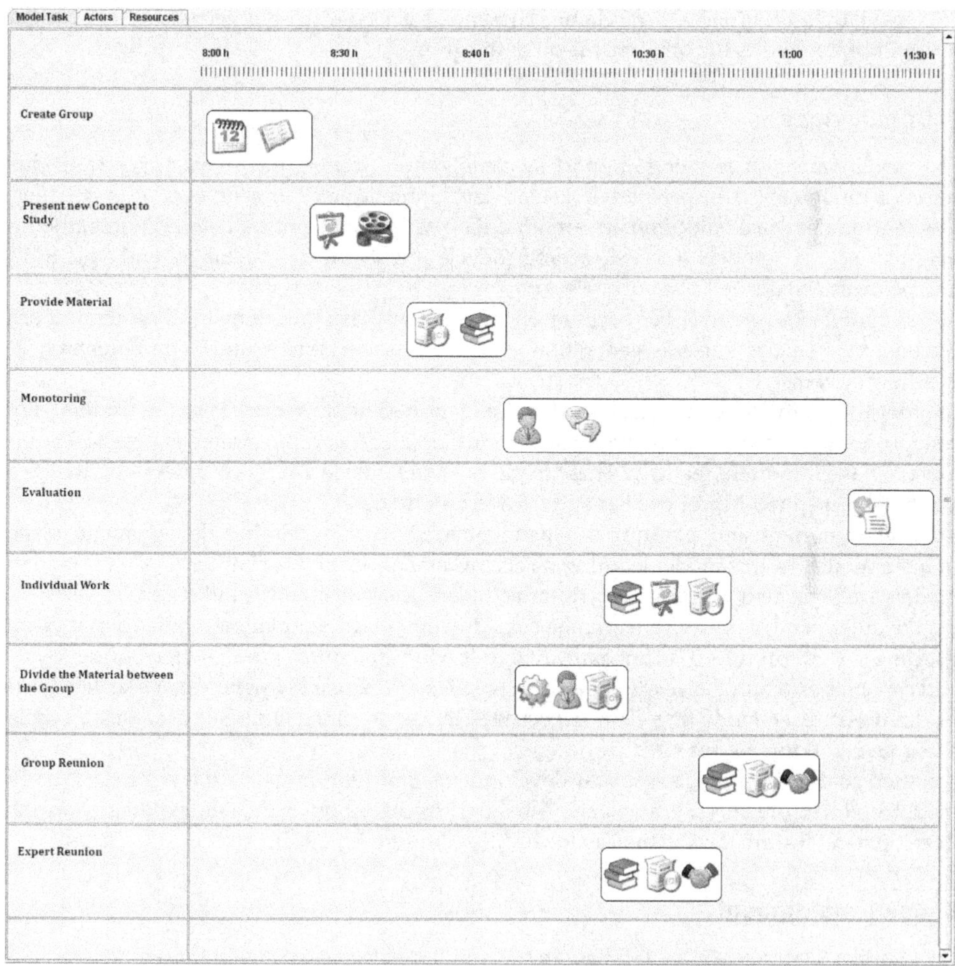

Fig. 16. Part of the used resources by each task of a puzzle activity modelled with eLearniXML notation.

4. Advising each group during the completion of the work: with the cooperative work development, the teacher loses the teaching role, as a direct transmitter of the knowledge, and he convert to an adviser. The student group activities and teacher supervision are supported by technology.
5. The result evaluation: It is undoubtedly one of the most controversial parts of the process, since the criteria and assessment instruments and qualifying must meet the same spirit as that the cooperative learning arises, the emphasis on positive interdependence. One possibility is that proposed by Aronson himself, who affirms that the correct way to qualify is: choose a person randomly from the puzzle group and evaluate him with also a randomly chosen subject. The score obtained by that person will be applied to the other members of the group.

5. Conclusions

The development of learning support systems suffers from a piecemeal process. In this sense, a model-based instructional system development environment was proposed and different models, task and domain, are identified as independent models. We identified a minimal set of models for e-Learning development in a systematic and, platform independent way.

In this chapter our interest has focused on two models: task and domain. Both models are considered essential for the generation aspire to automatically and semi-automatic e-Learning systems.

In order to specify e-Learning task models we identified many shortcomings in traditionally task proposals. A different manner to specify task in an e-Learning system is possible, but it must to have important features. These features were reviewed in this chapter and, finally, a Gantt chart-inspired is proposed as suitable for task model.

Another important and platform-independent model for e-Learning development is the domain model. In this model learning object are managed. In this chapter task and domain models are presented, analysed and described in an integrated and seamless way.

On the other hand, as a future work, the consideration of the adaptation capabilities of the e-learning system produced, in such a way that it will be adaptable to the distinct user needs and capabilities would be very desirable. It would require one key aspect that was left apart in the thesis: user modelling. This aspect was left apart since it clearly deserves a whole thesis just working on this topic.

Another goal is to provide a visual development tool that supports the edition of every model involved in an easy and visual manner, by using our previous experience in the development of similar tools such as IdealXML (Montero F. , 2005).

6. Acknowledgment

I would like to appreciate the ISE Research Group for its help to develop this work.

7. References

ADDIE MODEL. (s.f.); ISU College of Education. Recuperado el 2007, de http://ed.isu.edu/addie/index.html

Allen, J. (1983). Maintaining knowledge about temporal intervals. Communications of the ACM 26(11).

Aronson, E., Blaney, N., Stephan, C., Sikes, J., & Snapp, M. (1978). The Jigsaw Classroom. CA, Sage: Beverly Hills.

Baker, K. D. (2006). Learning objects and process interoperability. International Journal on ELearning, 5(1), 167-172.

Fardoun, H. M., Montero, F., & López Jaquero, V. (2009). eLearniXML: Towards a model-based approach for the development of e-Learning systems considering quality. Adv. Eng. Softw. 40, 12 , 1297-1305.

Guerrero García, J., Vanderdonckt, J., & González Calleros, J. (2008). FlowiXML: a step management systems. Int. J. Web Engineering and Technology, Vol. 4, No. 2, 163–182.

Hatzilygeroudis, I., Prentzas, J., & Garofalakis, J. (2005). Personalized learning in web-based intelligent educational systems: technologies and techniques. 11th International Conference on Human-Computer Interaction (HCII-2005). Las Vegas, Nevada, USA.

Heller, P., Keith, R., & Anderson, S. (1992). Teaching problem solving through cooperative grouping. En Part 1: Group versus individual problem solving (págs. 627-636). Am. J. Phys. 60(7).

Hill, T., & Westbrook, R. (1997). "SWOT Analysis: It's Time for a Product Recall". En Long Range Planning 30 (1) (págs. 46–52).

Johnson, D., Johnson, R., & Smith, K. (1991). Cooperative Learning: Increasing College Faculty Instructional Productivity. George Washington University: ASHE-ERIC Higher Education Report No. 4.

Limbourg, Vanderdonckt, J., Michotte, B., Bouillon, L., & López Jaquero, V. (2005). UsiXML: a Lan-guage Supporting Multi-Path Development of User Interfaces. En 9th IFIP Working Conference on Engineering for Human-Computer Interaction. EHCI-DSVIS'2004 (págs. 200-220). Springer-Verlag.

Maylor, H. (2001). Beyond the Gantt chart:: Project management moving on. European Management Journal, Volume 19, Issue 1, 92-100.

Mori, G., Paternò, F., & Santoro, C. (2002). CTTE: Support for Developing and Analysing Task Models for Interactive System Design. IEEE Transactions on Software Engineering, Vol. 28, No. 8, IEEE Press, 797-813.

OMG. (2004). UML 2.0 Superstructure Specification, Revised Final Adopted Specification. OMG.

OMG. (12 de June de 2003). MDA Guide Version 1.0.1. Retrieved from Object Management Group. Obtenido de http://www.omg.org/mda

Paternò, F. (2002). CTTE. The ConcurTaskTree Environment. Obtenido de http://giove.cnuce.cnr.it/ctte.html

Pinelle, D., Gutwin, C., & Greenberg, S. (2004). Collaboration usability analysis: task analysis for group-ware usability evaluations. En Interactions 11(2) (págs. 7-8).

UsiXML. (s.f.). USer Interface eXtensible Mark-up Language. Obtenido de http://www.usixml.org.

Wilson, J. M. (2003). Gantt charts: A centenary appreciation. European Journal of Operational Research, Volume 149, Issue 2, Sequencing and Scheduling.

Montero, F. (2005). IdealXML. Obtenido de Pattern-oriented tool IdealXML: http://www.usixml.org/index.php?view=page&idpage=34

Permissions

The contributors of this book come from diverse backgrounds, making this book a truly international effort. This book will bring forth new frontiers with its revolutionizing research information and detailed analysis of the nascent developments around the world.

We would like to thank Professor Elvis Pontes, Professor Anderson Silva, Professor Adilson Guelfi and Professor Sérgio Takeo Kofuji, for lending their expertise to make the book truly unique. They have played a crucial role in the development of this book. Without their invaluable contribution this book wouldn't have been possible. They have made vital efforts to compile up to date information on the varied aspects of this subject to make this book a valuable addition to the collection of many professionals and students.

This book was conceptualized with the vision of imparting up-to-date information and advanced data in this field. To ensure the same, a matchless editorial board was set up. Every individual on the board went through rigorous rounds of assessment to prove their worth. After which they invested a large part of their time researching and compiling the most relevant data for our readers. Conferences and sessions were held from time to time between the editorial board and the contributing authors to present the data in the most comprehensible form. The editorial team has worked tirelessly to provide valuable and valid information to help people across the globe.

Every chapter published in this book has been scrutinized by our experts. Their significance has been extensively debated. The topics covered herein carry significant findings which will fuel the growth of the discipline. They may even be implemented as practical applications or may be referred to as a beginning point for another development. Chapters in this book were first published by InTech; hereby published with permission under the Creative Commons Attribution License or equivalent.

The editorial board has been involved in producing this book since its inception. They have spent rigorous hours researching and exploring the diverse topics which have resulted in the successful publishing of this book. They have passed on their knowledge of decades through this book. To expedite this challenging task, the publisher supported the team at every step. A small team of assistant editors was also appointed to further simplify the editing procedure and attain best results for the readers.

Our editorial team has been hand-picked from every corner of the world. Their multi-ethnicity adds dynamic inputs to the discussions which result in innovative outcomes. These outcomes are then further discussed with the researchers and contributors who give their valuable feedback and opinion regarding the same. The feedback is then collaborated with the researches and they are edited in a comprehensive manner to aid the understanding of the subject.

Apart from the editorial board, the designing team has also invested a significant amount of their time in understanding the subject and creating the most relevant covers. They scrutinized every image to scout for the most suitable representation of the subject and create an appropriate cover for the book.

The publishing team has been involved in this book since its early stages. They were actively engaged in every process, be it collecting the data, connecting with the contributors or procuring relevant information. The team has been an ardent support to the editorial, designing and production team. Their endless efforts to recruit the best for this project, has resulted in the accomplishment of this book. They are a veteran in the field of academics and their pool of knowledge is as vast as their experience in printing. Their expertise and guidance has proved useful at every step. Their uncompromising quality standards have made this book an exceptional effort. Their encouragement from time to time has been an inspiration for everyone.

The publisher and the editorial board hope that this book will prove to be a valuable piece of knowledge for researchers, students, practitioners and scholars across the globe.

List of Contributors

Teodora Bakardjieva and Boyka Gradinarova
Varna Free University, Technical University of Varna, Bulgaria

Augustin Prodan, Mădălina Rusu, Cornelia Revnic and Remus Câmpean
Iuliu Haţieganu University Cluj-Napoca, Romania

Paulina Mitrea
Technical University Cluj-Napoca, Romania

Donika Valcheva and Margarita Todorova
"St. Cyril and St. Methodius" University of Veliko Tarnovo, Bulgaria

Aleksandra Werner and Katarzyna Haręźlak
Silesian University of Technology, Poland

Kamran Shaikh, Vivek Venkatesh, Tieja Thomas, Kathryn Urbaniak, Timothy Gallant, David I. Waddington and Amna Zuberi
Learning for Life Centre, Department of Education, Concordia University, Canada

Luigia Simona Sica and Alessandra Delli Veneri
NAC (Natural and Artificial Cognition Laboratory), University of Naples "Federico II", Italy

Orazio Miglino
LARAL (Laboratory of Autonomous Robotics and Artificial Life), ISTC -CNR, Rome, Italy

José Luis Alejandre, Ana Allueva, Rafael Tolosana and Raquel Trillo
University of Zaragoza, Spain

Guadalupe Martínez, Ángel Luis Pérez, Mª Isabel Suero and Pedro J. Pardo
University of Extremadura, Spain

Constanta-Nicoleta Bodea and Maria-Iuliana Dascalu
Academy of Economic Studies, Bucharest, Romania

Ajlan S. Al-Ajlan
Information System Management, College of Business and Economics, Qassim University, Kingdom of Saudi Arabia

Egons Lavendelis
Riga Technical University, Latvia

Salvador Otón, Antonio Ortiz, Luis de-Marcos, Sergio Mazo de Dios, Antonio García, Eva García, José R. Hilera and Roberto Barchino
Computer Science Department, University of Alcala, Technical School of Computer Science Engineering,
Alcalá de Henares, Madrid, Spain

Michael K. Badawy
Virginia Tech University, USA

Moise Gabriela, Netedu Loredana and Toader Florentina Alina
Petroleum-Gas University of Ploiesti, Romania

Habib M. Fardoun and Daniyal M. Alghazzawi
King Abdulaziz University (KAU), Jeddah, Saudi Arabia

Printed in the USA
CPSIA information can be obtained
at www.ICGtesting.com
JSHW011505221024
72173JS00005B/1204

9 781632 401670